Contents

Introduction

In the Middle East, where the United States government has applied double standards that have been detrimental to the lives of millions of people, new avenues of policymaking must be explored. Where a blind eye is turned to friendly governments who suppress their own people and the wrath of the US military is turned on "rogue states," can we help but ask which way the moral compass of US policy is pointing? This anthology of the Middle East writings of Richard Falk resets that compass and draws a new map for our understanding of the Middle East. A guiding principle that runs throughout Falk's writing is that the United States "has paid too much attention to inter-state relations in the Middle East and too little attention to the well-being of the people who live in the region."[1] With this attention to real people as his lodestar, Richard Falk has built, over the past 30 years, a coherent approach to issues related to the Middle East. Moreover, Falk has proven himself through these writings and through his actions to be an independent observer worthy of attention. His work provides a perspective that is not dominated by self-interest or the dictates of US foreign policy.

Falk's consistent assessment of issues regarding Iran, Israel, Lebanon, and Palestine has proven his to be a voice of reason in a discourse often bankrupt in its bias. For instance, when the UN Commission on Human Rights sought to establish a panel in October 2000 to investigate violations of human rights in the occupied territories as a result of the Al-Aqsa intifada, Falk—although American and Jewish—was seen as having the independence of mind to provide a true assessment of the situation on the ground. Although he specializes in international law, and has taught the discipline for more than 40 years, Richard Falk's understanding of Middle East issues transcends a simple legalistic approach. Instead, like Grotius (the "father of international law") before him, Falk has sought to blend "moral, legal, and political perspectives into a coherent conception of world order."[2] As Falk himself has noted, "Grotius was a person of deep conscience who was neither radical nor acquiescent, and who yet was deeply committed to leaving the world a better place than he found it."[3] In much the same manner, Falk's approach to the Middle East mixes those moral, legal, and political elements in an attempt to provide avenues by which a more humane, more peaceful horizon can emerge for the people of the Middle East.

Limerick County Library

30012 00433548 4

WITHDRAWN FROM STOCK

WITHDRAWN FROM STOCK

WITHDRAWN FROM STOCK

004335448
LIMERICK
COUNTY LIBRARY

UNLOCKING
the Middle East
The Writings of Richard Falk

AN ANTHOLOGY EDITED BY JEAN ALLAIN

327.73

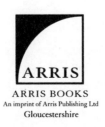

ARRIS BOOKS
An imprint of Arris Publishing Ltd
Gloucestershire

First published in Great Britain in 2003 by

Arris Books
An imprint of Arris Publishing Ltd
Unit 1A Fosseway Business Centre
Stratford Road
Moreton-in-Marsh
Gloucestershire GL56 9NQ
www.arrisbooks.com

Text copyright © Richard Falk 2003
Introduction copyright © Jean Allain 2003

The moral right of Richard Falk and Jean Allain to be identified as copyright holders of this work
has been asserted by them in accordance with the Copyright, Design, and Patents Act 1988.

ISBN 1-84437-004-6

All rights reserved
British Library in Cataloguing Data
A catalogue record for this book is available from the British Library

Printed and bound in Canada

To request our complete catalog, please call us at **01608 652655**,
visit our web site at **www.arrisbooks.com**, or e-mail us at **info@arrisbooks.com**.

Falk set out his greater vision in the following manner:

If, however, the purpose of our endeavors is to create a better world, then fantasy, whether self-deceived or self-aware, is of little help. We require instead a special sort of creativity that blends thought and imagination without neglecting obstacles to change. We require, in effect, an understanding of those elements of structure that resist change, as well as a feel for the possibilities of innovation that lie within the shadowland, cast backward by emergent potential structures of power.[4]

Falk demonstrates over and over again his deeply held belief that people, not politics or power, should come first. He is a "realist" to the extent that he believes that no venture into the future will succeed without anchors in the past, yet, he struggles to imagine what a more just society might look like. Such a struggle lead him, in 1976, to chair a committee on the protection of human rights in the Shah's Iran and in opposition to any US intervention in that country. The committee grew in stature as the revolution developed, and Falk was the first American to meet with the Ayatollah Khomeini and the revolutionary leadership after they had deposed the Shah. As part of the 1980 David Stoffer Lectures, Falk reflected on the role that the United States played in Iran by supporting the Shah despite the fact that he had "managed in the end to alienate 98 or 99 percent of his own population" (see Chapter 13).

He examines in such writing the type of US foreign policy that is based on protecting "isolated elites who desperately rely on their military prowess to resist" the flow of the people's agitation for a voice in the running of their own lives.[5] In doing so, he considers the role that international law played in the US–Iran hostage crisis. He questions the relevance of an international legal system that protects diplomats, while allowing those afforded that protection to undermine states. "One does not need to know much about Iranian history to know that the American embassy in Tehran," he writes, "was the center of the CIA plot in 1953" that brought the Shah to power. Falk continues: "The question must be asked: Why is the structure of international law so solicitous of the rights of diplomats and so indifferent to the rights of people?" He concludes that the challenge is to adapt international law "to the most basic rhythm of change [...] especially as associated with the resurgence of non-Western peoples in exerting control over" their own lives. And to pretend that the issue is only about the hostage in Iran "is to confirm the cynical view of international law as nothing more than a geopolitical tool."

His interest in the Iranian Revolution made him a *cause célèbre*, when a piece he wrote for the *New York Times* appeared under the headline

"Trusting Khomeini."[6] Falk found himself isolated and criticized by the likes of Anthony Lewis in columns and editorials (see Chapter 12). After the revolution, more critical editorials followed, asking why, after having been so vocal before the revolution, he was not speaking up now. Falk himself noted that he was in fact on a second committee that dealt with human rights in post-revolutionary Iran, but it gained little attention because it failed to have access to information and also because it was not as well financed as other groups. Included in this anthology is a piece that considers human rights after the revolution, but Falk contextualizes those abuses by first noting that the Shah's record was "one of the worst in a world notable for human rights abuse." He then considers the record of the Ayatollah Khomeini, stating that because of the "powerful outside interests [that] were aligned with the policies of the old order in Iran, an enormous incentive exists to discredit the new order." In 1981, Falk believed that sketching the prospects of respect for human rights in the immediate aftermath of the revolution could only be "incomplete and tentative"—but at least, he ventured

> let us not confuse the tyranny of the past with the problems of the present and future. Ayatollah Khomeini seems dedicated to evolving a form of governance for the people of Iran that includes a central commitment to social justice for the poor, a closing of gaps between social classes, and an elimination of the wasteful consumption and production patterns that grew up during the Shah's years.

With the human rights situation in Iran as a backdrop, Falk picks up, once again, the theme of the relevance of international law that protects diplomats, but does not deal with bringing tyrants to justice. He considers the monopoly that states have in creating international law and asks: "Why should governments alone establish the rules that govern behavior on the planet? Why should not citizens organize to insist on a framework of law that corresponds to a framework of minimum morality?" Falk looks to the Nuremberg principles and highlights the work of the non-governmental Russell and Basso Peoples' Tribunals to demonstrate that not only states have a claim on the law. He suggests that it "may be the moment for individuals, churches, and voluntary associations of various kinds to assert human concerns—that the future of international law is not a matter of governments only" (see Chapter 14).

Through these deeds and words, Falk's involvement in the Middle East emerged in the national media. For many years he felt the backlash created by his article in the *New York Times*, receiving hate mail and threats. But such was the life he had chosen; as he notes, criticism "goes with the territory." That territory—though Falk talks of it only reluctantly—is the territory of the intellectual.

In a passage in which he could have been speaking of Falk, Edward W. Said, in his 1993 BBC Reith Lectures spoke generally about the role of the intellectual in society:

> The intellectual is an individual endowed with a faculty for representing, embodying, articulating a message, a view, an attitude, philosophy or opinion to, as well as for, a public. And this role has an edge to it, and cannot be played without a sense of being someone whose place it is publicly to raise embarrassing questions, to confront orthodoxy and dogma (rather than to produce them), to be someone who cannot easily be co-opted by governments or corporations, and whose raison d'être is to represent all those people and issues that are routinely forgotten or swept under the rug.

Said then goes on to say that the intellectual does so on the basis of the following of a universal principle: "That all human beings are entitled to expect decent standards of behavior concerning freedom and justice from worldly powers or nations."[7] Falk's writings and public activities have always had their foundations in this universal principle.

Falk's intellectual credentials are most evident in his stand on issues concerning Israel. The universalism of the intellectual, notes Edward Said, means that one must take risks "to go beyond the easy certainties provided to us by our background, language, nationality, which so often shield us from the reality of others." For Falk, a New York Jew (even if his was an assimilationist family), this meant that he could not avoid being "confronted by many people at an early age who had a strong attachment to Israel." Falk posits that his Jewish heritage may have played a part, at least subconsciously, in his intellectual stands: "I think that Jews can go either way. They can either be completely absorbed by the establishment and want to be as much accepted by it as possible, or they can see themselves as marginalized and critics of those that are in power. And I certainly chose the latter approach." His politicization during the Vietnam era provided, or so he thought, a means of avoiding the issues surrounding Israel. "I decided that I should stay away from Middle East issues because I had enough controversy over my Vietnam stand and I knew that taking a position sympathetic to the Palestinians would create all sorts of additional agitation and I decided to avoid that." Eventually, his innate sense of justice compelled him to speak, as he "developed friendships with a variety of people from the region and felt it more and more artificial not to."

The first notable piece that Falk produced regarding Israel appeared in a 1969 edition of the *American Journal of International Law*. It dealt with the 1968 Israeli military raid on Beirut International Airport, which destroyed thirteen commercial aircraft, causing damage that at the time was estimated to be worth $43 million dollars. Israel justified its attack as retaliation for a specific act of individual (i.e.: non-state) terrorism, which had taken place against an El Al plane in Athens two days earlier. With this as a springboard, Falk considered the notions of armed reprisal that exist in international law. He found that the actions of Israel fell short of customary norms of proportionality, and further concluded that the UN Security Council resolution condemning "Israel for its premeditated military action in violation of its obligation under the Charter" as being "an authoritative pronouncement on the legal status of the Beirut raid." Yet, Falk was not satisfied with this outcome, as he noted that such international law did "not come to grips with the underlying policy setting" of the Arab–Israel conflict (this was soon after the 1967 war). The Security Council resolutions, he realized, were "not likely to engender respect"—and as a result, the issue was not settled. He then attempted to develop a process-oriented legal analysis[8] to suggest standards by which states might be justified in using retaliatory force.

In the next issue of the same journal, Yehuda Blum, then a senior lecturer in international law at Hebrew University, wrote that there was a "basic fallacy" in Falk's approach and questioned his integrity:

> It is of course idle to speculate on the reasons that could have prompted Falk to adopt this attitude. It is clear, however, that it has enabled him to accomplish at least two things [one of which is]: (a) to express displeasure with some of Israel's policies, and to bolster his censorial posture against her on the false assumption that her response must be judged by the law of peaceful relations between states....[9]

Blum goes on to discard Falk's investigation of ways that Israel might escape the dilemma of insecurity. For Blum, it was unacceptable to suggest that Israel accept the rules that apply to all states, as codified in the United Nations Charter. Falk refers to commentary such as Blum's as "cynical scholarship," which shall be turned to shortly.

But first, more on the shaping of Falk's understanding of the Middle East. He cites as one of the important influences on his view of the Middle East generally, and Israel more specifically, his meeting in Lebanon in the early 1980s with Yasir Arafat and other Palestinian leaders in exile. Subsequently, Falk was made vice-chair of an independent commission (headed by Sean McBride) investigating violations of international law in the course of the 1982 Lebanese War.[10] Much of his thinking on the issues related to that war made their way into a 1983 article in which Falk considered the US role in the region. Falk believes that the US consistently "subordinates moral qualms to strategic imperatives in carrying out its foreign policy, especially where important issues of critical resources and geopolitical rivalry are at stake," as in the Middle East. He notes that US criticism of Israel is "essentially hypocritical (that is, designed to improve its regional image rather than meant in any serious way as a comment on Israeli behavior)" and that in actuality, the relationship between the two is "stronger than ever." Falk places the Lebanon War in the greater context of the US policy of battling movements of national liberation; and, as such, demonstrates that Israel is carrying out US wishes by proxy. Falk notes that Israeli claims of invasion under the pretext of self-defense "certainly do not qualify," and that fighting the Palestinian Liberation Movement and Palestinians "en masse in Lebanon necessarily meant blurring [...] the distinction between civilians and soldiers, especially in relation to the refugee camps." He considers the high-tech nature of the Israel invasion, which targeted the innocent, and draws parallels to US tactics in Vietnam, concluding that Israel's war was a "species of sadism" (see Chapter 11).

With such views, it will come as little surprise that Falk has been the target of "cynical scholarship." In a 1991 edition of the *Harvard International Law Journal*, Falk co-authored a piece with Burns Weston, the Bessie Dutton Professor of Law at the University of Iowa: "The Relevance of International Law to Palestinian Rights in the West Bank and Gaza: In Legal Defense of the Intifada."[11] In the article they state their belief that peace and stability in the Middle East can only be achieved by ending the Israeli occupation of the West Bank and the Gaza Strip. The intifada was not only justified, but as Falk and Weston write, was seen by the Palestinians as being mandated "by the long duration and especially the harshness of the Israeli occupation, an occupation that has included and continues to include large-scale, severe, and persistent violations of the law of belligerent occupation and systematic deprivations of fundamental human rights, perhaps most importantly the right of self-determination." The authors agree with this assessment and go on to cite many sources to back up their claim, noting that these organizations "have abundantly and persuasively documented Israel's violations of the limited rights that the laws of war assures an occupied people; and they have done the same, too, regarding Israel's failure to uphold the international human rights of the

Palestinian people in general." On the basis of this assessment, Falk and Weston conclude that

> Israeli policies and practices over the last 23 years cannot convincingly be reconciled with these rules and standards of international law. Indeed, by its severity and cumulative impact, the pattern of Israeli transgression appears to violate, with historic irony, even the principles of criminal acceptability laid down at Nuremberg in 1945 to establish a framework binding upon all governmental leadership.

The *Harvard International Law Journal* conditioned its acceptance of their piece upon publishing a "balancing" piece. Falk and Weston, in their rebuttal to that commissioned piece, wrote: "There is a special sensitivity in scholarly and other circles within the United States whenever an analysis of Middle East affairs results in conclusions that are critical of official Israeli policy and practice. In this regard, for example, we note that the Harvard journal conditioned its acceptance of our article on its intention to solicit a "balancing" article, which itself implies that our assessments where somehow excessive, in need of balancing." In a rebuttal to that other article ("International Law and the Territories," by Michael Curtis of Rutgers University[12]), Falk and Weston wrote about the boundaries of scholarly discourse.

> [Curtis] writes, in our judgment, as an Israeli apologist who will go to virtually any length to discredit opposing views, no matter what the evidence. Part of his extremism involves a clever, but irresponsible, stratagem of role reversal, casting us as the polemicist and purporting himself to be the dispassionate scholar [...] His one-sided and selective use of history and authority to denigrate our evidence of Palestinian deprivation, his resort to diversionary arguments irrelevant to our thesis, and his *ad hominem* attacks upon our professionalism do not add up to a serious attempt at dialogue.[13]

As an example, Falk and Weston note the inability of Curtis to be objective with respect to the sources that they used in their original piece. Where Curtis claims that "[t]he international bodies on which Falk and Weston depend for support of their arguments have for many years adopted a double standard, prejudicial to Israel and aligned with Arab positions on the Arab-Israeli conflict," Falk and Weston retort

> We regard this contention as cheap polemics. After all, our main assertions have been confirmed by Amnesty International, the International Commission of Jurists, and the International Committee for the Red Cross [...] to call such sources biased is to depart from the boundaries of serious discussion.

Falk and Weston delineated Curtis's misrepresentations of their views, and concluded by turning the matter over to an invisible college of international scholars: "Of course, this claimed disparity between our approach and that of Professor Curtis cannot be definitively established by us. We leave that validation to the scholarly community and to the wider marketplace of further informed assessments."

Aware of the type of criticism that would be leveled against those who examined Israeli acts from the perspective of those that they affect, and not from the statist model, Falk has embarked on a number of studies related to Israel's illegal occupation of the West Bank and the Gaza Strip. In a 1988 symposium on Palestinian refugees, Falk pointed to the fact that Palestinians suffer a number of calamities, "most basic of all, of the hostile and brutally sustained occupation of their own homeland." Falk considers in detail the extent of the violations in the occupied territories and concludes: "Israel is predominantly and flagrantly in violation of the most fundamental humanitarian standards of international law," and that Israel's legal arguments fall short of "satisfying tests of persuasiveness." He argues that the number and prolonged nature of such violations goes beyond incurring the responsibility of the state for illegal acts and suggests "the appropriateness of supplementing the language of illegality with the language of criminality." In this manner, he notes that those responsible for such policies in Gaza and the West Bank should be held criminally liable for their actions (see Chapter 8).

In a panel discussion held the same year, Falk turned his attention to Israeli settlements on the West Bank and concludes that they represent "a massive, continuing violation of the laws of war." Falk considers briefly attempts by certain international lawyers to challenge the "overwhelming consensus of experts and governments" who support the view that the settlements "flagrantly" violate applicable international law. As he notes, such "arguments are so strained and artificial in character as to be hardly worth detailed refutation." He then goes on to consider attempts by Israel to establish facts on the ground, disregarding the rights of the local inhabitants, and thus reinforcing "the impression of the impotence of international law." Falk then considers the manner in which international law can play a role in the peace process. He notes that law may clarify the content of a "reasonable and fair solution" based on the right of the civilian population to "retain the societal integrity of their territory once occupation is ended." Further, he adds that international law requires the removal of the settlements, and thus "embodies an indispensable substantive precondition of an acceptable peace process." He argues that while full compensation to the settlement activities may be used as a "bargaining chip" during negotiations, it should not stand in the way of the "most vital claim": the end of the Israeli occupation (see Chapter 9).

Falk's expertise on the occupied territories was recognized by the United Nations in 2000 when he was asked by the Commission on Human Rights to participate in an inquiry examining the violation of human rights law in the occupied territories as a result of the Al-Aqsa intifada. In a section entitled "Clarifying the Context: Illusion and Reality," the Commission pointed out that the "commitment to objectivity does not imply a posture of 'neutrality' with respect to addressing the merits of the controversies concerning alleged violations of human rights and international humanitarian law. Judgments can and must be made." As such, the Commission, headed by John Dugard and comprising Falk and Kamal Hossain, concluded in March 2001 that it was "incontestable that the Israeli Security Forces [the Israeli Defense Forces and the Israeli Police Force] have used excessive and disproportionate force from the outset of the second intifada, whether their conduct is measured by the standards of international humanitarian law applicable to armed conflict, the codes of conduct applicable to policing in situations not amounting to armed conflict or by the open-fire regulations binding upon members of the Israeli Security Forces." The Report of the Commission highlights the Israeli policy of targeting specific individuals for political assassinations, the Israeli settlements in the occupied territories, and the deprivation of economic and social rights as a result of collective punishments (see the Appendix).

When speaking in a personal capacity about the findings of the Commission (see Chapter 5), Falk said that "you only need to have a 20-percent open mind in order to reach these conclusions that are critical of Israel on the main issues of international law and human rights." Falk notes that the frustration of the Palestinian people derives from two sources: the first is the oppression at the hands of the Israelis that permeates the totality of everyday life. The second is a response to a leadership that is perceived as having, for all intents and purposes, abandoned the Palestinian cause. While Israelis saw the 2000 Camp David Agreement as a major concession, the Palestinians, as Falk points out, saw it as a "bad bargain." It "failed in fundamental respects to deal with the creation of a viable sovereign Palestine, failed to deal with the refugee issue, failed to share rights to Jerusalem on an equal basis, failed to address the threat or irritant of persisting settlements." At its most basic level, the first intifada appears to have been a manifestation of the popular will to fight oppression as well as a demand from its leadership that the struggle bear fruit (see Chapter 7).

This understanding cuts to the core of the Inquiry Commission's findings. As the Report notes, when considering the Israeli–Palestinian conflict, one must never lose sight of the fact "that the Palestinian people are struggling to realize their right of self-determination, which by virtue of international law and morality provides the foundation for the exercise of other rights... [and] Israel's continued occupation of Palestinian territories has remained the most formidable obstacle to Palestinian self-determination." The right of self-determination of Palestinians is a topic which Richard Falk has turned to previously, although in relation to the "peace process" and the interim Oslo Accords. Falk was moved to place the notion of a "peace process" in inverted commas, because he believes that "a genuine peace process has to be something that is acceptable to both sides. And although the Palestinians may initially swallow this, I don't think they'll be able to digest it." Writing shortly after the signing of the 1993 Oslo Accords, Falk emphasizes the need to have more actors involved in the "peace process" due to the "disparity of power, wealth, influence, information, negotiation skills between Israel and the PLO" (see Chapter 5).

Falk contends that there can be no optimistic assessment of the Oslo Accords because they are too one-sided and Israel has "sought to push its advantageous position as fully as possible." Noting that the international community generally defers to the wishes of parties when negotiating international agreements, and that the disparity between the parties coincides with the United States' geopolitical interests, the Palestinians must look elsewhere for support. If Palestinians are to protect their claims to self-determination (in the true sense of the word), Falk argues that they must expand their grassroots activism, which could then be reinforced "by the transnational support of citizen's associations dedicated to peace, democracy, and human rights." This is necessitated by the fact that the Palestinian leadership of Yasir Arafat appears "autocratic and corrupt [...] content with a minimalist conception of self-determination." He concludes by arguing that "no matter how one-sided the agreed texts, Palestinian rights to self-determination are intrinsic and inalienable" and as such the end-point of "the peace process" is "not to be confused with the realization of Palestinian rights to self-determination."

XVI   UNLOCKING THE MIDDLE EAST: THE WRITINGS OF RICHARD FALK

While it is clear that Falk's writings have paid much attention to Palestinian self-determination, he has not neglected the right of the much larger grouping of a people without a state: the Kurds. Falk has noted that US policies regarding the Kurdish people are "essentially a dead end and reflect an absence of political imagination and a failure to help the peoples of the region achieve a better life for themselves."[14] In a 1992 article, Falk considers the plight of Kurds and the means by which they should proceed with their demands for self-determination. Falk considers whether demands for self-determination should aim toward a unified Kurdistan or limited self-rule within the five states in which the Kurds find themselves. Falk argues that the current period, with the end of the Cold War and the Iraqi defeat in the 1991 Gulf War, "contains the greatest opportunity for the advancement of the Kurdish struggle since the Ottoman collapse" (see Chapter 6).

Falk takes the reader through the evolution of the concept of self-determination but ultimately acknowledges that "the right of self-determination to be realized in practice does not have a definitive content or status but reflects both a contest of political wills and the play of forces." As such, he notes that "internal self-determination is more easily reconciled with some conceptions of international law and may be more in accord with the political prospects and relative capability of a captive and people or nation." He believes that if self-determination is to be a basis upon which Kurds ensure protection of their human rights, they may well be successful, but if self-determination is used as a basis for a claim of a secessionist Kurdistan, the "answer is more ambiguous." He concludes by calling on the Kurdish people to establish authoritative representatives who can take advantage of the current opportunity to place their demands forward "within as united a political front as possible."

Before presenting the above-mentioned pieces, the anthology provides readings that outline Falk's general bearings in unlocking the politics and religion in the Middle East. Falk asks, at a lecture he delivered in May 2000 at the American University in Cairo: "Can Political Democracy Survive the Religious Resurgence?" (see Chapter 3). He sees in this religious resurgence a form of resistance against globalization, in which the secular elite that control states, cannot (or will not) provide for people's most basic wants. Falk sees the militant examples of religious resurgence as a response "to this dangerous mixture of domestic governmental failure and global economic and cultural penetration." He points to the Islamic Revolution in Iran as a religious resurgence that was "inherently extremist and fanatically anti-modern and anti-Western." The resurgence was thus essentialized as a "declaration of war against American-led globalization," whereby "Islam" is seen as being monolithic and radical.

Against that backdrop, Falk notes that "religious resurgence" is not only an Islamic phenomenon; its weight has been felt in most countries. It is a result of the end of the Enlightenment as manifest in the failure of secularism to provide for the needs of the majority of the population. Falk speaks about two poles to be found within religious movements (as well as secular movements): one exclusive, which believes itself to hold the only truth; the other, inclusive, which affirms its own truth, but grants space for others. Falk then asks the question: "What if a secular state is confronted by a rising religious movement?" He points to Algeria and Turkey as examples of the state repudiating "moderate expressions of religious resurgence" only "to give rise to more extreme orientations." Falk contends that the danger to humane governance is not a consequence of religious resurgence, but the vulnerability of any society to political appeals based on extremism, be they religious or otherwise. In such a situation, what can a secular government do? It can repress or it can practice "preventive politics" by making itself invulnerable to appeals of extremism, whether religious or secular. This may be achieved, Falk purports, by encouraging inter-religious and inter-civilizational dialogue, by introducing a culture of human rights and civil society; and by seeking a balance between globalization and social well-being. What this requires then, is "a real social movement that is directed toward the re-empowerment of the state to act in a compassionate manner toward its own citizenry and not to serve only as an agent of global capital."

In a second piece on religion, Falk outlines an attempt to deal with the exclusion of Islam from a Western dominated international framework (see Chapter 4). Using as a starting point Samuel Huntington's *Clash of Civilizations*, Falk considers the evolution of "civilizational" participation in international affairs. He sees the establishing of a civilizational approach as having the potential to challenge the "hegemonic, almost monopolistic, dominance of statist identity" of the international system. What he seeks to explore is the discriminatory treatment that the Islamic world has faced in the participatory structures of international affairs. Falk considers the "geopolitics of exclusion" as reflected in a "false universalism" that is a product of the Eurocentric and Western-dominated international framework. An outgrowth of this domination is that "Islamic perspectives have not been equitably represented in key authority structures and processes of world order, which seems to account for the impression and actuality of an anti-Islamic bias in addressing policy issues of the global agenda." Falk considers the grievances that Islam has with its image in the West; he considers the extent to which Muslims have been excluded from various international areas "and subject to discriminatory regimes of control and prohibitions (i.e., Iraq and the Palestinians)"; and, as a result, calls for a "normative adjustment" to ensure the inclusion of Islam in the international system. In so doing, Falk seeks to fix "the framework to overcome the neglect of non-Western civilizations."

In the first two readings of this anthology, Falk's overall perspective on the region is put forward. In a 1991 edition of *Millennium*, Falk gives a nice overview of his thinking on numerous topics related to the region. He brings to the fore pertinent issues related to the Kurds, Kuwait, Israel, Lebanon, and the Palestinian struggle as a means of highlighting the regional vulnerabilities that have been brought on by geopolitics. From these cases, Falk sees certain discernible patterns: "the intrusion of geopolitics into a region of prime economic and strategic importance for ascendant global interests" means that no "autonomous political community at the state level" can exist. Further, he sees the persistence of the trend of the "refusal of geopolitical forces to take moral and legal arguments seriously, or to be guided in their policy-making by consideration of human rights and well-being of peoples." As a means of dealing with the Middle East, which finds itself captive to outside forces and led by "economic and political elites owing primary allegiance to the extra-regional geopolitical edifice of global power," Falk suggests that "[i]t is never too early to engage in resistance." He notes, however, that it is "difficult to conceive of a Middle East process of emancipation except by way of a fundamental reorientation of the political outlook which shapes the United States' policy." Falk concludes that such a reorientation would come at a heavy price, and notes that the interplay between "resistance and repression ensures that the logic of cruelty will continue to shape the politics of the region" (see Chapter 2).

In Chapter 1, an interview conducted at the Mena House, Richard Falk explains how his interests in the Middle East developed, and he looks back on these pieces to consider various issues. In such a manner, a sense of his commitment to the region and his perspective is unlocked. By focusing on issues that have not been given voice in the other readings, the interview fills gaps and gives further insights that demonstrate Falk's consistent and comprehensive perspective on issues relevant to the Middle East. Through the various readings presented in this anthology—be they interviews, panel discussions, speeches, or articles that appeared in periodicals or collected works—a comprehensive understanding of the Middle East emerges that is centered on placing people before politics. In such a manner, Falk demonstrates avenues by which the Untied States can escape its dead-end policies and cynical power politics. Richard Falk's work is not simply *a* perspective on the Middle East, it *gives* perspective. By demonstrating avenues by which the compass of foreign policy in the Middle East can be reset, Falk provides the moral political imagination so sorely lacking in US policymakers. Such avenues can lead to a more peaceful, more humane future in the Middle East. For policymakers and citizens willing to cross that threshold, this anthology may well hold the key.

—Jean Allain

The Middle East

Chapter One

THE MENA HOUSE INTERVIEW

JA: Richard, thank you for granting me this interview. I wanted to ask you about the extent to which your background and your chosen career as an international legal scholar has influenced your interests in the Middle East?

RF: I think it was unavoidable, growing up in New York City with a Jewish background, that I would be confronted by many people from an early age who had a strong attachment to Israel, who in the aftermath of World War II felt that the creation of a Jewish state was a historic sequel to the Holocaust, something absolutely necessary to the survival of the Jewish people, Jewish cultural identity. My own family was very secular in background, with very little emphasis on their own ethnic identity. I had almost no contact with my Jewish heritage as a young person, although living in Manhattan I knew a lot of people who were Jews. My own family was fully assimilationist—my father very strongly felt that the important thing was to be American, not a Christian American or Jewish American. He disliked the idea that you were loyal to another country as was implied by some Zionist commitments, so that is part of my background.

And I suppose another important element in my orientation toward ideas was a kind of identification very early in my life with the underdog. It extended even to sports. Most of my family were Yankees fans. You know the Yankees were world champions in those years. And I went all the way from my apartment in midtown Manhattan to watch the Brooklyn Dodgers play. They were at the bottom of the league, and it was plain even at the time that my own identity, in relation especially to my mother's very success-oriented family, was at stake.

The other part of my background that is relevant is that my father was a very forceful person, a lawyer and a naval historian, very conservative, and the lawyer for some of the most famous early anti-Communists who were émigrés from the Soviet Union, including Kerensky, who had been the

---

This interview was conducted on 15 May 2000 at the Mena House, which is literally in the shadows of the Great Pyramids of Giza, Egypt. Host to many historical events, it is best known as the place where Winston Churchill and Chiang Kai-shek met in 1943.

interim prime minister between the Czar and the Bolsheviks. I had known all these people as a kid, and became very friendly with them. And it made me—I suppose I was to some extent a reactive personality even then—uncomfortable with what I saw as political extremism of a right-wing nature. So I would question them, as a way of not being too bored by all this adult company. Though in my early adolescent years in my school, I generally followed my father's point of view. I remember writing an editorial supporting the Republican presidential candidate in 1948, the year I graduated from high school, so I had a kind of confused politics.

For a long time, I really was quite apolitical as a student and then became—I'll spare you some of the interim steps—politicized in the very early stages of the Vietnam War, somewhat by accident. I was then teaching at Ohio State. And I happened to read some things about the French experience in Indochina, and their efforts and failure to hold onto those colonial possessions. It struck me at that time very pragmatically that it was a disastrous enterprise for the US to try to reverse the outcome of a war waged against the French over the whole of Indochina, and then divide Vietnam and try to defeat the anti-colonial movement. So that politicized me very much, because this was very early (1960–61), when it was quite controversial to oppose the war. Later on, five or six years later, it became much more acceptable because the elite became divided itself, the media became divided, but in the early stage, if you look back, not a single member of Congress spoke against the war. The only two who opposed it, did so on constitutional grounds, that it hadn't been properly declared.

My two visits to North Vietnam during the war really transformed my thinking about the US government and the politics of the period. Initially, I went very reluctantly, but once I did, the visits changed me from a pragmatic opponent of the war to someone who thought about what the war really meant in human terms. I was very surprised that their leaders were not ideological fanatics but were real human beings with human intelligence and a lot of wisdom. And it's such a beautiful country. You saw how helpless they were under the higher technology weaponry being used against them. There was nothing to bomb in the country except churches and hospitals, nothing in the countryside, so that had a great ideological effect on me.

JA: How was it played out? You must have come under a lot of criticism for your stance against the war in Vietnam. How do you deal with that personally?

RF: Well, I respond to some of it and ignore some of it, and expect it goes with the territory. And then of course the other side is that it elicits a lot of positive things, too—even at Princeton in this period, the younger people were overwhelmingly on my wavelength. It was the older alumni who thought I should be dismissed from the university. But Princeton is a confident enough academic institution in that regard; they would have been just as happy if I hadn't been there, but they weren't about to get into another controversy by getting rid of me. And they actually treated me quite well during this period, which they didn't do to everybody.

But the Vietnam experience was relevant to the Middle East in this way: I decided that I should stay away from Middle East issues because I had enough controversy over my Vietnam stand and I knew that taking a position sympathetic to the Palestinians would create all sorts of additional agitation and I decided to avoid that. But then I developed friendships with a variety of people from the region and felt it more and more artificial not to, especially when I was invited to talk and to do things. Some of these people were quite prominent, like Edward Said and others, and so I gradually became more engaged in this cluster of issues.

My big commitment was in the aftermath of the Vietnam War, in the seventies. I came to the conclusion that Iran would be the next battleground for a US interventionary presence in a Third World country, because there were 45,000 American troops in Iran. The Shah had been put in power by CIA intervention and was extremely repressive, particularly toward the intellectual community and students, and there were a lot of Iranian students around in the United States and I was quite influenced by some of them. I became the chairman of a Committee on the Protection of Human Rights in Iran and Opposition to US Intervention. Very few people were interested in Iran at that point, so this little committee with almost no resources and no influence became very visible as the Iranian Revolution emerged, and I was invited to go to Iran and meet the leadership. I met Khomeini and the other leaders and went back a second time during the hostage crisis. I had some Iranian friends in the United States who went to Iran and became very prominent in the early stages of the Islamic government.

That got me into a great deal of difficulty, because I wrote an article at the invitation of the *New York Times* in 1979 on my meeting with Khomeini. They had covered him very little up to that point. I tried to write it carefully, but not being as negative as the general treatment in the US media of the Islamic challenge to the Shah. But the *Times* gave it a very inflammatory headline that I never saw, "Trusting Khomeini," and that generated a great deal of hate mail and threats for years afterward. And I was isolated by the *Times* by other things, like editorials and columns. Anthony Lewis wrote a column criticizing my views and there were some other editorials after the revolution saying that since I had been so active in opposing the Shah for his allegedly repressive practices, why wasn't I comparably active in opposing this new source of repression. In fact, I had been on a second committee that was trying to do something about the denial of human rights in post-revolutionary Iran, but it gained much less attention and there were other groups that were much better financed. And it didn't seem like something for which we had either access to information or clearly the basis, so it didn't amount to much. But this is a long-winded way of giving you some sense of how my Middle Eastern involvement emerged.

I went with Edward Said to Lebanon in the early eighties to meet Arafat and some of the other leaders, and that was the important step. And then I became the vice-chairman of a commission that investigated violations of international law in the course of the 1982 war. Sean McBride was supposed to be the chairman, but he was sick and I became the acting chairman. That was a very disturbing but interesting experience because we came to Beirut during the period when it was still under siege. It was quite dangerous—Beirut was being bombed and so we had to come in by ship. And because the Lebanese government was so upset, we were able to meet all the leading people in Lebanon. And then we went to Jordan where the Crown Prince received us, and we also met with some of the prominent Palestinian exiles. And then we went to Israel, where it was pretty dangerous for us to be, because the Commission was perceived to be critical of the Israeli invasion. So we had to register at the hotel under false names and things like that. But there were a lot of Israelis who were very opposed to the war, including a lot of military people, and we interviewed these officers. It started a kind of dissident movement there among the military, particularly the younger military. So it was an extremely interesting period. It was just before the terrible massacres at the two refugee camps of Sabra and Shatila. Part of the Commission went back to see the camp, which we had seen just before—they were in pretty bad shape then—but you can imagine what it was like after. And then we produced a report, which I think is a pretty good international law analysis. It was written essentially by Kader Asmal, who is now a minister in the South African government. The commission was small, but it was quite good. It had been constituted by some British members of parliament—it was basically a British initiative, by British people who were opposed to what Israel had done in Lebanon.

JA: Can you tell me a bit about your background in law? Why did you decide on law in general and international law specifically?

RF: Well, my father was a lawyer. I was a good athlete as a young person, in fact I had a major league baseball tryout and devoted a lot of my attention to that. I was a poor student. And I didn't know what to do. I went to a good New York high school, but I was a very mediocre student. Somehow I was able to get into the University of Pennsylvania, probably because my father had gone there. But I was on academic probation the first year. Partly because I was emphasizing sports—I was on the freshman basketball team, which was a big thing to be, because I had gone to a small high school, and there were many sports scholarship students, but I still managed to get on the team and also to play freshman tennis at the same time. And I gambled a lot, played a lot of poker and things like that. So I was really in pretty bad trouble.

Then a couple of kids asked me to room with them, and they were good students and I sort of felt that I had to show to myself and to them that I wasn't quite as much of a failure as I had seemed to be. And then I found that when I worked a little bit harder, I did well as a student, and furthermore that I enjoyed it. There wasn't such a big difference between almost or actually failing and doing really well. It was a mystery, because I almost didn't do that much more work. But I changed my outlook and I de-emphasized sports. Finally I dropped sports and became sort of belatedly culturally interested. I audited a lot of extra courses in fine arts and things like that. I had a very excellent undergraduate teacher in religious thought. And so I had a real transformation. Still I had no idea really what to do and I went to law school in circumstances of psychological drift, feeling law was a way of postponing a life decision for a few more years. It never occurred to me to think about an academic life, partly because of my background as a bad student and partly because, at least at that time, you didn't associate younger people with teaching. But then when I was in law school...

JA: This was at Yale?

RF: Yes, I went to Yale and I gravitated toward the more marginal courses, jurisprudence, commercial law. There were some broad cultural courses, and I became interested in Indian law, not the indigenous people, but the subcontinent. I studied Sanskrit and a lot of stuff that had nothing to do with being a big-time lawyer. My father was a Wall Street lawyer who had started in a small firm, but I knew I didn't want to do that. When I finished law school I had a Fulbright to India but the State Department cancelled it at the very last minute, on the grounds that India had not paid for grain and they were going to punish India by withholding these Fulbrights— punish them by not sending me and the others. They renewed it the next year, but then my father was sick, and I never did go.

But what happened was, because of this I had nothing to do very late in my last year of law school, and somebody got sick at Ohio State and they were so desperate to find someone that they contacted my international law teacher at Yale, Myers McDougall, and he very fortunately was a promoter of people. He had always picked out one or two people in each law school class. And I was one of the two people he had picked out in my class. So he encouraged them to hire me, which they did. And then it suddenly occurred to me that this was a very privileged life and I enjoyed it a lot. They were able to find a way for me to stay on, and the person who was normally teaching international law was very eager to have me stay, and so he very generously shared his courses with me. And I taught whatever no one else wanted to teach. So I was there several years, and in some sense, I never looked back, as it seemed to me a way of combining things that gave me a lot of freedom as a young person to pursue my own interests.

I then went to Harvard, while I was at Ohio State, and did a JSD degree. We had several very good people who were there at the same time. More intellectual stimulus came from the other students than from the faculty. The international law faculty was not that interesting. And they were very hostile to me because of my Yale background. Yale and Harvard—now there's an extreme dislike. It's more than ideological. People actually *disliked* each other. The worst grade I got at Harvard was in international law. I had gotten this Ford Foundation fellowship for young law teachers, supposed to rescue you from the hinterland for a year or so and let you audit courses, hang around, and read and write, if you wanted to. But Erwin Griswold, who was the dean then, and a very Calvinistic person, wouldn't let me do that. So that's why I ended up doing this work for the JSD, but that meant I had to take courses with undergraduates at Harvard Law School. So it was quite a challenge to my ego. I was an assistant professor taking the same exams as undergraduates. I survived, but didn't finish my degree until after I had been at Princeton, which had the same type of fellowship.

I didn't intend to really leave law school teaching. I was happy at Ohio State in the law school. But Princeton had this strange chair that they hadn't been able to fill, which had the requirement that you had to be trained in law but not too interested in it. And they somehow tracked me down at Ohio and gave me this very good offer. As a young person, they didn't hand me the chair immediately, but they didn't give it to anybody else either.

JA: This is the Albert G. Milbank Chair of International Law and Practice? Who was he?

RF: Albert G. Milbank was the founder of a very successful law firm in New York City, which is now called Milbank, Tweed, Hadley, & McCloy. He was probably the most prominent lawyer of his time. He was a lawyer for the Rockefellers and other very well known interests. A Princeton graduate who wanted Princeton to have a law school. And this was his way of saying, okay, if they won't give me a law school, at least they should do something in international law; then other people followed and created chairs in constitutional law and chairs in public law and history.

JA: Why did you stay at Princeton despite its not having a law school?

RF: There were two reasons that I articulated to myself why I preferred to stay at Princeton, although I had chances subsequently to teach in good law schools. The main reason, the main vocational reason, anyway, was that I hated grading law school exams. I absolutely detested it. And I was teaching large classes at Ohio State, a first-year required criminal law course. Also, I found the students who were studying in a non-vocational way more interesting, not necessarily brighter, but more interesting than the vocationally oriented students that one tends to have in law schools. So that was my explanation to myself as to why I decided to give up law school teaching.

JA: It's been said that while you "appear to be a member of the east coast Ivy League establishment," your writings reveal you to be "a free thinker, possessing radical solutions to man's problems on earth." Do you think this is accurate?

RF: Well, one of my characteristics, I suppose, is to find it difficult to merge my identity with collective institutions of any kind, whether it be church, state, or university, so I never conceived of myself as part of the Ivy League establishment. If you look at my resume, though, it looks like I am.

JA: But was there not the possibility of osmosis, in the sense that you could have fallen into line?

RF: I also had a kind of contrarian personality that led me to resist being defined by the expectations that flow from particular roles or particular institutions. And I have a sense of being on the side of the underdog and a motivation for justice.

The first politically active thing I did was when I was at Ohio State. There were black students who were not allowed to live in off-campus housing. And they were forced to pay double for inferior, totally inconvenient, housing. All this off-campus housing was owned by members of the university's board of trustees. Several of us young non-tenured faculty threatened a lawsuit. And the trustees backed down.

Maybe it's an individualism of sorts that led me to want to define my identity in a more personal, direct way. I always felt that one of the things that made academic life so desirable was that you were autonomous. You didn't get paid a lot and you didn't necessarily have a great deal of political influence, but at least you didn't have to serve any other master. You were ideologically free to pursue ideas that you felt were important and free to support causes that you believed in.

I think that sense of being an outsider has never left me—maybe my Jewish identity unconsciously accentuates this. Though I think Jews can go either way: they can be either completely absorbed by the establishment and want to be as much accepted by it as possible, or they can see themselves as marginalized and critics of those in power. I certainly chose the latter approach. There is a long tradition of Jewish dissidents.

I'm not a complete outsider, though, so it's been an ambiguous identity. I think the ambiguity exists partly because even though I might not think myself that I'm part of the Ivy League establishment, other people perceive me as such, and therefore I'm invited to do things that probably follow from that. I've been a member of the Council of Foreign Relations, for instance, for 30 years or so, probably just because I was a reasonably visible young Princeton professor at a time when the establishment had to reach out to new voices because it was being discredited by the Vietnam experience.

JA: Can you talk a bit about a problem that I'd like to raise about academic debates, especially in the United States, where people portray themselves as dispassionate scholars but often are mere apologists for the state of Israel. Can you tell us a bit about this, what you have termed "cynical scholarship," and expand on the level of intellectual discourse that you find in the United States?

RF: I think the problem of concealed ideology has particularly afflicted Middle East studies. And it has to do, I think, with the way in which those with a sympathy or ideological commitment to Israel have tried to use the academic arena as a site of struggle, so to speak, and to use the pretension of objective scholarship as an instrument of disguise and concealment. Because some very distinguished scholars have done this it's created a kind of establishment, an academic establishment that works very hard to discredit any views that are seen as dissident. And Princeton is one of the primary sites of this process. Edward Said has written about Orientalism and Bernard Lewis, who is probably the king of ideological concealment. It disturbs me a lot on intellectual grounds as well as on ideological grounds. Because I feel that the academic equivalent of the Hippocratic oath for doctors is the commitment to some kind of integrity, and that means showing your cards, being transparent. I'm obviously the last person to criticize someone for advocating certain controversial positions, but I think to do that while you're hiding beneath a veil of purported objectivity and neutrality is a very insidious kind of manipulation.

JA: Your scholarly output has been vast both in breadth and depth, yet discernible themes have recurred; I am thinking here, in particular, of one—the Nuremberg Principles. Could you explain why this has been a persistent theme in your writings?

RF: Sure. Well, as with many of my sustained interests, my concern with Nuremberg, the Nuremberg judgment, and the Nuremberg principles originated in the Vietnam controversy. I came to the conclusion, reluctantly, that the way the United States was pursuing the war in Vietnam, both in its use of force and the methods by which the war was being fought, could not be reconciled with the condemnation of German and Japanese leaders after World War II, and I began to articulate this perspective. It must have been very disturbing to people in government, to see themselves like this. Some of these people I had known from Princeton and Yale and so it was probably personally, more so than my general opposition to the war and my international law opposition to the war, the thing that agitated all opposition to me. And then, because it became very interesting to student groups that were opposed to the war, I was invited to university talks, sometimes in tandem with Telford Taylor, who had been a prosecutor at Nuremberg and was a very conservative person, a former general, who still wanted to argue the application of the Nuremberg principles in a fairly cautious way. He and I were ultimately put in a debating context. He had a very good mind, so it was a very interesting encounter. He wrote a book called *Nuremberg and Vietnam*, which more or less came to the same conclusions but ended with the idea that, and he quotes a French proverb: "This was worse than a crime; it was a mistake."

JA: And how would do you see those principles playing out in the Middle East?

RF: Well, one would have to say that a lot of the tactics relied upon by Israel to sustain its control over the occupied territories for all these years, including the invasion of Lebanon back in 1982, amount to crimes against the peace, and are war crimes in a Nuremberg sense. The reality seems to me to be that the Nuremberg framework established after World War II was a kind of victor's justice, but with the promise made by the prosecutors, most famously by the American prosecutor Jackson, that the principles being applied to the Germans at Nuremberg were going to govern the victors as well as the vanquished. And so I have written in the past that this Nuremberg promise has been broken by all the victors, not just the US, (and not just Israel, which of course was not part of the agreement) but by the Soviet Union, France, and the United Kingdom in different ways. And so one has to say that the importance of the Nuremberg principles, until the break-up of Yugoslavia and Rwanda, was as a source of resistance in civil society.

Nuremberg became important particularly for religiously oriented people, who wanted to base their opposition to Vietnam or nuclear weapons on some set of principles beyond their own beliefs. It was very important to Daniel Ellsberg when he released the Pentagon Papers. He very much wanted me to use the Nuremberg argument in his defense at his trial, which I did. I testified a great deal in trials in the period from the late sixties to the early eighties, which was not only Vietnam-era litigation but also for a lot of anti-nuclear and environmental activists. Radical Catholics like the Berrigan brothers. A Seattle group called Ground Zero that blocks the trains from delivering Trident Missiles to their submarine base. These people influenced me a lot in terms of understanding the struggle to make the Nuremberg principles part of the law of the land. The Nuremberg judgment hadn't done it, so it was up to civil society, up to the civil rights movement. To have civil rights, it depended on a lot of people keeping the ideal alive—and I do think that they kept the idea alive.

This made it less discontinuous to revive Nuremberg in the context of the former Yugoslavia, even though the revival was based on what I call the geopolitics of ambivalence—we really didn't want to intervene and take responsibility, but this was an easy thing to do, like sanctions. And so this was all a part of that process. But I think that the Pinochet incident and the move to establish an international criminal court and the experience at the Hague and Richard Goldstone becoming an international personality—now we are closer to really making the Nuremberg principles part of the living law of states.

JA: Considering the plight of the Palestinians under Israeli occupation, you stated that Israel's legal arguments fall short of "satisfying the test of persuasiveness" and that Israeli settlements are "flagrant violations" of applicable law. Could you maybe work through first of all what are the fundamental precepts of humanitarian law that would hold in Palestine?

RF: Essentially, the conditions governing belligerent occupation, for one thing, would require that Israel accept the Geneva Convention's framework. One of the cardinal provisions in that framework, Article 53, does not allow for population transfers, and that's very fundamental to the nature of a legitimate argument. Also, the underlying problem of the occupation is that it was carried on in defiance of UN Security Council Resolution 242, which calls for withdrawal. The persistence and the refusal to heed those resolutions created an underlying condition of illegality to the occupation.

But the establishment of the settlements and armed settlements in an occupied territory, combined with the imposition of collective punishment of the Palestinian inhabitants, demolition of houses, prolonged detention and torture under conditions of detention, almost acknowledgment of torture as a practice for eliciting information, creates a long litany of flagrant violations, both of international humanitarian law and human rights law, based on the fundamental protection of human rights. And the unwillingness to negotiate a withdrawal over such a long period of time, given this condition of illegality and criminality, created, in my view, at least a right of non-violent resistance. In that sense the intifada represented a legitimate form of resistance against a pattern of prolonged illegality.

JA: Could we move on to the notion of "Islam"? Could you maybe talk a bit about how Islam has been, let's say, re-emphasized in the Middle East, as a way of people seeking refuge in a movement that ultimately challenges the status quo?

RF: Well, I think that Islam represents a set of orientations and beliefs that are very committed to the autonomy of the region and its peoples and societies. And it was seen, first in the Iranian Revolution, as an extraordinary mobilizing perspective, especially under the stimulus of a figure like Ayatollah Khomeini. But even before that, Islamic thinkers, who had earlier been Marxists like Ali Shariati proved to have enormous appeal for young Iranians. And the essence of what occurred during the seventies and eighties was for those who wanted to challenge Western domination and the exploitative features of alien economic and political power; for them, Islam became a much more potent vehicle of resistance than Marxism.

There was always a strain of Islamic opposition to secularism. It was here in Egypt with the Muslim Brotherhood in the Nasser period. There was a lot of tension between President Nasser's form of nationalism and Islam. But it was at the margins of political life. What the Iranian Revolution did was to bring it to the center. And then it played into Western anxieties about what was happening in the Middle East, and to some extent Zionist and other forms of propaganda helped portray Islam and the Arab world as a source of terrorism. So people of the region were stereotyped and associated with a fanaticism and extremism that were thought to be one with Islamic fundamentalism. In many ways, the effort to discredit the Iranian Revolution proceeded under this rubric. And to some degree, there is a partial truth, of course—some of the most active manifestations of Islam tended toward extremism in early post-revolutionary Iran. But as with other revolutions, the process evolved, and now one can arguably say that Iran has the most vibrant democratic political system in the region.

JA: Would you say, for instance, that as much as the Iranian Revolution was a challenge to the West, in fact pluralism in Iran is more of a challenge to the Middle East, because it demonstrates that Islam can be democratic?

RF: Yes, yes and I think that's a very great challenge, particularly to the Sunni regimes, in the Gulf and elsewhere, that have purported to be very Islamic and at the same time are very repressive toward any kind of dissident views. What the Khatami government in Iran is showing, and also civil society philosophers like the Iranian Abdul Karim Serush, is that one can have a vibrant pluralism within the framework of Islam. And that this is not inconsistent with Islam—instead, it really vitalizes it. Everybody now says that the most intellectually exciting and diverse place in the Islamic world is Iran. If you go to bookstores there are more translations of Rumi and even of the romantic poets and of writings on the philosophy of science. So it's not just politics, it's opened a kind of cultural space, as well, which is quite remarkable.

JA: You have written about the "peace process" in quotation marks. Could you maybe talk about the difference you see between the peace that is being negotiated by Yasir Arafat and the Palestinian right to self-determination?

RF: Well I think that the peace process was initiated by Israel with US support and encouragement at a time when the Palestinian movement was at its weakest. It had imprudently supported Saddam Hussein in the Gulf War. It had lost a lot of its regional financial support and political backing as a result of that. And Arafat was at a stage in his own life where he probably was concerned that he was running out of time to establish a Palestinian state. So you not only have the asymmetry of power between the Israelis and the Palestinians, but you have this unfavorable set of conditions. It was a time when Israel thought it could make the Palestinians swallow a pretty unfair set of arrangements and call it peace. And for that reason, I think it's hard to really regard this as a genuine peace process, and that's why I use the quotation marks.

Because I think a genuine peace process has to be something that is acceptable to both sides. And although the Palestinians may initially swallow it, I don't think they'll be able to digest it. The next generation won't accept it; there are too many limitations on the Palestinian entity that will emerge. It seems dramatically inconsistent with Palestinian sovereignty to keep all the settlements. And some kind of participation in the administration of

Jerusalem would seem to be necessary. So this will have to be an armed peace that will be sustained by a structure of military dominance. In that sense, it's a continuation of the Israeli-Palestinian pattern that has existed since the 1948 war. It is very misleading to present this as a peace process.

At the same time, I'm not sure from the Palestinian perspective, what their alternatives are under these conditions. And whether the best thing to do here is to try to take what they can get and then work toward something more in keeping with the exercise of the right of self-determination. Certainly, if I were a Palestinian, I would not view this as satisfying the Palestinian right of self-determination.

JA: Switching gears, I wonder if you could meditate a bit about Israeli actions in Lebanon from a legal perspective?

RF: The Israeli occupations, that so-called security zone in southern Lebanon, was from the perspective of international law, a continuing act of aggression. It really had no foundation as a legal argument. So withdrawal is really just terminating an illegal arrangement; an illegal arrangement that brought great suffering to the people who were living there and probably deepened, in a very fundamental way, the tension between the Shi'ite and the Christian populations of Lebanon. Because Israel basically trained and employed this Christian army in southern Lebanon, it's very probable that the indigenous population will seek some kind of retribution. And because that is likely to happen, the Israeli-backed Lebanese militia will itself probably embark on some violence to intimidate the population. And I suppose that Hezbollah will try to make it clear that this is not going to change their basic struggle on behalf of the Palestinian cause.

JA: Could you talk about Hezbollah and their right to challenge the Israeli occupation?

RF: I don't know enough about the Hezbollah to really give a compelling response. It's certainly wrong to dismiss them as a terrorist organization. I think they are a genuine political movement that is quite comprehensive in its activities, that represents one form of struggle against the illegal status quo. Their tactics have sometimes violated the laws of war, but so have the retaliatory tactics relied upon by Israel. Certainly Israel has been responsible for killing many more civilians and innocent people in this period than Hezbollah.

JA: The strategic interests of the United States in the region are based on oil and Israel...

RF: ...and the attempt to keep countries other than Israel from acquiring weapons of mass destruction.

JA: Could you maybe talk about friendly governments that the United States has in the region? There are those who are friendly to the United States and those that are seen as "rogue states." Is it better for the people in the Middle East to be, let's say, under the umbrella of US hegemony or are they better off challenging the status quo?

RF: Well, that's an interesting question, and I don't think I can give an across-the-board answer. I think both positions cause a vulnerability—because if they become too subject to US hegemony, then they lose their own autonomy, their own freedom to develop in a way that is responsive to the needs and values of their society. And they're manipulated from outside.

If, on the other hand, they find themselves, in opposition, radical opposition, to the US, they're subject to interventionary initiatives of various sorts that can be very isolating and can impose tremendous hardship on the people. So that I think those societies fare best who steer a middle course and in effect, pursue a relatively pragmatic course. Recognizing that the US is a powerful presence in the region but at the same time, that it's not worth selling your soul to submit to that power. Easier said than done, to strike this middle path. If countries develop the kind of economic dependence that Egypt has, for instance, I think it becomes virtually impossible to take advantage of sovereign rights.

JA: Egypt receives the second largest sum of foreign aid from the United States and from international institutions, and yet it has a human rights record that includes systematic torture, and there are, depending on the sources, between 10,000 and 30,000 political prisoners, yet Egypt isn't seen as a rogue state. How do you explain the dynamic that allows Egypt to be a part of the international community in ways that Libya or Iraq can't be?

RF: Well, the perception of the moral standing of states is really manipulated by geopolitics to a very extreme extent. Both Egypt and Israel are the biggest recipients of foreign economic assistance, and they have among the worst human rights records in the world. And yet, as you say, they're not criticized, they are viewed as a benign presence in the region. And, in contrast, Iraq until the Gulf War had one of the best social records in terms of the well-being of its people of any of the countries in the region, as did Libya—Libya's is quite good—but they're categorized as rogue states.

Of course, when you categorize these states, which are weaker and isolated, as rogue states, it becomes a self-fulfilling prophecy. Because for them to hit back they have to do things that are outside the mainstream modes of conflict. So the weapons of the weak are characterized as terrorism, but the weapons of the strong are characterized as diplomacy and that creates a normative double standard of extraordinary proportions.

JA: May I ask you about US foreign policy in the Middle East and its geopolitics? In 1994 you spoke of a lack of political and moral imagination on the parts of policy makers in relation to the future of the Middle East. Could you expand on that view and explain a bit what you meant by that?

RF: I think American foreign policy toward this region has been exceptionally rigid in one sense, and unforgiving in another sense. And it alternates between being ultra-pragmatic and meting out harsh punishments. The history of the relationship with Iraq is very illuminating from this point of view. So long as Iraq was seen as a strategic player useful to the US, all that it did in its own society that was bad was completely overlooked. It was the recipient of military assistance, sophisticated weapons, and there were no problems raised, even about its program to build weapons of mass destruction.

It was, as is pretty widely documented now, encouraged by Washington to attack Iran because Iran was seen as the threat to American hegemony in the region after the 1980 revolution, and there was the hope that, at the very least, there would be a welcoming reception to the Iraqi invasion in the oil-producing province of Kuzistan in southwestern Iran. That didn't happen. The real hope, of course, was that the invasion would lead to the overthrow of the Khomeini government and the reversal of the revolution. It was a very Machiavellian kind of plot and it was completely cynical about the restraints of international law.

It also showed the way in which the UN was manipulated, in the sense that both the Soviet Union and the United States, despite the Cold War, were perfectly willing to see Iran attacked. So the UN stood to one side, as one of the longest wars and most devastating wars since World War II unfolded. The Soviet Union was worried about the spread of political Islam to central Asia and so they also shared the US view. In essence, I think the US has pursued control in the region to the greatest extent possible after the departure of the French and British, trying to make sure that Israel's security was not threatened, that non-Israeli weapons of mass destruction were not developed, and that cheap oil was available. The concern was not only about the access to the oil supply, but about the price—there was concern that countries like Iraq and to some degree even Iran, during the Shah period, were interested in higher-priced oil because they didn't have a diversified investment in the world economy as a whole.

These have been the guiding strategic ideas, and the human consequences have been consistently subordinated, and often sacrificed completely, to promote those very persistent interests. If you look back to the period of the last 50 or so years, these interests have not really varied very much, even if the balance has. For instance, until the 1967 War, Israel was seen as a strategic liability rather than a strategic asset. So that changed. Iran, of course, was seen as an ally until the fall of the Shah, and Egypt was seen as dangerous until Sadat. So one had these tactical adjustments, but the basic framework of the policy seems to me to have sustained remarkable continuity, and very little thought seems to have been given to how to bring peace and prosperity to the people in the region. It's a rich region, potentially, and a good deal of this oil wealth has been squandered without really doing very much for the people of the region.

Chapter Two

THE CRUELTY OF GEOPOLITICS: THE FATE OF NATION AND STATE IN THE MIDDLE EAST

The Tragic Predicament

The countries of the Middle East have been caught in a geopolitical trap throughout this century—a trap mainly not of their own making.[1] Their military capabilities have been too meager, compared to those of the West, to inhibit or resist intervention, and their oil too valuable to induce neglect. Other factors have aggravated or complicated this basic plot, but not fundamentally. Experiences of peoples in the region have varied for better and for worse, depending particularly on the character of their links with shifting geopolitical priorities that either mesh or clash with those priorities that serve wider interests or challenge their stability.

Within the broader setting of Middle Eastern political experience during this century, there are several notable structural features. Large established countries (Egypt, Turkey, Iran) have done better than those states that were generated by collapsing European colonial orders. Smaller countries have done better than the norm if their orientation was perceived as useful to reigning geopolitical forces and worse than the norm if their orientation was perceived as antagonistic to those forces. Strong states, reinforced by a unified nation, have done better; weak states, attempting to rule weak nations, are particularly vulnerable from within and without. No nation-state has been able to establish and maintain a constitutional democracy with a strong record of respect for law and human rights.

In this sense, the Middle East is a captive region and, so conceived, lacks the relative developmental openness that post-medieval European peoples experienced during their turbulent centuries of state-building. Whatever its difficulties, and there were many, modern Europe was not confronted with an external challenge that its members lacked the capacity to meet. Of course, it is analytically possible that had such a challenge existed, it would have induced region-building rather than state-building.

This piece first appeared in Millennium, *20.3 (Winter 1991): 383–393.*

The Middle East was subordinated before it embarked on modern state-building and was forced to proceed from a position of technological inferiority. In addition, the dynamics of Ottoman collapse, followed by European colonial demise, ensured the domestic presence of economic and political elites owing primary allegiance to the extra-regional geopolitical edifice of global power.

Against such a background, the peoples of the region have been victimized. The most pressing normative challenge is to mitigate geopolitical intrusions while encouraging the slower, but no less urgent, undertaking of re-imagining the contours of political community, and building popular support for pursuing such political projects.[2]

Some Comparisons

When Ayatollah Khomeini emerged from the obscurity of exile in 1978, he was insistent on distinguishing his "Islamic Revolution" from the media designations of an "Iranian Revolution." What underlay the distinction was the difference between spatial and religious boundaries as the key to collective identity and political community. This Islamic dream, or fantasy, as well as the more ethnically focused earlier call for "an Arab nation," continues to resonate throughout the region, especially among the poor. It is deeply threatening to the political leaders, especially those dynastic and despotic rulers who fear exposure of their paper-thin attempts to hide their allegiance to and dependence upon the non-Islamic West. The Shah was the perfect enemy for these deeply embedded indigenous tendencies (just as earlier he had been the darling of the West, loyal friend, and ardent modernizer). From this perspective, it was fitting that when powerfully challenged from within Iran, the Shah quickly drifted from being a seemingly invincible monarch to a feeble and pathetic figure, abandoned by everyone, even by the US government, which had intervened 25 years earlier, in 1953, to restore him to power. As long as he was in power, the Shah was revered in Washington, D.C. as the model of the Third World ruler, but once he became geopolitically useless, even granting him personal asylum became controversial and dangerously provocative.[3]

Nevertheless, Khomeini's vision, despite its seeming embodiment in Iran since 1979, was not realizable.[4] The statist capabilities of the region, reinforced by superpower anxieties, especially those in the United States, were determined to contain, if not crush, the Islamic counter-crusade emanating from Qum by way of Tehran. In the 1980s, the American fear of what became known in the West as Islamic fundamentalism exceeded

327.73

the worry about Marxism. Saddam Hussein, who during the preceding decade had been regarded as being in Moscow's camp, was now being courted and was even encouraged by US intelligence to embark on an aggressive war against Iran in 1980. Most expert commentators expected that the Islamic regime in Iran would be easily shattered or, at the very least, severely weakened. The Islamic Revolution emanating from Iran has, after all, been contained, despite the regional spread of Islamic militancy.[5]

Occupying a different trajectory, Kuwait was virtually a colonial invention: a way of holding on, yet letting go, in the confused process of picking up the pieces left by the collapse of the Ottoman Empire after World War I. Kuwait was a spectacle of a state created without struggle for the sake of a dynastic arrangement; possessing immeasurable wealth in the one resource upon which Western ascendancy rested, whether wittingly or not, Kuwait's vulnerability and dependence was ensured. While inventing states in the region, it would have been at least as plausible to have created a province in Iraq with the territory that became Kuwait. But Kuwait, so delimited, exceeded expectations. It was fabulously wealthy, its security was upheld because of its usefulness to the West and by its link to the Gulf sub-region, and it was surprisingly stable for almost 70 years in a region of intense turbulence. It is difficult to discern much of a Kuwaiti identity as that of belonging to a nation: Kuwaiti citizenship implied membership in a privileged commercial caste that generally denied access even to long-term resident Arabs unless they were born of a Kuwaiti father.

The complexity of what took place in 1990 defies any assured line of interpretation. The evidence is confused on the key question as to whether Iraq was enticed to invade Kuwait, thus providing the West with the pretext it needed and desired in order to destroy the Frankenstein in Baghdad it had earlier helped to construct. At a minimum, considering the evidence of an Iraqi threat, the geopolitical protection of Kuwait by the United States prior to August 2, 1990 was lax to the point of negligence, a reality as stark as the fury of the Anglo-American response after the Iraqi invasion. That Iraq was able to swallow Kuwait in a single gulp within a few hours confirmed its status as a dependent political entity in the region, a luxury enclave, secure only as long as protected from forces from without. The great risks and resources that were immediately devoted to the restoration of Kuwaiti sovereignty signify the geopolitical importance of retaining the Western grip on the region.[6] The United States, again for a rationale that remains partially obscure, was more interested in immediately destroying the Iraqi monster (yet, in the end, not interested in

OC4335-48
LIMERICK
COUNTY LIBRARY

destroying its embodiment—the person of Saddam) than in achieving the *status quo ante.*

As a preliminary hypothesis, let us assume that the US leadership, likely prodded behind the scenes by the Israelis, had grown convinced by 1990 that the time had come for some heavy geopolitical work of regional restructuring in the Middle East—a first phase in building "the new world order." As the end of World War I gave rise to the birth of Kuwait, so the end of the Cold War led indirectly, if temporarily, not only to its death, but also to its forcible resurrection. It is also tempting to draw an analogy between the collapse of a Soviet superpower role in the Middle East with the earlier Ottoman collapse. The end of wars are occasions for geopolitical restructuring, but within limits provided by the new framework of power. It is obviously a blunder to suppose a generalized fluidity. Saddam misread the geopolitical tea leaves, with disastrous consequences.

In both settings, the West was insistent, above all else, on resisting the play of regional forces of radical nationalism, whatever their form, as they were seen to pose potentially formidable threats to the retention of Western influence and privilege. In the new setting, the United States seemed particularly intent on preserving a political framework that stabilized global economic and strategic interests. Between the time of restructuring that occurred in the Middle East after World War I and after the Cold War, the geopolitical baton passed from Europe to the United States.

A second temptation is to compare and contrast Israel with Kuwait. As with Kuwait, Israel came into existence as a consequence of a major war that erupted in Europe. Further, Israel was allowed to emerge, in large part, as an artificial means to solving European problems that were unleashed by the Nazi program of genocidal anti-Semitism. As with Kuwait, but more assertively and effectively, Israel's image as a nation was conditioned by Zionist convictions, especially their exclusivist essence, of the promise of a Jewish homeland on territory sacred to the Jewish people. Within historical Zionism, many variations on this essential theme could be found, but the Israeli state, whatever its outlook on other matters, has never wavered in its commitment to Jewish ascendancy within Israel, as practice and as law.

Unlike Kuwait's, Israeli statehood was long preceded by a militant, ideologically coherent, and inspired nationalism that mounted strong and tactically shrewd resistance to the continuation of British colonial administration of its Palestinian mandate. Israel's existence was violently contested from the moment of its 1948 establishment by the arrayed Arab forces of the region. Unlike Kuwait, Israel was neither Islamic nor Arab, was not situated near oil, and boasted no special resources on which to achieve wealth, but it could draw heavily upon the financial and political resources of overseas Jews, especially in the United States and, to a lesser extent, in Europe. The Israeli government and people were firmly resolved to defend the territorial integrity of statehood, indeed to expand it, until death and destruction if necessary. Unlike Kuwait, Israel has fought wars against its hostile neighbors in each decade of its existence, winning each of them and gaining a reputation for its military prowess, yet remaining embattled and isolated. Israel has, over time, become a strategic partner of the United States in the pursuit of vital regional objectives. Indeed, as the Islamic pillars upholding Western interests have fallen or weakened, the Israeli pillar has seemed to grow ever firmer. A tangible expression of this perception is the pointedly clear signal associated with the public decision, shortly after the fighting ended in the 1990 Gulf War, to position American weaponry in Israel for the announced contingency of future regional use. For the United States to take such a step, and for Israel to agree, seemed a blatant acknowledgment of a strategy to keep the region in geopolitical bondage to the West for the indefinite future. It is symbolically revealing to note that Kuwait is the regional surety for access to oil while Israel is the foundation of military potency—the two integral dimensions of Western post-colonial hegemonic reality.

A comparison of Israeli and Palestinian national destinies is also illuminating, although bafflingly complex. The Zionist movement had spearheaded Jewish nationalism. The intense tragedy of the Holocaust alerted and mobilized world Jewry, whether previously Zionist or not, to favor the option of a secure Jewish homeland with a permanent guarantee to Jews of a right to return to that homeland. Israeli nationalism was far better prepared ideologically and militarily for political independence when it came in 1948 than were the inchoate forces of Palestinian nationalism. The response of the Arab governments to the United Nations' partition of the British mandate, Palestine, involved immediately issuing a military challenge to the Israeli presence. This proved to be a political disaster in almost every respect and contributed directly to a compounding of the Palestinian tragedy of exile and occupation. It was a glaring failure of Arab realism that substituted sheer emotion for a calculation of real possibilities. Not until Iraq resisted the United Nations' deadline of January 15, 1991 for withdrawal from Kuwait has there been an Arab disaster on such a scale, with the Palestinians once again made to bear a disproportionate, if incidental, burden of a failure of diplomacy—a failure for which they were not primarily responsible.[7]

From the perspective of community and identity, as distinct from the calculations of state power, it is not nearly as clear that, over the course of decades, the Israelis have won and the Palestinians lost. True, Israel established a strong state sustained by a fiercely loyal nation, effectively subsidized by and increasingly useful to extra-regional forces, but at a huge normative cost. Israel has been diplomatically isolated and repeatedly condemned at the regional and international level, has resisted efforts to strike an historic compromise with the Palestinians, has been continuously mobilized for war, has been compelled to devote a large share of its resources to the military, and has virtually relinquished the idealistic elements of the Zionist dream. Worst of all, it has revived its own heritage of persecution and suffering, both through the global expression of anti-Israeli sentiments, sometimes barely distinguishable from anti-Semitism, and through perpetrating a kind of holocaust on the Palestinians, as dramatized by the 1982 massacres in the Lebanese refugee camps of Sabra and Shatila.

During this period, the Palestinians have forged a political identity that is genuinely distinct. During the years of the intifada, they have managed to achieve a kind of heroic community of resistance, displaying the creativity and courage of the weak in their defiance of the strong. Despite this display of unity and will during this period of fervent struggle, the Palestinians moved toward reconciliation with the Israelis, expressing both an acknowledgment of the realities as well as a surprising sense of empathy for the otherness and humanity of their Israeli adversaries. Israeli intransigence, an expression of the deforming nationalism that has acquired state power in Israel, will undoubtedly drive the Palestinians back in the direction of despair or extremism, or both. As long as Israel is geopolitically essential, its intransigence is not a source of vulnerability— no more than Kuwait's extreme royalism and decadence was (or is).

What is most relevant to our theme are the strange, twisted destinies of these three nationalist movements that are caught up in such different ways in regional and global currents, that either open paths to statehood or close them down, and that form and deform collective identities and the shaping of political community. There are many other stories of nationalist hopes and geopolitical betrayal that are part of the larger narrative of the Middle East in this century. None is worse than the Kurdish story, almost no matter how it is told.[8] The Kurdish people were initially offered the prospect of an autonomous Kurdistan, a promise embodied in the Treaty of Sèvres, only to be withdrawn a few years later in the Treaty of Lausanne, by which time geopolitical calculations had shifted to the disadvantage of the Kurds. A main factor was the triumphal nationalism of Kemal Atatürk who promised to make Turkey a salient of Western-oriented modernization and a military bulwark against the projection of Soviet influence in a Mediterranean direction. The Kurdish identity was brutally suppressed in Turkey with hardly a whimper of protest from the West, and the Kurdish reality was subordinated to a regional design by the colonial architects of geopolitics. As a result, the Kurds were parceled out among five contiguous states, in each of which the Kurds suffered the fate of a persecuted minority. Furthermore, their fate was combined in cynical fashion with their utility as a pawn in regional political power games, and they were entwined in the wider tangles of geopolitics. When an oppositional foothold was sought in Iran or Iraq, the Kurds were encouraged, even incited, but when the compass of power turned toward stability, the Kurds were left to their statist fate, often a horrifying confirmation of Kurdish vulnerability.

Kurdish fortunes have risen and fallen on a geopolitical yo-yo that has been manipulated mainly by extra-regional forces. The Soviet Union encouraged Kurdish separatism in northeast Iran at the end of the Second World War as a way to weaken Iran and extend its own influence south. But when the Soviet military presence was effectively challenged by the United States in 1946, the central authorities in Iran once again harshly and discriminatorily integrated the Kurdish minority into Iran. During the 1970s, Iraqi Kurds were manipulated by Iran, with the encouragement of the US Central Intelligence Agency—a political dynamic generating an armed uprising. When the tensions between Iran and Iraq subsided in 1975, the Kurds were immediately cut off from their sources of assistance, clearing the way for the first of several waves of violent Iraqi repression that has included many crimes against humanity. This was a process which was repeated in the last stages of the Iran–Iraq War of the 1980s when poison gas was used against Kurdish villages while a ceasefire was being arranged in the external war. In the 1990 Gulf War, the Kurds were once again moved about the geopolitical chess board as expendable pawns. They were encouraged to rise up against Saddam Hussein during the period of fighting. They were then virtually abandoned in the face of Saddam's brutal reassertion of authority on behalf of Baghdad. Whatever ensues for the Kurdish people, it is evident that their sufferings illustrate too well the regional vulnerabilities and perils of a nation or nations without a satisfactory state. Almost 20 million Kurds have been far more victimized by the logic of geopolitical cruelty than have the far lesser number of Israelis and Kuwaitis. This is not because of a lesser quality of national consciousness.[9]

Lebanon provides a final example of regional vulnerability. In this instance, also, the state preceded the nation and was demarcated, for colonial reasons, in such a way as to encompass antagonistic "nations," which were defined by territory and religious affiliation and further riven by feudalistic structures. With a precarious brilliance, Lebanon survived, prospered for decades, and exhibited an unexpected durability until the mid-1970s by finding ways to serve outside and inside interests. Lebanon was a deliberately weak state governed in accordance with an intricate Christian/Moslem power-sharing formula, which was a mechanism for state power that was incapable either of protecting borders or of challenging decentralized bastions of power. Yet, Lebanon remained relatively secure for a long time as an outpost of financial convenience and cultural freedom for affluent Muslims. Because of this relative security, Lebanon was of special interest to Western forces and maintained a partial Western presence. Despite its persistence, the vulnerability was latent and exploitable, at will, by Lebanon's regional neighbors and with or without global incitement.

Fearing a challenge to prevailing structures (which were very highly valued by Western financial and touristic interests and, because of the prominent Maronite role in the country, regarded as partly Western), from radicalized Moslems inspired by Nasser, the US intervened in Lebanon in 1958 by sending in its marines. Stability restored, US forces withdrew. In the 1970s, Israel and Syria exacerbated internal Lebanese tensions and contributed to the onset of a long and destructive civil war that highlighted the inability of the Lebanese government to assert its domestic authority in the face of a crisis. Lebanese sovereignty was repeatedly violated; a strong Palestinian armed presence was maintained in the southern part of the country. The situation was greatly magnified by the reverberations of the 1967 Arab-Israeli War, especially the expulsion of Palestinian forces from Jordan in the wake of Black September. Israel responded to these developments by claiming a security zone near its border and by providing arms and guidance to a Christian militia that controlled the area.

Both Syria and Israel operated directly and indirectly in Lebanon.

The 1982 Israeli invasion was designed to upset permanently the Lebanese solution: by turning the state over to Israel's Christian allies, by driving the Palestine Liberation Organization into the sea, and by extending Israel's economic influence north. Israel's plan succeeded on the battlefield but not in subsequent phases. In the 1990 Gulf War, Syria's participation in the anti-Iraq coalition was purchased partly at the expense of Lebanese sovereignty in that Syria was given a green light to increase its presence and influence. Again, the reality of the Lebanese situation remains confused, uncertain, and unresolved. The experience of Lebanon illustrates one more variation on the theme of geopolitical vulnerability in the Middle East.

A brief comparison of Lebanon and Kuwait is suggestive. Both states are colonial creations, and both are incapable of defending their borders against stronger neighbors who, under expansionist leadership, are likely to turn aggressive. Differences exist, however. The Kuwaiti government was internally hard—fully capable of implementing a rigid and politically restrictive type of control. The Lebanese government, on the other hand, lacked both the mandate and the capabilities to manage internal sovereignty. The rigidity of the Kuwaiti system, although deeply unpleasant for much of the population, enabled its rulers to sustain their agency relationship to Western geopolitics. Arguably, Kuwait unduly jeopardized its survival by failing to be more accommodating toward Iraq, thereby heightening the prospect of invasion and occupation. Quite possibly, although it cannot be demonstrated, the Kuwaiti leaders counted too heavily on Iraq's comprehension of the geopolitical realities. This reliance possibly was encouraged by American advisors, either out of their own misperceptions or as part of the master plan to generate a war-provoking encounter.

In contrast, Lebanon lacked the means to safeguard its geopolitical status by upholding its internal sovereignty. As a consequence, it failed to constrain Palestinian revolutionary forces operating within its borders and repeatedly made itself a target of Israeli intervention. Israeli intervention subsequently served to validate Syrian intervention. Although the Lebanese leadership possessed a clear sense of their vulnerabilities, they lacked the cohesion and capabilities to prevent the erosion of their geopolitically grounded security. As in a Greek tragedy, from the 1960s onward, the leadership knowingly slipped toward the brink of national disaster.

Geopolitical Patterns

These five stories are extraordinarily dense and complex and could be told or retold in many different, even contradictory, ways. Nevertheless, certain patterns are undeniable: the intrusion of geopolitics into a region of prime economic and strategic importance for ascendant global interests; the inability, in such a setting, to achieve an autonomous political community at the state level, especially for smaller and weaker hinge states; the irrelevance of nationalist cohesion, or its absence, to the establishment and survival of states; and the refusal of geopolitical forces to take moral and legal arguments seriously, or to be guided in their policymaking by considerations of the human rights and the well-being of peoples. In contrast to the above patterns, there are those that focus on the importance of maintaining reliable regional strategic arrangements that facilitate the projection of military power on behalf of Western interests: control over oil and the security of Israel. The security of Israel is a goal that has become an end in itself, due mainly to the deep roots of Israeli participation in domestic politics of the United States. Because geopolitical factors cannot be reduced to materialist calculations, Marxist accounts of regional conflict are rendered suspect if they are exclusively relied upon to provide an explanation.

The patterns discussed above are not transparent, but definite tendencies may be disclosed that may reduce our susceptibility to false solutions. When America broke away from Europe, it broke free. In this century, Middle Eastern nations, especially those smaller or fragmented nations that were linked either to war-making in the region or to oil, have not had that possibility. The reality of nation and state is geopolitically embedded. The great advantage of Europe, in this regard, was that it invented the modern state and the accompanying idea of nation prior to the advent of geopolitics.[10] These political forms corresponded to the play of indigenous forces, were constructed on the basis of long traditions, and emerged in tandem with secular modernism that depended on the efficiency of larger economic units and on the gradual exclusion of religious criteria from the administration of political authority. The market and the bank replaced the church and the cathedral as the central symbols of worship.

The trauma of creating European nations and states (only rarely has a true correspondence been achieved, despite the claim of forging "nation-states") has been disclosed numerous times. The human costs were enormous and the resistance from within and without was ferocious, generating war after war and suppressing minorities and weaker peoples (and their cultures). Yet, it must be admitted, by establishing powerful identities and cherished feelings of community (with the notable exception of the Balkans), Europe is in the process of reforming its allegiances. Due to economic and political reasons, Europe is moving toward a regional identity that represents a new phase of adaptation to evolving international realities. As the core and main generator of the modern world system, Europe was overwhelmed by the centrifugal energies of this century: the rise to global eminence of the United States and the Soviet Union, their ideological clash, two world wars fought on European soil, the dissolution of the colonial order and the long Cold War that focused on Europe as the imaginary apocalyptic battlefield.[11]

Europe experienced the geopolitical backlash from the system it had invented and managed. But, as in the Middle East, that part of Europe perceived as useful to the hegemon was generally privileged, even as it was controlled. Europe is emerging from its long geopolitical ordeal by way of a shift from state to region as a basic organizing reality.[12] Within the region, identities as ideals can flourish without nearly so much attention to geographical boundaries. Whether the new Europe will generate a sense of regional community is far from assured. More likely, Europeans will reflect both more local identities of ethnic background and the globalized identity being forged by capital, media, and the popular culture. With regard to the latter identity, the United States, far more than the reconstituted Europe, is the source of new identities for Europeans. This is symbolized by the reliance on English as the regional language and by the kind of music, clothes, and food that provides young people with their global lifestyle.

Since 1945, Europe has been treated as subordinate to the geopolitical ambitions of the two superpowers. West Europe was favored in almost every respect as compared to East Europe. West Europe was perceived as a market and as an extension of the American way, whereas the East was seen as a security belt and as an extension of the Soviet way. But both parts of Europe were geopolitical objects rather than subjects. Even the countries of West Europe relinquished their authority over war and peace issues and over the outer limits of self-determination. When American strategists played their war games and evolved doctrines of limited nuclear war, the Europeans were only nominally consulted. Had containment failed, for whatever reason, the European survivors would lament the adverse consequences of geopolitical subordination. Current evolution in the European region can be seen as a mode to mitigate, if not overcome, such subordination.

Does the Middle East possess such mitigating options? It does not possess the capital and technological foundations to participate globally as an integrated unit. But it does have strong, effective, and unifying possibilities in relation to Arab and Islamic identity. It also has the experience of geopolitical manipulation, carried to the point of torture in recent decades, that would suggest the pooling of resources and energies. Egypt's Nasser pointed in this direction in the 1960s and Khomeini's Iran in a different way in the 1980s. Both projects were doomed by the partnership between entrenched indigenous interests and geopolitical strategies based, in the end, on divide and rule approaches.

Israel operates both as an agent for the American-guided geopolitical framework and as an independent actor with its own ambitions and tactics, although the two roles rarely diverge very far. There have been periodic tensions between the American interest in stabilizing Arab, Turkish, and Iranian co-agents of the geopolitical order, on the one hand, and the Israeli preoccupation with weakening any regional constellation of forces that may challenge its own security and ambitions on the other. These tensions have been resolved, mainly on the basis of a mutual awareness that the partnership is too valuable to both sides to be placed under any great strain.

Under this set of circumstances, are there images of political community and identity that can work in an emancipatory direction? Perhaps Eastern Europe is instructive in some general way. Only a decade ago, it appeared to be doomed to a period of indefinite geopolitical servitude.[13] When negotiated, the 1975 Helsinki Accords were seen as a means to settle legitimately the division of Europe, the division of Germany, and the entire European post-war order that was based on opposing blocs. (The Accords have been retrospectively and misleadingly reinterpreted as an instrument of democratization.) Popular forces in the East European countries did not accept their fate, nor, ironically enough, did the West European peace movement of the 1980s. Looking backward, we are mainly entranced by the breakdown of the Berlin Wall and the joyous young people waving German flags of unity. We tend to forget that this triumphal moment had been preceded by a willful community of resistance that operated against the grain of calculative politics. In Poland and Czechoslovakia, especially, the defiance and popular surge of resistance was a kind of intifada. The emergence of Gorbachev, his abandonment of the Brezhnev Doctrine (interventionism to preserve the unity of the socialist camp) and espousal of the Sinatra Doctrine ("I Do It My Way") changed and reflected the geopolitical realities that erupted in the great happenings of 1989.

The application of this European experience to the Middle Eastern situation is not plainly evident, although some suggestive propositions emerge: it is never too early to engage in resistance; the idea of political community belongs, in the end, to civil society, and can take or change shape with or without the encouragement of state structures; and the fate of political communities is decided by the specific interactions between indigenous forces and geopolitical structures. It is difficult to conceive of a Middle Eastern process of emancipation except by way of a fundamental reorientation of the political outlook that shapes US policy. Such a reorientation may be abetted by the extension of Islamic identity as a basis for political community—not an Islamicized state, but an Islamicized region. Such a region would not necessarily take the harsher confessional forms that we associate with Khomeini and his regional followers.

Because the world economy is dependent on the supply and pricing of oil and because the need for control of oil is linked to military superiority and to the maintenance of Israel as a secure base area, it is extremely unlikely that any basic regional escape from geopolitics will soon occur. There may be normative and tactical adjustments that reflect the ebb and flow of indigenous tendencies, including a remote possibility that Israel will be induced by some mixture of rewards and anxieties to establish a Palestinian homeland, even a state. It is possible that regional developments and Kurdish ingenuity can discover some political space for various types of self-determination and that Lebanon can reconstruct its sovereignty on some more tolerable basis than has existed in the recent past. These are niches of opportunity that exist within the geopolitical situation of the region, but they are extremely unlikely to relieve the peoples of the Middle East from their destiny of cruel subjection to the vagaries of geopolitics and its constantly shifting balances, which produce recurring torment for the most vulnerable and exposed societies.

Geopolitics seeks to stifle the political imagination, yet its designs are constantly challenged both by elements of surprise and leaders and movements that emerge and seek to strike back. In this regard, geopolitical structures of domination are never serene for long. The interplay of resistance and repression ensures that the logic of cruelty will continue to shape the politics of the region, perhaps periodically softened by horizons of possibility and hope.

Islam

Chapter Three

CAN POLITICAL DEMOCRACY SURVIVE
THE RELIGIOUS RESURGENCE?

I am conscious that trying to address these broad issues very much reflects the experience that one has in a particular place. I am sure that if I had been living here in Cairo, the way I would understand what is happening in the world would be different than it is as a result of living in the United States and working at Princeton. One of the things I have learned over the years is how important it is to see the political developments in the world from a variety of perspectives; perspectives that are influenced by culture, by the priorities of a society, by its historical background, by its philosophical traditions. All of that shapes one's understanding very decisively, and I think it is particularly true for Americans that we are conscious of telling the world how it should work and what is going on, and we are not very good at listening to what others are saying about what is happening in the world. And so I regard this opportunity to be here with you as partly a chance to listen, as well as an opportunity to talk.

One often conceives of a theme one is interested in talking about, and then when one comes to talk about it, one realizes that it exceeds one's understanding and comprehension, so it is a humbling experience as well as a challenging one to have this opportunity. I feel that most strongly about the theme that I have chosen for this lecture, which I put in the form of a question: Can political democracy survive the religious resurgence?

My main interest in this lecture is to explore a single overarching question: How should those of us committed to the ideals and goals of humane governance view and interpret the religious resurgence? And by humane governance I mean a combination of human rights and substantive democracy—that is, democracy that extends beyond participating in elections and pertains, or ensures, meaningful participation by the people of a society in the forms of governance that are established in that society. So the question that I am really trying to examine is whether religion necessarily poses a threat to the deepening of political

---

This lecture was delivered in the Oriental Hall of the American University in Cairo, Egypt, on 16 May 2000.

democracy. Should anti-democratic religious tendencies be allowed to play and win the electoral game? In this vein, can secular democracy survive the electoral game? And in this vein, can secular democracy survive those forms of religious resurgence that claim to embody the only past truth, especially when they manage to win the allegiance of the majority of a particular society? In other words, when a religious movement of extremist claims also has a democratic backing in the society, a majority backing, what then is the appropriate response?

My first comment is intended as a warning against premature generalizations here. The Russian novelist, Leo Tolstoy, famously noted that "happy families are all happy in the same way, but unhappy families are each unhappy in their own way." In my view, the problematic sides of religious resurgence are definitely linked to the circumstances of unhappy societies, and to the particularity that each such society is addressing. Generalizations about religious politics are likely to be misunderstood if they are not addressed to these specific set of circumstances. Each country is faced with the specific dilemmas born of its own history, particularly its way of experiencing the combined challenges of modernity, especially the impact of science and technology and the domination of economic globalization by Western interests, values, and projects.

Elsewhere I have argued that this combined challenge is producing a new geopolitics centered on the world economy and the rise of global market forces, and that is producing a changing role of the state because the state is finding that its freedom of action has been significantly reduced by the discipline of global capital. Global capital reduces the political space available to a state to enact policies that benefit its own society. The religious resurgence can be understood, as a first approximation, as one form of resistance against this overarching project of globalization.[1] But this resistance is immediately experienced most characteristically as a reaction to the perceived failures of each particular state, either its corruption or its capture by an elite that opens too wide the society to the forces of external capital and to the values of Westernization. The religious alternative offers such a society, and particularly those of its members who are left out of the globalizing equation, an alternative based on traditions of the sacred that can appear to be more closely and genuinely connected with the needs and aspirations of ordinary people than what is offered and delivered by secular leaders with their overseas bank accounts, their inefficient and corrupted bureaucracies, their dependence on foreign economic assistance, international loans, and global capital, and their subservience in relation to the geopolitical management arrangements that are being administered from Washington. Such arrangements involve the old geopolitics of military power, combined with the new geopolitics of consumerism and pop culture. The point is that many of the more militant examples of religious resurgence are responding to this dangerous mixture of domestic governmental failure and global economic and cultural penetration.

It is helpful, I think, to realize that this religious resurgence was not anticipated as recently as a few decades ago. On the contrary, the world seemed destined to travel a single path toward a secularizing modernity. It was widely believed, both by the Marxist–Leninist east and the Liberal Democratic west, that the key to human well-being was embedded in science and its technological applications to society. The disagreement was not about the character of progress, but it was about the modes by which society was organized in the service of this shared image of a science-based technology leading to progressive stages of human well-being. Both ideological contenders for world dominance during the Cold War based their public policy on claims of reason, promises of continuing material progress, and on the genuine belief that they were pursuing lines justified by an objective understanding of historical process. Religion under these circumstances was essentially irrelevant to such visions of the human condition and prospects for societal evolution. At most, religion offered private and personal comfort to individuals who did not seem strong enough to accept this supposedly dominant modernizing message most famously articulated by Nietzsche in the phrase "God is dead" or in the revolutionary call to action by Karl Marx who insisted that "religion is the opiate of the people." That is, it was keeping people unaware of their exploitation and therefore unaware of their own revolutionary potential, that religion was in that sense a drug that stilled the political mind and worked against the liberation of those that were oppressed by the existing order. Nietzsche's case was a more metaphysical claim that the civilization that was emerging had become autonomous—in the sense that its dynamics rested on the application of science to the human condition, and anything else was just a projection of an earlier stage of human evolution that required the metaphysical comfort of a theological explanation that there was a god who presided over the human experience.

I remember very well the degree to which religion was off the radar screen of public and political understanding during the late 1970s as the Islamic Revolution emerged in Iran. The US government had for so long nurtured the Shah's regime in Iran that it had completely focused its energies on the enemies to the left of that regime, so much so, in fact, that religiously oriented Iranian student groups in the United States and elsewhere were being habitually financed by the US government in order to provide a kind of counter to the Marxist student groups. There was no understanding of the mobilizing strength of religious opposition in Iran, of its political face of radical anti-Americanism, or of the thinness of support for the corrupt, decadent, and Westernized elite that dominated the Pahlavi palace. At the time, the Shah was viewed by Washington as the ideal Third World leader—a devotee of modernization Western style, receptive completely to global capital, and what Henry Kissinger at the time called "that rarest of things, an unconditional ally." Iran at that time supplied oil to Israel and South Africa, neither of which could acquire oil from the other members of OPEC. It is notable that just a year before the Islamic Revolution swept across Iran like a tidal wave, Jimmy Carter, a human rights advocate, chose to spend his first New Year's Eve as president in Tehran as the guest of the Shah. It was on that occasion that Carter made his notorious toast to the Shah and his regime, describing the Iranian government at that time as "an island of stability surrounded by the love of his people." Only months later it became evident that it would have been more accurate to describe the Shah's regime as "the center of turmoil surrounded by the hatred of his people," but of course such sentiments would not have been polite or well-received, particularly on New Year's Eve.

The Western image of the religious resurgence was initially shaped by its view of the Iranian Revolution. The image that was most relied upon was that of "Muslim fundamentalism," which was seen as anti-modern, anti-Western, autocratic, repressive, and, worst of all, the principal practitioner and exporter of terrorist forms of violence. Against such a political formation, all manner of opposition seemed justified, and it was led internationally by the two rival centers of geopolitical influence: the United States and the Soviet Union. Both saw the religious resurgence as a threat. The US lost control over Iran, a pivotal country in the region, and the Soviet Union feared the spread of political Islam to its Central Asian republics. Both silently backed Iraq's aggression against Iran in 1980 and made sure that the United Nations made no effort on behalf of Iran as the victim of aggression. Both underestimated the Iranian capacity to cope with a military invasion, and, despite the Iraqi high-technology weaponry and the disintegration of Iran's military establishment after the revolution, it turned out that Iraq was unable to inflict a military defeat upon Iran.

What is significant to understand is that there was an attempt to respond—by both superpowers at the time—to this religiously oriented government in Iran by mounting a military intervention that was carried out by Iraq, that then subsequently itself became the object of Western military action in the course of the Gulf War and the sanctions that followed.

This perception of the religious resurgence, as inherently extremist and fanatically anti-modern and anti-Western, is what fed a climate of opinion that regards our era as dominated by a new type of global struggle—essentially by "culture wars." This intellectual formulation in the West took two main forms—Huntington's "clash of civilizations," positing "the West against the rest" and viewing Islam as a coherent and militant challenger of the established global order. The other simplistic conceptualization was Benjamin Barber's "McWorld vs. Jihad"—an encounter between "the golden arches" of McDonald's typifying the spread of global capitalism and the holy war waged in the name of religious tradition against the Great Satan of American-led globalization. In other words, the emergence of the religious resurgence was seen as a declaration of war against American-led globalization. Both of these popularizing appeals to Western audiences essentialized the religious resurgence, treating Islam as monolithic, inherently violent, and necessarily resolved to engage in a sacred struggle against Western interests and values.

Such imagery, in my view, distorts the character of the religious resurgence in a dangerous and misleading way. To begin with, the religious resurgence is by no means just an Islamic phenomenon. It is truly global, and has made its weight felt in many countries of the world. Outside of Islam, there is the ascent to power of Hindu nationalism in India—the most populous democracy in the world. In Christian and Buddhist countries, the weight of a religious revival is increasingly felt in centers of political power. When lecturing a few years ago to young diplomats in Hanoi, Vietnam, I was struck by how much more these functionaries of a nominally Communist state were interested in Buddhism than they were in Marxism. That even in one of the few remaining countries oriented around a Marxist–Leninist perspective, the existential beliefs of the people in the society, including even the governing elite, are increasingly subject to religious influence. One notices at the present time that the greatest threat faced by the Chinese government since its revolution more than 50 years ago, is being mounted by an indigenous religious sect called Fulan Gong. In America too, religious evangelism and the entry of the religious right into political life has been the most notable development in recent years. In effect, the secularism of the kind that evolved out of the European Enlightenment, capturing the scientific imagination and then the political imagination, is now under siege in many parts of the world. To understand the relevance of this religious resurgence we must look at common global structural factors that are generating a religiously oriented backlash. These common structural factors underlie the commonality that is part of the pattern of religion emerging as a significant element in political life throughout the world.

Beyond this recognition, it is also crucial that we do not treat the religious resurgence as a homogeneous reality. Every great religion carries within its framework of teachings and interpretations a wide range of possible orientations. I find it useful to distinguish between exclusive and inclusive poles within each major religious tradition. The exclusive pole is one that believes that there is only one true faith, and that those that are outside that true faith are essentially part of an evil alternative, that there is a true path and other paths are false paths, and therefore it is only when the triumph of the true occurs that history is properly fulfilled. But the inclusive pole, while affirming the truth of its own tradition, grants space for comparable affirmations of other belief systems, both within its own religious space and beyond it. And it includes space for a secular orientation. Inclusive modes of religious orientation are fully reconcilable with the observance of human rights and the practices of democratic government, including an openness to the initiatives of a robust civil society.

What I am proposing is the de-essentialization of the debate created by the religious resurgence, and in doing this one also needs to take account of the exclusivist tendencies that can afflict secular attitudes toward political life. In other words, a variety of secular fundamentalisms can be intolerant toward alternative belief systems and repressive in response to religious practices. Such a pattern is sometimes manifest in Turkey, where the government has banished from its parliament elected delegates who wear a head scarf and prohibited political parties that advocate adherence to inclusive varieties of Islam. The point to be made here is that it is not religion as such that is the enemy of democracy and human rights, but exclusivist political claims that divide human society into those who are on the side of the angels and those who do the work of the devil. It is exclusivism that poses the threat—neither religion nor secularism as such.

Considering, then, the Islamic political experience it is notable that these patterns of emergence and diversity are present. There is no doubt that adherence to Islam is growing throughout the Islamic world, but is it growing in a homogeneous manner and in exclusivist directions? It is evident that a variety of moderate, inclusivist expressions of Islam are influencing political life in such countries as Malaysia and Indonesia. Indeed, Indonesia is experiencing a transition to democracy under the leadership of an Islamic figure, Gus Dur, after decades of cruel and corrupt secular military rule. More relevantly, Iran, which generated the initial backlash against political Islam, is now impressively, despite internal opposition, moving toward democratization, including a re-embrace of modernity and cultural pluralism. Even an expression of religious exclusivism, as the Iranian Revolution was in its earliest stage, can give way through its own internal evolution to much more inclusive interpretations of the relevance of religion to governance and political practice. Indeed, to gain access to the benefits of world economic development, it is more and more necessary to avoid the isolation of exclusivism, whether it be of a religious or secular character.

The Soviet Union, I think, substantially precipitated its collapse by a form of secular exclusivism that precluded the country's positive participation in the world economy. I was encouraged and moved by several prominent Iranian clerical figures who participated in a conference that I took part in a year or so ago, and their advocated reliance on the Universal Declaration of Human Rights as the most satisfactory starting point for initiating "a dialogue of civilizations" (of especial relevance to the three monotheistic religions). In other words, in the context of trying to create more mutual understanding, one of the avenues to that understanding is the recognition that the human rights texts, which have a Western origin, still provide the most useful starting point for civilizational dialogue. What impressed me at this meeting in Cyprus was that the initiative to use these texts in that way came not from Western scholars, but from Iranian philosophers and leading clerical figures. I think it is a recognition that a more inclusive set of potentialities depends on finding a normative language that is not limited or restricted to any single religious or secular tradition.

Such a background, then, poses the prudential question: What if a secular state is confronted by a rising religious movement? Should such a state presume that the movement is extremist and inherently a threat to democratic and humane governance? Ever since the Nazi Party in Germany under Hitler took control of the government there in 1933 as a result of a democratic election, there has existed a fundamental question about the limits of tolerance. Should a moderate political system defend itself against immoderate political challengers? And if it should defend itself, how should it do so?

Of course, in this part of the world the case of Algeria comes immediately to mind. Was it prudent and reasonable to ignore the will of the Algerian people by intervening against the FIS [Front Islamique de Salut]? Did the intervention shift the FIS from a moderate/inclusive approach to Islam to a more extremist/exclusivist version? We know that a bloody, costly civil war resulted from the secular backlash to this expression of religious resurgence. We cannot, of course, know what would have been the outcome of allowing Islamic-oriented leadership to govern Algeria. It would seem that a commitment to democratic procedures requires a society, under all but the most exceptional circumstances, to trust the will of its citizenry as expressed through the electoral process. In Turkey, as in Algeria and elsewhere, repudiating moderate expressions of the religious resurgence seemed likely to give rise to more extreme orientations. The test of a mature democracy is its capacity to allow shifts in political perspective and opportunity to compete for the allegiance of its citizens, and if successful, to govern in accordance with the constitutional framework. Therefore, I think that there is a strong pressure on any political system that conceives of itself as a democracy to accord a presumption of validity to the outcome of an electoral process, and as I suggest only in the most exceptional circumstance to question the validity of that electoral outcome by other than means of normal democratic opposition.

But what if the democracy in question is fragile and immature and the challenge that is being posed seems extremist and committed to the dissolution of democracy? What if the particular religious movement is suspected of hiding an extremist game plan behind a veil of moderation? These are difficult, essentially unanswerable, general questions that must be addressed in the crucible of specific struggles.

In an important respect I am contending that the danger to humane governance is not a consequence of the religious resurgence, but of the vulnerability of many societies to political appeals based on extremism, whether religious or not. This vulnerability is typically an expression of a failure by an existing governmental elite or leadership to meet the material and psycho-cultural needs of its people, especially those who are disadvantaged. A turn to religion as a political solution in these circumstances is generally an expression of societal desperation and of disillusionment with the promises and performance of secular government.

We are left, then, with two rather obvious conclusions: First of all, a democratic political culture faced with an anti-democratic religious movement seeking control of the state is confronted by a tragic predicament for which there is no way of avoidance. Either the challenge can be crushed by state power, which is itself an abandonment of humane governance, or the anti-democratic movement can be given control of the state, which risks, not only repression, but the end of democracy itself. This tragic predicament is a real one in circumstances where a society is confronted by this sort of extremist politics. Secondly, the best that can be done to avoid confronting such a predicament is to practice a form of preventive politics to make a given society and global political culture as invulnerable as possible to the populist appeals of extremism, intolerance, and violence linked to this kind of orientation. It is extremism, whether religious or secular, that poses the fundamental challenge, and not religion and secularism. It would be a mistake to aim for complete invulnerability to extremism, as that would imply an embrace of an extremist view toward extremism itself. You cannot, in other words, create absolute security for any political system except by becoming extremely oppressive in the process.

What is the best we can hope for to reduce the vulnerability of society to political extremism? In my view, that is the essential question that we confront. Recognizing this predicament that is posed by the challenge of extremism, how can we protect the vulnerability of society against such a danger?

Several things are important to encourage. The process of inter-religious and inter-civilizational dialogue and study seems to me a great help in reducing a collision of hostile stereotypes. It has been very important to increase the understanding of people in the United States that there are many forms of Islam, that there are many varieties of religious Islam that evolve democratically and in a manner that embodies human rights. And in the opposite direction, there are many forms of secularism that are oppressive and exploitative toward the citizenry. In effect, and this is a good thing to say in a room that calls itself the Oriental Hall, we must struggle against Orientalism in all its forms by knowledge and enjoyment of "the other" that exists in world society. In other words, we need not only tolerance toward the other but a celebration of diversity as the cultural foundation for a healthy political culture.

Additionally, it is of great importance to introduce an appreciation of human rights and civil society into our educational process at all stages—

from early primary education to advanced graduate study. The importance of human rights as a grounding for political life seems to me to be of great relevance to the current world situation. Michael Ignatieff has talked of the culture of human rights as the secular religion of our time, and I think that there is a sense in which what religion and secularism at their best have in common is an affirmation of human dignity and of the spiritual nature of the human experience.

Further, I think that a balance between globalization and social well-being is extremely important for the stability of political life within existing states. And this requires, in my view, a real social movement that is directed toward the re-empowerment of the state to act in a compassionate manner toward its own citizenry and not to serve only as an agent of global capital. What protects a society against political extremism is a socially empowered state that accords priority to the needs of its own society and is not only interested in facilitating the efficient investment of global capital. And in this sense, it is very important to separate the benefits of world economic development that arise from technological innovations from the predatory ideology of neoliberalism which is responsible for what I have been calling the social disempowerment of the state. In other words, we need as a democratic project to work toward a form of globalization that is not also a vehicle for neoliberal ideology.

Similarly, while participating in global cultural life it is important to nurture pride in the specific indigenous traditions of distinct language, art, and spiritual-philosophical thought. In this time of a homogenizing consumerist form of global economic development, cultural grounding in the traditions of particular societies is a way of avoiding being overwhelmed by a consumerist, heavily advertised imagery of what life is about.

What I think the religious resurgence offers humanity then, in addition to an alternative to corrupt forms of secularism, is a way of finding a spiritual sense of the human condition at a time when economic globalization is disseminating an ultra-materialist view of what human destiny is about. Thank you very much.

Questions, Comments

Dr. Saad Eddin Ibrahim:[2] Professor Falk, might you discuss the means by which you see the incorporation of religion into the political process?

RF: Thank you very much, Saad Ibrahim. In recent years, particularly, your own work has been a great inspiration to many of us in the West, who have tried to understand the democratic potential of societies in this part of the world. And I think your leadership and your journal *Civil Society* are vital resources for those of us living in the United States and elsewhere who don't have such immediate access to what is really the important political struggles that are going on here. I am very honored by your presence here.

I think part of the challenge to democratic political orders is to find ways of incorporating the religious dimensions of the political cultures that exist in each particular country. The form that that incorporation takes depends on the circumstances that exist in the particular society. For instance, if the governing process is too corrupt, then the incorporation can be a false form of solution to the fundamental challenges facing the society. I remember when I was in Indonesia, in the last stages of the Suharto regime, I had a conversation with Amin Rhys, one of the leading Islamic figures opposing Suharto, who at the time was acting as a religious adviser to the government, and he described his own role in the government, which he quickly changed, as one of what he called "positive co-optation." He felt it was a constructive incorporation, but he later found out that the corruption and the autocratic style of the Suharto government was so deep and the democratic opposition in civil society was so strong that he abandoned the government and joined civil society in seeking a new stage of political development for Indonesia. So I think one has to look at what the opportunities are for positive co-optation, and I think the creative leaders in this region are those who are seeking to encourage the inclusivist moderate forms of Islam, recognizing that Islam is an integral part of the political culture, and that what is threatening is not Islam but particular applications that are intolerant of difference and of alternatives and seek to impose a very literal reading of religious teachings upon society.

I think it is very important that the possibility of Muslim democracy and Muslim democrats be explored by academic discussion, by exchange of writings, by many means, because I still think that in the West, and particularly the United States, there is a very stereotypic monolithic view of what Islam represents and a fear that it is intrinsically anti-democratic. One has to understand that part of the American problem is also associated with certain domestic struggles in which the symbolism of Islam has been sometimes appropriated by very radical elements in American society that are seeking change, and so this reinforces a kind of stereotype of this great religion as being disposed toward violent solutions of political conflict.

Audience member: You mention that a mature democracy could allow for shifts in the framework a little bit, like a religious movement, except in exceptional circumstances. I was wondering if you could give us maybe a vague approximation of where the line between acceptable and exceptional circumstances would be and what a mature democracy's response might be to that challenge?

RF: Well, I was trying to dodge that question partly by saying that it is such an exceptional claim that it has to depend on the particularity of the circumstances. It is always easier looking back and with hindsight we make few mistakes; therefore the paradigmatic response would be to say it would have been good if democratic forces had defended themselves against Nazism in Germany in the 1930s, that Hitler was undisguised in his plans for creating a racist authoritarian form of government and a militarist form of government. It was not of course altogether clear that he would also initiate a genocidal policy. It is very difficult, I think, except for a set of criteria or guidelines that might be used. If there is significant evidence that an anti-democratic political tendency intends to dissolve democracy itself, if it believes that the governing process should not be subject to the consent of the citizenry, and if it is committed to a path of violence in dealing with its adversaries, then I think you have created the conditions where at least the question should be raised as to whether something should be done about the outcome of a electoral process that brings to power such an anti-democratic political force.

Audience member: I want to ask why the West, in the name of democracy, fights Islamic revivalism while we have the example of Iran, which is a democratic country, yet it had an Islamic Revolution, so it doesn't necessarily mean that Islamic revivalism is anti-democratic, And why, why does the West, in the name of democracy, fight Islamic revivalism? It can be fought in many other ways. In what way is fighting it through democracy, Islam, or whichever is their religious movements, anti-democratic? Is that right?

RF: If I understand correctly, the West uses a democratic argument to oppose Islam, which isn't itself in its essence anti-democratic, so why should a claim of democratic values lead to an anti-Islamic foreign policy? I think that it is not easy to give a convincing answer. It is linked again in some ways to the importance in the Arab/Israeli context of discrediting the Islamic world as the adversary of Israel. I think that was part of the origin of the stereotyping, and it was coupled by the portrayal of the Palestinian struggle as a terrorist movement. And this was then disseminated in terms of popular culture through movies that portrayed the Arab political activist in these very negative terms and linked that kind of activism falsely with Islam and then it was also linked to the Iranian Revolution, and the perception of the Iranian Revolution as opposing everything that the West, the liberal West, and the United States stood for. And Ayatollah Khomeini reinforced that impression by his presentation of the West as the Great Satan. So there were two kinds of exchange of stereotypes that fed extremist politics on both sides. What I guess I am trying to do is break that cycle of extremist imagery, which leads to ways of stereotyping the other and not acknowledging the humanity and the diversity and the potentiality of the other to generate a humane politics.

Thank you.

Chapter Four

FALSE UNIVERSALISM AND THE GEOPOLITICS OF EXCLUSION: THE CASE OF ISLAM

Civilizational Participation as a Human Right

In *Twilight of the Gods* Nietzsche insists that what makes Socrates interesting to the modern mind is not his thought or method, but the extraordinary societal significance for Athens of having taken so seriously such silly and banal ideas. I regard Samuel Huntington's "clash" thesis in a similar spirit. What is interesting is not the argument, as such, which seems both simplistic and implausible, but its extraordinary resonance around the world. I can recall no other short piece, including even the famous "X" article of George Kennan, that has elicited such an intense readership. My question, which anchors this paper, is this: What is this resonance telling us?

I believe that this resonance is closely related to the theme of this article. Namely, the emergent importance at this historical moment of civilizational identity as a potent political, moral, and psychological category that is an aspect of a more multi-faceted challenge to the hegemonic, almost monopolistic, dominance of statist identity bound up with the role of the state in the modern world order system. In fairness to Huntington, his starting-point is similarly conceptual, asserting that, for the long cycles of human experience, the significant unit of collective identity was something resembling what we now call a civilization rather than that which we label a state, the latter enjoying prominence only in recent centuries. Huntington, along with many others, sees the state as being in a waning phase, but unlike these commentators, he believes the defining emergent reality is not "the global village," or more dynamically, "globalization," but rather inter-civilizational reality.[1] For Huntington, this re-emergence of civilizational identity implies, above all, a reconfiguration of geopolitical patterns of conflict, which in its essence will result in a new

This piece is a revised version of a paper originally presented at a conference on "Universalizing from Particulars Islamic Views of the Human and the UN Declaration of Human Rights in Comparative Perspective," under the auspices of the Institute for the Transregional Study of the Contemporary Middle East, North Africa, and Central Asia, Princeton University, 24–26 May 1996. It first appeared in Third World Quarterly *218 (1997): 7–23.*

world order framework. My own view is less pronounced, although also questioning the intellectual viability of statist conceptions of world order, given the significance of global market forces and non-state political actors in the contemporary historical situation. I believe that the various dimensions of globalization, especially the economic and cultural dimensions, are of defining importance with regard to superseding a world order system based upon the interaction of sovereign states. Nevertheless I agree with Huntington to this extent: that inter-civilizational relations are newly of great significance for world-order thinking, and particularly so with reference to human rights, political ideology, and the future of nationalism. But, I should hasten to add, not primarily because of the issue of cultural relativism, and the related challenge to the purported universalist claims put forward on behalf of international human rights standards and procedures.

Rather my concern arises in relation to an exposed deficiency of the human rights enterprise, as broadly conceived, namely the discriminatory treatment of non-Western civilizations, and especially of Islam, with respect to participatory rights. My focus is not on the broad array of established human rights as such but on the posited human right to participate, directly or indirectly, in the authority structures, processes, and practices that together constitute world order as here defined and understood. Each element of this perspective requires some explanation and is somewhat controversial: How has Islam been the victim of discrimination in this world order sense? If this is so, in what respects does it raise issues that are properly treated as falling within the domain of human rights? And, even if it is granted that human rights can be encroached upon at a civilizational level, how can the character of such rights be validated and implemented, and by what means? Can international law be extended to serve as an effective vehicle for achieving equitable inter-civilizational participation in world order structures and processes without eroding its achievements in regulating state-society relations by way of protecting individual human rights?

Perhaps I can best clarify my point of departure by reference to what might be called "the geopolitics of exclusion," both with respect to the dynamics of global governance and those substantive and symbolic issues that seem to be of greatest concern to the Islamic world. By using such terminology, I am not implying a conspiracy among Western leaders to achieve such exclusionary goals, or even claiming a consistent, deliberate pattern of this character. Indeed, the implementation of exclusion occurs mostly as a result of what might be called "false universalism," depicting the particular and partial as if it were synonymous with the general, not only with respect to substantive results, but more crucially in relation to the processes by which these results are reached. Without entering upon the treacherous terrain of cultural constructivism, I attribute this false universalism mainly to the Enlightenment project, with its reliance on decontextualized reason, as embodied in the language, ideas, diplomatic style, experience, and rules of representation that originated in Western Europe and gradually evolved into a global framework of sovereign, secular, territorial states over a period of centuries that is conveniently, yet arbitrarily, linked to the Peace of Westphalia in 1648. This evolution is convincingly depicted by Stephen Toulmin in his book, *Cosmopolis*, which shares the view that the era of statist dominance is coming to an end, but he sees the sequel as global humanist, rather than as inter-civilizational or some more complex tapestry of overlapping and intersecting identities, a conception of world order that has often been analogized to the multiple, interpenetrating levels of authority associated with medieval Europe.[2]

In effect, the universalism that I am calling "false" is a mask worn to obscure Western civilizational hegemony. This mask has been worn so long that it is indistinguishable from the face itself for wearer and beholder alike. As would be expected, such a hegemony is far greater than the sum of its political, economic, and even cultural parts, as it is civilizational, including distinctive ideas, memories, beliefs, practices, misconceptions, myths, and symbols that go to the very core of human identity. In contrast, a true universality would acknowledge significant difference, as well as sameness, in constituting a world order based on procedures and norms explicitly designed to ensure equitable participation by each major world civilization.[3] Inter-civilizational equality, as a constitutive principle of world order, seems to add a category to what David Held, Daniele Archibugi, and others have been so usefully describing and advocating under the rubrics of "cosmopolitan democracy" and "cosmopolitan governance."[4]

My purpose here is not to enter into a discussion of the substance of difference, or matters of relative merit, but only to support the view that the neglect of civilizational participation for Islam has produced a series of partially deformed institutions, practices, and perceptions. In passing, it should also, of course, be understood that it is accepted that there is an enormous range of intra-civilizational differences in Islam that also need to be democratically negotiated as part of a human rights process.

My emphasis here is far more limited, and in a sense preliminary, to the effect that at this historical juncture civilizational identity is sufficiently genuine for a sufficient portion of the more than one billion persons on the planet who consider themselves Muslim to be treated as an essential category in evaluating the legitimacy of world order structures and processes.[5] Reinforcing this contention is the increasingly articulate expression of grievance and demand on the part of those who affirm their Islamic identity, and increasingly adopt a critical stance of normative and emotive distance from the Western-emplaced, still largely prevailing, structures and processes of world order, while themselves affirming the quest for peace and justice in the relations among the peoples of the world.[6]

The specific objective of this article is to link this analysis more directly to a concern with human rights. The contours of this concern can be briefly indicated: we are in the midst of a period in international history in which the normative architecture of international society has been increasingly expressed by reference to a human rights discourse that combines, somewhat confusingly, ethical, political, and legal perspectives; these perspectives are intertwined in various ways, but more in the form of claims, grievances, and practices than as stages in the articulation of binding rules and standards that are then implemented by those with the authority to interpret and apply "law." To a large extent, this human rights discourse is unavoidably perceived, with varying degrees of justification and opportunism, as tainted by false universalism and its relations to Western hegemony, one feature of which has been, and continues to be, the suppression of civilizational identity and difference, with a particular historical/political emphasis on the "threat" posed by Islam.[7]

This statement about the prevalence of human rights discourse can be literalized somewhat by reference to the embodiment of the human rights tradition in contemporary international law, primarily by means of a series of declarations and agreements affirmed by states, most notably including the Universal Declaration of Human Rights, the two Covenants of 1966, as well as through a series of regional formulations and more specialized conventions. On an intra-civilizational basis this tradition has been subjected to various kinds of assault, especially by those who affirm Marxist and socialist priorities and were offended by an overly individualistic conception of rights that included extensive protection of private property rights; in fact, although not as implemented, and even as appreciated, the human rights tradition as entrenched in international law carries forward a compromise between market-orientated individualism and welfare-orientated social democracy.[8]

Additionally, from the beginning of this century there have been imaginative and quite successful efforts, particularly by Latin American jurists, to challenge a series of exploitative and unequal relationships protected by international law in relation to foreign investment, extraterritorial criminal jurisdiction, and interventionary doctrines.[9] Such juridical critiques and innovations were framed as objections to the then prevailing character of inter-state, not inter-civilizational, relations, especially in the context of interventionary diplomacy. In the 1960s and 1970s this intra-civilizational critique from various Third World perspectives was generalized to emphasize the overall unfairness of the way rights and duties were distributed on a North–South basis, and was politicized within the United Nations, especially the General Assembly, in the form of calls for a "New International Economic Order" that were articulated in a series of declaratory, quasi-legal instruments.[10]

The categories of North and South were very generalized designations, as was reliance on the Third World or Non-Aligned Movement as a point of reformist reference, referring to historical, geographical, and developmental affinities, but not cultural or civilizational solidarity or encounter. These normative initiatives designed to promote mainly global economic reform were effectively disregarded as a result of a powerful market-orientated backlash associated with the neoliberal orientation championed in the 1980s by Margaret Thatcher and Ronald Reagan, and given the widening fissures in the Third World that resulted from modernizing strategies that yielded high growth rates and surging export markets for a series of Pacific Rim countries.

What has survived in the 1990s, at least rhetorically, from this effort to bring normative pressures to bear for the sake of a more equitable international economic order is "the right to development."[11] Whether this right has any operational content is doubtful, although important legal scholars have lent support to its validity. Although difficult to demonstrate, it would seem that the status of the right to development has shaped the way the international agenda on such other issues as environment, population, and human rights generally is addressed, as at important consciousness-raising UN conferences.[12] It is suggestive, however, of efforts to register as "a right" the perceived grievances of disadvantaged nations in relation to existing world order, and hence, is linked to an inquiry into how to overcome a circumstance of inter-civilizational inequity, although the unit of the claimant is not societal, national, or statal, but civilizational. These categories are overlapping rather than mutually exclusive identities.

The first truly inter-civilizational critique of the prevailing human rights discourse and its world order implications emerged, somewhat surprisingly, from the concerted struggle of indigenous peoples in the 1980s and 1990s.[13] This struggle took shape against a background (and foreground) of exclusion, discrimination, and persecution, even extermination, assimilation, and marginalization that were expressive of confusing admixtures of arrogance, racism, and ignorance. These extraordinary efforts of indigenous peoples to protect the remnants of their shared civilizational identity, an identity that was coherent and self-consistent only in relation to the otherness of modernity, achieved two results of direct relevance to this article: first of all, it exposed the radical inadequacy of a civilizationally "blind" approach to human rights, by which is meant the utter failure of the modernist instruments of human rights to take account in any satisfactory way of the claims, values, grievances, and outlooks of indigenous and traditional peoples; second, transnational activism by indigenous peoples in the last two decades has given rise to an alternative conception of rights that represents an articulation after a long process by previously excluded civilizational representatives.

In this regard, the contrast of this recent authentic expression of indigenous peoples' conception of their rights with that of earlier mainstream human rights instruments is revealing. Also revealing is a comparison between these efforts by indigenous peoples and the paternalistic efforts supposedly on their behalf in the marginal arena provided by the International Labour Organization. Such comparisons confirm the contention that participatory rights are integral to the acceptance of a political order as legitimate and to a reliable clarification of grievance, demand, and aspiration.[14] This alternative conception has been developed by indigenous peoples in an elaborate process of normative reconstruction that involved sustained, and often difficult, dialogue among the multitude of representatives of indigenous traditional peoples, especially as these have come together in recent years as the Informal Working Group on the Rights of Indigenous Populations, set up under the Sub-Commission on Racial Discrimination and Persecution of the Human Rights Commission that has recently taken the primary form of producing a Draft Declaration on the Rights of Indigenous Peoples, which is now being considered within the wider UN system. It is doubtful whether this declaration of indigenous rights will eventually be validated by state-centric procedures: in effect, these remain the gatekeepers within the UN system of the still ascendant false universalism.[15] The resistance being mounted in reaction to this more adequate expression of human rights as formulated by indigenous and traditional peoples in relation to their own destiny is mainly centered on certain perceived tensions that could result if the right of self-determination of indigenous peoples was to be legally confirmed. To what extent this struggle of indigenous peoples succeeds or fails is conceptually and substantively beside the point of this inquiry into Islamic exclusion, except to illustrate by analogy the surfacing of a different type of inter-civilizational challenge within the same approximate historical time interval.[16] Of course, the indigenous struggle also reinforces the point that unless authentic participation in the rights-creation process occurs, the results are not likely to be genuinely representative and the whole process will be regarded as illegitimate and alien.

Understanding the Geopolitics of Exclusion

At this point, it seems important to set forth the basic elements of the argument for "normative adjustment" in response to the inter-civilizational challenge being mounted from an Islamic perspective. Normative adjustment is understood in two senses: the reshaping of the human rights discourse to make provision for inter-civilizational participation; and the further legitimating of world order by improving the procedures for inter-civilizational participation and by establishing better means for inter-civilizational representation in the main authority structures of the world.

Although the wider conceptual and normative concern is one of inter-civilizational participation in general, my focus is upon the specifics surrounding Islamic exclusion and its implications. Arguably, a parallel inquiry could be made from a Confucian or Hindu or African perspective, as well as from a variety of indigenous perspectives. Further, to the extent that the analysis rests upon either the existence of a civilizational right to participate or the dependence of a legitimate world order upon equitable civilizational participation, then the wider inquiry is tied to this narrower one that dwells upon Islam. The narrower focus has the advantage of responding to the subjective side of civilizational exclusion in the crucial sense that Islam perceives itself as having been victimized within the framework of world order, and, in turn, is perceived in the West as posing a multi-dimensional challenge. It is important in light of this inter-civilizational interaction to assess whether there appear to be objective grounds for the subjective perceptions of grievance. It is in this spirit that the following steps in the argument will be taken:

(1) the psycho-political sense of grievance and significant difference that is characteristic of Islam's civilizational self-image in relation to the West and world order in general;

(2) a presentation of empirical, yet impressionistic, evidence in support of the view that Islam has been excluded from world order arenas and subjected to discriminatory regimes of control and prohibition;

(3) an insistence that the combination of perceived grievance and objective grounds provides the basis for "normative adjustment" so as to enhance the legitimacy of contemporary structures and processes of world order; and

(4) a conclusion that it would be useful to crystallize the case for normative adjustment by an extension of human rights to incorporate an essentially new right of civilizational participation, to be applied specifically to overcome Islamic grievances, but potentially available on a comparable basis for any civilizational unit of major stature in the present system of world order.

It is important, at this point, to recall the limited nature of this analysis: that the geopolitical exclusion of Islam is real, that it has negative world order consequences, that its rectification would be of benefit to Islam, and that expanding human rights coverage to include civilizational rights of participation provides one, but only one, mode of rectification.

Islam's Sense of Grievance and Difference

There is little doubt that a generalized Islamic sense of grievance overrides the very deep intra-civilizational cleavages (on the level of state, class, religious tradition, and geographic region) that currently exist in the Islamic world. Possibly less self-evident is an appreciation that this sense of grievance is coupled with an Islamic civilizational self-image that is capable of providing an alternative normative grounding for world order. The psycho-political confirmation of these assessments can be gleaned from many sources and is sufficiently established not to require elaborate documentation. I would refer anyone seeking such documentation to the range of presentations made at the Just World Trust (JUST) conference, "Images of Islam: Terrorizing the Truth," held in Penang, Malaysia in October 1995. For a more specific, sophisticated analysis of Islamic grievance and world order reconstruction, I rely principally on a book by one of the Penang participants, Ahmet Davutoglu's *Civilizational Transformation and the Muslim World*.

In a useful passage Davutoglu specifies the main elements of Islamic grievance in a manner that warrants extensive quotation:

There has been a tendency in recent years in Western political and intellectual center to misrepresent Muslim societies as incongruous elements in the international order. The issue of Salman Rushdie and the discussions of the Islamic dress code in France and Britain have provoked historical prejudices against Islam. The mass media has been extensively used to strengthen this imagination. Lastly, in the Gulf crisis, although the other front was also supported by many Muslim-populated states, Saddam has been misrepresented as the symbol of the increasing threat of Islamic fundamentalism.[17]

The point here is not to evaluate such a set of perceptions, but to set it off as representative of Islamic perceptions. In a similarly useful passage, Davutoglu extends this sense of grievance to the functioning of world order:

... the Muslim masses are feeling insecure in relation to the functioning of the international system because of the double standards in international affairs. The expansionist policy of Israel has been tolerated by the international system. The intifada has been called a terrorist activity while the mass rebellions of East Europe have been declared as the victory of freedom. There was no serious response against the Soviet military intervention in Azerbaijan in January 1990 when hundreds of Azaris were killed, while all Western powers reacted against Soviet intervention in the Baltic Republics. The international organizations which are very sensitive to the rights of small minorities in Muslim countries, did not respond against the sufferings of the Muslim minorities in India, the former Yugoslavia, Bulgaria, Kashmir, Burma, etc.... The atomic powers in some Muslim countries like Pakistan and Kazakhstan have been declared a danger when such weapons have been accepted as the internal affairs of other states such as Israel and India. Muslims who make up about 25 percent of the world's population, have no permanent member in the Security Council and all appeals from the Muslim World are being vetoed by one of the permanent members. The Muslim masses have lost their confidence in the international system as Neutral Problem-solver after the experiences of the last decade.[18]

Again it should be emphasized that it is not the accuracy, or even the reasonableness, of such assertions that is being argued (although they seem accurate and reasonable), but their representativeness.

The deeper argument, of course, moves beyond criticism to the claim that Western civilization as the dominant force in international life is having a destructive impact and that Islam, properly understood, presents the reality of a constructive alternative. Davutoglu also presents this case clearly, arguing, especially, that the economic globalization that he associates with the West is in the process of destroying the other "authentic cultures and civilizations" that together constitute world order.[19] In effect, Davutoglu argues that the Islamic recovery from a long period of suppression, culminating in the colonial era, offers the world a strong and coherent alternative to what he calls "the modernist paradigm."[20] In essence, then, the foundational premise of the argument here is the double Islamic awareness of grievance and self-limitation on one side and potential contributor to the emancipatory project of an ethically (and civilizationally) enhanced world order, on the other. In effect, in its more assertive expression, Islam and its proponents are committed to the rescue of the West (and others) from the calamity of modernism.[21]

Assessing Islam's Grievances

Accepting the anthropological insistence that all knowledge is "situated knowledge," reflecting the experience and outlook of the observer, and eschewing any pretension of an Olympian position above the fray, it still seems possible and useful to evaluate the reasonableness of Islam's sense of grievance and significant difference. Indeed, such an assessment underlies both the critique of false universalism and the argument favoring the incorporation of rights of civilizational participation into the discourse and protective framework of international law.

There is little doubt that much of the recent discussion of Islam and the West, whether in the form of journalistic portrayals or academic writings, is afflicted with the Orientalist construction of the other in stereotypical terms that validate hostile behavioral and policy responses. Since the globalizing hegemony of the West tilts this debate, especially by its dominance of TV, there is a strong disposition to perceive Islam as disposed toward violence and extremism, driven to terrorist action by hostility toward the West and Western values, and epitomized by Ayatollah Khomeini's Islamic Revolution and the ordeal of the hostage seizure in the US Embassy in Tehran that dragged on for many months until resolved in January 1981. This prevailing perceptual framework helps explain the extent to which the literature on Islam versus the West is preoccupied with the question of whether Islam does or does not pose a threat. Even the writings most sensitive to the Islamic reality[22] seek mainly to reassure the West that Islam is not as militant as often presented, that even political Islam is heterogeneous and not necessarily aggressive toward Western interests, and that it is important for the West not to make the Islamic threat into a self-fulfilling prophecy. What such perspectives tend not to do, except by way of acknowledging the historical extent of prior Western encroachment and abuse, is to examine the plausibility and structured character of Islamic grievances and the desirability of a world order reconstructed to take into account inter-civilizational identities and aspirations.

The main grievances enumerated by Davutoglu can be briefly considered in terms of their reasonableness.

Participation in the United Nations System

Despite having more than one billion adherents spread across over 45 countries, no permanent member of the Security Council is part of the Islamic world and, in most proposals for UN reform, calls for the expansion of the Security Council usually do not propose rectification. This, to be sure, in part, reflects the statist and Eurocentric origins of the United Nations at the end of World War II. And possibly it also reflects the failure of the Islamic countries to press harder for representation of this character in the most symbolically important organ of the United Nations. But the impression of exclusion is reinforced by the realization that none of the secretary-generals of the UN to date have been of Muslim faith, and very few of the important specialized agencies have been headed by a Muslim. Again this can be explained, in part, by the contention that officials are selected on the basis of secular criteria of merit and political support, not because of ethnic nor religious identity. Yet when combined with other factors, there would be reasonable grounds for believing that Islamic participation could make a difference with respect to the role of the United Nations on such issues as Palestinian self-determination and the status of Jerusalem, the approach to international terrorism, and the maintenance of the nuclear non-proliferation regime.

The Bosnian diplomatic process can also be viewed as one that denies the Islamic world a sense of equitable participation: each of the factions except for the main victims of atrocity and aggression, the Bosnian Muslims, were represented by an external actor with civilizational ties.[23] Turkey, the only European state with an Islamic identity and a steadfast member of the Western alliance, although highly secularized at the level of the ruling elites, was not included in "the contact group" of countries with a special role in the peace process, while Russia, with fewer claims in many respects, was. In isolation, this pattern in Bosnia would perhaps not warrant comment, but as part of the larger picture, it does seem to add a dimension to the geopolitics of exclusion.

Double Standards

Here again it is difficult to circumvent the subjectivity of interpretative standards. Nevertheless, the orientation of the media and of US foreign policy has seemed to produce consistent support for actors pursuing goals inimical to Islamic interests and opposition or indifference to issues of major symbolic and substantive concern to those with an Islamic interest.[24] To varying degrees the Arab–Israeli conflict has been dominant over many years, fostering an impression that Israeli violence against Palestinian refugees and others is generally acceptable as an act of war and expression of security policy, while Palestinian violence is treated as "terrorism" of a character that undermines whatever political and moral claims may exist to support the Palestinian struggle. Other conflicts that have involved Islamic victims of violent abuse, such as Bosnia, Chechnya, and Kashmir, confirm the accusation of double standards to the extent that it is probable that, if the identities of victim and perpetrator were reversed, the international response would have been different. Such a pattern exists, and although each instance can be partially explained by other factors, such as deference to state coercive power, deployed within territorial limits, or the unfeasibility of challenging major states acting within their own geographical zone of dominance, the cumulative weight of instances and the selective reliance on international law to condemn and condone gives the accusation of double standards a rather strong presumption of validity.

A Discriminatory Non-Proliferation Regime

Aside from China, the declared nuclear weapons states are Western in orientation, and they claim a continuing right and intention to retain possession of this weaponry of mass destruction and even proceed with further development. At the same time, states with genuine security concerns are being denied, to the extent possible, access to such weaponry. But even this dual structure is not being uniformly implemented. Communist states (North Korea) and Islamic countries (Iraq, Iran, Libya, and Pakistan) are the object of strong non-proliferation efforts, while the Israeli acquisition and development of nuclear weapons is completely overlooked and, according to some sources, deliberately facilitated.[25] The media reinforce this impression by writing about Pakistan's possible acquisition of nuclear weapons as creating the danger of "an Islamic bomb," although Pakistan's motivation is clearly directed at offsetting India's military, and probable nuclear, threat. No one would seriously write about "a Jewish bomb" or "a Confucian bomb" or "a Hindu bomb," and doing so about Pakistan's capability conveys the impression that civilizational identity does count, but only negatively, and only if it is Islamic! Such a double standard, as reasonably perceived from an Islamic perspective, is taken as irrefutable proof of an anti-Islamic structure of world order. Again there are extenuating circumstances, ranging from Israel's isolated and endangered circumstance (but would not such extenuation apply to North Korea, and to several other states seeking to possess a nuclear option?) to the Western impression that there is an Islamic threat that could materialize in a dangerous way if backed by nuclear weaponry. Nevertheless, the implementation of the global non-proliferation regime appears to have an anti-Islamic component.[26]

Punitive Peace

It is worth contrasting the way in which Serbia and Iraq have been treated after the cessation of hostilities—lifting sanctions and a rapid restoration of normalcy in one instance, compared to intrusive intervention and the maintenance of sanctions well-known to have caused prolonged great suffering and loss of life to the poorest sectors of Iraqi society without contributing to the downfall of Saddam Hussein's regime, in the other.[27] Janna Nolan points out that the insistence on the extensive demands for Iraqi-verified destruction of portions of its military capabilities, especially those relating to weaponry of mass destruction, "have some parallels to the Allied program to disarm Germany after World War I."[28] The failure of the Versailles punitive approach to a defeated enemy led to the abandonment of an imposition of humiliating and punitive conditions in the wake of military victory partly because it was seen as contributing to the rise of Fascism, but now it has been resurrected against Iraq, an approach extended in certain respects to Iran mainly by unilateral action. There seem good grounds, then, for regarding such policy approaches to countries in the Islamic world as part of the broader pattern of the geopolitics of exclusion, even to the extent of adapting the language of containment, central to the West's posture vis-à-vis the Soviet Union, in relation to Iran and Iraq. This latter policy is being discussed by Washington policymakers under the rubric of "double containment."

Policymaking and Participation in the World Economy

As with the permanent membership of the Security Council, the directorate of the world economy, the Group of Seven, or G-7, includes no Islamic state. Would not Indonesia, Malaysia, or Saudi Arabia have as good a claim as Canada or Italy? In an era of globalization, with the Asia-Pacific region in the ascendancy, it would seem reasonable to expect greater representation for Islamic countries. The same pattern of exclusion pertains, as well, to the Bretton Woods institutions that are administered by top officials normally drawn from the West. A further source of suspicion is the drastic, terminal manner of dealing with the disclosures of fraud on the part of the Bank of Credit and Commerce International (BCCI), leading to the immediate dissolution of the only international bank with primary Islamic funding and direction.[29]

Responses to Terrorist Incidents

There does seem to be a hostile attitude to Islam evident in the global media and Western governmental responses to incidents of major terrorism. This pattern was evident in the differences with which the US government responded to the World Trade Center bombing in New York City on 26 February 1993 and the bombing of the Federal Building in Oklahoma City on 19 April 1995. Perhaps most revealing was the reflex of suspicion directed toward political Islam, despite the timing of the Oklahoma explosion coinciding with the anniversary of the Waco, Texas raid on the Branch Davidian cult that was known to have agitated rightist militias and led several of them to contemplate retaliation. Further, the government reaction in the US was to investigate whether excessive force had been used in the Waco raid and to dismiss several of those in the government who seemed responsible, to pay compensation for Federal force used in another attack on a survivalist family in Montana, and to strengthen international laws on terrorism. The prosecutorial strategy included reliance on a conspiracy theory to reach those indirectly involved in the Trade Center bombing, especially the Islamic figure Sheik Rahman, while the indications are that the US government will limit its indictments arising from the Oklahoma incident to those individuals accused of being the actual perpetrators. A further difference is the removal of the trial for the sake of fairness to the defendant from Oklahoma, the venue where the crime was committed, while denying a similar motion for a change of venue to the Islamic defendants in New York, where the atmosphere was probably more adversely inflamed.[30]

Stigmatization of States as "Outlaw" or "Rogue"

The stigmatization of several states as "outlaw" or "rogue," especially by the US government, has again seemed to focus particular attention on the

Islamic world as the main irritant to world order other than that associated with such communist survivors from the Cold War era as Cuba and North Korea. Libya, Iran, and Iraq have been consistently so treated with varying degrees of justification, but reinforcing an impression that an Islamic orientation, if militant, will be dealt with as aggressively as possible, while non-Islamic states that violate basic norms of international law and offend the global conscience, such as Burma in recent years and South Africa during most of the apartheid period, are dealt with by way of "constructive engagement," either formally or informally.[31]

The Right to Democratic Governance

After the Cold War the West proclaimed its commitment to the spread of democratic governance, which meant especially the encouragement of constitutionalism in the form of multiparty elections. Yet its concern with the spread of political Islam apparently led it to overlook the coup that occurred in Algeria to deprive Islamicists of an electoral victory in 1990.[32]

The Unevenness of Compassion

Media treatments of Islamic suffering tend to be abstract, general, and scant, if given at all, and are dwarfed by repeated inquiry into the tactics and mentality of extremism. Little attention is given to understanding the moral and political pressures that might explain the desperation that induces such extremist acts as suicide bombings and the like. The support given by Palestinian refugees and some anti-Western governments (Libya and Iran) to horrifying acts of terrorism is appropriately noted, but not the Israeli calls for vengeance in ethnic terms (attacking Palestinians at random, chants of "death to the Arabs!"). These are delicate, complicated matters of assessment, but the imbalance is cumulative in that treatment of the suffering being experienced within the Islamic world tends to be comparatively much less sympathetic than that accorded to the provocations and tactics of its enemies. It is instructive to compare the small statistical advantage enjoyed by the house in gambling casinos, where the gambler will certainly lose if he or she keeps playing long enough. That is, a seemingly trivial imbalance in the appreciation of justice claims can register over time a decisive edge in support of the moral claims being favored.[33]

Recalling the analogy to the emergence of indigenous peoples as a claimant, the argument here is that Islamic perspectives have not been equitably represented in key authority structures and processes of world order, which seems to account for the impression and actuality of an anti-Islamic bias in addressing policy issues of the global agenda. Further, if civilizational rights of participation existed, such an impression and its reality would be diminished and the policies produced would probably be more balanced and viewed as such from Islamic perspectives, if assessed on an inter-civilizational basis. Such an analysis is minimalist in the sense that it does not give weight to the anti-modernist, anti-secularist, anti-globalization dimensions of the Islamic critique of the structures of world order or to the contention that positive Islamic contributions by way of balancing community values against individualist claims would contribute to a more stable foundation for social relations and inter-civilizational understanding.

The Difficult Challenge of Normative Adjustment

Normative adjustment implies a mutually reinforcing combination of moral, political, and legal developments, combined with supportive historical circumstances, if it is to achieve important positive results. Concretely, normative adjustment in relation to world-order conditions refers to alterations in patterns of practice and the modes of participation in authority structures and processes. It means overcoming grievances validated as reasonable. In the setting of this analysis it means connecting the grievances outlined in the prior section. With reference to Islam it means conferring and safeguarding rights of participation based upon civilizational identity. As such, this particular normative adjustment cannot be effectively achieved within the traditional framework of statism, even as modified to confer rights on individuals, minorities, groups, and— arguably—peoples.[34] As earlier discussed, the struggle of indigenous peoples, conceived as an aggregate reality that is superimposed on diverse distinct indigenous nations, comes closest to staking a claim of right on behalf of a civilization that seeks to be acknowledged as such rather than to be dissolved into constituent statist elements in line with Westphalian and post-Westphalian categories.[35]

The prospects for successful normative adjustment with respect to overcoming what has been called the geopolitics of exclusion are cloudy at best. For one thing, there is as yet no clear consensus that such exclusion is occurring, and those aggrieved have not chosen as yet to present their grievances in this manner. For another, there are strong policy grounds on the part of those social forces that benefit from false universalism to resist claims premised on the reality of civilizational identity and difference. Such resistance is likely to be particularly strong to the extent that an acknowledgment of bias would seem to benefit Islam. Finally, Islam is far from united in its self-definition with respect to normative adjustment, with some portions of the Muslim world accepting the premises of globalization, secularization, and a world order that remains constituted at the level of rights primarily by states.

The experience of normative adjustments is varied, but the study of past instances would be instructive in bearing witness to the intertwined role of morality, politics, and law. Among the instances that seem useful as precedents are the following: the prohibition of the international slave trade; the right of self-determination; the process of decolonization; the anti-apartheid campaign; the prohibition of genocide as a distinct crime; and realization of civil and political rights. Each instance is a complex narrative that generates a wide range of appraisals in terms of impact, but each discloses a degree of normative adjustment that resulted in some change in authoritative language and practices. It would also be illuminating to consider projects of normative adjustment that resulted in substantial failure: definition of aggression, establishment of a collective security system, and realization of economic and social rights.

The normative adjustment that is appropriate depends on the character of the grievances and the remedies being sought. My argument has been that the essential normative adjustment on behalf of Islam would be more equitable participation in authority structures (the United Nations, the administration of the world economy) and an acknowledgment of civilizational identity. Of course, even if such a position were to be generally accepted, difficult problems remain relating to representation and the contours of civilization units. All the same, certain favorable conditions exist with respect to the prospect for normative adjustment: the reality of an Islamic resurgence and sense of grievance; the established reasonableness of the core grievances; the political interest of non-Islamic leaderships to avoid a hostile inter-civilizational encounter and to neutralize any Islamic threat; and the similarity of these grievances to the claims of indigenous peoples. Thus, the moral and political preconditions for normative adjustment have been met to some degree but, as suggested, formidable obstacles remain.

Why Human Rights? Why a Civilizational Right?

A characteristic of the last half of the twentieth century has been to translate grievances into a legitimating process for their rectification by way of an acknowledgment of rights. This has occurred generally in relations between individuals and their governments, and then with respect to more specific categories of claims relating to group discrimination, children, women, environment and even food, peace, life, and development. Embodiment in the setting of human rights does not ensure behavioral implementation and enforcement. Reliance on human rights to alter conditions of perceived and actual injustice in the world involves all of the ambiguities and frustrations of "soft law."[36]

The main argument for suggesting a civilizational level of protection for human rights at this stage of history arises from the empirical circumstances that have been described, which have given rise to serious claims of grievance and pose dangers of conflict. The articulation of a right of civilizational participation would itself be a consciousness-raising educative process. An additional benefit would be to challenge the false universalism of globalization and suggest an alternative in the form of an inter-civilizational world order that combines the ecological and biological conditions of unity with the civilizational conditions of difference and self-definition.

There exists one important cost associated with the analysis of false universalism. It weakens democratic forces in existing Islamic states in their efforts to uphold a secular conception of relations between religion and the state, and to protect the freedoms and autonomy of individuals. In this regard, even if the human rights framework is vulnerable to the civilizational level of criticisms set forth, it is still valuable, even indispensable, in relation to struggles being enacted at the level of the sovereign state in such countries as Turkey and Egypt. In my view, this tension is essentially a creative one, invoking human rights norms as relevant, but fixing the framework to overcome the neglect of non-Western civilizations.

Self-Determination

Chapter Five

IMPLICATIONS OF THE OSLO/CAIRO
FRAMEWORK FOR THE PEACE PROCESS

Every peace process is distinctive, acquiring its own characteristics based upon the overall mix of circumstances that leads parties to an armed conflict to move, often unexpectedly and even abruptly, in the direction of "peace." Nothing is assured. Even the quest for peace itself cannot be taken for granted. Parties may pursue negotiations and a peace settlement for purely tactical reasons, to provide a lull in actual combat, to strike a sympathetic pose for the sake of world public opinion, or to create new conditions that would be more favorable upon the resumption of active hostilities. At the core of most diplomatic efforts to achieve peace is a negotiating process, the product of which will be an international agreement, or a series of agreements, to provide a framework for future adjustments and relations and to establish the modalities for the momentous shift from war to peace. Depending on its form, such an agreement may, to varying degrees, be obligatory for the parties and represent common ground in the event of further controversy about respective rights and duties.

The Oslo/Cairo framework for the Israel/Palestine Liberation Organization (PLO) peace process is definitely illustrative of such an effort to impart structure and to give guidance to the transition to peace after a long period of intense warfare. It was carefully negotiated by mutually acknowledged official representatives of each side, and it was ritualized in a ceremony on the White House lawn in September of 1993.[1] From outward appearances, the agreements negotiated seemed to provide a solid foundation for cumulative movement toward peace. There were, however, many treacherous difficulties that clouded expectations from the outset. It is the contention of this paper that if the peace process is to eventuate in peace, it will require reinforcement from time to time by external actors such as the United States, the European Union, and the United Nations.[2] Moreover, at the level of implementation, NGOs, transnational citizens' associations, and private diplomacy will turn out to be indispensable.[3]

This piece first appeared as "Some International Law Implications of the PLO/Israeli Peace Process," The Palestine Yearbook of International Law *VIII (1996): 19–34.*

First of all, the disparity in power, wealth, influence, information, and negotiating skill between Israel and the PLO has pervaded all phases of negotiation as well as the subsequent implementation; this multi-layered disparity has tilted the process very much in Israel's favor, especially in matters of interpretation and the political willingness of each side to go ahead to the next stage in the process. Of course, it is characteristic of such conflicts that a negotiated settlement exhibit a disparity between the parties, as was the case in Algeria in the negotiations between France and the FLN or in Vietnam in the negotiations between the United States and North Vietnam/National Liberation Front. In those instances, however, the "weaker" side at the negotiating table had essentially prevailed on the battlefield, and the "stronger" side had an urgent political need for an exit strategy. Here, the PLO was at the brink of defeat, if not collapse, and Israel had no urgent pressure to leave the occupied territories in the wake of defeat. In such circumstances, the disparity seems likely to express itself in the bargaining process, leading to a bad bargain for the weaker side and, absent wisdom on the stronger side, a nonsustainable arrangement that will engender opposition and resistance.

Secondly, each side in the process contained important minorities deeply opposed to allowing the Oslo/Cairo framework to become the effective basis of an Israel/Palestine peace. On the Palestinian side, Islamic Jihad and the Islamic Resistance Movement (Hamas) committed their organizations to a disruptive posture that included resorting to terrorism against Israeli targets of all variety, including civilians. On the Israeli side, extremists among the settlers and the Likud opposition opposed the whole idea of Palestinian self-rule, especially on the West Bank; the extremist and violent settler fringe resorted to terror tactics, most spectacularly the February 25, 1994 mass killing of Muslims praying at the Tomb of the Patriarchs in Hebron by a single Israeli militant, Baruch Goldstein.[4] Terrorist incidents causing Israeli casualties have generated demands for more effective PLO control of extremists among the Palestinians, and have led the Israeli government to repeatedly impose collective punishments, including the periodic sealing of Israel's borders. These steps denied Palestinians access to their Israeli jobs, and brought added hardship to a Palestinian society that had already been experiencing a steady and dramatic process of economic deterioration since the start of the arrangements brought into being by the Oslo/Cairo framework. Israeli officials have also threatened to halt the peace process indefinitely unless the Palestinian Authority suppresses anti-Israeli violence, even if the perpetrators were never within Palestinian-controlled areas.

Thirdly, the Palestinians living as refugees outside the West Bank and Gaza Strip were essentially unrepresented by the PLO during the negotiations. It remains to be seen whether some sort of right of return is incorporated into the peace process at some subsequent stage.

The interplay of these factors is complex and controversial, often being manipulated by various actors to demonstrate either that the peace process is failing due to its intrinsic weakness or that its essential integrity needs to be preserved in relation to extremists on both sides. This dynamic suggests a precarious situation dominated by political factors and remaining uncertain as to overall impact, even as the Gaza arrangements are extended to cover much of the remaining occupied Palestinian territory. Such a dynamic is in sharp contrast to other dimensions of the wider peace process, especially the Israel/Jordan agreements.[5] In this latter interaction the element of disparity, although present to a degree, seemed much less evident with respect both to the resolution of substantive issues and the relationship between the parties; furthermore, the outcome of the negotiations did not arouse extremist opposition of serious consequence on either side, particularly the Israeli side. This state-to-state relationship, barring truly fundamental changes in the underlying circumstances, seems likely to proceed in rough approximation to the terms agreed upon, although it may over time be linked once more to mutually acceptable arrangements on such unresolved regional issues as the future of Jerusalem, sharing of water rights, establishment of a Palestinian homeland, and Israeli abandonment of nuclear weapons.

For the present, negotiated arrangements between Israel and its neighbors are much more likely to be respected as feasible and mutually beneficial than are comparable Israel/PLO arrangements. Of course, the intense mutual entanglement of Israel and occupied Palestine makes this negotiation by far the most ambitious and difficult of the various negotiating tracks that together comprise the Middle East peace process. However, the limits of the state-to-state and regional peace process have surfaced both in relation to the US/Israeli-backed proposal for a Middle East Development Bank (with Gulf countries having second thoughts about entering so rapidly into close ties with Israel until more overall progress toward normalcy has occurred), and with respect to Egypt/Israel tensions over Arab adherence to an extended version of the Non-Proliferation Treaty despite Israeli non-adherence.[6]

An optimistic assessment could never have been responsibly made with respect to the Israel/PLO arrangements embodied in the Oslo/Cairo agreements: in part, the terms of agreement (reflecting the disparities) were too one-sidedly in Israel's favor, and at the same time the attacks on Israeli vital interests prompted by the flawed peace process have generated a political crisis in Israel that has placed the Rabin government on the defensive. This defensiveness led Rabin to suspend agreed-upon timetables for implementation of removal of troops and elections on the West Bank, and to seriously consider such radical solutions to the security challenge as the complete "separation" of the two peoples.[7]

In retrospect, it now seems absurdly inappropriate for leaders on either side of the negotiations to have been awarded a Nobel Peace Prize in 1994, although it is by no means the first time that the prize committee in Oslo has used the award to show support for unresolved moves in the direction of peace and reconciliation. Even earlier, when the prizes were announced, such recognition seemed like a mixture of forgetfulness about the past and wishful thinking for the future because it reflected the then-real acknowledgment that world public opinion was prepared to hope against hope, giving tangible expression to the view that what was started required courage and that symbolic moral support might help continue the process until it reached the desired outcome. A similar acknowledgment a year earlier by way of Nobel Peace Prizes to Nelson Mandela and F. W. de Klerk seems to have fared much better with the passage of time, reflecting both the quality of the individuals honored and even more so the degree to which the peace process in South Africa tangibly scaled back the injustices of apartheid. No such relinquishment of control has been evident on the Israeli side in relation to the Palestinian territories, not even as regards the initial transfers of authority. Instead, Israel has sought to push its advantageous position as fully as possible, thereby restructuring the disparities without seeking to transform them. This is reflected not only in extensive Israeli security claims even in relation to Gaza, but also by the provocative moves to expand Israeli settlements in West Bank areas slated for self-rule and by the obstacles placed in the way of Palestinian investment, trade relations, and employment. The extensions of Oslo/Cairo to the West Bank exhibit similar characteristics.

In effect, the Oslo/Cairo framework to support an ongoing peace process depended upon several kinds of action by the parties, especially Israel. To undercut extremism it was in Israel's interest to improve the lot of the Palestinians living under the Palestinian Authority as quickly as possible at the street level. Similarly, it was important for the PLO leadership to expand its political base in areas under its control by creating employment opportunities and improving life circumstances for Palestinians, especially those living in refugee camps. Further, when the Hebron massacre occurred, it would have been a moment for the Israeli government to rein in the settlements as part of its strategy to make the peace process a success.[8] Similarly, it seems destructive for Israel to blame Hamas terrorism on the enforcement laxity of the Palestinian Authority and to justify delays in negotiations or punitive countermeasures. These are precisely the results being sought by Hamas, and Israel thereby ironically provides ample incentive for the continuation of their activities. It would have been more useful for the Israeli government and media to focus Palestinian responsibility narrowly, thereby undercutting Hamas's terrorist incentive when Israel responds broadly and itself calls into question the peace process. What now seems to exist is a tacit conspiracy on both sides to ensure a substantial discrediting of the Oslo/Cairo framework, which has predictably produced the unwelcome outcome of strengthening the political leverage of extremist elements in both Israel and among Palestinians.

Against this background of uncertainty and deteriorating confidence it remains useful to evaluate the Oslo/Cairo framework from the perspective of the international legal order. Despite the difficulties described, both sides continue to express their grievances and disappointments with the agreements, and have, at this point, substantially agreed upon elaborate arrangements of a similar character for much of the West Bank. Even without the contextual difficulties that have been discussed, a negotiated peace process and its international legal implications need to be understood as possessing several special attributes.

The phrase "international legal implications" refers both to the rights and duties of the parties to the autonomy agreements so far negotiated between the PLO and Israel since the September 1993 Declaration of Principles on Interim Self-Government Arrangements (DOP) and to the relationship of this process to legal claims on a global level by representatives of the peoples involved, as well as by third-party governments, international institutions, and non-governmental organizations. It touches on the extent to which the texts negotiated and to be negotiated are authoritative and binding with respect to such matters as sovereignty, statehood, self-determination, refugees, boundaries, resources, Jerusalem, and protection of human rights.

Formally, these crucial issues remain contested and unresolved between Israel and the PLO, pending the conclusion of the permanent status negotiations that are not scheduled to begin soon, but must commence according to Oslo no later than two years after the start of the interim period.[9] A legal, political uncertainty affecting the whole process is the extent to which these parties have and will be treated as having the representational capacity to resolve issues that concern either Palestinians living outside the occupied territories or governments in the region with an interest in the process, particularly, arrangements for Jerusalem, water rights, and a Palestinian right of return. Even for Palestinians living under Israeli rule the representation issue is real. The PLO's authority and legitimacy have been under siege, not only from Islamic elements but also from progressive secular social forces. Some aspects of this present and future will be examined from the perspective of international law.

Deference

There is a strong tendency in international law to respect whatever framework parties to a conflict choose to resolve their differences, especially if undertaken against a background of prolonged warfare and with the encouragement of the international community. Disparities in power, negotiating competence, and knowledge between the parties are not treated as legally relevant; peace treaties imposed by battlefield outcomes in war are generally respected in international law, although acquisitions of new territory by force of arms have been legally problematic within the domain of the United Nations, regardless of what the parties may decide.

In addition, if the disparities seem too great, or political conditions change, legal deference to an earlier "peace process" may be dissipated by subsequent developments. Indeed, there is an important distinction between "legality" and "legitimacy" that may be relevant to the evolving PLO/Israeli relationship. This process, which has enjoyed widespread deference on an inter-governmental level and within the United Nations at its early stages, is increasingly subject to attack and wide criticism as "illegitimate" by Palestinians and by governments and international organizations. This is so both because the terms imposed on the Palestinian people fall short of their rights to self-determination and, on the other hand, because the PLO has failed to follow through in relation to either the Palestinian people or Israeli expectations arising from the agreed texts.

The Israeli leadership has already revealed its unwillingness to implement aspects of the early empowerment phases of the self-government provisions unless the PLO abides by its commitments (as interpreted by Israeli officialdom). This is especially true of the PLO's obligation to deny extremists safe haven and to sustain the security of Israelis living within the jurisdiction of its authority, as well as its alleged commitment to revise the Palestinian Covenant by removing challenges to Israel's right to exist as a state on its present territory. Various Palestinian leaders, representing different facets of Palestinian public opinion, have also challenged the capacity of Chairman Arafat to negotiate in secret and act unilaterally on behalf of the PLO. They have also complained about the alleged PLO failure to implement the democratizing provisions in the agreements in territory under its control.

So far the organized global community continues to treat as authoritative the PLO/Israeli peace process as negotiated by the parties. Paragraph 3 of the UN General Assembly Resolution 48/58, adopted December 14, 1993, "[e]xpresses its full support for the achievements of the peace process thus far," singling out the Declaration of Principles (DOP) as especially notable, and ends by urging "all parties to implement the agreements reached." This resolution was adopted by a vote of 155 to 3 (Iran, Lebanon, and Syria voting against), with one abstention (Libya), and was drafted by the key third-party states (Norway, Russia, and the United States) along with the active participation of the PLO and Israel. From an international law perspective, such an expression of consensus, reinforcing as it does the normal pattern of deference in the setting of a peace process, is, until repudiated or withdrawn, quite definitive in relation to states and the United Nations, with the possible exception of the four states that refused to support the UN resolution.

This prospect of deference is also reinforced by geopolitical considerations. First of all, continuing Israeli peace negotiations with Arab neighbors are leading toward a condition of regional normalization, although as yet incomplete and subject to shifts in attitude or even reversals. Secondly, the agreements so far negotiated facilitate the accommodation of the two overriding interests of the United States in the region: favorable access to oil and support of Israel. In this regard, a one-sided peace process is more likely to engender US deference than one that was more balanced in its disposition of controversial issues. This context is not favorable to the most fundamental Palestinian concerns and, arguably, has never been, although during the Cold War and in the course of belligerent relations between Israel and the Arab World, "the Palestinian card" was played by Arab governments and the Soviet Union as a dimension of opposition to Israeli statehood and expansion. At present, there are no strong incentives to play this card, except possibly on Syria's part, but even Syrian President Hafez Assad's diplomacy seems to be moving inexorably in the direction of a negotiated reconciliation with Israel. So far, the peace momentum has proved resilient, withstanding the psycho-political impact of the Hamas tactics, settler violence, Likud opposition, and Israeli punitive responses. At the same time, there are several indications in 1995 of a growing reluctance by Arab states to immediately accept Israel as a normal state when it comes to economic relations (e.g., Arab opposition to the Mideast Development Bank and withdrawal of potential Gulf state participants from joint ventures with Israel in the energy area).

Given this background, Palestinian prospects for the protection of both their broader claims to self-determination, statehood, and sovereignty, and their narrower claims to full implementation of the agreements, including provisions on democratization of the Palestinian governance process, will be dependent, to an unusual degree, on continuing, and even expanding, grassroots activism by Palestinians, reinforced by the transnational support of citizens' associations dedicated to peace, democracy, and human rights. The more extreme cases of East Timor and West New Guinea (Irian Jaya) are suggestive in that the circumstances of abuse have been deliberately overlooked by most of the international community because of the absence of geopolitical incentives to challenge Indonesia.[10] Indeed, without grassroots resistance and the efforts of transnational political forces, these issues would have disappeared into the black hole of geopolitics. The Palestinian plight is somewhat similarly situated, although the Islamic interest in the status of Jerusalem and concern about Israel's nuclear weapons and economic ambitions makes it much less likely that Palestinian concerns will be altogether neglected within wider regional and global political circles.

Sui Generis

The point here is a simple one: there is little relevant precedent. The PLO role in the Gaza Strip and Jericho, as well as elsewhere on the West Bank and in relation to Jerusalem, is embedded in a unique set of circumstances and shaped by the interactions of the past several decades of occupation, which have influenced the conditions imposed on the partial transfer of authority to the PLO in a variety of fundamental respects. The persistence, and even expansion, of Israeli settlements and security zones give these interim arrangements a particularly unresolved, precarious character. The structures and circumstances of dual authority are quite an anomaly in the post-colonial era where the exercise of rights to self-determination normally extinguish enclaves of foreign privilege at an early stage and imply an unconditional transfer of sovereign rights as a matter of right. The arrangements for Hong Kong after 1997 or in the various parts of the United Kingdom (Scotland, Ulster, Isle of Man) are illustrative of self-rule, dual, or incomplete sovereignty. Yet the anomalies here are, for the time being at least and from the perspective of the agreements themselves, subordinate to the deference accorded whatever texts are negotiated, especially as argued above, since the agreements reached are the essence of a peace process instituted to supersede a condition of prolonged and bitterly resisted belligerent occupation.[11]

In the end, the acceptability of the process will depend, of course, on the success of the status negotiations that are supposed to begin within two years after the inception of the interim arrangements and end within five years of this date. If the peace process goes forward, even if more slowly than agreed upon, the supportive consensus of Resolution 48/58 in the UN holds firm, and the PLO remains sufficiently credible among Palestinians and on the international level as the sole legitimate representative of the Palestinian people, then the prospects are reasonably good that the agreements as negotiated will remain generally authoritative from the perspectives of international law. But if any one of these conditions further weakens, then the agreements seem vulnerable to a variety of lines of stress and outside attack, including repudiation, and are not insulated by any earlier persuasive precedent or wider doctrine. Even a Likud victory in the forthcoming 1996 elections would cast severe doubt on the arrangements already agreed upon and implemented.

With respect to international law, the disparity between the two sides reflected in the one-sidedness of the arrangements is both the strength and weakness of the peace process. It is the strength because, to date, the process has been guided essentially by one side according to its priorities, and it is the side with superior access to the media and to the geopolitical forces in control of the world order. It is the main weakness of the process because this one-sidedness, if effectively exposed, undermines the legitimacy of whatever has been agreed upon, especially if the Palestinians themselves, either by way of the PLO or in opposition to its leadership, regard the agreements as not satisfying, within a reasonable time interval, their basic aspirations for sovereignty, statehood, and improving material conditions. Despite their one-sidedness in Israel's favor, the agreements are also vulnerable to varying degrees of repudiation or non-implementation on the Israeli side, possibly either by a return to control of the Likud or by escalating violence against the Israelis. This vulnerability has already been manifest, especially with respect to Israel's refusal to abide by the agreed timetable on elections and empowerment and its insistence on taking whatever security measures it deems necessary, even if their enactment imposes unwarranted hardship on the Palestinians.

Status

On a textual level, the Palestinians arguably have lost ground in their basic quest for statehood and sovereignty, while the PLO has gained in its external contention of representing the Palestinian people, as epitomized by the signing ceremony on the White House lawn and by the abrupt transformation of Yasir Arafat from "terrorist" to normal political leader entitled to treatment equivalent to that accorded a head of state. With some irony, this external acceptance of the PLO, as represented by Arafat, is coupled with an internal erosion of the PLO's claim to be the authoritative representative of the Palestinian people and with increasing Palestinian dissatisfaction with the results and style of Arafat's leadership, which now ironically includes serious abuses of democratic elements and rights of Palestinians living under the jurisdiction of the Palestinian Authority.[12]

The negotiating framework and the agreements issuing forth reflect this underlying ambiguity on matters of status. As never before, the state of Israel operationally accepted the PLO and Arafat as diplomatic equals, as "parties." Yet formally and textually, as well as in substantive arrangements, inequality of status was enshrined throughout the process. The Preamble of the DOP identifies the Palestinian party as "the PLO team (in the Jordanian–Palestinian delegation to the Middle East Peace Conference)," while the Israeli party is described simply as "[t]he government of the state of Israel," a status confirmed by the September 9, 1993 exchange of correspondence. In later documents the PLO is simply described as such, given an authoritative relationship to the negotiations to establish a Palestinian Interim Self-Government Authority, and Arafat, in the September 9 letters with Rabin, undertakes without deadlines to submit to the Palestinian National Council proposals to make "the necessary changes" in the Palestinian Covenant in accordance with the PLO acceptance of Israel's right to exist as a sovereign state.[13]

Throughout the agreements, there is no acknowledgment whatsoever of Palestinian sovereignty over the West Bank, Gaza, or Jerusalem areas, and no implication that the Palestinian Authority is a vehicle for emerging Palestinian statehood. Numbered paragraph 4 in the May 4, 1994 exchange of letters specifies that Arafat will "use the title 'Chairman (Ra'ees in Arabic) of the Palestinian Authority' or 'Chairman of the PLO,' and will not use the title 'President of Palestine.'" This attempt to circumscribe the Palestinian status is further confirmed in Article VI of the Gaza-Jericho Agreement by denying the Palestinian Authority "powers and responsibilities in the sphere of foreign relations" and throughout the interim arrangements by severely restricting the Palestinian role even in internal security to the extent that Israelis are affected. At the same time, Israel acknowledges the PLO's right to negotiate with foreign governments and international organizations on matters pertaining to economic development, aid, cultural, scientific, and educational matters.[14]

Prior to the peace process, the PLO was recognized as the government of the state of Palestine by more than a hundred countries, and had many diplomatic representatives and facilities at different levels abroad.[15] In the interim arrangements, despite the PLO having a territorial base of governmental control for the first time, the legal competence to engage in foreign relations is narrowly circumscribed, including either the establishment of Palestinian diplomatic facilities abroad or foreign facilities in Gaza or Jericho. Additionally, Israel claims an informal authority to regulate entry, including that of foreign heads of state, as seen in the incident over Benazir Bhutto's proposed visit to Gaza in the fall of 1994. Rabin rebuffed Bhutto by attacking her lack of "manners," evidently because of her failure to obtain Israel's approval of the visit before announcing her intention. The fact that the visit did not take place lends credence to the perception that Israel retains many of the operative rights of occupation, even if it has redeployed its troops.

It is uncertain how practice will evolve. Will there be a tacit tolerance by both sides of gaps between the textual denials of emerging Palestinian statehood and the behavioral expressions of it, or will Israel press the issue that the Palestinian Authority lacks the formal or substantive attributes of sovereignty? How will third parties, whether states or international organizations, treat the issue? How will the PLO?

The issue of status casts a shadow over the nature of the agreements. Because the Palestinian side is so far definitively not treated as a state in the negotiating process, and the PLO has accepted this diminished status, the agreements reached are not treaties in a technical sense under international law. Yet, the White House signing and endorsement, the diplomatic rituals emphasizing the equality of the parties, the Norwegian role in encouraging the negotiations, the tendency in recent customary international law to give respect to the outcome of self-determination negotiations conducted with a non-state actor, and the UN expressions of formal support have definitively internationalized the process, at least for the present. This gives the PLO a state-like role in the process and makes the resulting arrangements treaty-like for most purposes. Of course, the PLO and the Palestinian Authority would not currently have full access to any arena that restricts participation to states (e.g., the International Court of Justice).

In these regards, some language in Article XXIII (5) of the May 4, 1994 Cairo Agreement is of potential relevance to the Palestinian side:

> Nothing in this Agreement shall prejudice or preempt the outcome of the negotiations in the interim agreement or on the permanent status to be conducted pursuant to the Declaration of Principles. Neither Party shall be deemed, by virtue of having entered into this Agreement, to have renounced or waived any of its existing rights, claims or positions.

Such an "escape" clause seems inconsistent with the substance, tone, and language of the agreements so far negotiated, but it gives a legal basis in the future to the reassertion of claims relating to Palestinian sovereignty and self-determination that have been so far not explicitly acknowledged. This clause also gives Israel the possibility of reasserting territorial claims to the West Bank, as would likely happen if the Likud were to resume control of the negotiating process.

The early disputes under the agreements have confirmed that Israel holds the main cards and intends to play them aggressively, suggesting that the rate and quality of implementation of the agreements will depend almost exclusively on the will of the Israeli government. This Israeli advantage is accentuated by the failure of the PLO to move swiftly toward a more democratic relationship with Palestinians under the jurisdiction of the Palestinian Authority. Such a development raises to prominence a neglected and generally unanticipated dimension of the peace process, namely, the legal vulnerability under the agreements of the Palestinians who are seeking to uphold human rights and achieve democratic governance. Unlike rejectionist elements (e.g., Hamas), Israel seems to view democratically inclined Palestinians as a matter for the PLO to handle as it sees fit. Despite its claim of support for a democratic Palestinian entity, Israel does not appear distressed by the suppression of these Palestinians, possibly because it may prefer to deal with the autocratic and corrupt rule of a PLO leadership that is content with a minimalist conception of self-determination. In that way, the PLO can more easily be held accountable, which allows Israel to avoid confronting the broader demands of Palestinians who insist on a much fuller exercise of the Palestinian right to self-determination.

Among the legal issues posed here is the extent of Israeli responsibility for violations of human rights of Palestinians as a result of the activities of the Palestinian Authority, recalling that Article XIV of the Gaza/Jericho Agreement pledges both sides to proceed separately to carry out their respective responsibilities on the basis of international human rights standards and the rule of law. Events to date involving arbitrary arrests, allegations of torture and intimidation, interference with freedom of the press and rights of free expression make it evident that such Palestinian concerns are not fanciful, but also that Article XIV's legal commitment is being ignored, at least by the two negotiating parties. If the Israeli government does not press such claims on behalf of the Palestinians, it would seem that the UN would still be in a position to do so to the extent that Israeli occupation has not yet been terminated in the sense decreed by Security Council Resolutions 242 and 338, and sovereignty has not been transferred to an emergent Palestinian state. Israel retains, at least during the interim period, extensive security and economic prerogatives as well as plenary control over foreign relations, Israeli settlements, and other responsibilities and duties that arise from this evolving set of circumstances.

Self-Determination

Not only is the issue of eventual Palestinian statehood and sovereignty suppressed (along with Palestinian claims in relation to Jerusalem), but more remarkably, the right to self-determination of the Palestinian people is never explicitly and unconditionally affirmed in the arrangements negotiated to date. Instead, the DOP unsatisfactorily refers in Article I under the heading "Aim of Negotiations," to "a permanent settlement" after the five-year transitional period "based on Security Council resolutions 242 and 338." It will be recalled that Resolution 242 was adopted in the aftermath of the 1967 war, having as its central tenet Israeli withdrawal from the territory it occupied in exchange for being accorded security by other states in the region, yet without ever specifying precisely what is meant by withdrawal or territory. Palestinian claims were at the time dealt with in the resolution as a peripheral matter, not even by direct reference, but within the presumed ambit of clause 2(b) of the resolution, which refers to the "necessity... for achieving a just settlement of the refugee problem."

It is plausible in the present climate of expectations to assume that achievement of such a just settlement would only be possible within the setting of a Palestinian homeland enjoying comprehensive sovereign rights, including some participation in the administration of Jerusalem. Whether such a just settlement also implies that all refugees claiming a Palestinian national identity would enjoy a right to return, and whether the exercise of this right would eventually be regulated by the Palestinian governance process that will be established is uncertain. There are also complex issues arising from the Israel-Jordan Peace Treaty signed without Palestinian participation yet addressing issues that bear on self-determination for the Palestinian people, such as economic control over West Bank resources and responsibility for controlling access to Islamic holy places in East Jerusalem.

Resolution 338, adopted in 1973, merely reiterates the imperative of implementing Resolution 242 by way of negotiations, and sheds no further light on the status or extent of Palestinian claims. By the textual language these resolutions would be quite consistent with a transfer of sovereign control over the occupied territories to Jordan (or any other entity), provided Israel withdrew its military forces and that some agreed arrangement of "the refugee problem" was achieved. It is somewhat astonishing that the PLO negotiators have accepted this outmoded textual framework as the agreed basis for a permanent settlement of the conflict, presumably obliging the Palestinian people to accept the land for peace formula enshrined in Resolutions 242 and 338 without any assurance on broader claims. The dynamics of the actual negotiating and implementing process have been far more favorable to the satisfaction of Palestinian claims for substantial sovereignty by way of a Palestinian state located within the occupied territories, but this has yet to be reflected adequately in the language of the formal texts that have emerged from the negotiations. The surmise of a state is based on the consequences over time of de facto self-rule. Yet such a surmise is suspect until the status of Israeli settlements and security rights are clarified in relation to the final outcome of the peace process.

As has been pointed out by Palestinian critics of negotiations to date, Gaza and the West Bank have been shifted from "occupied territory" to "disputed territory."[16] Such a change gives the contemplated Israeli "withdrawal" a more problematic character, making natural the retention of extensive residual rights and privileges, especially with respect to security and economic development, and the settlements as exempt from territorial law. The requirements of Resolution 242 are thereby reduced to the outcome of negotiations in a context of gross asymmetry and deference, reinforced by an Israeli tendency to seek as favorable a bargain as possible, allegedly, in part, so as "to sell" the process and arrangements at home, and in the face of stiff domestic opposition.[17] Article V of the DOP leaves open the shape of the permanent disposition of issues, including "Jerusalem, refugees, settlements, security arrangements, borders, relations and cooperation with other neighbors, and other issues of common interest." The same Article also confirms that the "permanent status negotiations should not be prejudiced or preempted by agreements reached for the interim period." Such a mandate allows for the possibility that the permanent status negotiations will move toward a more comprehensive understanding of Israeli withdrawal that would by itself be compatible with the exercise of Palestinian self-determination (unless self-determination is understood formalistically as whatever designated leaders of a people agree to even in circumstances of virtual compulsion).

Implementation

Many fundamental issues with respect to the peace process are unresolved at this stage, including the degree to which a successor government in Israel or a different Palestinian (or PLO) leadership would be bound by agreements negotiated and partially implemented, especially if important obligations were breached by either side. Since the DOP and other arrangements are not technically treaties, their international character can be denied, although the involvement of other governments, the formalization derived from the White House signing, and the UN General Assembly endorsement create a strong presumption that both sides have good faith legal obligations to carry out the agreed arrangements without retaining any option to repudiate. Of course, the test of the political viability of the process is likely to come about if there is a drastic change of government in Israel, if Arafat loses control of the PLO, and if and when permanent status negotiations get under way and raise the crucial long-term issues of statehood, sovereignty, Jerusalem, settlements, and external refugees.

During the interim period, assuming that the leadership on the two sides is stable and remains committed to the negotiating process, it is likely that inter-governmental disputes will be resolved by diplomacy, and that the Palestinian Authority will gradually acquire a de facto statist character even if implications of statehood are resisted de jure and Israeli settlements and security roles create major inroads upon the sort of territorial supremacy normally associated with statehood. The longer the interim process drags on and the more extremist opposition on both sides gains support, the less likely it is that the process can be maintained in its present form.

What about the provisions for elections and the constitutional arrangements proposed for the Palestinian Authority in the Agreement on the Gaza Strip and the Jericho Area, and more broadly in the West Bank? Suppose these undertakings are not implemented or are further delayed, which has occurred, and Palestinians are subjected to autocratic and inept rule, deprived of political participation, human rights, and basic material necessities. Suppose further, as seems likely, that neither Israel, the United States, the UN, nor even other Arab governments lend support to such charges of non-implementation, especially if other aspects of the process are going forward relatively smoothly. How, then, can the rights of the Palestinian people be upheld? It is here that the informal roles of NGOs in reinforcing governmental and inter-governmental procedures could be crucial. It would be of great legal relevance to have reliable monitoring procedures in place that identify, expose, and evaluate allegations of non-implementation of the democracy and constitutional portions of the peace process, and issue periodic reports; similarly, with respect to human rights. The UN retains a special responsibility toward the Palestinian people living in the occupied territories, at least until Security Council Resolution 242 is fully implemented, and this includes the protection of human rights. The challenge is to activate this latent legal responsibility by mobilizing effective political pressure through exposing violations, giving the prospect of exposure some possible deterrent effects on the governance approach adopted by the PLO and the Palestinian Authority.

The other confusing context, with respect to implementation, is the degree to which Israel/PLO negotiations can extinguish or supersede the legal claims of unrepresented parties. Because of the overall interest in peace, reinforced by regional and global geopolitical factors, there is a tendency to disregard third party interests, especially if not effectively voiced in the form of objections. UN resolutions of support for the existing framework of negotiations and arrangements give a legal coloring to this disregard. It might be appropriate to urge the UN General Assembly to request an Advisory Opinion from the International Court of Justice on such outstanding matters as the status of Jerusalem, the rights of Palestinians living outside the Gaza Strip and West Bank, and the distribution of water rights.

Conclusion

At this stage, from the perspective of international law, it is difficult to provide any clear guidelines as to the likely reception of the peace process under international law, especially as it pertains to the protection of human rights of Palestinians subject to the authority of the Palestinian Authority. The fluidity of the situation makes it critical for all concerned parties, especially those associated with the rights of citizens and the Palestinian diaspora, to posit their legal claims and grievances at an early stage in as effective a form as possible. This is particularly true with respect to those claims not likely to be protected by the perceived self-interest of the two negotiating sides and of no distinct interest to the US government.

It is in relation to human rights, democratization, and constitutional governance that grassroots Palestinian initiatives, reinforced by transnational citizens' associations, may yet have their greatest contributions to make, especially if substantiated by independent academic analysis and respected media accounts. In other words, the human rights dimensions of the peace process, if implemented, will likely depend upon the capabilities and imagination of an emergent and genuine, even if yet still weak and uneven, global civil society.

Such dependence is likely to diminish to the extent that the authority structures of emergent Palestinian statehood are effectively democratized, although this is not likely to be brought about by the peace process itself, but by activism within Gaza and the West Bank, reinforced by a more mobilized external public opinion. In the end, the role of international law is likely to relate to the mobilization of world public opinion in support of Palestinian non-governmental efforts to achieve constitutional democracy, including human rights, especially the core struggle for statehood and the full exercise of self-determination. No matter how one-sided the agreed texts, Palestinian rights to self-determination are intrinsic and inalienable, meaning that their existence may be obscured for a time, but never truly lost.

The test of this process of establishing normalcy will be widened as Israel relinquishes control over a substantial portion of the West Bank. Despite Israel's retention of security rights and settlements, the Palestinian reality is likely to be strengthened by these developments to the point where the operational situation is one of a Palestinian state, although qualified in its sovereign rights, vulnerable to intervention, and not able even to assert itself formally in many international arenas including the United Nations. If such is the end-point of "the peace process," it is not to be confused with the realization of Palestinian rights to self-determination.

Chapter Six

THE KURDISH STRUGGLE FOR
SELF–DETERMINATION AFTER THE GULF
AND COLD WARS

Fragmentation of the Struggle and its Goals

At a dinner in Istanbul with Kurdish journalists and academicians in early 1992, I was told by a young sociologist that he had just finished a survey of Kurdish attitudes toward different solutions to the Kurdish problem. His principal finding was that Kurds living in the Middle East were generally in favor of modest solutions within the boundaries of existing states, while Kurds living in exile were overwhelmingly in support of the establishment of a single sovereign state, to be called Kurdistan, that would provide a homeland for all Kurdish people. Whether or not the study would satisfy social science standards of rigor, it did seem to correspond with my own impressions and to identify important conceptual issues: what is the authoritative way to express the overriding Kurdish demand for self-determination? Who, if anyone, is empowered at this stage to speak on behalf of the Kurdish people as a whole? Or alternatively, should Kurdish self-determination be understood in pluralist terms, as having several distinct embodiments paralleling the separated existence of the Kurdish people over the course of the last 70 years?

Such issues of political identity bedevil almost all movements of peoples for self-determination but seem more currently central to the Kurdish situation as compared, say, to the Tibetan or Palestinian movements. In part this reflects the long-imposed period of fragmentation of the Kurdish people during the present century and the evolution of Kurdish political consciousness under diverse and difficult circumstances in a series of distinct sovereign states. In fact, the Kurdish struggle in recent decades has been primarily waged on a state-by-state basis with seemingly autonomous movements in each country that on occasion are openly hostile toward one another.[1] There are also variations of the contention found in some scholarly writing that the Kurdish people have been

This article first appeared as "Problems and Prospects for Kurdish Struggle for Self-Determination after the End of the Gulf and Cold Wars," Michigan Journal of International Law *15.2 (Winter 1994): 591–603.*

traditionally disunited, even beset by inner antagonisms as a consequence of a predominantly tribal organization and consciousness, a reality accentuated by their living in largely mountainous terrain.[2]

A further reinforcement of this impression of contemporary Kurdish disunity is the absence of any pan-Kurdish leader with high international visibility of the sort possessed by the Dalai Lama or Yasir Arafat. The outstanding Kurdish leaders in recent decades have all been associated with Kurdish movements at the national level, although success in a particular setting is generally celebrated at the international as a step toward achieving the wider Kurdish program. But even this assertion needs to be qualified, as efforts by Iraqi Kurds to consolidate their autonomy during 1991 came into conflict with the use of Iraq as a sanctuary and base area by guerrillas of the revolutionary Kurdistan Workers' Party of Turkey (PKK).[3]

Despite these intra-Kurdish tensions, the following statement expresses this wider sentiment of Kurdish solidarity in relation to the establishment of Iraqi Kurdistan as a constituent element within a federated Iraq: "The declaration of federalism has been greeted in all the regions of Kurdistan as the beginning of concretization of the dream of self-determination of the Kurdish people."[4] The same source goes on to assert that these Iraqi developments constitute a "highly symbolic act" that needs to be associated with the Treaty of Sèvres,[5] which proposed, in the aftermath of the collapse of the Ottoman Empire, the creation of a single Kurdistan covering the entire Kurdish region. Also mentioned was the establishment of the Kurdish Republic of Mahabad[6] in 1946 by the Iranian Kurdish people. Of course, the nonsustainability of these latter symbolic experiences suggests a double ambiguity when it comes to their invocation: first, the impulse to celebrate historical failures as successes tends to accentuate, rather than diminish, the modern Kurdish tragedy; second, the lumping together of the Iraqi federation, Mahabad, and Sèvres emphasizes the uncertain links between affirming aspirations for a single Kurdish state and for the more limited plan of seeking self-determination within the existing and firmly entrenched state structure in the region.

Often in discussions of the Kurdish right of self-determination these issues are not clearly identified. On the one side, the situations of Kurds in Iraq, Turkey, Iran, Syria, and the former Soviet Union are discussed as essentially separate concerns, but at the same time the plight of the Kurds is, nevertheless, treated, even in the technical literature, as a single, integrated misfortune.[7] Clarifying these issues of self-definition, to the extent possible, is itself a political challenge of some importance to the

Kurdish people, and has a decisive bearing on the capacity to pose the overriding question of self-determination for the Kurdish people within international arenas in a convincing way at this time.

Current uncertainty about the appropriate focus for the expression of Kurdish self-determination can be grasped by setting forth the main alternative approaches:

(1) The right of self-determination is to be understood as inhering in the Kurdish people and to apply to the whole of historic Kurdistan.

(2) The right of self-determination is to be understood as belonging to the Kurdish peoples and to apply separately in relation to the states wherein these peoples live; however, the form and depth of self-determination may vary in its implementation from state to state, depending on both the political will of the Kurdish movement and its degree of success in achieving its goals.

(3) The right of self-determination is not yet clearly associated with either (1) or (2) or, alternatively, (2) may be a stage in a process that would only be consummated by (1); a further possibility here is that an ambiguity of intention with respect to the scope and depth of self-determination serves the current interests of the Kurdish people as a whole, combining tactical flexibility in existing contexts of struggle—which are national in scope, internal in depth, and uneven in prospect—with an underlying strategic vision that remains committed to the eventual establishment of a single Kurdistan.

If indeed the dominant Kurdish position is currently understood as some variant of (3), it should be appreciated that such a view possesses both serious weaknesses from the perspective of building a Kurdish support movement on an international level and definite strengths in terms of accommodating the complex historical circumstances of power and struggle. These weaknesses center on the impression of incoherence and amorphousness that has come to be associated with the Kurdish movement, making it far more difficult for non-Kurds generally sympathetic to the struggles of oppressed peoples either to identify closely with the Kurdish struggle or to accord it a high priority on the global agenda of unresolved grievances. Whether or not such solidarity at a global level is important for Kurdish success at this time is difficult to say. It should be appreciated that compared to the Palestinian and Tibetan struggles, the Kurdish struggle confronts even harsher geopolitical realities—both in the form of a regional consensus favorable to the maintenance of all existing states within their current boundaries and support for the regional status quo by influential outside actors, including the United States.[8] In retrospect, perhaps the Kurdish turning-point was to swallow without any effective appearance of unified resistance the Treaty of Lausanne[9] that not only extinguished the pledges of Sèvres,[10] but also ratified a political framework that effectively distributed the Kurdish people among five distinct political entities, each achieving sovereign status.[11] Kurdish political self-consciousness seemed insufficiently evolved in the period after World War I to offer effective resistance to these essentially European colonial machinations.[12] In this regard, Kurdish political consciousness may not have been less developed than that of many other peoples, considering that the colonial order remained firmly in control throughout the non-Western world, although the persistence of tribal loyalties may have facilitated oppression. Further, the regional colonial project in the Middle East was influenced by the success of Kemal Mustafa Atatürk's nationalist program in Turkey that promised "Westernization" and was compatible with British colonial designs in the region, which centered on oil and the maintenance of a strong buffering link with Central Asia and India. Atatürk absorbed a significant portion of the Kurdish people in the course of establishing the modern Turkish state; once Turkey was accepted as a political reality, then colonial interests, dominated by the British, were best served by keeping the remaining Kurds as national minorities in Iran, Iraq, and Syria, thereby creating better prospects for viable states in the region.

There are two further preliminary questions of a conceptual character. The right of self-determination to be realized in practice does not have a definitive content or status but reflects both a contest of political wills and the play of forces. It is possible that a territorial state will acquiesce under certain conditions to claims of self-determination, even of a maximalist, secessionist variety. It is reported, for instance, that the Belgrade government headed by Slobodan Milosevic in the former Yugoslavia was prepared in 1991 to accept the secession of Slovenia, despite being resistant to other secessionist claims.[13]

Exercising fully a given right of self-determination need not imply separate statehood or the dismemberment of an existing territorial state. Self-determination in a variety of formats can be fulfilled within existing states and is sometimes referred to as internal self-determination.[14] The pursuit of internal self-determination is more easily reconciled with some conceptions of international law and may be more in accord with the political prospects and relative capabilities of a captive people or nation. At the same time, as the experience of the Iraqi Kurds during the past

twenty years in particular shows, internal self-determination may itself be a
snare and delusion, leaving predominant power in the government of the
encompassing state, thereby consigning the captive people to a
circumstance of permanent vulnerability.[15] Those in control of the central
governing process can bide their time, reasserting oppressive control as
opportunities arise, a pattern descriptive of the relationship between Iraqi
Kurds and Baghdad during the period of Saddam Hussein's rule. Of course,
the presentation of historic opportunities works in both directions, and the
current success of Iraqi Kurds in achieving de facto autonomy seems
organically connected with the Gulf War and its horrifying aftermath.[16]

The Evolution of the Right of Self-Determination

An understanding of the evolution of the right of self-determination is
important for appreciating the complexities and ambiguities of the Kurdish
experience. The idea of self-determination expressed, in part, the gradual
identification of statehood and political legitimacy with the theory and
practice of nationalism, as opposed to that of empire with its multi-nation
character. Its relevance was dramatized by Woodrow Wilson's espousal of
self-determination as a constitutive principle of peace in the altered
international order that he favored in the aftermath of World War I. Wilson's
concerns were explicitly directed at the future political arrangements
planned for the defeated Austro-Hungarian and Ottoman Empires, but
their realization was thwarted and distorted by the interposition of the
colonialist schemes of the victorious European states. Self-determination
was not written into the Covenant of the League of Nations and was
relevant to postwar arrangements only to the extent consistent with
geopolitical considerations. As Hannum expresses this pattern: "It should be
underscored that self-determination in 1919 had little to do with the
demands of the peoples concerned, unless those demands were consistent
with the geopolitical and strategic interests of the Great Powers."[17]

   Also at this time self-determination was subordinated to considerations
of territorial unity for existing states. In a dispute concerning the future of
the Aaland Islands, which the League confirmed as part of Finland despite
acknowledging both the Swedish ethnic character of the population and
its preference for union with Sweden, it was definitively concluded in
1920 that the wishes of a part of an existing state had no legal basis for
claiming a right of secession and that claims of self-determination on
behalf of an ethnic minority were not legally relevant.[18]

   The strengthening of the right of self-determination has been a gradual process, given a definite, if opportunistic, push by the Soviet-led socialist countries as an aspect of their wider struggle to oppose and weaken the colonial order. Self-determination is affirmed in the UN Charter, both in Articles 1 and 55, but ambiguously as a "principle" rather than as a "right." In both charter references, self-determination is coupled with the "equal rights" of states, suggesting more the notion that all states are entitled to pursue their own course free from outside interference rather than that captive "peoples" are entitled to autonomy, or possibly even secession, if that is their will.

But the anticolonial struggle, as it gained momentum after World War II, established self-determination as a right of peoples subject to colonial rule to pursue and achieve full political independence. As expressed in the famous Declaration on the Granting of Independence to Colonial Countries and Peoples,[19] the scope of the right of self-determination is broader than the explicit circumstances of colonial subjugation. For instance, the first two operative clauses of the declaration state:

(1) The subjection of peoples to alien subjugation, domination, and exploitation constitutes a denial of fundamental human rights, is contrary to the Charter of the United Nations and is an impediment to the promotion of world peace and co-operation.

(2) All peoples have the right to self-determination; by virtue of that right they freely determine their political status and freely pursue their economic, social, and cultural development.[20]

But one must also acknowledge the declaration's characteristic limitation on the exercise of self-determination: that "[a]ny attempt aimed at the partial or total disruption of the national unity and the territorial integrity of a country is incompatible with the purposes and principles of the Charter of the United Nations."[21]

The next important formal step in the UN era was the inclusion of the right of self-determination in the common Article 1 of the human rights covenants of 1966, the International Covenant on Civil and Political Rights[22] and the International Covenant on Economic, Social, and Cultural Rights.[23] In these covenants the enunciation of the right in the context of setting forth a framework for the general exercise of human rights is not tied to the colonial setting: "All peoples have the right of self-determination. By virtue of that right they freely determine their political status and freely pursue their economic, social, and cultural development."[24] Here, the right of self-determination seems to pertain to peoples, including those trapped within existing states, and is so located in the treaties as to constitute a collective precondition to the exercise of individual human rights. Also, it is not qualified by any reference to the primacy of the principle of territorial integrity of existing states, implying a guarantee of fundamental human rights for all peoples regardless of their political circumstances.

The Declaration on Principles of International Law Concerning Friendly Relations and Co-operation Among states in Accordance with the Charter of the United Nations[25] further solidified the importance of the right of self-determination and set forth some influential, although confusing, language about its appropriate application. The right of self-determination is treated as one of seven basic principles of international law, and it is acknowledged that it can be realized by different modalities, whatever status is "freely determined by a people," whether it involves claiming a new state or some kind of association with or within an existing state.[26] The idea of territorial integrity is reaffirmed, but in more conditional terms that leave openings for exceptions. The language is important enough to set forth:

> Nothing in the foregoing paragraphs shall be construed as authorizing or encouraging any action which would dismember or impair, totally or in part, the territorial integrity or political unity of sovereign and independent states conducting themselves in compliance with the principle of equal rights and self-determination of peoples as described above and thus possessed of a government representing the whole people belonging to the territory without distinction as to race, creed, or colour.[27]

The formulation raises the question, "What if the state in question is not conducting itself in compliance...?" Also, exceedingly important in assessing the evolving right of self-determination are patterns of practice indicative of boundaries and trends in the exercise of the right of self-determination.[28] The statist character of the Cold War period was very strong. No instance of secession, save that of Bangladesh, which was facilitated by the interposition of the Indian Army, occurred in the period 1945–1990. But with the ending of the Cold War, statist discipline broke down, especially in connection with the breakup of the Soviet Union and Yugoslavia. In both instances, for various moral and political reasons, powerful states either welcomed the breakup or were indifferent to its consequences.[29] The earlier bias in favor of territorial unity of existing sovereign states was cast aside without any serious attempts at principled justification. It is difficult to assess what sort of precedents have been created, especially as the ultra-nationalist fallout from this spate of secessionism has yet to abate. It is possible that this recent experience will produce a backlash that weighs sentiments against self-determination claims with separatist implications.[30] More likely, however, is the more tentative reaction that continues to accede to or resist self-determination claims based on the play of geopolitical forces rather than upon the relative merits of the moral and legal case. In this sense, despite the evolution of the rights of self-determination, itself largely a reflection of political pressures, the overall situation remains not drastically altered from what it was in the period after World War I, except that colonialism of an overt sort has passed from the scene.[31]

Geopolitics and the Prospects for Kurdish Self-Determination

The complex Kurdish experience over the course of the century highlights both the relevance and cruelty of geopolitics. Kurdish vulnerabilities have been consistently manipulated by outsiders, offering either temporary encouragement for the active pursuit of self-determination or occasions for the abrupt abandonment of the Kurdish struggle in the course of striking a bargain with anti-Kurdish statist forces in the Middle East. The lesson here is not one of determinism, but of relevance. It is important on the Kurdish side to assess their geopolitical options in any given setting as an aspect of their struggle, taking risks and setting goals accordingly, not only avoiding naive trust in the motives of outsiders but also grasping real opportunities presented by a shifting historical scene.

The moral, political, and legal strength of Kurdish claims to self-determination remains in the background. This strength was acknowledged at the very outset of the development of the right, as Wilson intended, above all, for self-determination to apply to the non-Turkish peoples caught up in the Ottoman Empire. In Wilson's Fourteen Points (of 1918), Point Twelve addressed the issue directly: "XII. The Turkish portions of the present Ottoman Empire should be assured a secure sovereignty, but the other nationalities which are now under Turkish rule should be assured an undoubted security of life and an absolutely unmolested opportunity of autonomous development...."[32] Presumably, even in 1918, not all of historic Kurdistan was situated within the Ottoman Empire, part having been incorporated into the modern Persian country of Iran and a small part belonging to the Soviet state.

Kurdish aspirations were directly safeguarded in the Treaty of Sèvres[33] negotiated between Great Britain and defeated Turkey in 1920. It provided for independence from Turkey in those parts of Anatolia where Kurds were in the majority[34] and set forth a political mechanism for the establishment of a Kurdish state that was to have encompassed the *vilayet* of Mosul (later located in Iraq), including imposing a legal commitment both on the Turkish government to facilitate the process and on the Allied Powers to accept such an outcome.[35] Sèvres was never ratified, and the political realities were decisively altered by Atatürk's victory in Turkey, consummated by the defeat of Greece in 1921. The British easily accommodated these changed circumstances, entering into the Treaty of Lausanne with Turkey in 1923, which never even specifically mentioned Kurdish national rights. In the new order, Mosul, constituting what would have been southern Kurdistan, became a part of Iraq. The basic British concern being the oil in Mosul—a subject of an earlier British/French rivalry and compromise, Britain's interest in Kurdish self-determination was both instrumental and short-lived. Arguably, this outcome was influenced by Kurdish miscalculations, generally earlier siding with Atatürk in the struggle against the Armenian Christians, unduly reliant on assurances of Kurdish autonomy. Perhaps, also, the Kurdish people were insufficiently united and organized in defense of their own aspirations, and they failed to realize what a crucial moment in history the circumstances in their region after World War I presented.

Few observers in 1918 would have guessed that the vague promise of a Jewish homeland in the Balfour Declaration would result in Jewish statehood before the acknowledgments of Kurdish national identity would have led to Kurdish statehood. There are important lessons to be learned, of success and disappointment, in these two disparate experiences, each shaped and deformed by the outcome of major wars within the region and beyond. Perhaps the central lesson is the relevance of a focused movement that represents and unifies the people in question. A secondary lesson is the importance of becoming a subject of geopolitics rather than being continuously cast in the role of object.

On the basis of the status of the right of self-determination and recent practice, the Kurdish legal position is strong, although not without severe obstacles and problems. The main challenge arises because as of 1993, the Kurdish population is spread out as a series of large national minorities in established, independent states that are members of the United Nations. There is no doubt that the UN coalition could have included among its Gulf War aims the grant of a right of secession to Iraqi Kurds, a posture justified by systematic and severe oppression, including crimes against humanity culminating in the use of poison gas against the village of Halabja in 1988, in the aftermath of the Iran/Iraq War.[36]

The main coalition states seeking maximal regional support in opposition to Iraq realized that emphasizing Kurdish rights would be a divisive element. In addition, Kurdish pressure on an international level was minimal, easily being ignored by major states, especially the United States, with its main preoccupation being directed at preventing the spread of Islamic fundamentalism. This led US policy planners to maintain Iraq's territorial unity in relation to Iran. The other regional countries with Kurdish minorities used all of their diplomatic leverage, especially Turkey, to discourage setting an Iraqi Kurdish precedent. If television had not dramatized the plight of Kurds fleeing to the Iraqi mountains in the immediate aftermath of the Gulf War, it seemed likely that nothing at all would have been done to oppose Saddam Hussein's vengeful and genocidal attempts to destroy the Kurdish people in Iraq.

Can reliance on the Kurdish right of self-determination help protect the Kurdish peoples and serve as the basis of their future emancipation? If self-determination is taken to be a foundation for the exercise of human rights, then the answer is clearly yes, although with varying prospects on a state-to-state basis. If self-determination is viewed as the basis for claiming a right of secession, then the answer is more ambiguous, given the strong states that would have to accede, their shared interest in discouraging effective Kurdish autonomy, and the interest of the United States in stabilizing the regional status quo. It is ambiguous because of the degree to which the distinct peoples caught up in the former Soviet Union and Yugoslavia were able to succeed in establishing their own states; it is no longer credible to block secessionist claims by reference to ironclad support for the territorial unity of existing states.

The Kurdish position on self-determination needs to be recast in light of these various considerations, but especially, to the extent possible, in a manner that expresses a consensus among various Kurdish tendencies. One issue of importance is whether to accept the course of the last seventy years and define self-determination pluralistically in relation to distinct conditions in the various states, suggesting the existence of separate Kurdish movements, relegating the pan-Kurdish state to the domain of utopia or restricting its relevance to matters of cultural identity. It is also possible to reassert the pan-Kurdish state as a legitimate political goal, relying on the evidence that its failure to materialize was a casualty of colonial machinations and that its continuing denial is a violation of the normative order that evolved during the UN period and was associated with the repudiation of colonialism and related forms of alien subjugation. Given Kurdish numbers, self-identification, and association with specific territory over a period of at least 2,000 years, and given the consistent Kurdish experience of abuse and discrimination within the existing states in the region, a maximalist case for claiming rights of self-determination on behalf of the Kurdish peoples exists. Yet given the strength of statist and adverse geopolitical forces, as well as the fragmented character of the Kurdish movement, an argument for more modest or minimalist claims on behalf of the various Kurdish peoples may seem currently persuasive. Only the Kurds themselves can make these choices, but the failure to do so is likely to lead to new frustrations.

The current period of regional and global fluidity contains the greatest opportunities for the advancement of the Kurdish struggle since the Ottoman collapse, but it is also fraught with traps and dangers. It is urgent that the authoritative representatives of the Kurdish people act on the basis of this challenge with as much understanding as possible and within as united a political front as is attainable.

Palestinian Occupied Territories

Chapter Seven

PROTECTING PALESTINIANS

I will speak today mainly from the perspective of the Human Rights Inquiry Commission (HRIC), which I have served on as a member. The HRIC was established by the Human Rights Commission in Geneva at the behest of the Economic and Social Council of the United Nations and it visited the Israel and the Occupied Palestinian Territories of Gaza and the West Bank in mid-February, 2001. This experience made a very powerful impact on the three of us who were members, and confirmed our sense that this was indeed a difficult assignment. The results that we reached reflected our best effort to look at the evidence as impartially as possible and to obtain as much contact with prominent Israelis as was feasible. The government of Israel declined to cooperate formally with the HRIC. At the same time, the Israelis did not obstruct our efforts, except to discourage several prominent people from talking with us. We did have the opportunity to meet with General Shlomo Gavit, who was the administrator of the West Bank and Gaza between 1967 and 1974. We made it a point to arrange appointments with a wide range of Israeli academicians and civil society leaders. We also tried to take into account the official submissions that Israel made to the Mitchell Commission and their response to Mary Robinson's High Commissioner of Human Rights Report. Both of these Israeli statements are very detailed documents. But I think the conclusions that we reached are convincing. The three of us on the commission were unanimous on matters large and small, even though we have come from very diverse backgrounds.[1] I came away from the experience of assessing allegations directed at Israeli practices with the sense that you only needed to have a twenty-percent open mind in order to reach conclusions that are critical of Israel on the main issues of international law and human rights. You don't need to have a balanced mind—that is not necessary, although it is desirable of course. It is almost inescapable, confronted with Palestinian reality, not to reach the conclusions that we reached (see the Appendix for the full report).

A speech delivered at the Center for Policy Analysis on Palestine, Washington, D.C., on 20 April 2001.

We had meetings with the representatives of the European Union in Jerusalem who shared our overall understanding of the issues, and who encouraged our commission to reach the strongest possible conclusions. They seemed eager to put pressure on their governments to adopt positions critical of Israel's approach to the Palestinians, especially during the second intifada. Similar views were expressed by the leading international civil servants who are now dealing daily with the Palestinian people and by both Israeli and Palestinian non-governmental organizations. In other words, there is a consensus that holds Israel directly responsible for grave breaches of international humanitarian law and for fundamental violations of human rights. That is a view that is unfortunately not so easy to grasp by reading the media in this country. It is easier to realize the Palestinian ordeal in Europe, somewhat easier; and it is, as I say, impossible not to grasp the essential character of Israeli oppression if you are confronted with the reality directly. In that sense, there is no substitute for having the experience of being in Gaza and the West Bank. The actual circumstances of the Palestinians are worse than my moral imagination is capable of depicting, and I have always thought I had an active moral imagination.

The most fundamental realization is that the present modalities of Israeli occupation and conflict impose on every Palestinian a daily ordeal. The uniqueness of this situation in my view is that there is no way to avoid this ordeal if you are physically present in Gaza or the West Bank. Of course, those who live in the refugee camps experience the ordeal in an even more intense fashion (that includes more than 50 percent of the population of the territories and quite a bit over that in Gaza, and somewhat less in the West Bank). If the Palestinian diaspora is included, then the proportion of Palestinians who remain refugees is close to 70 percent.

It is important to recognize that the situation for the Palestinians has changed for the worse, even since late February when I was there, that the interaction between the Palestinians and Israelis does look more and more like a war of attrition and less like an intifada. From the Palestinian side, I suppose, the preferred terminology is "a war of attrition"; from the Israeli side, the conflict is regarded as a "low-intensity conflict"—to use the prevailing jargon relied on by strategic think tanks. That was not yet the case when we were there. There were isolated instances involving exchanges of gunfire, but it was essentially still a civil disturbance in heavily occupied territory that was being repressed with great brutality and with excessive violence.

I think in order to understand the interaction of the two peoples it is important to recognize the fundamental difference in the circumstances of their existence: Israel is a powerful military sovereign state that has enjoyed an unusual period of material prosperity during the Oslo Peace Process. During these years the material conditions of the Palestinians dramatically declined from their already low level in 1993. Israel enjoys the status of being a sovereign state with full international access and it has, of course, as its very active friend and supporter the most powerful country in the world. And beyond that, it exerts what might be called information hegemony. Israel constructs the sense of reality about the conflict that 99 percent of the people in this country accept. And it is a construction of reality that not only shifts responsibility to the victims as the conflict unfolds, but also shapes public understanding of what is a fair solution for the two peoples. The image of a fair solution—and this includes identifying which side is responsible for the breakdown of the Camp David talks and the intifada that followed—has been badly distorted. The Israeli view of what is a fair solution is based on starting from a baseline of the present facts on the ground. This includes taking as legitimate all the illegalities of the Israeli occupation that have been imposed on the Palestinians since 1967. Most dramatically, such baselines mean regarding pre-1967 Israel (78 percent of the original Palestine) as belonging definitively to Israel and it means accepting the existence of 190 Israeli settlements. Negotiations then involve compromising quantitatively on the remaining 22 percent of the territory, as well as on the settlements. The compromise so reached would incorporate most of the results of the earlier conquest. It would exclude weighty issues arising from the 1948 expulsion of Palestinians from some 530 villages, thereby avoiding issues associated with the Palestinian right of return that are very fundamentally connected to the prospects of the Palestinian refugees. These exclusions from peace negotiations amount to saying that international law is not relevant to the peace process, and that the peace process is just a compromise based on the interaction between the rich and powerful state of Israel and the dispossessed Palestinian people, who are poorly represented by a leadership obsessed with establishing a Palestinian state, but with only a minimal commitment to representing the refugees both within and without the occupied territories. Such a structure of inequality makes any diplomatic process likely to reflect overwhelmingly these power relations. Such a prospect is underscored by an Israeli disposition to insist on an asymmetrical outcome that would not provide the Palestinian people with a viable and independent sovereign state, and would not, as a result, realize the Palestinian right of self-determination.

I think it is very important, particularly in the United States, to question this media hegemony exercised by Israel and to challenge it to the extent possible. Also, it is extremely important not to accept the kind of diplomacy, championed by the United States and Israel during the Oslo process, that renders international law and human rights irrelevant to the diplomatic process. The US/Israeli insistence during the Oslo years was that since there was a negotiation going on, objections to Israeli practices were not appropriate. If objections were made, for instance, to the settlements or to other violations of Palestinian rights, it was said: "This will be settled by the peace process in the final status phase." The self-serving contention was that it would be disruptive of the peace process to call attention to these sorts of issues. I believe that if there is ever to be a real peace process, international law and human rights will be integral to the process from its inception, and not something to be promised as an outcome of the process. And that insistence is crucial to an appropriate construction of the relevant reality for the diplomatic process.

In approaching the main violations of international law and human rights, it is important to realize that both Israel and the Palestinians hold self-justifying views of what is occurring within this latest phase of conflict. In other words, a very wide chasm separates the perceptions of reality of the two sides, and this chasm has widened for most Israelis and most Palestinians since the breakdown last September of the so-called peace process. It relates very much to a sense of who is responsible for the violence that started after Sharon's visit to Harem al-Sharif. The Israeli center and even moderate left accept the view that was recently articulated by Yossi Bellin in the New York Times that Israel had made a very generous offer that gave into the main Palestinian demands, and was on the verge of acceptance by Arafat, and that there were only a few details to be resolved. From this perspective, the rejection of this offer by the Palestinians indicated their unwillingness to accept a reasonable solution by the most forthcoming Israeli diplomacy to date. The rejection needed to be understood as a Palestinian embrace of a maximalist challenge directed at the legitimacy of Israel as an established state. Israelis seem to believe that this pattern alters the conflict, giving Israel no alternative but to treat the Palestinian challenge as a form of warfare.

The Palestinians, of course, regard the efforts to make them swallow the agreement as both a failure of their own leadership, to the extent that it was seemingly on the verge of accepting the bad bargain that was being proposed, but also that the proposal itself failed in fundamental respects to deal with the creation of a viable sovereign Palestine, failed to deal with the refugee issue, failed to share rights to Jerusalem on an equal basis, failed to address adequately the threat or irritant of persisting settlements within the Palestinian territories, and accepted an outcome that would fragment Palestinian territory and confer total border control on Israel.

Another aspect of this contradictory perception relates to the settlements themselves. We were convinced as a commission that most of the violence in the early portions of the intifada was related to the defense of the settlements and the access roads leading to them. Almost none of the Israeli casualties resulted from the violence of the demonstrations. It was clear that Israelis tended to marginalize the importance of the settlements. They tended to say, "Oh—it is a bargaining chip," or that the leadership didn't want to confront the settlers before peace had been arranged. Therefore the Israeli leadership indulged the settlers, and even permitted their expansion of these settlements during the Oslo process. I don't think the puzzle of the settlement expansion has been adequately understood at the international level. Such a concern falls outside the context of the Commission report. In my view, the expansion of the settlements is part of a psychological war being waged against the Palestinian people on behalf of a vision of Greater Israel: to the extent that these settlements are continuously expanding in space, in population, and in number, a process reinforced by a network of expensive bypass roads that have been constructed in the West Bank, it casts doubts as to whether Israel ever intends to withdraw, and by so doing creates an uncertainty in Palestinian minds that is part of the overall way in which Israel has responded to this second intifada. And for the Israeli right, the settlements are connected with a commitment to establish Israel along some lines that far exceed the 1967 borders. In other words, one never really knows what the future will bring, and it cannot be treated—as Thomas Friedman and others have done—as simply a matter of Israeli lunacy to expand the settlements under these circumstances of an ostensible search for peace. The settlement dynamic has to be viewed as a more fundamental ambivalence on the part of the Israeli mainstream as to whether it is possible or desirable to seek a negotiated outcome of the conflict. The settlements are a way of Israelis saying to themselves and to the Palestinians: we might make this conflict permanently irreconcilable, and then we will be able not only to have this expanded zone of territorial control, but by purporting to seek "peace" on the basis of a bargain that the Palestinians would have to reject, then it will be possible to pin blame on the Palestinians for the failure to reach a peaceful solution.

Of course, the other deeply embedded and vastly different perception is about what constitutes security. Much of what Israel has done in the course of the second intifada has the character of collective punishment on a massive scale, directed at squeezing the entire Palestinian population, economically, societally, and psychologically. Every Palestinian has been rendered vulnerable and endures daily consequences of closures, checkpoints, incursions, and random attacks. The political assassinations, with their seemingly random hit list, seem designed to create an awareness that no matter who you are and what you do, Israel has the capacity to kill you at their discretion, and without any obligation to come forward with evidence or justification. Some of the targets of political assassination have been individuals with surprisingly close connections to Israeli peace groups. They have not always been the Hamas operatives or militant terrorists that the Israeli government claims. Take for instance the case of Dr. Thabat Ahmed Thabat. He was a dentist working in close collaboration with some of the Israeli NGOs that we met with in Jerusalem. They said to us, "He was our friend," "He was our partner," and besides that, "He could have been arrested." The Israelis knew exactly where he went each day. He regularly entered Israeli territory and passed through Israeli checkpoints.

So his assassination has to be viewed as a psychological tactic that says: if Dr. Thabat is a target, then every adult Palestinian is a potential target. This inevitably causes an acute level of anxiety, which we encountered among Palestinians. There are hardships enough to make the population anxious without such lethal provocations. The Israeli public, with some notable exceptions, lacks any real understanding of this daily ordeal of suffering that the Palestinians are experiencing, and there is little indication of empathy. There is a saying on the part of some activists in Israel: "the West Bank is farther from Israel than Thailand." This combination of proximity and ignorance reminded me a lot of what white middle-class South Africans were saying about the African townships during the apartheid period. They often claimed that the oppressive circumstances of Africans and of the townships was an invention of the international media, and that most Africans in South Africa were quite content with the political situation that existed. South African whites were really saying such things and even seemed to believe them. It is quite extraordinary what people can make themselves believe.

Very briefly, it is possible to summarize the findings of our commission. The conclusions reached are somewhat self-evident, following directly from Israel's approach since the onset of the intifada and with respect to the reaction to Sharon's visit to Al-Aqsa Mosque on September 28, 2000. Israeli police units relied on excessive and disproportionate use of force, shooting unarmed demonstrators, deliberately shooting to kill, and deploying snipers at the scene of demonstrations. It is worth stressing that during the early phases of this second intifada there was no Palestinian gunfire and what violence occurred inflicted no casualties on the Israelis. In these circumstances, there was no pretext for using snipers and sharp-shooters. Their active role from the very beginning of the response to these Palestinian demonstrations was itself shocking. The first and most major conclusion of the commission was that Israeli use of force was excessive and in violation of international law.

A second conclusion involves a legal condemnation of extra-judicial assassinations by Israel that have been officially proclaimed by high military and political officers of the Israeli government. Such assassinations are grave breaches of the Fourth Geneva Convention, Article 147, and of international humanitarian law. We also concluded that the settlements and their extension are both intimately connected to the violence of recent months, and are a source of continuous provocations. This pattern violates directly the Fourth Geneva Convention, which makes the settlements themselves illegal. Our further conclusion was that the Israeli reliance on closures, curfews, and the destruction of Palestinian civilian property violates fundamental, economic, and social rights, and is, as I suggested earlier, a severe form of collective punishment. Such behavior by Israel is in flagrant violation of its legal duties as an occupying power.

And finally, we found that the treatment of Palestinian refugees is an intensified version of this violation of fundamental economic and social rights. Palestinian refugees in particular are vulnerable in a manner that other refugee communities around the world are not. This anomaly was not intended. Actually, Palestinian refugees were supposed to be protected by a UN Conciliation Commission that was established in 1948 as a supplement to the UNRWA role in providing humanitarian assistance of a material sort. We were told over and over again by UNRWA officials that they were reluctant to say anything about the violation of human rights of the Palestinian refugees because this might likely jeopardize their humanitarian work. And yet, the protection role assigned to the UN Conciliation Commission never became operational, leaving Palestinians out in the cold for decades. The UN entity has existed on paper since 1948 and continues to exist as a kind of ghost structure. It has no budget and no operating role. Because of this special regime, Palestinian refugees have not been under the authority of the High Commissioner of Refugees and therefore do not qualify for standard forms of protection normally granted to refugees. According to Article 1(D) of the 1951 Convention on the Status of Refugees, if a protective regime does not operate as intended, then that refugee community in question is supposed to be reassigned to the UN High Commission of Refugees, but this has not happened in the Palestinian case. The result has been that one of the largest and most severely abused refugee communities in the world finds itself unprotected, in a situation of legal and political vulnerability. The refugees are particularly victimized by the recent Israeli policies of closure and blockade that prevent those that live in the refugee camps from continuing to hold gainful employment and often from being unable to receive medical attention.

Let me say, in conclusion, that the sorts of things the Commission recommended follow directly from our findings and are rather obvious. There is, first of all, a strong recommendation to establish an international protective presence in the Palestinian territories along the lines unanimously supported in the Security Council (but not acted upon because of a veto by the United States).

A second recommendation calls upon the parties to the Geneva Convention to take urgent steps to secure the implementation of its provisions, which is a formal obligation of all those that are members of the Geneva Convention. It is relevant to note that both Israel and the United States are parties to the Geneva Conventions of 1949, and they are duty-bound to comply and take steps to ensure compliance.

A third area of recommendation concerns the refugees. Steps need to be taken to secure credible protection for Palestinian refugees living in Gaza and the West Bank. It is necessary either to bring the UN Conciliation Commission into real operation at once or to make sure that the High Commissioner of Refugees does assume responsibility for what is happening to the Palestinians in this period of severe Israeli oppression.

A fourth recommendation urges a clear expression of the general understanding that settlement activity is illegal, a flagrant violation of Article 49(6) of the Fourth Geneva Convention, and should be stopped and reversed at once. A fifth recommendation mandates an end to the violations of international humanitarian law, such as assassinations and the destruction of property.

I wish to make one observation about the destruction of property that bears on the whole presentation that I have made. It is to take note of its cruelty in concept and application. We spoke to many of the people along the access roads to settlements who had been displaced from their homes. The Israeli bulldozers would typically arrive between midnight and two in the morning, give inhabitants seven minutes of warning to vacate their homes, and then proceed to destroy houses, as well as trees, wells, and farm buildings. We observed no genuine security justification for such behavior, and even if there had been, Israel could have proceeded in a more considerate manner: giving notice, providing alternative housing, offering compensation, and making a demonstration of security needs. This Israeli pattern of housing demolition is a microcosm of an overall approach to the Palestinian civilian population. Palestinians are not treated as "protected persons" as legally required by the Geneva Conventions, or even with a minimal respect due to all human beings. It is, of course, traumatic in the extreme to lose one's home and livelihood as a result of a midnight action of this sort, especially when these individuals are not accused of anything.

Our commission was appalled by this pattern of Israeli disregard of Palestinian well-being. It was also disappointed by the unwillingness and inability of the United Nations and Europe to do more to expose this humanitarian catastrophe and to organize a protective response of some kind.

Responses to Questions

Several of these questions directed at me ask in differing ways, "What can be done in practical ways to change the approach to the conflict in this country?" A wonderful question, but if I had an answer, I wouldn't be here—I'd be carrying out a plan. You have to understand that issues about ideas promoted by the mainstream media are really expressions of power and influence. There is no magic vitamin that you can give editorial writers so that they will discharge their responsibilities more reasonably and live up to their pretensions of journalistic objectivity and balance. It is an issue of countervailing power. Those who favor Israel have brilliantly used their wealth and power to create a certain sense of reality that prevails and distorts perceptions. Until that sense of reality is challenged by countervailing power it is wishful thinking to feel that if you could only talk to the *New York Times* or the *Washington Post* and take them out and show them what is going on in the occupied territories, then their columns would reflect the true situation. Maybe one out of a thousand such people will change their views when confronted by the facts. As I said at the beginning, you need only a twenty-percent open mind to present the competing claims in the manner of our commission. Most Americans are at about a three-percent level, and so the issue is how you get the other seventeen percent—you need the twenty percent. Most people holding positions of influence are in some sense responding to social forces, and they have been shaped and created for many years by those social forces. The ways in which this pro-Israeli construction of reality has been foisted on the American people are subtle and pervasive, and quite unique for a foreign policy issue. You don't find the same degree of bias in Europe, for instance. And if Europe was less passive in relation to the US, which is a legacy of the Cold War, then some pressure to help the Palestinians would be mounted. Europeans are so accustomed, except to some degree the French, to relying on the United States in international settings, that there is no willingness to push a policy in defiance of the United States. There is a book that was written in Japan called *The Japan That Can Say No.* We need that book in Europe, *The Europe That Can Say No.* Better, we need a political movement that will say no, but intelligently and instructively.

Our commission had the experience in Geneva, for instance, that leading European ambassadors were saying privately, "we completely agree with you, but we can't do anything." This deference is an addictive habit. Addictive habits are usually escape mechanisms. There are powerful diplomatic forces that underpin the present policy posture, and there are economic forces, and there are military forces. There is a European sense that the longest period of peace has depended on heavy US involvement, and so there's an uncertainty as to what will happen if the United States enters a new isolationist phase. There are a lot of anxieties in Europe about repudiating this post-World War II structure. It's a tricky obstacle to overcome. And, of course, I did not mean to imply that the settlements were in any sense virtual, or were not responsible for real daily suffering, abuse, outrage. Settler violence has been one of the worst features of this second intifada. I took that for granted in talking with this audience.

What I wanted to emphasize is that beyond all this that is well understood there are some inexplicable aspects. We may ask from a rational point of view: Why do those Israeli leaders who say they want peace engage in the expansion of settlements? The evidence suggests the need to search for hidden factors, concealed motives. What are the Israelis intending by building these expensive bypass roads, billions of dollars invested, if they really want a peaceful relationship with a real Palestine in the future? The Israelis are too smart to do that mindlessly, and so there must be some other agenda. So what is that other agenda? The only thing that I am smart enough to figure out is it has to do with the psychological warfare that is trying to keep the Palestinians off balance and to preclude their perception of a stable reality that allows for hope in the future. I saw the suffering of Palestinians and our report confirms its depth and breadth. And beyond the oppression, there are larger designs on the part of Israel— to break the will of Palestinians to resist, to fasten only to the territories a permanent structure of dominance.

Chapter Eight

LEGAL REFLECTIONS ON THE
ISRAELI OCCUPATION

I am very grateful to the organizers of this conference for taking such
an initiative at this time. There is no situation in international affairs
that so strongly demands an international response as does the
continuing character of the Israeli occupation of Gaza and the West
Bank. An intensifying consensus virtually independent of political
outlook as to the underlying Arab-Israeli conflict now agrees that a
humanitarian challenge exists requiring resolution by way of Israeli
withdrawal. Necessarily, when speaking at a safe distance from the actual
circumstances of jeopardy, it is essential to proceed with care and
deference to the well-being and sensitivities of the actual participants in
this ongoing struggle to establish secure control over this contested land.
At the same time, it is also true that as human beings living in a world
that is connected inevitably and in many different ways, we are all
implicated directly and indirectly by injustices that are tolerated, or even
facilitated, particularly if the perpetrators enjoy a certain kind of
economic and diplomatic blessing from the governments of countries to
which we as individuals owe a particular allegiance.

Therefore, I think that at this stage of reflection the peoples of the
world are obliged to recognize that no circumstance of injustice is
removed from their proper sphere of concern and response because its
locus of harm is situated within the territory of a foreign state.
International law of human rights is overwhelmingly dedicated to the
protection of all persons, but especially those who are most vulnerable
to abuse, whether the underlying circumstance is one of war or peace,
and whether the persons affected are fellow-residents or tormented in
distant lands.

---

*The following piece was a paper presented at the International Symposium on "The West Bank
and Gaza Strip: The Problem of Palestinian Refugees and Non-Refugees, 8–10 July 1988, at
Queen Elizabeth House, University of Oxford. It was published in* Journal of Refugee Studies
2.1 (1989): 40–51.

International Law, Human Rights and the Palestinian Problem

There are in the world today various categories of refugees, displaced persons, and populations living under alien military occupation, who are trapped in unresolved political collisions of opposed nationalisms. These situations generate some of the most appalling circumstances of mass distress in the world as a whole. And among all of these classes of victims that are so much part of the history of our time, the Palestinians are particularly prominent, having suffered so many severe ravages from such diverse sources, over an extended stretch of time, and with no end yet in sight. These are ravages of dispossession, of recurrent war and civil strife, of disintegrating colonial rule, of crude geopolitics and great power manipulation, and, most basic of all, of the hostile and brutally sustained occupation of their own national homeland. The intifada has disclosed, with anguished clarity, the fundamental unity of the Palestinian people in asserting at great cost a claim to self-determination that can only be satisfied by the acquisition of statehood. Such unity of objectives is, as we all realize, beset by many deep cleavages among Palestinian political groupings as to preferred tactics and goals, as to the style and person of leadership, and as to the character and scope of a minimum solution. The PLO headed by Yasir Arafat remains the commanding and legitimate voice, but he is subject to several challenges from fringe Palestinian factions, and from various political forces in the Arab world that manipulate and abet Palestinian factional strife.

Having said this, I share with Adam Roberts his concern about the difficulty of applying international law in a constructive manner in such an inflamed setting of seemingly irreconcilable perceptions of the respective rights and duties of these antagonistic parties. It is also important to discourage the polemical use of international law as a propaganda instrument that is more an expression of conflict than a source of guidance as to its proper mediation and eventual transcendence. The authority of international law will be strengthened only if specialists maintain their objectivity to the extent possible, and seek to interpret impartially the complex interplay of facts and applicable legal rules and principles.

The Extent of Violations

At the same time, however, it seems to me obligatory for those who interpret legal rules and principles to identify extreme situations as such, and that if a responsibility for generating an extreme situation is one-sided, then the legal conclusions must be correspondingly one-sided. If one side, for whatever reason, commits gross violations of applicable legal standards, then a definite legal judgment to such an effect is in order, even if it offers a political justification to the other side and reinforces claims that its adversary is guilty of violations. There is often a considerable gray area of indeterminacy when it comes to assessing legal responsibility, either because the facts are obscure or the law variable, or because of some combination of these factors. At the same time, patterns of violations often establish a clear burden of responsibility, and it is up to an independent analyst to pronounce upon such a state of affairs. Impartiality should not be confused with balance, in the sense of a symmetrical apportionment of responsibility. A balanced or equivocal assessment is only appropriate if it corresponds to the actual circumstances. In my judgment, the Israeli role in the occupied territories does not any longer, if it ever did, admit of an equivocal legal assessment. Israel may not be the exclusive violator of international law (and human rights norms), nor is it completely without justifying arguments for many of its most contested policies, but, on balance, Israel is predominantly and flagrantly in violation of the most fundamental humanitarian standards of international law and is guilty of wrongfully disregarding Palestinian rights of self-determination. Israel's legal arguments fall well short of satisfying tests of persuasiveness on the critical issues in contention.[1]

The international law of war embodies minimal humanitarian values that are seeking to provide certain vulnerable individuals and groups protection against the arbitrary power of the modern state as wielded in the midst of war. The task of serious scholarship in this sort of belligerent setting is to encourage the fulfillment of the constructive potential of international law to reduce the vulnerability of the civilian population.

A basic question of method bears on what can be done with international law to mitigate the vulnerability and the suffering of those who are innocent; that is, those who are not formally engaged in armed struggle and are civilian inhabitants of the land that is the scene of fighting. Abstractions dehumanize and depersonalize the victims of militarist tactics of control and intimidation.

Therefore, it is my judgment that the principal responsibility here is to consider the suffering of the Palestinian people to be a consequence of systematic violations of the minimum standards of protection that are embodied in an international treaty that is widely accepted—by the governments of the region, by the superpowers, by Israel itself. There has been a systematic and massive series of deliberate violations of the most flagrant kind of the Geneva Convention IV, which offers a series of protections to the civilian population, as extended and elaborated by the Geneva Protocols of 1977, whose specifications are mainly declaratory of pre-existing legal obligations. Israel's failure to sign and ratify this latter treaty text does not necessarily exclude these legal guidelines from relevance. This form of protection arising as an incident of the humanitarian law of war is reinforced by the customary international law of war, and the closely associated international law of human rights, and proceeds from an overarching legal (and moral) principle to avoid the unnecessary infliction of suffering on civilians and to respect the innocence of civilian status.

At this stage, given developments of recent months, the only real question that seems to me important to raise is whether the character of these violations of the law of belligerent occupation by Israel is of such an intentional, systematic, and severe character as to make inappropriate a reliance on the mere language of illegality. To keep accumulating evidence of Israeli violations fails to express the seriousness of the pattern of Israel's behavior, which deliberately and consistently nullifies the custodial role of a belligerent occupant. In my judgment, the Israeli refusal to adhere to Geneva IV standards is by now so well documented, pervasive, and sustained as to suggest the appropriateness of supplementing the language of illegality with the language of criminality. To speak of illegality means the allegation is one of an intentional violation of legal standards that engages governmental responsibility; to charge criminality is to allege a willful violation at high levels of civilian and military authority that engages the personal responsibility of those who act on behalf of the state, knowingly or in circumstances where they should know of such patterns of pronounced illegality.

The factual issue involves the assessment of Israeli behavior as establishing beyond reasonable doubt a pattern of deliberate violation of the rights of vulnerable people. It would appear that this behavior, carried on systematically over a number of years and leading to much suffering on the part of the Palestinians, does pose a serious challenge to any objective commentator on international law, a challenge one cannot avoid. Acknowledging the seriousness of the shift, the cumulative record of Israeli illegality now constitutes the basis for alleging crimes of state. This inference of criminality arises from patterns of gross violation and from Israel's abuse of its custodial role as belligerent occupant of Gaza and the West Bank, and is quite independent of an acceptance of the underlying Palestinian claim to exercise rights of self-determination in the disputed territories.[2]

This line of thinking rests upon the tradition of accountability established after World War II, which regards systematic and continuing abuse of civilians under a position of belligerent occupation, in situations vulnerable to governmental authority, as constituting crimes against humanity.[3]

Such conduct was punished in situations of occupation, you will recall, in the aftermath of World War II. The occupation policies of the German and Japanese military authorities were then scrutinized by special tribunals from the point of view of imposing individual criminal liability for systematic severe violations of international law, as well as from simple allegations of illegality. Part of the post-1945 development of positive international law was to establish this framework of criminal accountability as a legal precedent for the future.[4]

In sum, then, an objective assessment of the facts and legal circumstances pertaining to the occupied territories makes it virtually irresistible to anyone who approaches these issues from a neutral perspective to conclude that Israel is guilty of crimes of state with regard to its occupation of Gaza and the West Bank. Such a conclusion is important for several distinct reasons:

1) to reinforce Palestinian contentions and the repeated conclusions reached by international institutions;

2) to strengthen the resolve of external actors to build pressure upon Israel to uphold the guidelines of international law so long as occupation lasts;

3) to establish a legal duty on the part of foreign governments to refrain from steps that could be interpreted as supporting or strengthening the Israeli occupation.

In the background, of course, is the apparent inability of Israel to obtain an acquiescence in its occupation except by "criminal" modes of administration. In this regard, and quite apart from pronouncing upon the final arrangements suitable for Gaza and the West Bank, the demand for Israeli withdrawal from the territories seems to rest on a solid legal foundation, and from the viewpoint of law should proceed at this stage without even awaiting a negotiated bargain.

This conclusion is reinforced by the evident, if ambiguously acknowledged, Israeli intention to convert its provisional presence as belligerent occupant into a permanent presence as de facto and de jure sovereign. This Israeli intention is established by deeds as well as by words, but most especially by the encouragement of Israeli settlements in the territories as a continuing and expanding process.[5] The 1988 new coalition government headed by Shamir has "compromised" with its Labor Party partners by agreeing to accept eight as the limit on the number of new settlements per year in the occupied territories.

Prolonged Occupation and the Crisis in International Law

What is at stake is whether Israeli patterns of practice on the issue of settlements have led to the subversion of belligerent occupation as a legal status. The establishment of these settlements has created a circumstance that has been generally regarded as either partial annexation or de facto annexation, and as creating a set of conditions pertaining to the future that makes it exceedingly difficult to uphold Palestinian rights of self-determination.[6] The existing customs and treaty rules of international law are dominated by the idea that an occupation of territory that arises as an incident of war should be dealt with as a matter that is temporary and subject to a return of the territories to the rightful sovereign at the earliest feasible date. It can be acknowledged that reasonable controversy surrounds the identity of such a rightful sovereign with respect to Gaza and West Bank, and even of the modalities to resolve this issue. What is not in reasonable doubt, however, is the lack of any credible Israeli sovereign claim to these territories, and therefore the settlements issue places Israel in a posture of continuing and blatant defiance that goes back virtually to the start of the occupation in 1967.[7] This impression is also confirmed by the Israeli policy of continuing to encourage new settlements and by continual acquisition of public and private lands for the benefit of the settlements in the occupied territories, as well as the appropriation of resources, including water rights, and by the encouragement of settlement by Israel accompanied by subsidies and assurances of the permanence of Israeli control.

It is reasonable to conclude at this time that the Palestinian character of these territories has been definitively and repeatedly affirmed by a combination of expert commentary on rights and duties under international law and the overwhelming consensus of the organized international community. In essence, sovereignty with respect to the occupied territories continues to reside with the Palestinian people. This Palestinian identity of the territories limits the Israeli role to that of, at most, a belligerent occupant with security claims and custodial duties. Israel can claim in relation to this role quite broad discretion to uphold the security of its occupation, including arguably even the need to establish certain restrictions on the activities of the inhabitants. Yet the security rationale cannot be vaguely invoked to cover anything undertaken by the Israeli administrators, and it certainly cannot justify residential settlements that are built in furtherance of the maximalist vision of "Greater Israel" that lays claim to the West Bank on behalf of the state of Israel. This claim has been decisively rejected by a variety of influential international assessments, most definitively by the original UN partition of Palestine, upon which Israel's own claim of statehood depends so heavily. At this stage only the mechanism and scope (territorial extent) of Palestinian self-determination is indeterminate, not the locus or authoritativeness of the right itself.

Although the history of the right of self-determination is complicated and confusing, it seems clear that by the mid-1980s the status of this right was based upon a combination of international legal doctrine, political acceptance, and moral authority. At present, the ethnic and cultural identity of the indigenous population, the persistence of the Palestinian struggle, the widespread diplomatic recognition accorded the PLO, the weight of public opinion, and the balance of judgment within the United Nations make Palestinian claims to statehood, at least in the occupied territories, a valid, if only inchoate, and legally authoritative application of the principle of self-determination.

Proposals for Reform

The crisis in the character of international law in relation to this set of circumstances arises because Israel as the occupying power denies the obligation to respect this underlying Palestinian identity of the territories. Further, Israel ignores the international community judgment and disregards it repeatedly. And by this insistence and defiance, a pattern of both resistance and massive suffering has emerged in reaction to engulf the issues. The existing rules of international law, as incorporated in the Geneva Conventions and the Hague Regulations, are not written to cover such extreme circumstances. There is a need for a further development of international law at this time; what would be most helpful would be an international convention on the consequences of prolonged military occupation that has evinced sufficient evidence of a deliberate campaign to impair rights of self-determination, as embodied in international law and as they inhere in the resident population. As soon as "hostilities" are concluded, the belligerent occupant has a duty to arrange its withdrawal as soon as practicable and to do nothing to diminish prospects for an orderly transfer of administrative authority.

There are several reasons to propose such a formal convention at this time. The specific intention here is to illuminate the injustice of the existing structure of occupation in Gaza and the West Bank, and also to propose an appropriate way to address the situation faced by inhabitants who find themselves being "colonized" by an alien power against their will and under the pretext of "belligerent occupation." It is a pretext whenever, as in Gaza and the West Bank, the occupying power advances claims to transfer its own population to the territory under occupation or appropriates for its own benefit land and other resources. To implement these overriding goals a clearer legal grasp of the realities of the situation of the inhabitants might help frame the political debate in such a controversy as to the outer limits of discretion enjoyed by the occupying power.

First of all, it seems to me that where there has been prolonged military occupation, not only should the laws of war continue to apply, but also international legal standards of human rights should be brought directly to bear on behalf of inhabitants.[8] At minimum, the Universal Declaration of Human Rights, which has enjoyed the status of universal international law, should be extended to the circumstances of such a prolonged occupation. Secondly, where a period of ten years or more has transpired, and the belligerent occupation has not been terminated, then it seems to me appropriate to establish some kind of international procedure to protect the rights of the inhabitants to acquire control over their political destiny, if that is their desire, as evidenced by an internationally supervised plebiscite or, at the very least, to confirm that a circumstance of continuing belligerence exists and justifies the extension of the inherently provisional status of "belligerent occupation" for a further period.

There needs to be, in other words, some automatic mechanism for challenging, reassessing, and, if appropriate, terminating belligerent occupation after a certain period, especially if a showing can be made of either an intention by the occupant to create the basis for permanent domination or a clear cessation of hostilities. In the context of such a ten-year limit, it would be important to have available a procedure to handle the assured devolution of political power to a governing process that would be constituted within such a territory. Possibly, one aspect of such a process would be to convene a constituent assembly representing the inhabitants that would be charged with proclaiming a state or other entity as the legitimate voice of the people held under prolonged occupation and threatened by the realities of creeping annexation. Once so proclaimed, outside governments and institutions could endow the new entity with added legitimacy by according recognition and attaching full legal consequences to the changed status of occupation.[9]

A convention of this sort, which addresses prolonged occupation under conditions roughly comparable to those that exist in Gaza and the West Bank, would fill an important gap in international law. The Geneva Conventions and Protocols, as currently drafted, do not cover the most disturbing features of prolonged Israeli occupation, especially the implementation of ambitions to incorporate the territories under Israeli sovereign control and steps taken to preclude the realization of Palestinian rights of self-determination. The Geneva Conventions remain relevant to identify multiple Israeli infractions of minimum humanitarian expectations of legal conduct, but by itself this record of persistent violation does not undermine Israel's right to carry on the occupation. International law as evolved in the setting of occupation is mainly of a humanitarian character that addresses political problems only indirectly by way of responses to felt problems that emerge in different circumstances. We have in this occupation a circumstance that has been long deplored by the great majority of governments throughout the world. There has not been a satisfactory response on the part of Israel. Governments seeking to improve the protection of the inhabitants could make use of the International Law Commission, which is a UN expert body, to draft a convention on prolonged or superseded occupation and rights of resistance. It is certainly also possible for a group of international lawyers interested in this problem to put forward on their own at this preliminary stage such an idea along these lines in the form of a draft proposal. It is very important for public opinion to appreciate that international law is no longer exclusively an instrument of governments. It is possible to give legal expression to the will of the peoples of the world and their grievances, and various informal "legal" arenas can operate directly as an innovative source of international law. This possibility is already widely operative in relation to fundamental human rights. We are accustomed to such popular claims as, for instance, when the Solidarity movement in Poland invoked the International Labour Organization's standards as a way of grounding their objections to policies of the Polish government that denied rights to workers and their organizations. It is widely understood that this sort of popular claim is generative of new legal standards and operates as a kind of legal precedent for the future. Obviously, such proposals for legal reform are framed against the background of realities of political power, making it exceedingly difficult to implement at this time the call for expulsion with respect to Gaza and the West Bank. An assured precondition to effectiveness is sufficient pressure mounted at an international level that includes serious support by the US government. Even in the absence of such a prospect, clarifying the right of the people subject to this type of occupation might help shape international public opinion and strengthen the policies and resolve of governments and international institutions that are trying to respond to the situations that exist.

Conclusion

The effect of this analysis is to underscore how inappropriate it has become to treat the situation in the West Bank and Gaza as if it involves only the Israeli failure to show respect for a series of specific laws of war contained in Geneva Convention IV that deal with belligerent occupation—even though this failure alone would be ample ground for persistent international concern. At this stage, both the character of Israel's prolonged occupation and the nature of Palestinian resistance have transformed the legal character of the situation into one of an encounter between alternative and antagonistic destinies for the land and the people.

The existing situation requires a different type of legal focus, one that does address the real aspirations of the people at stake, and that tries to interpret their situation in a way that is more responsive to the actual circumstances that they have been confronting, that is, as collectively resisting a condition of annexation being established under the formal guise of prolonged belligerent occupation. In fact, Israel itself has always denied even the applicability of the laws of war as a matter of legal duty because of its contention that this is not technically an instance of belligerent occupation in a formal sense, and because its sovereign claims in these territories are at least equal to, or arguably superior to, that of any other people or state, including those made on behalf of the Palestinians.

The specific context of Israeli occupation reinforces this line of interpretation. In the course of more than twenty years of occupation Israel has deliberately maintained an aura of ambiguity about both the character of its relationship toward the occupied territories and its ultimate intention. To a degree this uncertainty flows from the differing views of Israel's Labor and Likud parties, but it is deeper than this. On the one side Israel has purported to be the legitimate sovereign authority of the territories as a consequence of its conquest of the territory and the absence of any prior sovereign claim that warrants respect. Israeli authorities claim that when they entered in 1967, they encountered a legal vacuum, and that therefore Israel could have established itself as a sovereign power. At the same time, Israel has, for diplomatic reasons at various points, refrained from pressing this maximalist position, and endorsed and bound itself to apply the international consensus embodied in UN Security Council Resolution 242, the core obligation of which is to confirm Israel's legal duty to withdraw from the territories occupied during the 1967 war. This resolution can be reasonably interpreted as a continuing and conclusive acknowledgment by Israel of the provisional character of its rights on the West Bank and Gaza, and as effectively acknowledging and establishing its status as belligerent occupant, nothing more, and possibly as something less, considering earlier arguments.

Furthermore, in the Camp David process, Israel, even as represented by the Likud leadership, accepted the conception of a legally prescribed devolution of authority to the Palestinian people by way of the obligation to ensure autonomy for the territories. It is true that autonomy for the Palestinians seems to locate sovereignty over an autonomous Palestine in the state of Israel, but without political discretion to alter the basic character of the territories or to deprive Palestinians of political, cultural, and economic control. The idea of autonomy was promoted at the time as a formula to achieve Palestinian self-determination without jeopardizing Israel's security, including its longer-term interest in avoiding the creation of a fully independent PLO state based in these territories. At any rate, Israel acknowledged in the Camp David process that the operative life of the territories should eventually be administered by and for the Palestinians, even though Israel was allowed to retain most of the attributes of sovereignty, as well as to encroach on the basis of its presumably extensive security interests.

It is, of course, this failure to interpret Palestinian self-determination as entailing statehood that helps explain the Arab rejection of the Camp David approach. This rejection was partly because "autonomy," whatever it might have become, was less than the form of "self-determination" that the main representatives and friends of the Palestinian people insisted upon; partly that "autonomy" was not an assured development or one with clear attributes as it was set forth in agreements, and partly that the Palestinians were not themselves participants in the Camp David process. As was widely expected by critics of Camp David at the time, even the inadequate promise of autonomy was an empty one that amounted to a betrayal of Palestinian rights: the real agreement at Camp David involved land for peace between Begin's Israel and Sadat's Egypt, a return of Sinai in exchange for an end to Egyptian belligerency toward Israel, coupled with a definitive Egyptian acceptance of Israeli claims to legitimate statehood.[10] In the end, it can be argued that Egypt's unauthorized representation of Palestinian claims was null and void, an infringement upon Palestinian rights of self-determination, not an exercise of these rights. From this it follows that the Camp David agreements lose their international status as treaty instruments, at least so far as the Palestinian question is concerned.

As indicated, the international level of policy has been confused and complicated as well by the Israeli domestic political debate between the Likud and Labor. Whether that debate really bears on the issues of occupation is itself inconclusive, because both Likud and Labor have consistently denied that minimum content of the Palestinian consensus on self-determination, namely, representation of the Palestinians by the PLO and the formation of a Palestinian sovereignty. So given the extreme unlikelihood of the Palestinians accepting a solution outside of that framework, it seems to cast doubt on the meaningfulness and relevance of the tactical dispute between these two Israeli political parties, a dispute which is worth mentioning if for no other reason than because it is treated as relevant in many international discussions.

Let me close by saying that I think it is desirable for international law to be brought to bear fully on this situation. The standards that exist raise the most serious and—it seems to me—irresistible basis for alleging an underlying series of violations that relate to the core of Israel's presence in the territories, and create a legal foundation for Palestinian and international demands for immediate Israeli withdrawal.

Beyond this, international law should adapt to the unique situation created by the prolonged character of Israeli occupation. This circumstance calls urgently for response additional to those associated with violations. The further issue concerns the legitimacy of the opposing underlying claims to the territories. Until Israel accepts the weight of international public opinion, it seems appropriate for legal specialists to endorse Palestinian rights of resistance in the occupied territories and to censure Israel's contentions that it is entitled to use whatever degree of coercion is needed to punish breaches of public order. In effect, the legal argument supported here is that Israel has by now forfeited the security rights that might have accrued to it initially in its role as legitimate belligerent occupant. Over the years Israel's annexationist presence in these Territories has operated as a continuous provocation to the Palestinian population, and their posture of resistance appears to be proportionate and justified under the circumstances. Furthermore, the political conditions in the region, although strained and disruptive, provide no pretext for Israel to sustain its occupation for more than two decades. A secure withdrawal has long been feasible, virtually from the termination of hostilities in 1967. Israeli responsibility for the provocations, its loss of status as belligerent occupant, and the unacceptability of authorizing Israeli coercion against repeated, fundamental, Israeli provocations are each part of the overall picture.

Of course, the conduct of Palestinian resistance is itself governed by the constraints of the humanitarian law of war, which implies an obligation to restrict armed struggle to military personnel and targets, or to those who officially serve in the Israeli civilian administration.

Chapter Nine

THE STATUS OF ISRAELI SETTLEMENTS UNDER
INTERNATIONAL LAW

Over the years since 1967 there has been considerable analysis of Israeli settlements in the occupied territories from an international law viewpoint. I believe it is reasonable to conclude that an overwhelming consensus of experts and governments, as well as the competent organs of the United Nations, supports the view that the establishment of these settlements flagrantly violates applicable rules and standards of international law. No one has developed the legal reasoning in support of such a conclusion with greater clarity and authoritativeness than my fellow panelist, Professor T. M. Mallison, generally working in collaboration with his wife, Sally Mallison. There is little that I can add to the persuasive conclusions reached by the Mallisons in a series of valuable publications.[1]

Of course, their assessment has been challenged by several specialists in international law who adopt positions closely identified with official Israeli thinking. Professor Yehuda Blum, who served for several years as Israel's UN ambassador during the period of the Begin government, has advanced the argument based on the so-called "missing reversioner" that, in effect, questioned the sovereign claims of any foreign government to the West Bank, and, thereby released the government of Israel from those constraints embodied in the international law of belligerent occupation.[2] By invoking the Zionist claim of historic title to "Greater Israel" embracing the provinces of Judea and Samaria, Blum also asserted a basis for claiming Israeli sovereignty. Somewhat analogously, Professor Eugene V. Rostow of Yale Law School argues that the absence of any resolution of the underlying territorial status of these occupied lands results in a continuing lease of life for the Palestine Mandate under whose terms, the argument runs, Jews can settle throughout the mandate territory, including the occupied territories on the West Bank.[3] Their arguments are so strained and artificial in character as to be hardly worth detailed refutation. Suffice it to say that the entire organized international community, including on

---

This piece first appeared in the Department of Palestine Affairs, ed., The Israeli Settlements in the Occupied Arab Territories *(Washington, D.C.: League of Arab States, 1988) 317–325.*

several occasions even the United States government, shares the view that Israel's maximum legal claim on the West Bank is based on its temporary supervisory control of the territory as a result of belligerent occupation, and hence subject to the Fourth Hague Convention of 1907, and, more significantly, the Fourth Geneva Convention of 1949, Relative to the Protection of Civilian Persons in Time of War.[4] Once these provisions are made relevant, their application is impossible to reconcile persuasively within the Israeli settlements policy and practices. As a consequence, it is a diversion to argue, as Professors Blum and Rostow do, that the disputed sovereignty of the territory allows Israel's occupation to avoid being assessed by reference to the standards imposed by the international law of belligerent occupation. To argue that the Palestine Mandate survives is to ignore both terminating acts by Great Britain as mandatory power and the unanimous intention of the United Nations to substitute its partition plan for the mandate, as of May 14, 1948. It is perverse in this setting to invoke the Namibia litigation in the World Court, which sustained the survival of the mandate as the sole means to avoid the full consequences of South Africa's extension of its system of apartheid to the detriment of the inhabitants of the territory administered under the same "South-West Africa." More pertinent is the action by the political organs of the United Nations to revoke South Africa's authority as mandatory power, and its substitution of the organized international community, as embodied in the United Nations on the widely accepted reasoning that there was no other way to carry out "the sacred trust of civilization" on the primary issue of well-being of the inhabitants. Here, such reasoning does pertain as a new set of post-mandatory circumstances involved with legal and political consequences, despite the aura of ambiguity that arose from the Arab governments' refusal since 1948 to accept the legitimacy of partition of the mandate, and their recourse to war and a state of belligerency as an expression of the political depth of this refusal. In my view, such a stance, however interpreted, does not provide Israel with any justification for avoiding international legal obligations toward territories occupied subsequent to 1967, nor does it compromise the political rights of the inhabitants to a destiny independent of Israel.

More important, to be sure, is Professor Allan Gerson's argument that the special, prolonged character of Israel's occupation makes it a trustee-occupant rather than "a belligerent-occupant."[5] The effect of the distinction is to give Israel greater discretion during the period of occupation, provided only that it acts for the benefit of the inhabitants as determined by the Israeli government. Gerson acknowledges that the inhabitants possess a legal entitlement to some reasonable form of autonomy to be shaped by an eventual agreement among governments and political entities that partake of an overall negotiated settlement between Arabs and Israelis. Here again, the legal argument rests on little more than the personal authority of this author. There is no real support in the relevant legal literature or in the appraisals of legal status made by competent international organs for such a position. Similarly, various ingenious proposals for regarding the territories in question as having a distinctive status of "associated statehood" also fail to meet any of the general tests of legal acceptability. At best such proposals are expressions of the political opinion of a particular author that ignore the international consensus insisting since 1967 that Israel refrain from "creating facts" that alter the character of the territory or make its occupation acquire over time the character of permanence. The establishment of settlements is so objectionable precisely because the settlements, especially the larger post-1977 suburban ones, manifest a clear intention to maintain a permanent presence. Nor are the settlements attractive proposals on either political or moral grounds, as they basically have the effect of depriving the civilian population of the central effort of international law to guard against encroachment by the occupying power upon their economic, political, and cultural rights. The whole purpose of the law of war is to accord this protection as effectively as possible in circumstances of combat and post-combat occupation where uncertainties persist as to the eventual disposition of territory. Throughout this protracted occupation the inappropriateness of any permanent Israeli presence has never been questioned by the organized international community that has confirmed total withdrawal from all occupied territory, and it is expected to be a central feature of any resolution of the basic conflict. "Total" has been understood to mean not only administering forces, but also settlements and settlers. Given the identity of the occupied societies, there is no doubt about their refusal to be integrated, directly or indirectly (economically, culturally), into the state of Israel.

The Israeli position has been to create facts, establishing settlements as permanent encroachments upon the occupied territory, promoting integration with Israel's economy (exports, jobs) in utter defiance of both international law and the repealed manifestations of the will of the organized international community and the inhabitants on the subject.[6] This process has now reached such extraordinary proportions that an estimated 42,500 Israeli settlers living in 118 settlements widely distributed geographically among an Arab population of about 800,000 have acquired control over 52 percent of the 5.5 million dunums of land on the West Bank, as attested to by the latest publication of the widely quoted Benvenisti study. The Israeli official position, reflecting the influence of Blum's argument, is that Israel is not obliged to apply the Geneva Conventions on belligerent occupation because there was no legitimate sovereign displaced by the so-called "defensive conquest" of the territories in 1967. Israel goes on to argue that as a matter of discretion, it has administered the territory in harmony with these conventions, interpreting Article 49(6) in the narrowest possible way so as to exclude an inference of violation. The plain wording of 49(6), as well as authoritative interpretations of applicable law, including by specialists within the US government, refute this Israeli claim.[7] There is no effective way to reconcile the settlements with the international law of belligerent occupation.

The more recent stance of the US government is to suggest that legal assessment of the settlements is an obstacle to the peace process.[8] The argument here seems to suggest that the settlements are a *fait accompli*, and, hence, their ultimate disposition would have to await the implementation of the second phase of the Camp David Accords or some analogous process to resolve outstanding issues in dispute between Israel and its Arab neighbors. In this view, to argue back and forth on the legality of the settlements is a meaningless propaganda battle that enables both sides to avoid a peace process. The most that the Reagan administration has done is to call upon Israel to establish a freeze on further settlements so as to promote Arab-Israeli negotiations. This element of the Reagan Plan, put forward on September 1, 1982, has been superseded to a large degree by Israel's refusal to halt the settlement process, creating a situation that is now claimed by some observers to have established a relationship on the ground that is tantamount to annexation. Even a freeze would not be very meaningful at this stage. President Reagan had further confused the situation by apparently contradicting earlier US assessments when on February 2, 1981 he declared at a press interview that the settlements were "legal." Quite obviously, no legal weight should be attached to an isolated and unsubstantiated pronouncement by a political leader.

The argument I would like to stress here is how to regard the relevance of international law in light of these developments in the eighteen years of occupation. To summarize, first of all, the legal status of Israeli activity on the West Bank is most appropriately treated as an instance of belligerent occupation. Israel is bound by these legal standards, and the establishment of settlements on the scale that has occurred and for the professed purpose (at least after the accession to power of the Likud in 1977) of realizing historic dreams to "Greater Israel" is a profound, continuing violation of international law of gravest consequence for the rights and prospects of the Palestinian inhabitants of these territories, severely complicating their supreme rights of national self-determination.

Secondly, Israel has consistently defied the virtually unanimous views of impartial legal experts, of the United Nations, and even of its closest supporter, the US government, with respect to its obligations under international law as pertaining to the territories occupied during the 1967 war. Not only has it failed to comply since 1967, but it has deliberately proceeded to create a set of circumstances making it increasingly difficult to bring satisfactory political arrangements into being, thereby jeopardizing for the indefinite future the well-being of the inhabitants. That is, the cumulative effect of Israeli violations of international law is to deprive the civilian population of the occupied territories as a whole of their most basic concern to avoid having the pretext of occupation achieve many of the results of conquest or annexation. Meron Benvenisti's West Bank Data Project has received wide attention as an authoritative account of the magnitude of the settlements process, especially with respect to land alienation. Since the study is based in Israel and Benvenisti was the former deputy mayor of Jerusalem, the project has an added quality of credibility, and indeed its findings do seem both accurate and alarming, fully confirming Arab allegations of a consistent pattern, accelerated after 1977, of establishing a set of conditions assuring permanent effective de facto sovereignty no matter what was the de jure solution evolving out of diplomatic maneuvering. Benvenisti's further contention that the situation is not irreversible, and that a circumstance of virtual annexation has resulted, could play a destructive role in negotiation, influencing perceptions as to what is reasonable. In my view, the situation has assumed the appearance of irreversibility, but with fewer than 50,000 Israelis living among 800,000 or more Palestinians, the situation can be reshaped to fulfill nationalist aspirations if the political will is present and supported. It is not, in this sense, helpful to accept uncritically Benvenisti's interpretations of the present situation.[9]

Finally, despite the overwhelming evidence of these violations and their harmful effects, available political leverage has not been brought to bear. On the Arab side, rhetorical denunciations of these illegal policies, repeated year after year, have served to reinforce the impression of the impotence of international law and of the relative indifference of Arab governments. Even along the channels of international law, available options have not been used. For instance, the Security Council or General Assembly could request an Advisory Opinion from the International Court of Justice on the disputed legal questions. Even if blocked in the Security Council by a US veto, the Assembly could seek confirmation of its international law positions, generating some further political pressure.

More to the point, of course, is the United States refusal to back up its legal assessment with some pressure by way of diplomatic persuasion and economic policy. Given Israel's high level of dependence on US foreign aid, especially considering the high costs associated with subsidizing the settlements, it must be realized that the US government by its failure to assert leverage is an accomplice to the illegal policies. To take the view that these levels of illegality are a distraction from the search for "peace" is to depreciate, possibly unwittingly, the value of international law in general, as well as to contradict earlier official views on the precise issues. From almost any point of view the US government, by this stance, assumes a measure of direct responsibility for these illegal policies that so severely impair the human rights of the civilian population of the occupied territories.

On the basis of this line of analysis it might seem as if international law has no practical bearing at this stage on the search for peace and justice in the Middle East. Such a skeptical conclusion would miss my main argument. To be sure, if the main antagonists treat international law as irrelevant, then indeed it is. Israel, and to a lesser extent, the United States, have a clear incentive to dismiss international law (including with the scholarly form of dismissal, such as the strained interpretations of the legal issues of Blum, Gerson, and Rostow). After all, international law, reasonably and authoritatively understood, condemns their settlements policy, and hence, their entire posture toward a resolution of the basic conflict. It is pure polemics to contend, as Gerson does, that the legal issues get in the way of the peace process. These issues only get in the way of the Israeli one-sided definition of the peace process, that is, a conception of peace that is a bargain struck at an inter-governmental level that neglects the rights of those Palestinians victimized by the occupation of their lands since 1967.

Looked at from the Arab-Palestinian side, the peace process should be understood in a quite different way. For one thing, it is one role of international law to help clarify the content of a reasonable and fair solution. Especially here in the setting of the humanitarian goals of the laws of war, it is essential to emphasize the fundamental right of the civilian population in a territory subject to belligerent occupation to retain the societal integrity of their territory once occupation is ended. The Israeli settlements, hardly even making a pretext of military necessity, represent an undisguised plan to shift resources and effective sovereignty from the inhabitants to the settlers, thereby greatly limiting the actual significance of steps that might be taken to relinquish control and grant some kind of autonomy or even independence to the territories. Since the implementation of international law requires the removal of the settlements, it embodies an indispensable substantive precondition of an acceptable peace process. To insist on the relevance of this implementation helps justify the demands that must be made from the Arab–Palestinian side in negotiations. Otherwise, a political bargaining process is likely to accept the status quo on the ground and merely alter the superstructural elements of status and political identity. Put differently, international law is important both for bargaining purposes and to clarify a reasonable substantive solution. In this sense, having international law on one's side means much more than a propaganda advantage.

Finally, in this specific setting, there is no way to protect the basic interests of the civilian population except by insisting upon implementing their rights under international-law. To lose sight of this feature is to accept the recent US position that the international law issue should be avoided because it is an obstacle. My point is that it must remain an obstacle if a satisfactory solution is to be achieved, not for carrying on debate, but to reach an acceptable outcome in accord with the agreed political framework set forth in Security Council Resolution 242. It is up to Arab–Palestinian diplomats and advocates to make clear the principled basis of their stand on the international-law status of the settlements. Such a stand is also an implication of the wider insistence of international law that it is inadmissible to achieve territorial changes as a result of the use of force.

In conclusion, the establishment, expansion, character, and scale of the settlements represent massive, continuing violations of the laws of war. In a technical sense, this accusation engages Israeli responsibility at the governmental level. The Palestinian civilian population has not been protected, but rather has been exploited in a wide variety of ways, most fundamentally, by taking steps associated with permanent encroachment on resources, economic and cultural life, and political independence under the guise of "occupation" achieved as a result of military action.

At minimum, compensation is due. Here, however, the reach of international law exceeds the political necessities of a fair solution. The entitlement of the civilian population to compensation is more "a bargaining chip" at this stage than it is a vital ingredient of a solution. To insist, in other words, on complete compensation could indeed make international law an obstacle rather than an instrument in the search for a just peace. It is critical, in other words, to distinguish reliance on international law for the practical expression of an essential position in a negotiating setting from a more academic appreciation of the literal merits of competing views of a political dispute. It would not serve the interests of the aggrieved Palestinian civilian population to insist on this overall satisfaction of their legal rights as a condition for moving ahead on the most vital claims.

Lebanon

Chapter Ten

THE BEIRUT RAID & THE INTERNATIONAL LAW
OF RETALIATION

O n the night of December 28, 1968, eight Israeli helicopters took part in an attack on the Beirut International Airport. Israeli commandos descended from six of the helicopters (the other two hovered above) that had landed either on runways or at the hangars of the airport. All commercial aircraft belonging to Arab airlines were destroyed by explosives being placed in the nose-wheel well and in the undercarriage well of each plane. The attack resulted in the destruction of thirteen planes whose worth has been estimated to be $43.8 million.[1] Additional damage has been reported done to hangars and other airport installations. Lebanese sources report that two Israeli commandos were injured by gunfire from airport guards. There was no loss of life.

The Beirut raid was defended by the Israeli government as a retaliation for an attack by two Arabs two days earlier, on December 26, upon an El Al passenger plane at the Athens airport. The Athens attack was the work of two men, Mohmand Mohammed Issa and Maher Hussein Suleiman, who belonged to the Popular Front for the Liberation of Palestine.[2] The terrorists used gasoline bombs and submachine guns to attack the El Al Boeing 707 as it was preparing to take off with 41 passengers and a crew of 10 on a flight bound for New York City. One passenger, an Israeli engineer named Leon Shirdan, was killed by machine-gun bullets that penetrated his plane window. Israeli reports suggest 86 piercings of the fuselage from the cockpit to the tail, with many of the bullet holes through windows at seat level.[3] Greek authorities have charged the two Arabs with first-degree murder, a crime subject to the death penalty in Greece. The Greek magistrate, Nikolas Stylianikis, disclosed that the defendants said, despite the character of their attack, that they had been under orders from a Popular Front official in Beirut to destroy the El Al plane but not to kill any of the passengers.[4] The two Arabs had traveled from Beirut on Lebanese travel documents provided to stateless persons.

This article first appeared as "Beirut Raid and the International Law of Retaliation," American Journal of International Law *63.3 (July 1969): 415–443.*

The Popular Front for the Liberation of Palestine has been operating in Lebanon rather openly since the June 1967 war, with the knowledge and apparent acquiescence of the government.

On December 29, Lebanon requested an emergency session of the UN Security Council to consider its charge that Israel had committed a "wanton and premeditated attack" upon the Beirut International Airport. Israel also requested an urgent meeting of the Security Council to consider its counter-charge that Lebanon was "assisting and abetting acts of warfare, violence, and terror by irregular forces and organizations" against Israel.[5] On December 31, after a considerable period of debate, the Security Council, by a vote of 15–0, unanimously adopted a resolution censuring Israel for the Beirut raid.[6] The preliminary language of the resolution emphasized that the attack was "premeditated and of a large scale and carefully planned nature." The resolution indicated that the Security Council:

1. Condemns Israel for its premeditated military action in violation of its obligations under the Charter and the cease-fire resolutions;

2. Considers that such premeditated acts of violence endanger the maintenance of the peace;

3. Issues a solemn warning to Israel that if such acts were to be repeated, the Council would have to consider further steps to give effect to its decisions;

4. Considers that Lebanon is entitled to appropriate redress for the destruction it suffered, responsibility for which has been acknowledged by Israel.[7]

On the evening of December 31, a rocket bombardment of Kiryat Shmona, an Israeli town close to the Lebanese border, was presumed to be the work of the Popular Front, in effect a counter-retaliatory use of force. The attack killed two Israeli civilians; a third inhabitant died from a heart attack that appeared to have been provoked by the raid. The rocket bombardment evidently originated from Lebanese territory and the nature of the rockets suggested that it was an act of irregular forces. Israel has not brought this attack to the attention of the Security Council. There have been a series of minor incidents along the frontier between Israel and Lebanon, both before and since the Beirut raid, leading to what has been described by both governments as a deteriorating border situation. Shortly after December 28 Lebanon also complained to the UN Mixed Armistice Commission about Israeli reconnaissance flights over Lebanese territory, especially those associated with the inspection of the damage done to the airport.

These basic facts surrounding the Beirut raid are, by and large, not in dispute. The relevant context is, of course, both intricate and indefinite, and might be enlarged by either side in contradictory ways. It seems helpful to consider several additional features of the context. The first is an antecedent. On July 23, 1968, an El Al plane was hijacked by three Arab guerrillas while the plane was subject to Rome air traffic control and, possibly, still in Italian airspace en route from Rome to Tel Aviv. The plane was forced to land in Algiers. The non-Israeli passengers were released, but the Israeli male passengers and crew were held until August 31, when they were released in exchange for some Arab common law criminals imprisoned in Israel, in a transfer arranged under the auspices of the Red Cross.[8]

The second event, a consequence of the Beirut raid, was the formation of a new government in Lebanon that has indicated its intention to join more actively in the struggle against Israel. At the time of the Beirut raid the Lebanese Premier was Abdullah Yaffi, a moderate on Arab-Israeli relations and the leader who assumed responsibility for keeping Lebanon out of the June 1967 war. Yaffi has now been replaced by Rashid Karami, who has a reputation of favoring a somewhat greater Lebanese effort to achieve military preparedness, as well as the acceptance of a more active role in opposing Israel.[9] In June 1967, Karami was prime minister of Lebanon and ordered the army to advance on Israel, but the army refused to obey.

The third event involved the execution of fourteen men by the Iraqi government in punishment for allegedly spying on behalf of Israel. Eleven of these men were put on public display in Baghdad on January 27, 1968, in a very provocative fashion, involving mass demonstrations to celebrate these hangings and intense public displays of anti-Israeli feelings. This gruesome event was accompanied by reports of Israeli concern about the welfare of 3,000 or so Jews living in Iraq and intimations from the Iraqi government that additional spy trials were going to be held. Nine of the men hanged were Jews and so, too, were many of those (reported to be about 60) being held for subsequent trial as Israeli spies.[10]

Israel, although very explicitly disturbed by these events in Iraq, refrained from any action in retaliation. The reason given was that Israel does not engage in reprisals as a punishment for what is past, but only as a warning about what is to come.[11] Such an explanation of Israeli restraint is not altogether convincing on these grounds because of the prospect of future trials and executions. More convincing as an explanation, however, was the apparently influential diplomatic protests received by Iraq from many parts of the world, including the Pope, the dissociation of other Arab countries from the Iraqi action, and the fear that retaliation might jeopardize further the welfare of the Jews still living in Iraq. Despite these considerations, there was speculation that Israel might launch an air attack against Iraqi military units stationed in Jordan.[12] It may be that one further pressure against retaliation was the adverse reaction of the international community to the Beirut raid. This pressure could not be openly acknowledged by Israeli officials without tending to give weight to the deliberations of UN organs that have been growing increasingly hostile to Israel's position in the overall Arab-Israeli dispute.

A fourth event of some significance was the attack on February 18, 1969, also by four members of the Popular Front for the Liberation of Palestine (apparently operating out of the group's headquarters in Jordan) on an El Al plane as it was about to take off from the Zurich airport. Six persons on board were injured and one of the assailants was killed by an Israeli security guard who was on board the plane. Israel refrained from any specific retaliation; its officials blamed the Zurich incident on "the climate of forgiveness" within international society in relation to Arab governmental responsibility for the Athens attack. The Zurich attack was condemned by UN Secretary General U Thant, who stressed the seriousness of this new occurrence, especially its terroristic impact on innocent travelers, and appealed to Israel to refrain from retaliation. Both the repetition of the Athens incident after such a short lapse of time and the recollection of the very strong Israeli act of retaliation at Beirut led to much greater attention being given to the Zurich incident than had been earlier given to the Athens incident. Israel used its posture of restraint after Zurich to appeal for world support to secure better protection for its international aviation flights. A formal statement attributed to the Swiss Cabinet indicated that the attack at Zurich was viewed by Switzerland as an act of armed intervention for which Arab governments would be held responsible if investigations disclosed governmental links with the attack at Zurich;[13] in fact, on February 28 the Swiss government delivered formal notes of protest to Jordan, Syria, and Lebanon, in which the attack at Zurich was condemned and in which each of the three governments was urged to take steps "to prevent any new violations of Swiss territory."[14]

A further event occurred on February 24, 1969, when an Israeli air strike was carried out against two major guerrilla camps of Hama and Maisalun located close to the city of Damascus in Syria. There was unofficial speculation in Israel, as a result of the timing, that these camps

were attacked in partial retaliation for the Zurich incident; other
motivating circumstances were a bombing of a Jerusalem supermarket a
few days earlier that had resulted in the death of two Israeli students and
an upsurge of Arab commando activity in the vicinity of the Golan
Heights.[15] To attack Al Fatah bases in retaliation for activities of its rival
organization, the Popular Front, appears at first to be rather surprising,
especially as Al Fatah had not been responsible for any of the attacks on El
Al and had indicated its determination, in differentiation from the Popular
Front, to focus its use of violent means upon military targets.[16] If Israel,
however, regards itself as confronted at this point by an adversary relying
primarily on a multifaceted liberation strategy employing a variety of
terrorist tactics, then responses would seem rational that weaken this
overall paramilitary capability or that emphasize the collective
responsibility of all liberation groups for any acts of terror. Also, far less
adverse international reaction seems to arise if retaliatory uses of force by
Israel are directed at Arab military and paramilitary targets. Evidently, for
instance, the attacks on the Syrian bases resulted in fairly large Arab
casualties and yet failed to provoke any sense of international opposition
to the Israeli action. Unlike the Beirut raid, an attack of this kind on bases
seems well assimilated into the structure of international expectations
about tolerable levels of Arab–Israeli violence, given current levels and
forms of conflict and hostility.

Certain Special Contentions

Both Lebanon and Israel have advanced very special claims in relation to
their conduct. Lebanese officials have denied any specific responsibility
whatsoever for the Athens attack, although the work of the Popular Front,
including these specific acts, received praise from Lebanese leaders.[17] The
Popular Front has freedom of movement in Lebanon and has been allowed
officially to recruit members and support in the Lebanese refugee camps
containing some 140,000 Palestinians, and to disseminate propaganda
throughout the country. Since the June war this activity has been stepped
up and the Popular Front has been allowed to carry on its full program,
including the planning of commando raids such as the one that took place
at Athens. Premier Yaffi described the work of the Arabs who participated
in the Athens attack as "legal and sacred."[18]

Both sides have been very displeased with the outcome within the
Security Council. The Lebanese had sought more definite action,
including a commitment to Chapter VII sanctions that would assure action

against Israel, and not just words of censure.[19] The Arab countries and their supporters have argued that Israel has been found guilty of many Charter violations by the Security Council, but that nothing has been done as yet to secure Israeli compliance with the directives of the UN organ.

Israel, in contrast, argued that Security Council condemnation is without any significance because the organ is so one-sided in its composition and its assessment of responsibility.[20] Israeli spokesmen have pointed to the failure of the Security Council resolution even to refer to the earlier Athens raid or to the general Lebanese role in tolerating, at the very least, the active use of its territory to mount terroristic activities against Israel.[21]

From the perspective of international law, three very important sets of issues are raised by the Beirut raid and its interrelations, with the principal contentions advanced by the adversary states:

(1) The quality of governmental accountability for terroristic acts that have some link with territory and the rights of response enjoyed by the state that is the target of such terror; this problem is accentuated in the special case where the locus of terror is within a third state and the tactic is to disrupt the security of commercial airline service;

(2) The legal status of action by organs of the United Nations in a situation wherein the decisional process is politically one-sided and voting behavior appears less concerned with the specific merits of the disputes;

(3) The residual competence of an aggrieved state to use force against a state that persistently refuses to adhere to the recommendations and decisions of the United Nations.

These areas of concern are central to the realization of security and justice in the contemporary world. In particular, in the Middle East the principal antagonists hold sharply contradictory conceptions of the nature of a just outcome. These conceptions govern the perception of any particular sequence of events, such as those surrounding the Beirut raid.[22] Such events provide a rather clear "case" that helps focus an inquiry into the relationship between law and behavior in the Middle East.

Often particular situations, such as the dispute arising out of the Beirut raid, are instances of more general problems of conflict that may arise in several quite distinct settings throughout international society that call for somewhat distinct treatment. The conflict between "territorial sovereignty" and "liberation" is one such contemporary problem that takes several distinct forms in different parts of the world. These distinct settings should be borne in mind whenever a legal analysis is made. Otherwise particularities of fact and policy preference may distort the search for more general principles of assessment. In a legal system as consensual as international law it is especially important to regard particular cases as instances of general problems. For this reason it seems appropriate to mention some of the other settings wherein the broad policy issues at stake in the Beirut raid are presented.[23]

Terror, Liberation Movements, and the Processes of Social Change

In any social system in which strong claims for change are advanced, the threat or use of force is likely to play a major role. International society lacks any effective legislative process that might facilitate peaceful adjustment to changes in value and power structures. The idea of national sovereignty, the sanctity of domestic jurisdiction, and the absence of central sanctioning procedures work against the nonviolent implementation of the will of the international community on matters of social and political justice. The modern state often enjoys a great technological advantage over its population in a struggle for political control, especially if the struggle assumes a military form.[24] To overcome this disadvantage, social forces favoring change have used techniques of coercion that give a maximum role to their distinctive capabilities. Recourse to terror and random violence has been a principal tactic of the dispossessed, insurgent, revolutionary faction seeking to gain control over the machinery of government of a state. The rise of communism, the rapid collapse of colonialism, the formation of "liberation" movements to deal with racism and residual colonialism in southern Africa, and the predominance of the Afro-Asian outlook in the General Assembly are among the factors that have given prominence to terror as an instrument of political change and as a "legitimate" tactic of military struggle.[25]

The use of an external base to mount an insurgent campaign also enjoys a recent tradition of respect in the West. It is relevant to recall the role and status of "governments-in-exile" during World War II and the generally heroic imagery used to describe anti-Nazi terrorism in German-occupied Europe. The idea of "liberation" was very strongly endorsed by conservative governments generally committed to the status quo in international society, including the leading colonial powers. And even in more recent times the United States has given "aid and comfort" to anti-Castro exiles who have proposed to liberate their country by violent means, most spectacularly at the Bay of Pigs in April 1961.[26]

The principal point is that the politics of terror and the use of exile sanctuaries to disrupt "the enemy" society enjoy an ambiguous status in recent international experience. All principal states in the world have, in some situations at least, given their support to such practices. Therefore, the approval given to the liberation movements and their tactics of terror by the Arab governments is quite consistent with the behavior of other governments seeking a revision of the status quo, but unwilling or unable to make an orthodox military challenge or to negotiate a satisfactory diplomatic compromise.

The status of "liberation" movements and their practices has not been dealt with in any systematic and non-polemical fashion by either diplomats or experts in international law.[27] Governments that have been among the most enthusiastic sponsors of recent liberation activity have also been among the most ardent advocates of adherence to the principle of nonintervention in the affairs of sovereign states.[28] Such an apparent contradiction arises from simultaneously seeking national autonomy for their own society and the drastic revision of certain foreign societies. The pursuit of such a combination of goals tends to undermine the status of rules of restraint, as well as to diminish the force of legislative claims. One or the other priority would be consistent with legal authority, but not both, manipulated to suit specific preferences of a particular government.

Reprisals, Defense against Terror, and the Maintenance of Minimum Order

The kind of sporadic violence associated with liberation movements presents difficult choices to the target government, especially if its general orientation is unpopular within the regional and world community. For one thing, the terroristic acts are rarely of sufficient salience to command widespread attention from world public opinion. For another, there is normally a partially successful effort to dissociate the liberation movement from the government of the territory wherein exist facilities for training, financing, sanctuary, and guidance. The sponsoring government attempts to minimize its accountability for the conduct of violent operations by the liberation movements, and there does exist a wide range of variation as to the extent and character of control (or even knowledge) possessed by the territorial government over the conduct of specific guerrilla operations and the formation of more general liberation strategy.[29] Finally, the organized international community at the regional and the world level may endorse the objectives of the liberation movement to such an extent as to make censure, much less opposition, impossible for the target state to obtain. The use of terror as an instrument of change is given a certain legitimacy, then, to the extent that its use receives the endorsement of international institutions.[30]

These problems of response are even greater in a situation in which the terrorists' activity involves attacks upon commercial aircraft carried out in a third country. The Palestinian perpetrators of the Athens incident expected, presumably, to be apprehended and punished under Greek law for the common law crimes that they had committed. But this hardly offsets the damage done, by way of real loss of life and inconvenience to passengers; but even more, by way of making people everywhere quite hesitant to fly on airlines that are likely to be endangered en route. What is the victim government to do? It hardly makes sense to hold the Greek government accountable in any way, provided it carries out the provisions of its criminal law and, perhaps, issues a protest to the governments giving sanctuary to a liberation movement. The only effective target of response would involve inflicting unacceptable damage upon those governments that can impose limits upon the tactics used by the liberation movements. In the Arab setting, at least since June 1967, it is not even clear that the Arab governments have much leverage over the activities of the principal liberation groups within their territory. These groups currently enjoy such strong popular backing that some Arab governments (most obviously Jordan) would risk their stability and jeopardize their popular backing if deliberate and overt measures to control a liberation movement were undertaken as official policy.[31]

The government of the target state is presented, then, with a difficult choice among options in trying to devise an effective response against terror of this externally-based variety. Its defensive options are much more likely to be limited to regular sorts of military operations. The extremist commitment of terrorist groups means that their leaders are virtually undeterrable by any kind of responsive violence. In fact, responsive violence of an inter-governmental kind, such as the Beirut raid, may actually prove of positive benefit to the liberation movement, inducing the territorial government to declare openly its support. The most generally effective defensive maneuver is to seek and destroy guerrilla training camps and bases. The only other kind of effective defensive measure is one that inflicts injury upon the foreign government such that it will be induced to suppress or curtail the activities of the liberation movement. In both instances, the target state tends to appear to be making a disproportionate response, the scale is large, and the form of operation is overt. In addition, such military action is undertaken by the regular military forces of the government against a foreign state; as such, the *prima facie* indication of a UN Charter violation seems much more clearly established, and especially so if the state pursues a domestic or international course that is widely unpopular to begin with. Without centralized impartial fact-finding procedures, the state that acts overtly and on a large scale is much more likely to be regarded as the one that has endangered peace and initiated "aggression."[32] In effect, traditional legal criteria create a certain asymmetry in favor of the use of more covert and irregular forms of violence across international frontiers. Of course, this asymmetry should be balanced against the central bias of international law in favor of the incumbent government and the absoluteness of its authority over the territory under its control. Such a government can resist with legal "impunity" claims for change, however widely and deeply supported as just and reasonable.

In such a situation there is hardly an alternative to violence for the advocates of change. Similarly, a state that is the target of persistent terror has virtually no effective response, in the event that the foreign government is unable or unwilling to suppress the terroristic tactics of a liberation movement, other than recourse to what is traditionally regarded as "aggressive" war. Israel in 1956, and again in 1967, was "provoked," in effect, by its inability to maintain its national security, given its vulnerability to penetration and harassment by externally based terrorists. In the last analysis, protection may involve conquest of the territory from which the terrorism emanates. The logic of self-help which continues to underlie the search for security in a world of sovereign states may encourage this sort of border-crossing military operation, although the provocation does not constitute "an armed attack" and the response is difficult to classify as an instance of "self-defense." The paradoxical relationship between the status of violence and the procedures of social change is a central deficiency of the present structure of international legal order, especially evident at a time of emergent claims for social and political justice.

The Limits of UN Authority, Traditional Great Power Diplomacy, and Nuclear Proliferation

The general problem of curbing this kind of disruptive pattern is accentuated, as has already been suggested, by the character of the United Nations.[33] The United Nations is capable neither of implementing the justice demands of those groups that seek objectives approved by the world community nor of policing compliance with its prohibition upon recourse to violence. The geopolitical and ideological splits in international society generally prevent any kind of operative consensus arising out of UN activity. As a consequence, nineteenth-century patterns of alliance diplomacy assume great prominence in the effort to moderate the course of conflicts carried on at the regional level. Patterns of Great Power competition and coordination provide the fuel for arms races, the incentive for compromise and settlement, and the basis of uneasy forms of temporary equilibrium. The prospect of easy access by secondary states to nuclear weapons technology may even mean that a state unwilling to risk the sacrifice of its interests by a Great Power ally will seek to develop its own nuclear deterrent.[34]

International society is vulnerable to a series of disruptive conflicts that involve various kinds of externally-based insurgent operations challenging the control of an incumbent regime. These conflicts are particularly resistant to settlement because the stakes of the conflict are perceived by participants in such contradictory terms. Quite often the issue is nothing less than the political identity of the state. Resentments are so deep and bases of power so divided that reconciliation appears virtually impossible. Victory, defeat, stalemate, or a temporary truce are the only plausible outcomes.

International law is conditioned in its operation by this international setting. The remainder of this article seeks to clarify the legal situation by examining two topics: first, to present briefly the traditional rule-oriented static analysis of respective rights and duties of parties to such a conflict and to point out the inadequacies of this approach for these sorts of problems, and second, to offer a more process-oriented legal analysis that works toward a multidimensional conception or test of relative legality.

The Beirut raid will be used as "the case" that illuminates broader issues of legal approach and disposition. The approach urged is one that could be adopted either by an official advising a government on the legal implications of a proposed course of conduct or by a diplomat, civil servant, or expert seeking to pass judgment on adversary appeals to international law.

Traditional Legal Perspectives: Analysis and Appraisal

My purpose is to illustrate the traditional mode of analysis with sufficient clarity and fairness to provide an adequate background for the proposal of an alternative mode of legal analysis.

There are several kinds of legal issues that are raised by the Beirut raid: (1) What is the legal status of a reprisal claim? Under the UN Charter? Under customary international law? What is the relationship between charter law and customary international law?

(2) Does the Beirut raid constitute a reasonable exercise of the right of reprisal?

(3) Does the Security Council resolution of December 31, 1968 constitute a definitive legal assessment of the conflicting contentions of Israel and Lebanon?

The Legal Status of Reprisals

The prevailing expert view is stated clearly by Ian Brownlie:

> The provisions of the Charter relating to the peaceful settlement of disputes and non-resort to the use of force are universally regarded as prohibiting reprisals that involve the use of force.[35]

It does seem appropriate to conclude that the UN Charter prohibits all forms of forcible self-help other than the exercise of self-defense within the meaning of Article 51.[36] The Security Council clearly confirmed this view of the legal status of reprisals under the charter when it acted to censure Great Britain for carrying out a reprisal against the Yemeni town of Harib on March 28, 1964, in retaliation for alleged Yemeni support of the anti-colonial struggle in Aden. The resolution passed by a vote of 9–0, with two abstentions and had as its initial operative clause the Council conclusion that it "*Condemns* reprisals as incompatible with the purposes and principles of the United Nations."[37] Israel has not even claimed that the Beirut attack was an exercise of the right of self-defense, but rather has rested her case on the right to retaliate against Lebanon in view of its alleged connection with "the Athens incident." Israeli Chief of Staff General Yetzhak Bar Lev, has been quoted as saying that the Beirut raid was a reprisal the purpose of which "is to make clear to the other side that the price they must pay for terrorist activities can be very high."[38]

It seems clear that on the doctrinal level Israel is not entitled to exercise a right of reprisal in modern international law. Such clarity, however, serves mainly to discredit doctrinal approaches to legal analysis. International society is not sufficiently organized to eliminate forcible self-help in either its sanctioning or deterrent roles. Therefore, each reprisal claim needs to be appraised by reference to these two roles. Israel contended that the Beirut raid was a sanction imposed as a consequence of Lebanese responsibility for the Athens incident. Assessing the reasonableness of these claims involves a complex inquiry into the overall factual context. The legal rules of prohibition isolated from context offer very little guidance for the conduct of such an inquiry, except to the uncertain extent that they embody various policies about the minimization of violence in the adjustment of international disputes.

The Right of Reprisal in Customary International Law

In view of the inadequacy of Charter doctrines either to provide authoritative guidance or to give insight into the comparative merits of legal positions in the Beirut context, it would seem appropriate to consider the question by reference to pre-Charter legal conceptions contained in customary international law on the subject of reprisals.[39] For a valid exercise of the customary right of reprisal it is necessary to satisfy three main requirements:

(1) That the target of the reprisal be guilty of the commission of a prior illegal act directed against the claimant state;

(2) That the claimant state make an effort to obtain redress from the target state;

(3) That the damage inflicted in retaliation be roughly proportional to the damage initially inflicted.[40]

In relation to the controversy over the Beirut raid it is difficult to apply these standards. It is especially difficult to determine whether the Lebanese government should be properly held responsible for the commando acts of the Popular Front at Athens. Does the Lebanese failure to take reasonable steps to suppress the activity of the Popular Front on its territory establish a sufficient link to make it responsible for the specific acts of the organization?[41] Can the failure of the Lebanese government to disavow the terrorist acts or warn the Popular Front to cease such acts be used to constitute a post-facto ratification that establishes the link? The need to make this kind of demonstration would appear strong in view of Lebanon's special effort, unlike that of any other Arab state,[42] to remain at peace with Israel.[43] Israel's reprisal claim seems to fall short of satisfying the test for the first legal requirement.

Israel did not protest to Lebanon in any public forum about its responsibility for the Athens incident, nor did it demand redress prior to its raid on the Beirut airport.[44] There is no indication that the Israeli government issued a public warning to Lebanese officials that they must take steps to curtail the operations of the Popular Front.[45] The record suggests that the Israeli decision to raid the Beirut airport was not preceded by any reasonable effort to obtain pacific redress. Thus the Israeli claim also appears to fall short of the second reprisal requirement.

It is difficult to apply the test of proportionality to specific factual circumstances. How does one weigh the loss of an Israeli life at Athens or the harassment of El Al operations against the destruction of civil aircraft and other equipment valued at more than $43.8 million or the blatant military incursion upon Lebanese territory? In terms of international salience the Beirut raid seems to have been disproportionately greater than the Athens provocation.[46] It was a larger, necessarily spectacular military operation carried out on an inter-governmental basis.[47] It is fair to ask, however, "Proportional to what?" If the Israeli raid is understood as a reprisal for the willingness of the Lebanese government to tolerate operations by the Popular Front on its territory, then the Beirut raid might be regarded as proportional to inducing greater government control (although probably ineffective to achieve it). The application of this third requirement, and to some extent the first as well, depends on whether the delinquency of the Lebanon government is regarded as its complicity in the Athens incident or its toleration of the activity of the Popular Front on its territory. Israel did not clearly communicate the character of its claim, although it seemed specifically related to safeguarding the operations of El Al rather than punishing Lebanon or inducing the overall suppression of the Lebanese activities of the Popular Front.

The reprisal argument turns out to be weak if the events that are appraised concern only the Athens incident and the Beirut raid. The reprisal argument is far stronger, however, if based upon the connection between a Lebanese-based liberation movement operating with government knowledge and approval and the Beirut attack calculated to influence the leaders of the government to alter this course of policy. The fact that the raid may have produced the opposite effect, moving the Lebanese government into a position of more overt support for the liberation efforts of the Popular Front, is of no legal consequence; such an effect bears, if at all, on the political perspicacity of Israeli policymakers. Such a consideration is also of reduced significance if the Beirut raid was directed toward warning all Arab governments, not only Lebanon, that the security of Arab airlines would be disrupted if these governments failed to prevent terroristic acts against El Al. The effectiveness of the Beirut raid in communicating this claim can only be judged after the lapse of a period of time and by evidence of whether the Arab governments do take measures to discourage liberation groups from disrupting El Al.

The customary international law of reprisal does direct inquiry at more specific features of the context than does a mere assessment of the compatibility between the Beirut raid and Charter norms. At the same time, the inquiry is necessarily inconclusive because there is no agreed way to frame the basic issue as to the relationship between liberation activity and the target of a reprisal claim.[48] Furthermore, traditional inquiry relies on far too restrictive ideas about how to assess a particular claim. There is a need to assess a claim by reference to what constitutes reasonable behavior under all of the relevant circumstances.[49] Among the relevant circumstances is the inability to secure territory against terrorism if a neighboring country provides support, or even merely a sympathetic sanctuary.[50]

A special situation exists, however, when a series of terroristic incidents is undertaken by adversary states to disrupt the security of national society. It becomes somewhat more artificial in such a situation to assess the legal status of a retaliatory act in isolation from this ongoing and cumulative process of incitement through liberation activity. The situation in the Middle East is one of quasi-belligerency in which there is an agreed cease-fire and a de facto situation of hostility that frequently results in inter-governmental violence.

We need to evolve a legal framework that is able to deal with a situation of prolonged quasi-belligerency. Such a framework would at least have the advantage of overcoming the dichotomy between war and peace, and would be more sensitive to the continuities of terroristic provocation and retaliatory response such as are evident in the Middle East.[51]

The Status of the Resolution of the UN Security Council

The Security Council resolution of December 31, 1968, (1) confines the context to the facts of the Beirut raid, and (2) holds Israel responsible for the damage done. The resolution was unanimous after debate by both sides. States normally friendly toward Israel, including the United States, joined in voting with the majority. The resolution is a formal act of the international institution most competent to consider such questions and an authoritative determination of the respective merits of the adversary contentions.[52] There appears to be no valid legal basis for Israel's evident refusal to accept the formal conclusion of the Security Council as entitled to respect by its government.[53]

The Foreign Minister of Israel, Abba Eban, has suggested that "The UN does not express the idea [of international order] with any effectiveness in its present composition."[54] But one can hardly imagine any alternative composition of the Security Council that would have given a much more favorable review to the claims of Israel. Since the end of the June war of 1967 Israel has been increasingly isolated diplomatically. This isolation is partly a consequence of an Israeli insistence upon securing certain territorial and economic advantages from its military victory in 1967.[55] The attitudes that dominate world community procedures have been oriented against Israel as a consequence of this underlying feature of the conflict, and this orientation shapes the approach of UN organs toward specific issues or "events."[56] The failure of the Security Council resolution to widen the ambit of its concern (1) to include the condemnation of Arab terrorism, such as the Athens raid, and (2) to encompass the responsibility of the Lebanese government for the control of terrorist activity emanating from its territory is probably properly understood as part of the wider judgment that has been passed against Israel by the Security Council.

Under these circumstances, it is to be expected that Israel will contend that the United Nations is not prepared to deal fairly with specific instances of Arab-Israeli charges and countercharges.[57] On another level of response, it is not surprising that spokesmen for Israel point out that some states joining in the resolution of censure have been completely unmoved by UN censure of their own conduct. A most obvious and prominent recent example concerns the failure of the Security Council to censure by formal resolution the Soviet military occupation of Czechoslovakia in August of 1968.[58] The conclusion seems evident:

(1) The Security Council resolution, despite its technical character as a recommendation, is an authoritative pronouncement on the legal status of the Beirut raid;

(2) The quality of authority exercised, however, is diluted by the extent to which "the event" was approached with a disposition against Israel arising from the overall political setting of the Arab-Israeli dispute;

(3) The "duty" of Israel to comply with the terms of the resolution is qualified by its status as a recommendation (rather than a decision) and is impaired by the extent to which other states, including members of the Security Council, have themselves recently acted in defiance of UN directives.[59] There is no established tradition of governmental respect for adverse UN determinations.[60] Quite the contrary.

It seems proper to conclude, then, that the United Nations has passed judgment against Israel but that this judgment does not mean very much, given the structure and prevailing habits of international society.

Appraising the Beirut Raid: The Search for a Legal Method

Earlier sections of the paper have tried to demonstrate that:

(1) The legal rules and standards embodied in international law do not come to grips with the underlying policy setting provided by the Arab–Israeli conflict;

(2) The determinations of the Security Council are authoritative, but are nevertheless not very likely to engender respect.

At the same time, it is important to sustain some framework of constraint in circumstances of conflict such as exist in the Middle East. There is, in particular, a need to establish indicators of reasonableness that can be applied to appraise specific flash-points in a setting of continuous conflict. These indicators can influence, above all else, national decision-making processes to adopt a course of conduct that tends to appear reasonable from an objective or third-party point of view. The structuring of expectations, those of the adversary and of the community, are normally the principal purpose of retaliatory uses of force.[61] More specifically, the chief Israeli purpose (presumed and disclosed) in attacking Arab aircraft at the Beirut Airport on December 28, 1968, was to communicate a message about the disruption of Israeli civil aviation to Lebanese government leaders, secondarily to other Arab governments giving support to liberation movements, and thirdly, to other governments concerned with the Middle East.[62] In such a context of conflict, world public opinion can become influential should it crystallize in favor of one party in a dispute; this influence can affect what the parties regard as a reasonable basis of settlement, and hence, the shape and prospects for a negotiated settlement. In this sense, the censure by Pope Paul VI, the imposition of an arms embargo on Israel by France, the replacement of the Yaffi regime by the Karami regime, when added to the unanimous censure of the Security Council, make the Beirut raid a costly act from Israel's point of view.

In brief, the reasons why it is costly are as follows:

(1) It worsens Israel's diplomatic position within the international community, alienating friendly and more neutral governments and hardening the attitude of more hostile governments.

(2) It gives the impression, created by the evidence of censure at the international level, that Israel is relying upon excessive force to impose its will on weaker countries; such an impression creates, in turn, greater toleration for counter-violence, including Arab terrorism.

(3) It seems to work against the diplomatic effort to secure a negotiated or agreed-upon settlement of the underlying conflict.

(4) It leads Israel to assume a militarily defensive posture in response to international censure, thereby putting itself into an adversary relationship toward the rest of the international community, according greater strength to more militaristic perspectives within its own elite, thereby inclining the government to even greater reliance on force (rather than persuasion) in future instance.[63] There is, in other words, a dangerously escalatory cycle generated by any use of force that has been perceived as excessive in third-party contexts.

The principal point is that a retaliatory use of force that is perceived as excessive tends to engender a variety of bad consequences, including some that may be detrimental to the user. The further point is that rules of international law, as traditionally conceived, are too rigidly formulated to give appropriate insight into the factors that shape a decisional process of government and thus does not, in a realistic way, help officials or observers identify when a use of force is "excessive." The excessiveness of a particular use of force depends upon a combination of objective and subjective (value and ideological outlooks) factors, including the effort at justification made by the claimant state.[64] A more useful conception of international law than the specification of categorical rules would be the enumeration of objective factors likely to shape authoritative judgment and expert commentary. Such an enumeration would be useful for legal advisers to the adversary governments and to those passing judgment on contested behavior.

A rule of conduct isolated from context is often too abstract to guide choice and action. The more significant the connection between the overall context that conditions the action and the particular choice and act, the more difficult it is to make beneficial use of rule-guidance. The situation is subject to such a variety of relevant considerations that a generalized rule is unable to offer much guidance for those entrusted with the responsibility of specific governmental policy. A list of policy considerations can be used by the claimant government to shape its course of conduct to assure the achievement of its own ends. These considerations are only part of the input that enters the decisional process. At times, for instance, conduct that appears highly "illegal" by reference to past appraisals might be deemed essential to sustain the security of the state. But if it is demonstrably essential, then the policies supporting defensive force would tend to mitigate or even overcome any perception of "illegality."[65]

The principal objective reasons why the Beirut raid seems illegal are as follows:

LIMERICK
COUNTY LIBRARY

(1) It involved a governmental use of force by Israel in retaliation against non-governmental provocation.

(2) It involved holding the Lebanese responsible for the Athens incident without the production of sufficient evidence establishing a direct link between the Beirut government and the Arab terrorists.

(3) It involved recourse to force without any prior recourse to diplomatic remedies in a situation where no necessity for immediate recourse to retaliation was demonstrated to exist.

(4) It involved the destruction of what appeared to involve an excessive amount of property in an unusually spectacular and inflammatory fashion, thereby constituting an affront to the dignity and security of Lebanon.[66]

These elements of the Beirut raid seem to underlie the objective side of the international judgment, explaining, for instance, the hostile reaction of Pope Paul VI and the United States government to the Israeli conduct.[67] A greater sensitivity to these factors might have shaped the Israeli action in a manner that would have been both more effective to attain the end in view and less at variance with community perceptions of lawful conduct. In the paragraphs that follow, some effort is made to suggest a suitable framework for claims to use force in retaliation against prior terroristic acts.[68] This framework embodies certain general policies concerning the use of force in periods of peace:[69]

(1) That the burden of persuasion is upon the government that initiates an official use of force across international boundaries;

(2) That the governmental user of force will demonstrate its defensive character convincingly by connecting the use of force to the protection of territorial integrity, national security, or political independence;

(3) That a genuine and substantial link exists between the prior commission of provocative acts and the resultant claim to be acting in retaliation;

(4) That a diligent effort be made to obtain satisfaction by persuasion and pacific means over a reasonable period of time, including recourse to international organizations;

(5) That the use of force is proportional to the provocation and calculated to avoid its repetition in the future, and that every precaution be taken to avoid excessive damage and unnecessary loss of life, especially with respect to innocent civilians;[70]

(6) That the retaliatory force is directed primarily against military and paramilitary targets and against military personnel;[71]

(7) That the user of force make a prompt and serious explanation of its conduct before the relevant organ(s) of community review and seek vindication therefrom of its course of action;

(8) That the use of force amounts to a clear message of communication to the target government so that the contours of what constituted the unacceptable provocation are clearly conveyed;

(9) That the user of force cannot achieve its retaliatory purposes by acting within its own territorial domain and thus cannot avoid interference with the sovereign prerogatives of a foreign state;

(10) That the user of force seek a pacific settlement to the underlying dispute on terms that appear to be just and sensitive to the interests of its adversary;

(11) That the pattern of conduct of which the retaliatory use of force is an instance exhibits deference to considerations one through ten above, and that a disposition to accord respect to the will of the international community be evident;

(12) That the appraisal of the retaliatory use of force take account of the duration and quality of support, if any, that the target government has given to terroristic enterprises.

Conclusion

There are several parts of the approach to the kind of legal analysis recommended in this article: (1) a depiction of the central policy issues embodied in the underlying conflict; (2) a check-list of objective considerations relevant to the assertion and appraisal of a claim by a state to make a retaliatory use of force.

The Beirut raid was an event situated in an unusually complicated politico-military setting. Its assessment as a legal act is not a dichotomous "either/or" judgment, nor should its legal appraisal be isolated from antecedent or subsequent conduct. The essential problem confronting Israel is the design of a response against provocative terror carried out by liberation movements enjoying varying degrees of tacit and overt support from various Arab governments. This single problem is related to the overall search for a resolution or stabilization of the conflict in the Middle East, a conflict that is dangerous to both regional and global stability, containing even some threat of igniting a world war fought with nuclear weapons.[72]

The role of legal analysis is to facilitate the process of shaping and judging action: specifically, to promote constructive effects to the actor and to the community. The assumption underlying such an approach is that the primary role of international law is to help governments plan how to act, rather than to permit some third-party judge to determine whether contested action is legal or not. In fact the function of the third-party judge can be performed properly only by attempting to assess in what respects and to what extent the governmental actor "violated" community norms of a prescriptive nature. Given the present character of international legal order, the essence of law consists of an interactive process of communication among governments and between governments and international institutions as to the character of acceptable behavior. The more this communication is premised upon a consensus as to relevant considerations and the more it reflects the dominance of objective over subjective factors, the more plausible it becomes to say that international law is playing a significant role.[73]

The Beirut raid exhibits a failure of the appropriate legal considerations to guide the Israeli government's claim to use force in retaliation against terroristic provocation. This failure is important because of its bearing on world attitudes toward the relevant merits of the adversary positions of Israel and the Arab states on the underlying issues, including a peaceful settlement on mutually acceptable terms, as well as attitudes toward the whole matter of the existence of the state of Israel. It is also important because retaliation across frontiers against terroristic activity has significance in several other world contexts: Southern Africa, Latin America, and Southern Asia. It is, finally, important because the claim to be acting in a retaliatory capacity is one that involves recourse to self-help that is generally only available to the strong against the weak. As such, the ethics of retaliation is related to the role of military superiority in shaping the resolution of international conflict. Yet the vulnerability of some states to an externally-based and supported liberation movement points up the artificiality of territorial boundaries. It is arguable that in certain situations actions against terror in the form of striking at the camps and sanctuaries amounts to extraterritorial police enforcement.[74] A reprisal, such as the Beirut raid, seeks to influence the target government to suppress or regulate terrorist activity within its territorial limits; it can be understood as a demand for cooperative law enforcement. If this demand is refused, then the state that is a target of the activity is confronted by a difficult choice. It can either tolerate the foreign sanctuary or it can violate the international boundary. If it does the former, then its enemies often grow stronger and its security diminishes, whereas if it does the latter, then it often puts itself in the position of appearing to be the violator of international peace, the initiator of aggression; in time such a state risks becoming an international pariah. Israel's dilemma in the Middle East is of this sort. The best way out of this dilemma is for Israel to achieve greater sensitivity to world-order considerations, especially on matters bearing on the basis for permanent reconciliation. There is a need for reciprocity and mutuality in the course of clarifying the line of ultimate solution, as well as in maintaining a tolerable degree of domestic security during the difficult interim period.

International lawyers can contribute greatly to the quality of world order by working out a systematic framework for the assessment of claims to use retaliatory force. This article is a first step in this direction.

Chapter Eleven

RETHINKING US–ISRAEL RELATIONS
AFTER THE LEBANON WAR

There is a strange incoherence evident in recent discussions about US relations with Israel. On one side, Israeli foreign policy has been subjected to an unprecedented barrage of criticism centering on Israeli unreliability as an ally and on the country's expansionist goals. On the other side, the outcome of its most controversial undertaking, the 1982 invasion and occupation of Lebanon, has been openly celebrated by American leaders, creating, in Henry Kissinger's words, a situation in which "the possibilities for negotiation have never been better."[1]

Incoherence here, as is often the case, arises from the presence of inconsistent elements. It is generally true that American leaders resented the unilateral character of Israel's attack on Lebanon and had apparently even used gentle diplomatic pressures in the months preceding June 1982 to discourage it. Similarly, Washington definitely seemed displeased by the defiant postures of Begin and Sharon, as well as by the fact that the United States was perceived as having been somewhat tainted by Israeli tactics in the war, including the widespread use of American-supplied cluster bombs in violation of congressional restrictions, the prolonged siege of Beirut, and subsequent Israeli complicity in the Shatila/Sabra massacres.

At the same time, the US government realized that the Israeli attack on Lebanon, and indeed the very extensiveness of it, produced enormous benefits in relation to the wider goals of American foreign policy. Above all, Israel demonstrated that being an ally of the United States was far more beneficial than being allied with the Soviet Union, especially when it came to a range of combat circumstances. Israel's military outperformed that of Syria, and to a less impressive extent that of the PLO, demonstrating the gaping technological disparities in the quality of the weaponry provided by the two superpowers. Presumably this message in America's favor is being interpreted by governments throughout the Middle East and beyond as a matter of the highest diplomatic and strategic priority.

This piece was first published in Johns Hopkins University's School of Advanced International Studies SAIS Review *3.1 (Winter–Spring 1983): 43–63.*

Furthermore, the long-term US resolve to contain radicalism in the Middle East was definitely bolstered by Israel's defeat and dispersal of the PLO, which even now remains, alongside Islamic fundamentalism, the main regional expression of radical nationalism. The Israeli victory also severely weakened the position and the capabilities of Lebanese radical elements, which were mainly Muslim and closely allied with the PLO. And not only were Palestinian nationalism and Lebanese domestic radicalism dealt heavy setbacks, but the war created a situation that enabled Israel to reshape decisively the Lebanese government under right-wing Christian auspices, assuring a Lebanese foreign policy and economic program oriented toward the West. As it happens, Lebanon's postwar leadership has indeed turned out to be anti-Palestinian and pro-American, but without being at all willing to bestow upon Israel any economic or diplomatic rewards for its facilitative role. The new Lebanese leadership seems determined above all else to avoid taking the Sadat path, despite the extent to which their power derives from the heavy Israeli investment in the Christian Phalangist cause since the 1975–76 civil war period and possibly before. Phalange hostility to a Palestinian presence within Lebanese boundaries is a definite contribution to Israeli security; that alone may be quite enough to validate the war effort in most Israeli eyes.

As far as the United States goes, there have been no ambiguities or disappointments as regards postwar Lebanon, and the only wider concern involves Egypt's political future. Amin Gemayel has turned to Washington in the most unabashed fashion possible, asking for an expanded American military presence and offering the prospect of a secure "friend." Unlike Egypt at the time of Sadat's original peace initiative, Lebanon has no long history of bloody wars with Israel aside from the problems associated with the PLO presence in southern Lebanon. Yet Israeli planners are undoubtedly disturbed by Amin Gemayel's diplomatic stance, and they are possibly even galled by the refusal of the US government to be more supportive in other respects, considering the extent to which Israel paid the costs in blood and reputation for the results that seem to enhance the American role in the area to such an extent. For the Phalange, now that the PLO is out of Beirut and southern Lebanon and they dominate the government, Israel has nothing further to offer, except of course a rapid and complete withdrawal. The legitimacy and stability of the new Lebanese leaders are enhanced by putting all their Western eggs in the American basket. They realize that, unlike the case with Egypt, the Israeli occupation of Lebanese land is not, at least not yet, a bargaining tool.

As a religiously divided polity, the new Lebanon is likely to do better internally and internationally by pressing on its own for unconditional Israeli withdrawal and by emphasizing its solidarity with the basic objectives of overall Arab policy. Therefore, Amin Gemayel's request for more American marines in Beirut symbolizes a special insistence that a line can and must be drawn by the new Lebanese leadership between establishing a positive relationship with the United States and keeping its distance from Israel. Relying on world public opinion as well as on the stated intentions of the parties to the conflict, including Israel, Lebanon hopes to enlist the aid of the United States in bringing pressure to bear on Israel (and, of course, on Syria and the PLO) to withdraw from Lebanese territory without offering *any* quid pro quo.

One extraordinary feature of the postwar situation is that the United States has emerged as the critical diplomatic actor for all sides in the conflict. This is a remarkable achievement, considering the extent to which Israeli military capabilities and diplomatic freedom of action are a direct result of the scale and virtually unconditional nature of US support. The Lebanon war underscored to an even greater extent than the Kissinger diplomacy in the aftermath of the 1973 war and the Camp David process that the United States is the only superpower that counts when it comes to the core of the Arab-Israeli conflict. The PLO imaginatively used the circumstances surrounding its agreed departure from Beirut to establish a virtual negotiating relationship with the United States, thereby further diluting its being dismissed as a mere terrorist organization. In this regard, the PLO manifested a keen appreciation of the extent to which their future is tied to gaining legitimacy in Washington's eyes. Surely Robert W. Tucker goes too far, as is his bent, when he suggests that "if America does not resurrect the PLO, it can no longer have a meaningful political life."[2] Nevertheless, it is startling to realize the total ineffectiveness of Soviet support for the PLO at the moment of their extreme crisis. It has to be a humiliation for Kremlin policymakers to observe the PLO leadership acting as if only the United States can help them realize their fundamental goals, and, similarly, it has to be heartening to the White House that its claim to regional leadership is currently being acknowledged across the entire spectrum of political actors.

The same line of reasoning applies with as much force to the Arab world as a whole. Despite a posture of anti-Israel diplomacy carried on especially within the cushy safety of the United Nations, the Arab governments, despite their oil and money, turned out to be non-actors at the moment of truth for the PLO, particularly during the siege of Beirut. Whether radical or moderate, the Arab leaders symbolized their impotence by sending the foreign ministers of Saudi Arabia and Syria to Washington in the midst of the crisis, virtually in the role of petitioners.

And finally, the harshness of the Israeli disposition to terrorize the Palestinian camps (ironically in the name of fighting "the terrorists") led to a series of moves that culminated in the Shatila/Sabra massacres. These gruesome undertakings clearly weakened Israel's position vis-à-vis Washington and in relation to its own people, and it also stimulated mutual recriminations between Phalangist and Israeli leaders, each eager to shift blame to the other. One consequence was for Israel to give up certain secondary war objectives, including its earlier apparent ambition to establish political and economic hegemony in Lebanon. In this context, also, the United States became the immediate beneficiary. Its hands were apparently clean, although its hasty withdrawal of United States marines days prior to the assassination of Bashir Gemayel and reported CIA special links with Elie Hobeika, who was evidently the commander of the militia forces that entered the camps, have raised suspicions of American foreknowledge.[3] The United States, together with France and Italy, were urged after the massacres to reconstitute the multilateral force by the new Lebanese government, and Amin Gemayel definitely accused Israel of causing this latest round of Palestinian misfortunes, even to the bizarre extent of denying in public any Phalange participation in the massacres. The willingness of the media to let Gemayel get away with this fabrication has to be viewed as one of the marvels of self-imposed censorship.

It is against this general background that changes in the American relationship with Israel need to be understood. In a geopolitical sense, Israel has never before delivered so much to the United States, and in a form that has not strained the American relationship with the wider Arab forces in the region, not even with Egypt, at least not yet. Also, Israel, now rated the fourth military power in the world by the Institute for Strategic Studies in London, has established itself beyond doubt as "a strategic asset" in the region, perhaps the best overall hope for the maintenance of Western hegemony in the Middle East.

In these circumstances, mainstream critics of Israel's behavior toward Lebanon are straining hard to be convincing. I tend to accept Robert W. Tucker's view that many criticisms of Israel by prominent mainstream political figures confuse disapproval of its policies in a moral sense with an attack upon their political consequences. As Tucker puts it: "The moral critique is important because what has so often been presented as hard-headed political analysis is, when its surface is once scratched, moral preference masquerading as political analysis."[4] The outcome in Lebanon, because of long-range American goals in the region, has to be viewed as by far the greatest and possibly the only major foreign policy triumph to date by the Reagan administration. It is true that the longer-term implications of these events are not yet fully evident, but even if these should prove to be adverse, virtually every government is notoriously indifferent to the deferred costs of its short-term successes. And in regard to such long-term implications, the Reagan leadership seems to have seized the opportunity to demonstrate its will to stabilize the overall Israeli–Palestinian relationship in what is being generally seen as a constructive fashion. The revival, in a somewhat altered form, of the Camp David conception of Palestinian autonomy on the West Bank and Gaza, as well as opposition to Begin's policy of establishing still more Israeli settlements on the West Bank, does represent a longer-term view by Washington of the gains to be secured from the Lebanese invasion. Kissinger's sense of a negotiating opportunity and his thinly veiled threats to King Hussein to bring him to support the peace process at this time, represent the prevailing American view that now is the moment to restructure the Israel-Palestine relationship on a more permanent and satisfactory basis. It is also likely that because of their desperate circumstances of dispersal and vulnerability, most of the PLO leaders will be more receptive than ever before to such minimalist offers of a homeland. Begin's resistance to the American initiative is partly ideological—some would say theological, for Begin does not want to qualify Israel's claimed divine sovereign rights over Judea and Samaria—and partly prudential, in that the Likud Party leans toward annexation and territorial grandeur, while the Labor Party prefers to exert indirect control by way of autonomy arrangements to produce an eventual confederation between a Palestinian homeland and Jordan. Israel continues to be united in its resolve to overcome the Palestinian problem by crushing Palestinian nationalism. It is for this reason that mainstream Israelis, whether they prefer the annexation or the autonomy route, join in their opposition to the PLO playing any role in the peace process. By excluding the PLO and Arafat, Israel could signal the defeat of Palestinian nationalism at the very moment that Palestinian claims for national self-determination were, at last, apparently being heeded. Even King Hussein made it clear that to resolve the Palestinian problem without the PLO is a contradiction in terms: "I believe the PLO is the sole legitimate representative of the Palestinians, and I can't see how the Palestinian problem could be resolved without the participation of the Palestinians in every phase of the effort."[5] Whether the PLO is flexible enough at this stage to increase the pressure by according Israel unconditional recognition remains to be seen, especially as Israeli leaders would undoubtedly interpret such a gesture at this stage as an expression of PLO weakness.

In any event, images of a long-term solution that involve a largely nominal conception of a Palestinian homeland and that contemplate the exclusion of the PLO from political control are unlikely to succeed even at the initial negotiating stage, if for no other reason than that the Palestinian people overwhelmingly regard the PLO and Yasir Arafat as the only legitimate vehicles for the realization of their national aspirations. Actually, the PLO stand against Israeli forces massed around Beirut last July and August has strengthened their leadership claims within the Palestinian movement, a reality possibly offset by the resurfacing of PLO factionalism in the aftermath of the departure from Beirut. Even if obstacles could be removed and the negotiations could somehow succeed and the PLO could somehow participate in the process, the outcome would not likely bring a lasting peace unless a far more generous conception of a Palestinian homeland (in terms of both power and land) was achieved than that contemplated by the Reagan plan. This plan actually represents a long step backward from the image of Palestinian autonomy contained in the Camp David agreements, which included a mechanism for possibly more genuine Palestinian self-determination on the West Bank after the initial interim period of five years. But my point here is that Israel's entry into Lebanon has given renewed prominence to a long-range peace process, has drawn the Arabs closer to a position of legitimizing Israel's statehood, and has even lead the PLO to scale down its demands. These developments make it difficult to maintain that the war in Lebanon had negative political effects, even from a long-range American outlook.

For these various reasons, then, I share the Tucker conclusion that criticism of Israel cannot be explained at this stage by contentions that its invasion of Lebanon harmed the national interests of the United States. Furthermore, when a close ally produces politically beneficial results of the magnitude of those achieved by Israel for the United States in the Middle East, it is highly unusual to endorse moral objections to its behavior. Even the United States, more moralistic than most states in its diplomacy, consistently subordinates moral qualms to strategic imperatives in carrying out its foreign policy, especially where important issues of critical resources and geopolitical rivalry are at stake, as here. This pattern of subordination has been notably evident during the Reagan years.

Why, then, the moralizing here? Or is it moralizing? Surely, one line of response has to do with the visibility of the war and its victims. Seeing Palestinians, especially children, caught up in the horror of the experience elicits moral anguish that is quickly turned into criticism of the perpetrator of the violence. This kind of general criticism of Israel came mainly from the public and from liberal journalists. More influential, possibly, were the critics who understand that war and foreign policy are not shaped by moral outrage. It was these critics of Israel who tried to make their moral position "heard" in centers of power by couching their objections to Israel's behavior in the pragmatic terms of geopolitics.

Yet beyond these explanations lies the main reason for such criticism, and this reason is associated with various conflicting pulls on American diplomacy in the Middle East. The US government is seeking to play a double role in the region as both regional peacemaker and as Israeli partisan. It is amazing that this double role can be sustained, considering the extent of American support for Israel and the pain and humiliation that have resulted for the Arab world from Israel's ability to impose its will by force of arms. The US government maintains its credibility by distancing itself periodically from official Israeli policy. This distancing is especially important at a time when Israel's leadership appears extremist and unyielding, or when Israel has moved on to yet another military victory. Therefore, the critique of Israel rests as much on the character of the American role in the region as it does on any genuine divergence between Israel and the United States. In this essential respect, then, American criticism, whether political or moral, is essentially hypocritical (that is, designed to improve its regional image rather than meant in any serious way as a comment on Israeli behavior).

As with other alliance relationships, there are areas of conflict and disagreement between the United States and Israel. The United States seeks, it would seem, uncontested spheres of economic and diplomatic influence in as many Arab countries as possible. Therefore, Washington undoubtedly resents Israel's wider ambitions that appear associated with its role as occupying power in Lebanon, and to the extent that Tel Aviv relies on this role, there is a tendency for the United States to perceive Israel as a rival and to exert leverage against it, even hinting that there may be limits to future American support if Israel remains noncompliant. American leaders also do not appreciate Begin's blunt approach to the Palestinian question, objecting more on grounds of style than substance, and preferring the more genteel claims of dominance put forward by the Labor mainstream in Israel.

In this context, the Begin style matters. For one thing, the US government as Israel's benefactor expects more consultation and deference, or at least contends that it does. Begin's apparent defiance, expressed in an abrasive idiom, exaggerates an earlier and consistent tendency of Israeli leaders to implement their views of their state interests by creating facts that the outside world must accept as a new status quo. Such a style causes some official American discomfort, even a certain amount of mild censure. Recent pre-Lebanon instances of Israeli unilateral action, such as the proclamation of Jerusalem as Israel's capital, the destruction by air attack of Iraq's Osirak nuclear complex, and the annexation of the Golan Heights all enjoyed bipartisan support in Israel and were evidently undertaken without advance American clearance. Of course, the United States, given its various aspirations in the region, may often prefer Israel's unilateralism to being drawn into a closer and more complicit relationship to these provocative Israeli initiatives. American leaders do not seek to be identified with policies that repudiate both international obligations and the views of the overwhelming majority of governments, including America's closest allies. This apparent absence of prior American notification, at least at official levels, creates pressures on the United States to join in on movements for Israeli censure. That is, the particular character of the special US–Israel relationship, necessitated by the American double role in the region, creates an impression at a time of controversial Israeli behavior that the United States is joining in with the critics. Because the Israeli attack on Lebanon and its subsequent actions were exceedingly controversial and prominent, the impression of a critical US response was fostered, and was reinforced by many private voices expressing distress over events in Lebanon. This impression is misleading; the actualities of the relationship (diplomatic support, financial and military aid) are stronger than ever, although more critical voices will probably be heard in Congress and elsewhere for a while.

Perhaps it was inevitable that against this background, allegations of anti-Semitism would be made by Israeli supporters. Why, it can fairly be asked, should an effective ally be castigated by moral yardsticks normally reserved for enemies? And why was Israel chosen for such intense moral scrutiny in a world where atrocities and militarism are the order of the day?

It is certainly true that some prominent moralists, at best rather marginal presences in the foreign policy debates of leading states, seemed to weigh in unduly heavily on Israel, exaggerating early in the war the extent of the damage and the numbers of casualties caused by the Israelis in southern Lebanon, and drawing far-fetched comparisons between Hitler and Begin, or between Israeli and Nazi behavior. And even later on, so the response to these critics goes, the casualties caused by the Israeli bombardment of Beirut were trivial compared to earlier large-scale air attacks on cities (e.g., during World War II). And perhaps most tellingly, although the Shatila/Sabra massacres were carried out by members of the Lebanese militia, most of the critical attention has been concentrated upon Israel's alleged responsibility, which was at most indirect. When no Israeli involvement was apparent, as in the case of earlier massacres in recent Lebanese history, for instance at the Tal Zataar refugee camp back in 1976, such events received far less international scrutiny and censure. Taken as a whole, do not such considerations constitute evidence of an intention to isolate Israel as a pariah state? And is not this intention associated with historic persecutions of the Jews, now partly transferred into an effort to mistreat the Jewish state of Israel? Are not those who offer criticism of Israel in these circumstances contributing to such a campaign, and therefore, are they not, whether knowingly or not, even whether Jewish or not, acting in effect as anti-Semites?

This argument takes on greater force if the moral argument is refuted as in itself unwarranted and unreasonable. Tucker's counterattack, the most well-reasoned argument on behalf of Israel currently available, rests on the following central assertion: "The Israeli objective in Lebanon—and in Beirut—was no more and no less than the objective of any belligerent; the surrender or the destruction of the enemy's armed forces. If this objective is illegitimate, then the objective of any armed force in war is also illegitimate." And as far as conduct of the war is concerned, Tucker claims that since Israel did its very best to minimize destructive effects, "the charge of indiscriminate warfare is one made either by those with a special axe to grind or by those who quite simply reject the necessities of war."[6] Those with an axe to grind are presumably anti-Israeli beyond the circumstances of the encounter, and hence must at the very least be suspected of ulterior, presumably anti-Semitic, motives.

Some commentators go even further in this direction, contending that any criticism of Israel, in the context of a continuing Arab rejection of Israel's right to exist, represents a deliberate effort, in the words of the president of the Zionist Organization of America, Ivan Novick, "to place Israel in jeopardy."[7] Novick urges true supporters of Israel to practice "discipline," by which he apparently means the inhibition of all public criticism. To criticize Israel is to do more than to censure particular Israeli leaders or policies. Novick contends that "it is the Jewish people that are maligned in the eyes of the non-Jewish world by the words and actions of those who now congratulate themselves because they have the so-called courage to speak out against Israel."[8]

In fact, Norman Podhoretz broadens the countercharge, arguing that this anti-Israel outburst is not only without doubt an exhibition of anti-Semitism, but that it also represents a "sure sign of failing faith in and support for the virtues and values of Western civilization and of America in particular."[9] He makes the full burden of his extraordinary polemic clear in a closing blast: "I charge here that anti-Semitic attacks on Israel which have erupted in recent weeks are also a cover. They are a cover for a loss of American nerve. They are a cover for the acquiescence in terrorism. They are a cover for the appeasement of totalitarianism. And I accuse all those who have joined in these attacks not merely of anti-Semitism but of the broader sin of faithlessness to the interests of the United States and indeed to the values of Western civilization as a whole."[10] This is an extreme position that makes support for Israel in the circumstances of its Lebanese invasion a litmus test for one's overall moral credibility as a member of American society.

Writing a shorter subsequent piece after the massacres, Podhoretz reiterates this stand, contending that "by the standards both of international law and of simple common sense it should have been obvious that the PLO and not Israel was to blame."[11] The overall pattern of destruction in the war, including the Israeli bombardment of schools, hospitals, and residential sections, should be attributed to the PLO, which situated its munitions and fighters in places normally off limits to attack. Likewise, responsibility for the massacres should be assigned mainly to the Christian militias and the PLO, with Israeli leaders having at most some subordinate responsibility for these events, especially General Sharon, who should be charged with "negligence" in relation to these events.

Podhoretz means to argue that no critic of Israel's role is an innocent, merely giving vent to an honest difference of opinion, presumably a vital citizen function. Rather the critic is "an enemy" in the fullest sense of the term, not only of Israel and the Jewish people, but of the United States as well, and even beyond that, of Western civilization in its entirety.

Taking account of such charges is difficult, especially as there is a tendency on the part of some critics, as Tucker noted, to hide their moral criticism in a political form, and in this form such criticism is so unconvincing as to require special explanation. A further problem arises because moralizing critics (for instance, Anthony Lewis) did overstate the scale of Israeli wrongdoing in Lebanon, thereby creating a "credibility gap."

I share Podhoretz's assessment of the connection between what Israel did in Lebanon and what official America stands for in the world today, but I draw the reverse set of normative conclusions from this fact. There are no convincing grounds on which to condemn Israel for its policies toward Lebanon since June, from the viewpoint either of the geopolitical goals or of the moral guidelines that have directed American foreign policy since 1945. By trying to utterly destroy a movement of national liberation in a Third World country, Israel was carrying out a policy that has had the bipartisan commitment of the United States foreign policy establishment in response to revolutionary nationalism all over the world. What Israel did to the PLO is what the United States is currently trying to do, although somewhat more indirectly, to nationalist movements throughout Central America. Indeed, if the rightist governments of the region enjoyed a comparable military edge over their neighbors as that enjoyed by Israel in the Middle East, they would be encouraged, at least covertly, to carry out armed attacks designed to rid the Caribbean of the established governments of Cuba, Nicaragua, and Grenada. Even as matters now stand, "friends" of the United States throughout the world are being encouraged to join in the struggle against all movements of national revolution, which is in essence what the PLO represents in the Middle East. Of course, there are some crucial regional variations that explain differences in approach. The United States is inhibited to the extent that it seeks to reconcile its support for anti-Israeli moderate Arab regimes with its support for Israel, and this complicates from time to time the character of its relationship with Israel. Unlike the Central American countries, Israel is, of course, a very vibrant society with strong ambitions of its own. Israel's increasingly regional conception of its own security makes it a competitor and rival, as well as a more formidable partner than the typical Washington-dependent Third World regime.

And yet, the fundamental question posed here is whether the United States wants to associate its national identity and national interests with continuing to provide arms and encouragement to anti-revolutionary forces around the world. The Lebanese case was comparatively easy in the sense that some moral and political ambiguities existed. The PLO was intruding upon Lebanese sovereignty. The Palestinian presence was resented by many components of Lebanese society, including many Shiites in the south. The balance between Christian and Moslem rule had broken down to such an extent that the formal government situated in Beirut was unable to assert its authority almost anywhere in the country. To approve of the Israeli attack in these circumstances would, in addition to inflicting great losses upon the PLO, set the conditions for a diplomatically favorable form of stabilization for Lebanon.

And surely the sanction for the Israeli operation must have been implied, at the very least. Sharon and other Israeli officials had been relatively open since at least the end of 1981 about their intentions to move against Lebanon; only the timing and the extent of the invasion were left uncertain. American officials contend even in private that they put some pressure on Israel to avoid an attack earlier. Surely there was the expectation in Washington that the attack would nevertheless come as soon as a suitable pretext was found. In these circumstances, the United States could have made its opposition to such an attack on Lebanon more definite and public and tied it to the flow of arms and money to Israel. Instead, US representations were cordial and vague, and more consequently, the flow of arms shipments to Israel in the months prior to the invasion was expanded dramatically as compared with the arms flow for the preceding year.[12]

If we accept an international political order without norms, then Israel's invasion cannot persuasively be faulted on geopolitical grounds, Yet the whole weight of international efforts, led by the United States throughout this century until quite recently, has been to deny states the discretion to wage aggressive wars, except in carefully delimited circumstances of self-defense. In circumstances of far greater "terrorist" provocation, when Israel joined in 1956 with England and France to attack Egyptian forces in the Sinai, the United States sided with Soviet-leaning Gamel Abdul Nasser of Egypt to demand their withdrawal. The June 3 attack on Shlomo Argov, Israel's ambassador in London, apparently carried out by Palestinian enemies of the PLO, and contrived claims of intolerable levels of cross-frontier terrorism in the Galilee region, both clearly seemed to be pretexts for Israel's invasion, and certainly did not qualify as "self-defense," no matter how elastically that term might be understood. Furthermore, the scale and the goals of the invasion bore no proportional relation to these alleged justifications for it. Therefore, the question of backing or at least endorsing "a war of aggression" was fairly obviously involved for United States policymakers.

Yet this does not account for the sheer intensity of the criticism of Israel in these circumstances. Here, I think, the underlying moral implications of the policy objectives of Israel became vivid beyond all ambiguity. Israel was, as Tucker suggests, doing little more than pursuing belligerent objectives by relevant means, and it even displayed a certain concern in aspects of the war for limiting civilian casualties. Nevertheless, the nature of the belligerent objectives of Israel in the context of its conflict with the Palestinians necessarily posed moral issues of a sort that did not in any sense arise, despite a similar one-sidedness of the results of combat, in the context of Israel's war with Syria. Fighting the Palestinians en masse in Lebanon necessarily meant blurring in all sorts of ways the distinction between civilians and soldiers, especially in relation to the refugee camps. In Moslem areas of Lebanon, such as Sidon and Tyre, it meant gathering the entire civilian population and removing for "interrogation" and detention a high proportion of all the Palestinian males, identified for the Israeli occupying forces by hooded informers, a selection process reported by residents to be highly arbitrary. It also included taking steps to prevent the rebirth of a militant Palestinian presence in Lebanon, which was clearly interpreted by Sharon, Eitan, and the rest of the Israeli leadership as requiring the devastation of the Palestinian camps as well as the demoralization of their inhabitants to an extent that can only be described as "terroristic." Not unreasonably, given its mission, Israel's struggle against the PLO is being waged in such a way as to destroy Palestinian national identity. This goal requires the relevant population to renounce as fully as possible their national aspirations and explains why Israel seemed intent on removing or destroying even the cultural and intellectual archives of the Institute for Palestine Studies in Beirut, as well as the private libraries of noted Palestinian scholars. In this respect, the campaign against the PLO definitely recalled other anti-guerrilla wars, including the war waged by the United States against the National Liberation Front in South Vietnam, and, more distantly, the war waged by the United States against the Filipino independence movement at the end of the last century, as well as the dispossession of the Indian nations, a process spanning the entire history of the American people. It is not surprising that Israel's campaign against the PLO, the first sustained military encounter with its Palestinian adversary (as distinct from doing battle with the armed forces of Arab states), provoked for the first time defections by prominent Israeli military officers who objected to the nature of the mission entrusted to them. To ask military officers, for whatever reasons, to attack women and children, or to bomb hospitals or refugee camps, is to create a political crisis for any society that takes pride in its moral traditions and sense of decency.

As in the case of Vietnam, the problems associated with an encounter between high- and low-technology adversaries were important. The kinds of weaponry at the disposal of the two sides, as well as the tactics and goals being pursued by the high-technology side, gave the war the debasing quality of a slaughter, rather than the quality of military combat. This particular kind of one-sidedness was made dramatically evident during the siege of Beirut, and was, of course, underscored by nightly televised reports. Israeli battlefield commanders could attack targets of their choice in Beirut at will from the air, the sea, or by means of long-range artillery with no Palestinian capability for a military response. The battles then acquired the quality of the Israeli side coolly calculating how much pain to inflict, and where and how. This central characteristic of the military campaign was accentuated by Israel's reliance on precision-guided munitions that could definitely pinpoint targets for destruction, and this contributed even further to the sense of this war as a species of sadism. In these circumstances, then, the vivid portrayal of bombed hospitals, orphanages, and schools contributed to an impression that civilian targets, without any relationship to PLO combat capabilities, were being deliberately struck.

The devastating high-technology attacks on the Palestinian camps, including Shatila and Sabra, which preceded the events of September 16–18, produced heavy casualties, mainly among women and children. This type of "massacre," because it is carried out from a distance, creates a strong sense of dis-ease among those who have objected consistently to waging modern war against a national revolutionary movement of this sort. The massacres merely extended a building sense of outrage, just as the massacre at My Lai confirmed rather than established for moral critics of the American involvement in Vietnam the basic structure and character of the overall war effort.

The Israeli government reacted to news of the massacre in a manner that corresponds with its official posture toward the war and its overall claim of being a humane government. After efforts failed to minimize the extent of the harm, the Israeli leadership tried its best to deny, or at least to minimize, its complicity. To accommodate domestic and international pressures, the Begin government moved to establish a judicial board of inquiry whose mandate was restricted to the circumstances of the September events in the two camps. The massacre was implicitly treated as a grotesque aberration of the war effort, rather than as its continuation by other means. For instance, Sharon in his speech to the Knesset on the massacres used the word "wonderful" to characterize the Israeli war effort up until the Shatila/Sabra killings.

In fact, Israeli high-technology attacks on the camps, including those in southern Lebanon (Ein al Hilweh, Rashidye, Miyemiye), as well as those in the Beirut area (Burj al Brajneh, Shatila, Sabra), inflicted heavy casualties mainly on civilians. The pattern of bombing, as well as the extensive use of cluster and phosphorus bombs, disclosed objectives that could in no normal sense be described as "military."

In these overall circumstances, whether Israeli officials actually planned or anticipated the massacres is almost beside the point. The Israeli entry into West Beirut, and its gathering up of Lebanese militias with a notorious hatred for the Palestinians in the inflamed aftermath of Bashir Gemayel's assassination for the express purpose of entering the camps for purposes, in Begin's words, of "liquidating the terrorists," was the willed creation of a situation in which such an atrocity would occur.[13] What is more, the overall attempt to destroy the camps as places of habitation, which was clearly a major Israeli war objective, was hardly distinguishable in effect from consummating that objective by hand-to-hand, low-technology combat. It is not surprising that Israeli officers in command positions exhibited such a low degree of sensitivity to what was happening in Shatila and Sabra as these events unfolded. From a functional point of view, nothing spectacularly different was taking place.

Israeli leaders and supporters make special moral claims on behalf of Israel relating to its very existence as a state, as well as to its leadership, and to its conduct of military operations. As a result, deviations from acceptable moral standards of behavior by Israel are more salient, and they create a sharper tension between image and reality than most such deviations. Again the parallel with the American experience in Vietnam is clear, as in this case also, believers in America's moral exceptionalism found the disclosures of the actual character of the war deeply disturbing, initially resisting the evidence, then trying to cordon it off as an aberration. This logic of the war was made equally manifest by the American reliance on B-52 planes to devastate the countryside from altitudes so high that the planes were unseen and unheard by the peasants below and by face-to-face killing with small arms in Vietnamese hamlets like My Lai. The full realization of this brutalizing logic of counterinsurgency warfare has been resisted by most Americans to this day, enabling its repetition in new settings with altered doctrines and justifications. The reality of civilian slaughter can be sufficiently blurred as an aberration incidental to acceptable modes of warfare in order to quiet moral anxieties unless it assumes the shape of a deliberate massacre at close quarters. Perhaps more fundamentally, the use of high-technology weaponry tends to numb moral sensibilities to such a degree that only objections on the fringe arise, and these can be discounted as being either hypersensitive or as flowing from political enemies. In effect, objections are dismissed as coming from those who would obscure their partisan politics by displays of moral outrage, a process opposite to the one Tucker primarily addresses.

The case for reassessing the special relationship of the United States with Israel is mainly a case for reassessing the wider relationship between the United States and the Third World in the specific circumstances of the Middle East. It can be argued that recent levels of American economic and military support for Israel are disproportionate to its importance as an ally. It seems, however, like a strange moment to mount such an argument, considering the large geopolitical gains that seem to have accrued to the United States from Israel's recent policies.

More plausibly, yet quite cynically, it might be thought that Israel promoted American interests very significantly by means of its invasion of Lebanon, but that its future role as an ally is more problematic. It could be argued that in light of the controversial character of Israeli aggressiveness and because of its defiant diplomatic style, now is the opportune moment for American foreign policy to redefine its relationship with Israel by adopting a genuinely independent line on Middle East issues, reinforced by shifts in aid policy. Such distancing would now seem more acceptable to domestic public opinion, if undertaken deftly, and would jeopardize neither the gains arising from the dispersal of the PLO or the shift that took place in internal Lebanese politics.

What might such a distancing entail? It would look toward a stable resolution of the Arab-Israeli conflict along lines far closer to the Arab position put forward this September in the Fez proposals than the current expression of American views contained in the Reagan plan. In particular, such an altered approach would involve the acknowledgment of the PLO as the Palestinian negotiator and lend support to the demand for an adequate Palestinian homeland enjoying the status of a state. To resolve the conflict will require more than Israeli-American minimalism, even should the present circumstances of the Palestinians induce a temporary and expedient acceptance of minimal terms. After all, the Germans accepted the Versailles Treaty after World War I. Versailles was an imposed settlement that humiliated the German people and helped create the climate for a re-emergent militarism and for political extremism. Hitler, genocide, and World War II were the results. After World War II a much more moderate "peace" was imposed, and Germany generally has flourished despite its divided state, and the lure of extremism and militarism has been resisted. I would not push such an analogy too far, but I think it is unwise to favor a minimalist solution for Palestinian claims.

To achieve a resolution, the United States would have to back up its call for a freeze on further West Bank settlements with a conditioning of aid, or a portion of aid, on Israeli compliance. Yet, what is in fact opportune by way of such realignments would undoubtedly be effectively presented as "opportunistic" by the strongly entrenched pro-Israeli forces in this country. This prospect, surely anticipated by politicians, would seem to be a formidable obstacle to change, especially as a fairly strong pragmatic argument can be made for continuity in special relationships, including the one with Israel. Israel is the only assuredly pro-Western presence in the region and its help could be needed to oppose the rebirth of revolutionary challenges from the Palestinians or from others, and also to maintain a favorable strategic balance for the United States throughout the Middle East. Thus, I think it likely that the United States might push in the direction of encouraging an internal Israeli return to Labor party leadership, but not push so far as to weaken Israel's position as the dominant military force in the region whose strength includes its special relationship with the United States. This slight shift in the tone of the relationship would not alter its substance—the level of aid, the degree of collaboration between the two countries, the continued support for Israeli minimalism on the core issue of Palestinian rights.

Realignment is also not seen as a justifiable reaction to the Shatila/Sabra massacres, except as a cover for a change of heart toward Israel for other reasons. The massacres were a manifestation of the underlying Israeli resolve to liquidate the terrorists, and there is no discriminating way to do this, as the overall tactics of the Lebanese invasion demonstrated and as Israeli policies on the West Bank since 1967 confirm. These massacres were horrifying in their every aspect, and their occurrence created the circumstances by which the fuller meaning of the suppression of the Palestinian movement became manifested. This is possibly best summarized by a member of the militia forces who responded to a question about why women, even pregnant women, and children were being killed: "Pregnant women give birth to terrorists. Children, when they grow up, will become terrorists."[14] To a certain extent, the realities of Palestinian political consciousness in the refugee camps lend some credence to this statement. In fact, the alienated circumstances of growing up in a refugee camp help to accentuate real Palestinian deprivation, as well as their resolve to carry on the armed struggle. Most PLO fighters grew up in the camps.

Israeli policy, generally operating in a less literal way, reflects its acceptance of this same totalist way of thinking. Israeli leaders justify their willingness to let the militias go into the camps for the acknowledged purpose of liquidating the terrorists, which seems to mean any Palestinian male, whether armed or not. Israeli observers of the events in the camps, shrinking from the full, literal implications of their anti-Palestinian policies, apparently perceived it as a massacre only because women and children were being killed. But to assume that every Palestinian male was "a fighter," much less a "terrorist," just because he was there in Shatila or Sabra with his family is to assume that Palestinians are terrorists per se (that is, to be male and Palestinian is to be a terrorist).

Such Israeli totalism was also demonstrated by the mass removal of Palestinian males from the Sidon and Tyre region. It was even more evident in the attempt to make the camps uninhabitable, especially considering that the Palestinians, including women and children, had no other place to live. And, finally, it was evident in the pattern of attacks on these camps, areas where few fighters were present and where the main victims of attack, as borne out by hospital and death records, were women and children. It was also borne out by the apparently deliberate bombardment of hospital and medical facilities, and by treating the Palestinian (Red Crescent Society) medical staff as if they too were engaged in "terrorism."

The massacres by themselves were only extensions of an underlying Israeli policy, although to be sure it was misguided to undertake them because of their horrifying effects on public opinion. At the same time, the massacres by themselves do not form the basis for a policy shift. Such a basis could only be provided genuinely by reconsidering the US commitment to the military logic of smashing movements of national liberation.

Perhaps, however, policy shifts occur in a messier way than by principled acknowledgment. The renewed pressure on Israel to move toward some kind of Palestinian solution could represent, at least in this context, a repudiation of the politics of massacre. Yet whether this pressure will be meaningfully sustained is unclear, and whether the American conception of the solution is sufficiently broad to transform the underlying Palestinian–Israeli conflict is most uncertain. There is no indication at this time that the United States has renounced its overall counterrevolutionary stance, whether that be exercised against the Palestinians or any other Third World people. Quite the contrary.

Renunciation would imply a new orientation of American leaders toward security. It would imply a willingness to accept the outcome of the self-determination struggles going on around the world, even though the victory of radical nationalist forces may result in added influence for anti-Western elements. Moving toward a non-interventionary diplomacy would also imply a different sense of geopolitical identity. It would imply an understanding that our security is primarily related to the economic, cultural, and political strength of our own society, and that the resources and attitudes required to support and to engage in interventionary diplomacy drains our physical and moral strength, involves us in debilitating over-extensions, and generally makes the survival and well-being of America more problematic. We are nowhere near risking such a reorientation at present. Neither opposition politicians nor public opinion yet perceives the full dangers of a militarized foreign policy, except to a very limited extent, and this change is recent, partial, and without much policy impact as yet as regards the nuclear arms race. The freeze movement expresses, primarily, a public demand "to stop" rather than "to change."

American interests would be served by a renunciation of counter-revolutionary approaches to security everywhere, including in relation to the Palestinians. I believe that Israel would benefit as a society, and would have a better prospect of prospering and surviving, if it too came to affirm the legitimacy of the basic Palestinian claim to have their own homeland, and to allow the realization of this claim in a manner that did not merely shift to a new context the realities of Palestinian humiliation and deprivation. As the world works, the Palestinians need a homeland that functions as a state, they need their own chosen leaders (that is, the PLO), and they need land that is not penetrated by Israeli settlements (even at present Israel maintains more than a hundred settlements in the occupied territories—many of them little more than armed bases—exercises direct ownership over 27 percent of the West Bank, and has access to 65 percent of all West Bank land; besides, it proposes almost doubling the number of settlements and increasing to 100,000 from the current 25,000 the number of Israeli settlers by 1987). In effect, a reversal of policy is required, a reversal that can come about only through the acceptance of a different vision of Israeli security as well as of its character as a nation. The implementation of such a reversal, if the political will existed, would not be so difficult, and would involve the resettlement of some 25,000 Israelis. This is a minor undertaking in the context of a new peace process. Because the West Bank (plus Gaza) is already densely populated and resource-poor, it would also be desirable if Jordan would dedicate some additional land to the Palestinian homeland, possibly underutilized portions of the East Bank. Jordan, too, has a strong interest (centering on its majority Palestinian population) in non-minimalism as the soundest basis for long-term peace and security.

The predominant Machiavellian mindset is almost certain to remain stuck in the mires of dispossession, violence, and, ultimately, massacre. Only a different conception of security and self-esteem can yield new policies. This process can happen in the United States without occurring in Israel. It could occur in Israel without taking place here. It could even occur in both countries simultaneously. It is not likely to occur by degrees, but rather in some abrupt fashion. The redesign of fundamental policy, premised on an altered image of interests and aspirations, does not appear likely in either country as matters stand, but for the first time in many decades it seems at least possible to bring such a drastic perspective into the debate.

In these circumstances, those who purport to censure critics of Israel or of the Israeli–American relationship are locked into a dogmatic, authoritarian stance, which includes a refusal to distinguish between the well-being of Israel as people and nation and the wisdom and acceptability of the policies pursued by a particular Israeli government or set of leaders. If the nature of the Israeli–American relationship is adverse to the well-being of both countries, as this is best understood, then it would be damaging to withhold criticism. "Discipline" does not mean refraining from criticism, but rather making it persuasive, forceful, and constructive. To characterize it as "anti-Semitic," "anti-American," or "anti-Western" is merely to bully those who advocate changes of direction.

At the same time, to the extent that critics were half-hearted or incoherent in their analyses or prescriptions, and yet relied upon a heavy moralizing rhetoric, it is fair to point these discrepancies out, as Podhoretz effectively does, and even to raise certain suspicions about a secret agenda that might include anti-Jewish sentiments. Even Novick has a point when he condemns those who criticize Israel about its role in the massacre or some other such discrete aspect of Israeli policy because they inevitably weaken its overall anti-PLO, anti-Palestinian enterprise. To the extent Israeli security is based on that enterprise, criticism of its tactics should be kept confidential and out of the media, because the issue is mainly one of public relations and technique. Of course, Podhoretz and Novick would not welcome an endorsement along these lines, but it seems to me implicit in their advocacy.

A middle position, apparently encompassing such influential supporters of Israel as Michael Walzer and Irving Howe, is to try to reconcile their moral consciousness with the revealed truths of the Lebanon war. This reconciliation comes down to a repudiation of the Begin/Sharon approach, and a conviction that the supposed moderateness of the Ben Gurion/Meir tradition of Labor leadership is the answer. Unlike the unconditional apologists, holders of such a position draw a sharp distinction between Israel as a nation (which they passionately support) and Israel as a state represented by a particular government (which they may or may not support). Here, the publication of criticism is essential, as what is being attempted is to exert sufficient pressure to realign Israeli domestic politics, and even outside criticism may be necessary or even essential to do this if the situation grows serious enough. These critics (and possibly all genuine critics) are concerned about the double effect of such a public show, as it inevitably also strengthens those anti-Israeli elements that are anti-Semitic in principal motivation.

At the same time, the evident assessment of these intermediate voices is that "the soul of Israel," in Howe's phrase, depends on a public repudiation of the Begin/Sharon direction, and that signs of Jewish acquiescence in it will otherwise give rise to an even more intense anti-Semitism.[15] And, indeed, the outbursts of violence against Jews in Europe seemed to be responsive to the siege of Beirut and to the overtness of the Israeli connection with the massacres. This position, perceived and presented as a "moderate," "humane," or "intermediate" stance is, from my point of view, extremist. It accepts as legitimate the politics associated with the dispossession of the Palestinians and embraces the fiction that the PLO is not the appropriate representative of the national movement. At best, it looks toward a Versailles-like peace treaty with the Palestinians, that is, a minimalist "homeland' created in such a way as to assure a perpetuation of Israeli hegemony.

I see no conflict between the well-being of Israel and the realization of national rights for the Palestinians. As such, it would be "hostile" to withhold criticism, although it is necessary to understand that the proposed reorientation of security enjoys scant current support in the United States or Israel.

Conclusion

The Israeli-American special relationship exemplifies mainstream geopolitics. Within this framework, the relationship has been, on balance, validated by the Israeli invasion of Lebanon, and it is the very excesses of Israeli policy that have, at least for now, produced a favorable set of results for the United States, not only in the region, but beyond. Criticism within this framework, except for detail and style, is not warranted, and tends to be vulnerable to the sort of counter-statements coherently, if acidly, made by Tucker and Podhoretz.

In this essay, I have tried to develop a line critical of the framework itself that rests on a different conception of security, one that repudiates the need for either Israel or the United States to use their military power to smash national movements in the Third World, of which the Palestinian movement is a prime case, but only one instance. Opposition to American support for Israeli policies, then, rests on many of the same pragmatic and normative grounds that pertained to the opposition to American involvement in Vietnam. The main difference, of course, is that Israel is an ultra-efficient power center with an excellent prospect of prevailing for years to come. But to prevail in this manner is to assure the militarization of its domestic life, the diversion of needed resources from its economic development, and to further a rapid regional arms race that will likely eventuate in an Islamic bomb, and then will perpetuate an Israeli-Islamic or Israeli-Arab regional nuclear arms race, and possibly, of course, an actual test of wills and capabilities.

Changing the American relationship with Israel in any significant respect is likely to depend on changing fundamental American attitudes toward Third World foreign policy and its Middle East applications. Minor shifts in tone and style are the most that can be anticipated, and these do not touch closely the core issues. The prospect of the withdrawal of American support would certainly have the effect of opening the debate in Israel and would create greater "space" for approaches that seek to rely on non-military conceptions of stabilization and security. Of course, it is probable that an anticipation of an American shift would, at first, intensify

Israeli militarism and provoke an even greater polarization of opinion in domestic Israeli politics, but there seems no other path that leads away from the dead-end of inflicting crushing defeats of one sort or another on the Palestinians and their political movements, a futile course as a solution. The vast Arab-Islamic hinterland will always allow the Palestinians to regroup and mount a new challenge based on altered power configurations. It is too early to assess the future, but Palestinian future prospects might be soon revived by a breakdown of Israeli-Egyptian relations, a development that could once more create the terrible sense in Israel of being beleaguered, dependent on US support, and doomed to a national destiny of permanent warfare.

Let us hope that some of these considerations begin to create new awareness in both Israel and the United States. Otherwise, the best one can reasonably expect is further bloody encounters.

Iran

❧

Chapter Twelve

THE NEW YORK TIMES TRILOGY

"Trusting Khomeini," by Richard Falk

Part of the confusion in America about Iran's social revolution involves Ayatollah Ruholla Khomeini. More even than any third-world leader, he has been depicted in a manner calculated to frighten.

President Carter and Zbigniew Brzezinski have until very recently associated him with religious fanaticism. The news media have defamed him in many ways, associating him with efforts to turn the clock back 1,300 years, with virulent anti-Semitism, and with a new political disorder, "theoretical fascism," about to be set loose on the world. About the best he had fared has been to be called (by *Newsweek*) "Iran's Mystery Man."

The historical record of revolutionary zeal's degenerating into excess is such as to temper enthusiasm about Iran's future. Nevertheless, there are hopeful signs, including the character and role of Ayatollah Khomeini.

An early test of his prospects is being posed by the outbreaks of violence in Tehran and elsewhere in the country. Some chaos of this stage of the revolutionary conflict was virtually inevitable, given the cleavages and climate of intensity in Iran. It is uncertain that Ayatollah Khomeini can control the extreme left or even those segments of his own followers who bear arms. What happens in the next few days is likely to determine both whether the movement's largely non-violent record will be spoiled further and whether a new political order can be successfully brought into existence.

In recent months, before his triumphant return to Tehran, the Ayatollah gave numerous reassurances to non-Moslem communities in Iran. He told Jewish community leaders that it would be tragedy if many of 80,000 Jews left the country. Of course, this view is qualified by his hostility to Israel because of its support of the Shah and its failure to resolve the Palestinian question.

He has also indicated that the non-religious left will be free to express its views in an Islamic republic and to participate in political life, provided

This exchange of articles appeared in the New York Times *on the following dates: Falk's "Trusting Khomeini," 16 February 1979: A27; Anthony Lewis's "Trusting in Illusions," 12 March 1979; and Falk's "A Balance of Hopeful Signs," 28 March 1979: A24.*

only that it does not "commit treason against the country" by establishing foreign connections, a lightly veiled reference to anxiety about Soviet interference. What the left does in coming days will likely indicate whether it will be seen as treasonous.

To suppose that Ayatollah Khomeini is dissembling seems almost beyond belief. His political style is to express his real views defiantly and without apology, regardless of consequences. He has little incentive suddenly to become devious for the sake of American public opinion. Thus, the depiction of him as fanatical, reactionary, and the bearer of crude prejudices seems certainly and happily false. What is also encouraging of close advisers is uniformly composed of moderate, progressive individuals. For another thing, the key appointees to the provisional government include Mehdi Bazargan, the Prime Minister, Karim Sanjabi, leader of the National Front Political federation, and Daryoush Farouhar, deputy leader of the National Front; they are widely respected in Iran outside religious circles, share a notable record of concern for human rights, and seem eager to achieve economic development that results in a modern society oriented on satisfying the whole population's basic needs.

In the political background, of course, is a strong active sense of deference to the views and judgment of Ayatollah Khomeini. This is not a matter of coercion or even agreement but of the special character of the movement. It is inconceivable, for instance, for some one as devout as Mr. Bazargan to govern without manifesting naturally and without any compulsion, acute sensitivity to the values of Shiite Islam, including responses to Ayatollah Khomeini's views. Yet, as every religious leader is quick to underscore, the Shiite tradition is flexible in its approach to the Koran and evolves interpretations that correspond to the changing needs and experience of the people. What is distinctive, perhaps is its concern with resisting oppression and promoting social justice.

As if to contrast his vision with that of the Shah's rule, Ayatollah Khomeini said recently, in France, that in any well governed society "the ruler does not live very differently from the ordinary person." For him to be religious is to struggle for these political goals, yet the religious leader's role is to inspire politics, not to govern. Hence, it is widely expected that he will soon go to the holy city of Qum, at a remove from the daily exercise of power. There he will function as a guide or, if necessary, as a critic of the republic.

In looking to the future, Ayatollah Khomeini has spoken of his hopes to show the world what a genuine Islamic government can do on behalf of its people. He has made clear frequently that he scorns what he considers to be so-called Islamic governments in Saudi Arabia, Libya, and Pakistan.

Despite the turbulence, many non-religious Iranians talk of this period as "Islam's finest hour." Having created a new model of popular revolution based, for the most part, on non-violent tactics, Iran may yet provide us with a desperately needed model of humane governance for a third-world country. If this is true, then indeed the exotic Ayatollah may yet convince the world that "politics is the opiate of the people."

A Reply from Anthony Lewis: "Trusting in Illusions"

Shortly before Ayatollah Khomeini returned to Iran, he was visited in Paris by an American group that included Ramsey Clark, the former Attorney General, and Richard Falk, Professor of International Law at Princeton. The Americans came away from the meeting with reassuring words about the Ayatollah's moderation and fairness.

"The depiction of him as fanatical reactionary and the bearer of crude prejudices seems certainly and happily false," Professor Falk wrote in the *New York Times*. He said that picture of Khomeini had been drawn in the United States in a calculated attempt to frighten people.

The American press had "defamed" Khomeini, Professor Falk wrote, attributing to him "efforts to turn the clock back 1,300 years," and to establish a "theocratic fascism." History did show the possibility of revolutionary zeal "degenerating into excess," Professor Falk said, but in Iran there were "hopeful signs" to the contrary, "including the character and role of Ayatollah Khomeini."

"What is also encouraging," he added, "is that his entourage of close advisers is uniformly composed of moderate, progressive individuals."

In this uncertain world any of us who makes firm predictions may be embarrassed: newspaper columnists included. But the description of Ayatollah Khomeini and the shadowy figures around him as "moderate" and "progressive" in the Western sense of those words, has turned out to be outstandingly silly.

Since taking power Ayatollah Khomeini has set out without equivocation or disguise to turn the clock back and give Iran a theocratic regime. He has called, for example, for a dismantling of "all European criteria built in to the judicial system." Among other things, then, there should be no appeals in civil or criminal cases:"Every hearing must end in a final, absolute decision in a single phase."

Several generals and other charged with resisting the revolution have been executed after secret trials, under circumstances unknown even to the new government. Religious courts set up outside the framework of the civil law have sentenced people to flagellation for such things as drinking liquor.

Ayatollah Khomeini has also directed a sweeping rollback of rights won by women in recent years, including the right to divorce. He has questioned a 1975 law restricting polygamy. He has ordered women to be "properly dressed," a phrase widely taken to mean the veil.

Women have been marching in protest against the turn of events. And according to an account by Youssef M. Ibrahim of the *New York Times,* other Iranians are alarmed—lawyers, civil libertarians, oil workers, the new white-collar class. An editor wrote "The people did not rise and make supreme sacrifices in order to revert to another type of oppression."

Then there is the case of Khomeini's Prime Minister, Mehdi Bazargan. Professor Falk wrote—last January—that Mr. Bazaragan, who had a "notable record of concern for human rights," also had "a strong active sense of deference to the views and judgment of Ayatollah Khomeini." This was "not a matter of coercion," he said, but of natural "sensitivity to the values of Shiite Islam, including responsiveness of Ayatollah Khomeini's views."

Mr. Bazargan has in fact found his relationship with Ayatollah Khomeini so difficult that he has twice threatened to resign. He has been distressed at learning of executions only after the event. He has said of the "committee of sides" around Khomeini: "They persecute people, they arrest people, they issue orders, they oppose us, they are against our appointments. Our day has been turned into night."

None of this should have been any great surprise. Ayatollah Khomeini had put his views on the record with unusual forthrightness. He said he wanted Iran to be governed strictly by the laws of Islam and he meant it.

Why, then, did Professor Falk expect anything different or tell us to? I think he was carried away by opposition to the Shah. He had long argued correctly that the Shah was a tyrant who had lost the support of his people. In urging the end of US backing for him, Professor Falk was led to picture the alternative—the Ayatollah—as congenial to American liberal opinion.

To think that way is to forget a lesson of Vietnam. We went wrong there in large part because we tried to apply American ideas, without understanding a very different culture. It was just as distorted to analyze the fundamentally Islamic Revolution in Iran in Western terms.

Professor Falk was one of those who criticized American support of a corrupt regime in Vietnam. But the point was not that the alternative was a government of Western liberals. It was that American intervention was fruitless and destructive.

The illusion of American omnipotence did terrible damage before it ended Vietnam. But illusions of all kinds are dangerous in world politics. No one should have expected Iran under Ayatollah Khomeini to be comfortably liberal—or stable.

Falk's Reply: "In Iran, a 'Balance of Hopeful Signs'"

In his March 12 column, "Trusting in Illusions," Anthony Lewis attributes a position to me that I scarcely recognize and then proceeds to demolition.

It was never my view that Ayatollah Khomeini would (or should) strive for a "comfortably liberal" republic. How irrelevant it is to conceive of this singular revolution in such provincial terms. The mistake, I think, is that Mr. Lewis believes inwardly that wherever Anglo-American jurisprudence is denied or absent there lurks darkest evil.

I stand by my earlier view, despite some troublesome developments, that, given the situation and the past, a balance of hopeful signs remains present in Iran. Every revolution goes through a period of vengeful retribution. This was true even for the American revolution. In Iran, where state crimes against the people were so extreme and massive in extend during the Shah's long reign, the popular demand for retribution is especially intense. And with weapons so widely dispersed, it was critical for the authorities to act quickly and decisively.

Casting aside the human rights of anyone accused of crime is not a pretty spectacle, but neither is a rampage of private vengeance, the likely alternative. If this phase of retribution can be brought to an end soon and its application generally confined to those prominently associated with the worst atrocities of the Pahlavi period, then we may still conclude that violence has been minimized and that Khomeini's movement has weathered the attributive storm as well as any major revolution.

For those who were so exquisitely silent for decades while thousands perished in jails, before firing squads, and through police and army violence in the streets, this sudden solicitude for human rights in Iran seems most strange. Especially strange given the continuing routine of abuse in Saudi Arabia, Pakistan, Egypt, indeed throughout the region. To single out Iran for criticism at this point is to lend support to that fashionable falsehood embraced by Mr. Lewis, that what has happened in Iran is the replacement of one tyranny by another.

Of course, the Iranian Revolution is far from over, as the mass demonstrations of the women's movement and the left make evident. Yet if these struggles can go on without producing bloodshed or repression, then the cause of popular democracy will have taken a giant step forward since Pahlavi times. Given our complicity in the past sufferings of the Iranian people, it seems proper, and even prudent, to defer judgment.

Chapter Thirteen

INTERNATIONAL LAW & THE US RESPONSE
TO THE IRANIAN REVOLUTION

In truth, I have been so concerned about the central features of the Iranian Revolution and the United States' response to it, that I have hitherto paid little attention to its various legal implications. Although this may be a commentary on the limited relevance of international law to such political turbulence, it is probably more a personal matter of having become marginally involved with the more dramatic aspects of the encounter between the United States and Iran.

I think that the question whether at this historical moment law can play a positive part in a world of change, ferment, and chaos is an especially crucial issue for Americans to address. I think we have failed to grasp the degree to which the United States is currently viewed by the rest of the world as being part of the problem of world order rather than of its solution. At the same time, we have a fantastic reservoir of self-righteous moralism, a moralism that seems directed at telling others how to solve the problem.

President Carter's human rights diplomacy is only the most recent example of a major American foreign policy initiative premised on the notions that human rights are a good and necessary thing for other societies; that human rights have to do only with foreign policy; and that somehow or other we Americans have reached a domestic level of political and moral development that allows us to export for the benefit of others our societal achievements under the label of human rights. This kind of imperial outlook, to put it provocatively, is not only short-sighted; it also prevents our hearing much of what is happening in the rest of the world.

Adlai Stevenson a long time ago said that the one item of technology most needed by the United States is a hearing aid. There is an East European joke about Stalinist architecture that conveys the same idea: One of the things that Stalin imposed on the countries of East Europe was to insist that each of them have an enormous ugly building housing the Ministry of Culture right in the middle of each capital city. The joke is that

Originally part of the 1980 David Stoffer Lectures.

two people are talking, it could be anywhere—Warsaw, for example—and one asks the other, "Where do you get the most beautiful view in Warsaw?" The other replies, "From the top of the Ministry of Culture, of course." "Why?" "Because that's the only place in Warsaw you can't see the Ministry of Culture." We have a Ministry of Culture view of the rest of the world, especially of the Third World, and correcting the myopia of that view is a crucial precondition, in my judgment, for allowing international law to perform in a positive way in the world.

There is a very quick answer to the question of what role international law can play, but it is an uncongenial answer for the short run, given the consensus that exists in this country. The best answer is to allow international law to become an instrument for accommodating the flow of history at this particular time. (This, of course, requires renouncing the current use of international law as an instrument that basically tries to inhibit that flow.) And what is the strongest element of the flow of history? It is the continuing process of national, economic, political, and cultural self-assertion going on throughout the world and particularly in the countries of Asia, Africa, and Latin America. This self-assertion is more extensive than the quest for full independence that we have come to associate with the decolonization movement. It centers upon the achievement of economic and cultural autonomy. The struggle to achieve economic and cultural autonomy waged against various forms of postcolonial domination often involves an encounter with Western interests and values. This encounter is the essence of what has made the Iranian Revolution problematic for the United States government since the outset.

The Iranian Revolution was waged against the postcolonial, yet still imperial, structures of economic and cultural domination; United States resistance to that struggle was expressed through our support of the Shah and all he stood for. Henry Kissinger reveals much along these lines in the six pages devoted to Iran in his memoirs. He refers to the Shah as a gentle human being and calls him "that rarest of things, an unconditional ally."

Kissinger makes such comments in reference to a leader in a country blessed with abundant natural resources, especially in the form of oil and gas, who yet managed in the end to alienate 98 or 99 percent of his own population. No revolution in history has obtained such nearly total mass support from all social classes. Every other revolution has split the population, with some important segments defending the old order. In Iran there was such an overwhelming popular mandate for the revolution against the Pahlavi dynasty that the struggle could rely upon nonviolent tactics until a final weekend of armed conflict in February 1979. These tactics were practicable because, in the end, even the military forces were unwilling to fight on behalf of the regime and continue to shoot their unarmed brothers and sisters, as had been done throughout 1978. Moreover, there was no support among Iranians for a governing process that had systematically used torture against its suspected opponents, including many children of the middle classes. The societal effect of such repression was to estrange even those elements of society with vested interests in the status quo. The Shah's regime had managed to stimulate an enormous flow of money into the country in a way that benefited only a tiny minority of the social order, leaving the great mass of people in a rage. The population knew that much money was flowing in, and they also knew that their lives were generally getting worse, not better.

The flow of history (a shorthand label for patterns of development) must be seen as going along with these kinds of movements for self-determination, which are incipient throughout the Third World. And yet the United States continues to build its foreign policy around isolated elites that desperately rely on their military prowess to resist that flow. And so we are perceived around the world—as is the Soviet Union, increasingly—as a reactionary force in the fundamental sense of using our military power to reverse this flow of history in support of the reactionary political and cultural forces that exist within a foreign society.

To place this controversial point in the present context, we can see that it is impossible to adjust to the flow of history in the Middle East generally and yet simultaneously pursue a foreign policy hostile to the Palestinian Liberation Organization. It is impossible because the PLO, for better or worse, represents the agent—the symbolic agent—of the most sacred political cause in that region. Even leaders as generally reactionary as King Hussein and the Saudi Arabian royal family, as much as they perceive the PLO as a threat to their stability, are forced for the sake of their own fragile legitimacy to affirm the right of the PLO to represent the Palestinian cause. I mention this aspect of the situation to underscore the increasingly isolated diplomatic position of the United States in the world. When a powerful country is as isolated diplomatically as we are becoming in relation to controversial international issues, it tends to increase its reliance on military power for the pursuit of national interests. We are being forced onto a tremendously dangerous terrain of militarism in the nuclear age; this is a terrain in the Middle East setting where vital economic interests are at stake and where, at some point, a mixture of Soviet and American miscalculations could very easily produce a situation that leads to general war. In this regional setting, then, it is not only a matter of adjusting to the flow of history, but also a matter of averting catastrophe.

Finally, on the kind of role international law can play at this time, I would say that it has to be a role shaped as much by values as by interests; it has to be sensitive to cultural and religious configurations as well as to the orientation of the elites and of those who control the formal governing process in foreign societies. Building an American foreign policy around our "friends," however oppressive and reactionary they are, is a recipe for both moral and political disaster. It compels our foreign policy to contradict hallowed traditions of our domestic heritage: those of supporting the right of people to control their own economic and cultural and political destiny.

The last preliminary issue that I would raise is the meaning of being "objective" in relation to the role of law in a crisis such as exists in US-Iranian relations. Most of us are so caught up in the reality of our national and socio-economic identities that we inevitably view the rest of the world, and we view a situation like the one in Iran, through the partisan perspective that our government propounds and our media reinforces. Objectivity in an interdependent world requires us to free ourselves as much as possible from our state and class identities when we grapple with questions of international conflict. In other words, these issues of respective rights in international conflict should look the same whether one is looking at them from Newark, Copenhagen, Tokyo, or New Delhi. That is to say, there should not be one set of answers for each place that merely disguises in legal jargon subjective preferences that, with respect to international legal analysis, depend upon adding a planetary identity to the more traditional loyalties, including loyalty to nation and state. These traditional loyalties range from one's individual identity, to family, to neighborhood, and to country. All those ties are fine as aspects of a total conception of loyalty. But if one is trying to understand complex issues from an adequate world order perspective, then one must try, it seems to me, to transcend the particularity of time and space, and to look at a given situation as nearly as possible from what I view as an objective standpoint. This objectivity does not mean that one is not concerned with values. It represents, in the main, an effort to avoid interpreting facts and norms in a self-serving way.

From this basis, I would like to say a few things about the role of international law and its relevance to the Iranian crisis. There is an ironic element about this current preoccupation with the Americans held hostage in Iran since November 1979. These Iranian developments are clearly of great moment for most Americans. It has even been an occasion for celebration by international lawyers because for the first time in a long while, our leaders have taken international law seriously in a major international crisis. As we know, there is nothing worse, especially for lawyers, than being ignored. Therefore, the juridical silver lining of the Iranian crisis consists in the readiness of even the President of the United States to describe American policy toward Iran by frequent reference to our national rights under international law. This relevance of international law has not generally been acknowledged by our leaders. We must ask, why is it true now? Why, in this crisis, do we find Jimmy Carter, in his first major speech concerning the hostages, mentioning international law no fewer than nine times?

For perspective, it might be helpful to recall the discussion of the relevance of international law after the Cuban missile crisis in 1962. Shortly after those momentous events, there was a famous meeting of the American Society of International Law, at which Dean Acheson, then a distinguished former secretary of state, and other jurists were talking about the relevance of international law to that crisis. Acheson began his remarks with this elegant little anecdote: "To talk of the legal aspects of the Cuban incident reminds me of the story of the women discussing the quiz program scandals. One said that she felt the scandals presented serious moral issues. The other answered, 'And I always say that moral issues are more important than real issues.'"[1] Acheson's point, of course, was that legal issues are not real issues when the sovereignty of the United States is at stake.

Acheson's views upset some of the assembled international lawyers, but most of them generally accepted this scornful attitude as an amusingly realistic way of looking at the relevance of international law. Most of the books about the Cuban missile crisis contain not a single reference to international law. The only people who took international law seriously in reference to the crisis were a few international lawyers, particularly those who were involved in making policy within the government, such as Abram Chayes, who was legal advisor during the crisis.

Let me give you another example. The legal advisor during the United States' intervention in the Dominican Republic in 1965, Leonard Meeker, was bold enough to develop in public an international law justification for that intervention. He said with reference to the Dominican circumstances that we must not become trapped by what he called "a fundamentalist view" of international law. Rather, our view should be flexible enough to serve the realistic needs of United States foreign policy in a period of great challenge and crisis in the world.[2] A country possessing both military power and an individual trained in a good law school could always find a nonfundamentalist way to justify in legal language any foreign policy initiative whatsoever. In the hands of the powerful, in other words, international law is either dismissed with a flick of the wrist (Acheson) or manipulated to cloak dubious exercises of state power (Meeker).

Let me resume now my inquiry into why, in this crisis, the United States leadership felt that international law was a good thing. Jimmy Carter is no more law-oriented than other recent American leaders. His motivations have to be understood as political in the broad sense. After the embassy seizure, the Carter administration had no high cards to play that weren't manifestly self-destructive. There was no Entebbe option. That is, there was no way to use military force so as to achieve a solution that would reflect the relative power of the two countries.

Second, international law as written down in the books seems to be quite helpful for Washington. On the main issues, it supported the United States's contentions. For example, there was no question that diplomatic personnel and premises are, by virtue of the Vienna Convention on Diplomatic Relations, entitled to unconditionally immune treatment. Therefore, to the extent that the Iranian government endorsed the seizure of the embassy and hostages, it seemed to commit a clear violation of international law.

Third, international law gave little aid and comfort to the Iranian grievances. It seemed to confirm that the United States possessed the discretion to admit the Shah and, especially in the absence of an extradition treaty, to allow him to remain in the United States indefinitely. Even if an extradition treaty had existed, it is very unlikely that the kinds of charges that have been generally alleged against him would constitute extraditable crimes. Here, then, was a situation in which international law was as clearly as possible on our side in a dispute where the practical constraints discouraged the use of military power.

The fourth favorable factor in this situation was that the existing world institutional structures, the International Court of Justice and the United Nations, seemed available to endorse the legal correctness of the United States' position, thereby adding weight to the American demand that Iran release the hostages unconditionally. Indeed, the International Court of Justice and the Security Council did both unanimously confirm the main

United States claim. Although this juridical support has not led to the release of the hostages, it built some domestic and international support for recourse to a more coercive approach. Therefore, the American threat to impose economic sanctions on Iran was made to rest on a solid foundation of legal right, given the prior recourse to the Court and the Security Council. Furthermore, since nothing else could be done, making use of these legal procedures in this situation seemed to reduce domestic pressure on Washington to take more drastic action even if self-destructive. So, one of the contributions of international law in this setting has been to make it appear that the Carter administration, that is, the political leadership in this country, was doing something tangible on behalf of the hostages in a context where in truth there was not much that could be done.

Since military power was not available and the Iranian government was not impressed by our legal arguments, no easy solution has been forthcoming. One avenue of approach was to use the international institutional framework embodied in the United Nations for mutual settlement. This framework, however, was largely invalidated for this purpose by the United States' efforts to secure United Nations support for its claims.

Part of the puzzle for the Carter people all along has been how to give something away without seeming to do so. In other words, how does one acknowledge the claims of the Iranians while resisting the accusation of critics at home, especially in an election year, that blackmail has prevailed? That is the puzzle. You cannot get the hostages out without doing something to satisfy Iran's grievances against the United States. And yet it is difficult to do something for Iran without committing political suicide back here. That is one of the reasons why the hostages have been held so long (although there are other reasons, especially internal Iranian political struggles). It is easier to be critical than wise. If one were trying to devise a policy that would keep the hostages in the embassy as long as possible, but unharmed, it would probably resemble the policy we have been pursuing. The problem could be much worse. We could be pursuing a policy that would result in harm to the hostages. But we are neither prepared nor able to pursue a policy of getting the hostages released, and nothing is more likely to keep them there longer than the sanctions. Everyone knows that, and yet we proceed along the sanctions route.

So one asks why impose sanctions, if everybody knows it will result in the hostages being kept longer. Sanctions are not going to break Iran's will (and everybody knows that too)—so why? The fundamental answer relates to what I would call bureaucratic momentum. Once a country like the United States has claimed to be legally right, it is politically inhibited from achieving its goals by making concessions. The other side's refusal must be met with some kind of force. In this case, the next step of sanctions is not what Washington wants. Whatever else, virtually no one expects Iran to release the hostages because it is being threatened with deprivations of one sort or another. Ayatollah Khomeini is a leader renowned for his refusal to back down under pressure. His achievements are associated with exactly the opposite disposition, to persevere on a course once charted, however great the odds or risks. At this stage, then, it seems that pursuing the legal path further is counterproductive from the point of view of achieving a favorable outcome.

The way in which international law has been used in this crisis has contributed to an inappropriate escalatory logic. Establishing the rightness of one's legal case inhibits making the sort of concessions required in this instance to obtain conflict resolution. It was one thing to have legal claims endorsed, but it was quite another matter to take this endorsement too seriously, for the consequent momentum was inconsistent with the primary objective. At the same time, to have recourse to legal procedures and then ignore their outcomes is to reinforce popular skepticism about international law.

It has not been, in this connection, worthwhile to secure endorsement by the United Nations of the United States' legal position. To Iranian eyes, this endorsement represented an invalidation of the United Nations as a framework for conflict resolution. They perceived the United Nations response as one-sided: the UN addressed the seizure of the hostages but did not look at either the questions of the Shah's crimes against the Iranian people or the complicity of the United States in subverting the constitutional order of Iran back in 1953. Therefore, in the early stages of the encounter, Khomeini and the revolutionary leadership in Iran withdrew authority from their representatives to allow the United Nations to participate seriously in the resolution of the conflict. The Iranian position did soften somewhat later when a United Nations commission of inquiry was formed to report upon Iranian grievances.

A final criticism of the way international law has been used in this crisis involves the Canadian role in hiding and spiriting out of Iran six Americans who escaped to the Canadian embassy on the day of the seizure. People laugh, and with some justification, when Iranian Foreign Minister Sadegh Ghotbzadeh says that Canada shall pay for this transgression. Part of his contention turns on Canada's having forged visas and passports to arrange the exit of the Americans from Iran. There is a clear violation and abuse of diplomatic prerogatives. Its celebration in the United States demonstrates that "international law" is treated as irrelevant the moment it interferes with our own freedom of action.

The basic perception here is that the United States has used international law seriously and intelligently in this crisis, but this does not indicate that we are moving toward a law-oriented world system. It merely tells us that when military power is unavailable, law can, to some extent, fill a political vacuum that might otherwise exist. It is clear that to have an effective international legal order will require several types of global reform. One approach would be by way of improved capabilities for enforcement. But suppose the determination by the International Court of Justice were enforced in this instance. To take law seriously in this way is not necessarily what we want. It would lead almost certainly to the killing of the hostages and to the destruction of the oil fields; it would be costly in geopolitical terms. It would mean economic disaster for Western Europe and Japan, and it might easily lead to general war. In short, we do not want such enforcement of the mechanisms imposed on a world system dominated by separate sovereign states.

One could well argue that an international mechanism for investigating crimes of state would be useful. It would have been helpful, at the time the crisis originated, to have had an existing procedure in place that would have allowed the United Nations to receive immediately and automatically all allegations concerning the Shah's crimes of state. There would have been no semblance of an opportunistic bargain for the hostages struck under the pressure of circumstances. Rather, this mechanism could have provided a meaningful forum for people who feel that they have been victims of state crime. I think there is some feeling, in the United Nations at least, that this is a sound idea and that there is a need for such a mechanism. But my guess is that its creation is not likely in the years ahead because there are too many skeletons in too many governmental closets. If you create a mechanism for dealing with the Shah, what do you do about Cambodia, the Soviet Union, Saudi Arabia, and at least 117 other consistent violators of human rights in the world? Where do you logically draw the line? Which again suggests that there is little to be done, either practically or morally, in a world order system that is generally dependent on the authority of governments at the state level. Apparently, crime can be dealt with by international action when it is marginal to the established social order, but if it exists at the core, then it is very difficult to mobilize any effective means against it. There is no institutional foundation for imposing normative authority. Therefore one must understand that the core of this world order system is corrupted by the commission of massive violations of human rights by the overwhelming majority of governments. This reality inevitably stymies efforts to strengthen present international arrangements on behalf of the aggrieved peoples of the world.

Finally, it is necessary to face the fact that this kind of political and moral paralysis emphasizes the inadequacy of the present world order system. This is a system that is virtually without institutional means and wholly lacking in both moral authority and political procedure: it is a hopeless structure for dealing with the problems presented by the US-Iran encounter. I think many people have acknowledged this individually, but it is not likely to be acknowledged by the responsible political world leaders because they see no alternative to the state system of which, not incidentally, they, as actors on the world stage, are beneficiaries.

It has been said that the United Nations is the largest pressure group in the world for diplomatic immunity; one of the few things all governments have in common is their interest in upholding, under most conditions, each other's prerogatives. In this context too, I think it is unlikely that the difficulties in Iran will result in a positive learning experience. Furthermore, and more fundamentally, we now face the darker side of legal clarity in these circumstances. What sort of clarity is it that does not acknowledge the contrary side of an argument—that does not acknowledge the side of the argument that says: "Yes, diplomats should be secure and immune, and diplomatic premises must be protected; but what about the constitutional order of the states in which they operate?" How can we say that a system deserves respect if it permits the use of a foreign embassy for the purpose of undermining the constitutional order of a state? One does not need to know much about Iranian history to know that the American embassy in Tehran was the center of the CIA plot in 1953 that has been widely acknowledged and documented in recent years. It was this plot that brought the Shah back to power in defiance of the constitutional process of Iran; American embassy personnel helped train the Iranian secret police. The question must be asked, why is the structure of international law so solicitous of the rights of diplomats and so indifferent to the rights of people? What is the real explanation of this double standard?

The explanation is, of course, political: the powerful are better protected from the weak than vice versa. There is no way Iran can intervene significantly in the constitutional processes of the United States. The interfering of the powerful in the affairs of the weak is a consistent aspect of international relations that throughout history has provided the powerful with two sets of interests: they want strict rules covering their immunities and loose rules governing their rights to intervene.

Why should the weak acquiesce? Why should they accord this system legitimacy at a time when the flow of history suggests that all states should be treated as genuinely independent and equal? There is a system of at least formal equality, which suggests in the altered circumstances of the present that concerns be treated more symmetrically than in the past.

Similarly, why is extradition more readily available for "terrorists" who commit anti-state crimes—hijacking a plane, for example—but unavailable for heads of state who commit arbitrary executions and torture thousands? Why is there no symmetry between the law regarding hijackers and the law pertaining to tyrants? Again, we face a situation in which the governments of the world have a common interest both in developing fairly strong anti-terrorist laws (with some exceptions) and in retaining discretion to grant asylum to state criminals. These criminals are protected as though they were prisoners of conscience. Originally, the idea of diplomatic asylum was intended to protect prisoners of conscience from persecution in their country of origin. Now it has been extended to protect those who engage in the most brutal and repressive denials of conscience, helping such miscreants escape prosecution and punishment. And, perhaps most perniciously of all, it shields discredited leaders from any procedures of account developed on behalf of the people they governed abusively.

It is evident, I think, that this one-sidedness gives international law little political and moral credibility within a revolutionary atmosphere such as exists in Iran or in many parts of the Third World. Moreover, among intellectuals and reformers throughout the non-Western world, this imbalance built into international law discredits its claims to regulate behavior. What I would suggest in closing these remarks is that if we are serious about creating an effective legal order in the world, we must first be prepared to address the situation of this one-sidedness. As long as we close our eyes to it while trying to benefit from it, international law may provide us with a rhetorical whip but it will not command respect in most parts of the world, because it will be perceived in this era as nothing more than a whip used by the strong to torment the weak. For any legal system spontaneously to generate respect and authority, there must exist a correspondence between the perceived equities of the subjects and the system itself. This is especially true of international law, which is a voluntary legal system. There is, of course, no world government; law without government works on a moral level only if widely held values are embodied. A legal system of this sort is effective only to the extent that its subjects are willing to obey, and there is no reason for such willingness if the structure discriminates against many of its subjects. Dean Acheson said that the United States can cast law aside because its sovereignty is at stake; why can't Ayatollah Khomeini say and do the same thing? After all, who sets the rules of the game? Always, the dominant actors do. And once those rules are set, why can't the other side play by them as well? To me, the essential challenge is to adapt international law to the basic rhythm of change going on in the world today, especially as associated with the resurgence of non-Western peoples in exerting control over the political, economic, and cultural domains of their national existence. To narrow the legal focus to exclude such concerns, as has been done by the US government in the hostage crisis, is to confirm the cynical view of international law as nothing more than a geopolitical tool of use in a situation where practical inhibitions make it undesirable to rely on superior force.

Chapter Fourteen

HUMAN RIGHTS AFTER THE
IRANIAN REVOLUTION

In early 1979 a revolutionary movement toppled the Shah of Iran. It was a startling development for many reasons. Here, we consider only some aspects of its human rights significance. The rationale for the revolution was centered upon the rights of the Iranian people to rise up against the bloody tyranny of Pahlavi rule. Gross violations of human rights by the Shah's regime were attested to by a variety of impartial investigating groups. Indeed, it was widely accepted in international circles that the Shah's human rights record was one of the worst in a world notable for human rights abuses.

After the revolutionary seizure of power under the leadership of Ayatollah Khomeini, a new governing process was responsive to the will of the revolutionary forces and initially operated without benefit of any constitutional framework of constraint. The first of the three parts that comprise this piece considers the special question of human rights observance and violation in the atmosphere of revolutionary immediacy. In particular, charges against the revolutionary leadership are examined in the context of post-Pahlavi Iran.

As of October 1979 a new situation arose as a consequence of the Shah's admission to the United States to receive medical treatment. On November 4, 1979, militant students seized the American embassy in Tehran and held hostage there for months some fifty Americans who were officially connected in various ways with the exercise of diplomatic functions. The student leaders, supported by mass demonstrations and Khomeini himself, demanded the physical return of the Shah to face criminal charges in Iran, as well as to return to the Iranian people the billions allegedly plundered through corruption by the Shah, his family, and his entourage. The first question is whether it is appropriate to charge a deposed ruler with crimes of state and whether there exist moral and political, if not legal, means by which to achieve jurisdiction to prosecute.

This article first appeared as "Human Rights after the Iranian Revolution," in Human Rights and State Sovereignty, *edited by Richard Falk (Holmes & Meier Publishers, 1981).*

At stake here is the effort to enforce human rights against the class of violators in their individual capacity. Such claims are an extension of the Nuremberg idea of imposing criminal responsibility upon defeated leaders in war to the quite different setting of prosecuting deposed tyrants in times of peace. Second is the question as to whether, in the setting of the encounter between the United States and Iran arising from the hostage crisis, the existing structure of international law is not one-sided. That is, international law upholds the immunity claims of the American diplomatic personnel, but it fails to uphold either extradition claims directed at the Shah or charges that the American embassy in Tehran has been used to encroach upon the political and personal human rights of the Iranian people.

The assessment of human rights in revolutionary settings is an understudied topic of considerable importance. Each circumstance is unique, but with common features. An old order has been repudiated, while a new order has yet to be formally crystallized. Legal outcomes are fluid, and may appear arbitrary and cruel. Can international law provide some minimum criteria for the administration of justice in such situations?

Preliminary Notes on Human Rights in a Revolutionary Situation

The Iranian Revolution took power in the late 1970s largely by nonviolent means: a general strike, repeated mass demonstrations, cassettes bearing the messages of exiled leader Ayatollah Khomeini, photocopy machines coordinating and reporting on the movement largely through the mosque network of mullahs. It was also a popular revolution enjoying overwhelming support from the Iranian masses, as well as more reserved backing from all parts of the country and among all social classes. It was, of course, a revolution inspired by Shi'ia Islamic thought and tradition, indigenous to the Third World, owing virtually nothing to the great Western revolutionary experience emanating from the American, French, and Russian revolutions. It was also a religious revolution, the fervor of the masses and the authority of the leader organized around a sacred mission to overthrow the oppressive Pahlavi dynasty of the Shah and establish in its place an Islamic republic, but with the support of many liberal secularists.

The success of this revolution seemed at the time to offer great hope to oppressed peoples elsewhere, especially in Muslim countries. The Iranian Islamic Revolution demonstrated once and for all that the relation of forces between ruled and ruler in a Third World society has not decisively shifted from the people to the state, even to a highly militarized state closely allied to the United States. Iran represented such an important case because the populist possibility seemed so remote in the region, until it exploded into success. The Shah's apparatus of state power was immense, given the scale of Iranian society, reinforced by a ruthless and large secret police and various categories of armed forces available for use against unarmed opposition to the rulers of the country. Also, the Shah had built up a network of supporting links with outside governments that included, among others, favorable relations with the United States, the Soviet Union, and China, as well as with regional neighbors including Saudi Arabia, Egypt, and Israel. As activists in the Khomeini movement liked to put it, "We won although the whole world was against us."

What is important is the confirmation that relative power in a revolutionary situation is more a matter of political will and revolutionary leadership than military and paramilitary capability. The Iranian success resulted from the mobilization of the Iranian people on the basis of leadership and beliefs that had intense mass appeal and deep domestic roots. In that sense, the activation of the Shi'ia perspective by Ayatollah Khomeini and its ideological expression in the influential work of Ali Shariati were crucial catalysts. In the end, however, it was the willingness of the Iranian masses to persist in challenging state power, carrying on with their demonstrations despite the Shah's willingness to inflict widespread casualties with heavy machine guns, helicopter gunships, and tanks. The best estimates are that between 20 and 65 thousand Khomeini supporters were killed in the streets of Iranian cities during 1978.

At the last stage of the revolutionary struggle—that is, between the time that the Shah left on January 16, 1978, and resistance by Iranian armed forces collapsed a few weeks later—the regime was virtually isolated from the Iranian people. No significant social remnant was willing to lend its support to, much less fight for the survival of, the Pahlavi order. In February, small arms were distributed to the people in great numbers. During the last stage of struggle against the Shah, crowds chanted "Leaders, leaders, give us guns." At issue was achieving total control over the state, including its military bureaucracy, as well as protection against the violence of internal security forces. The revolutionary leadership was not prepared to reach a negotiated settlement with the military leadership that left the command structure of the Shah period intact. The Allende experience in Chile indicated to Iranian leaders how dangerous for their survival it could become if their governing process went ahead with plans to implement a radical social and economic program while relying on a hostile bureaucracy inherited from the Shah era. At the same time, this insistence on a complete victory over the old order led the Iranian revolutionary movement to shift and stiffen its tactics at the end in the direction of armed struggle. This terminal violent phase was brief, centering on the weekend of February 11, 1978, but it did alter the character of the revolutionary orientation toward the role of violence in the struggle. The dissident elements in the armed forces and the guerrilla groups (People's Fedayeen and Mujahedeen) carried Iran just over the brink of civil war before securing the de facto surrender and dissolution of the armed forces loyal to the Shah.

This type of ending also meant, however, that at the moment of victory the stage was set for an orgy of retribution. One of the first tasks for the Khomeini movement was to establish minimum order in an atmosphere of accumulated rage and in a situation in which the means to pursue vindictive justice were available to a population long abused by a repressive, bloodthirsty tyranny. In understanding the early weeks of revolutionary governance, this crucial background element must be kept in mind. It helps explain the rush to judgment with respect to those accused of criminal abuse as officials in the Shah's regime.

In addition, although the morale of the armed forces was shattered, its leadership remained at large and unreconciled to the revolutionary outcome. Ibrahim Yazdi, originally designated by Khomeini to be deputy prime minister for revolutionary affairs, contended that a principal reason for the summary executions was the persisting fear that a more orderly process might expose the country to a desperate coup attempt by the remnant of pro–Shah forces. Later developments disclosed darker motives, including some suspicion that the insistence on closed, summary trials of leading Shah figures followed rapidly by their immediate execution was designed as a cover-up, a deliberate effort to avoid compromising elements of the new Iranian leadership that may have opportunistically cooperated with the Shah's regime or with the United States government at earlier times. A distinctive feature of the Iranian Revolution was the absence of a victorious revolutionary army to protect the new state—in fact, the most experienced pro-movement armed units formed out of the mass movement were of an essentially left socialist character and soon found themselves at odds with the orientation of the leadership in the post-revolutionary situation. In the early weeks the Khomeini leadership, aside from its hastily organized popular militia, contrived in part to contain the

Iranian left, which quickly changed its relationship to the new rulers from ally to adversary. The revolutionary leadership seemed without any capacity to protect itself against a counterrevolutionary thrust, whether mounted from without or from within the country, or possibly a mixture of the two.

There are other factors. As with any revolution, an artificial unity against a common enemy suppresses cleavages until the moment of victory. The Shah was such a hated enemy that the level of unity temporarily achieved was tactically very effective, but it was especially deceptive. When the Pahlavi dynasty collapsed these cleavages came to the fore. The left was immediately eager to establish its presence and to claim for itself a share of credit for the victory. The armed struggle groups, militant for many years, had given many martyrs to the revolution. They were insistent on being recognized and given a part to play in the emerging post-revolutionary governing process. And the main ethnic minorities—Kurds, Azerbaijanis, Baluchis, Bakhtiaris, Arabs, and Turkomans—who together make up just under half of Iran's population, seized the opportunity, possibly abetted by outsiders, to assert their persistent demands for autonomy and an acknowledgment from the new leadership of their rights as "peoples" under international law to claim self-determination for themselves. This challenge confronted the new leadership with an immediate threat to the territorial integrity and political unity of the state. Besides, ethnic separatism in Iran, while genuine, has also frequently provided a fertile ground for foreign intervention. It is reasonable to suspect that both the Soviet Union and the United States would make whatever use they could of these separatist tendencies to weaken the new government in Iran, especially if eager to show its incapacity to maintain order in the country.

In addition, many special concerns subordinated to the common objective of the revolution surfaced with the explosive ferocity that comes after a long period of confinement. The manifestations of intense internal concern over women's rights can be, in part, so understood. Women, who participated so bravely in the struggle against the Shah, were determined that their status be upgraded in an emergent Islamic republic so as not to perpetuate, and even intensify, a long cultural tradition of gender repression. Women who had actively supported the revolutionary cause became fearful that under the influence of Islamic thinking their circumstances would actually deteriorate if compared to the generalized secular oppression of Pahlavi rule, and its obsession with Westernization.

In addition, never far from the concerns of the new leaders, of course, was the fear of outside intervention. Iranian memories of the American-sponsored coup in 1953, which toppled the Mossadegh government, remained vivid. In fact, a preoccupation with avoiding its repetition exists, perhaps accounting for the unexpectedly secular, Westernized quality of Mehdi Bazargan's first cabinet, a reformist orientation that seemed inconsistent with the revolutionary mandate, possibly intended to reassure Washington and Europe. Indeed, appointing such a moderate provisional government at the outset of its authority over the country agitated the more militant and fundamentalist elements in the Khomeini movement. Revolutionaries wondered, in light of this provisional government, about the genuineness of its revolutionary and Islamic content. It is in this light that we must understand the dispositions of Khomeini's religious advisors as the main source of political direction in this period, to some extent formalized in the Revolutionary Council.

It is against such a confused background that we consider the outlook for human rights in Iran in the period immediately following the revolutionary success. It is, of course, a hazardous moment for conjecture. The situation was changing rapidly, and would continue to do so in the years ahead. There was, as yet, no coherent governing process. Not everything can be known even now about what happened, and why. We lack access to the rationale of leaders. An unresolved power struggle soon erupted within the revolutionary leadership, with the more secular forces on one side (associated with Bani Sadr), and the insistently religious forces on the other (associated with Beheshti), both seeking the undivided backing of Khomeini. Events superseded every attempt at diagnosis, and yet the interplay of human rights concerns within the fluid revolutionary situation of that period of early revolutionary rule is still an appropriate focus for inquiry and evaluation.

Nevertheless, it is important to put what is now known in some perspective, if only to correct fashionable distortions. Because such powerful outside interests were aligned with the policies of the old order in Iran, an enormous incentive existed to discredit the new order by highlighting its faults. The most prevalent way to achieve this result with the collaboration of the world media is to point up human rights abuses to an extent that gives credence to a most malicious construction of reality, namely, that what has happened in Iran was that one tyranny had been replaced by another, and that what had previously existed was at least friendly to the West and to modernity.

Such claims were deceptive, and often outrageous, and pointed to the need for a different type of assessment. First of all, it is necessary to compare the post-Shah situation with the situation under the Shah. Second, human rights in Iran have to be understood within a regional and cultural context where levels of abuse are widespread and severe. Such comparisons in time and space are not meant to excuse the violations of human rights that have occurred in Iran, but merely to expose the motivation of those who suddenly devote disproportionate attention to abuses in Iran. Many of those new "voices of conscience" were exquisitely silent during the long years of repression by the Shah and remain so about the routine of systematic abuse in those neighboring states with more Westernized geopolitical orientations.

Here, briefly, the attempt is to take account of this context, while exploring the prospects for human rights during the early stages of post-revolutionary Iran. From the perspective of later decades, the struggle for human rights and democracy in the Islamic Republic of Iran has been continuous, with impressive degrees of success and dismaying setbacks.

Repression under the Shah

The evidence of torture, summary execution, denial of minimal rights of the person, and the absence of a democratic process, was well-documented during the entire period of the Shah's rule. Even the most cautious outside observers of the human rights situation in Iran confirmed this impression.[1] Amnesty International issued a report late in 1978 indicating the continuation of systematic torture.

The Khomeini movement emphasized its opposition to the repressive features of the Shah's rule. Many members of the revolutionary leadership were personally abused by the SAVAK, spending years as victims of various forms of harassment and in jail. No rights of discussion or criticism were permitted by the Shah, and not even the intellectual preconditions of democratic process existed. Students periodically disappeared from classes. Signs of opposition, such as demonstrations or meetings, were brutally broken up by government security forces. Iranian students abroad were subject to surveillance and cruel punishment upon their return if political activity hostile to the Shah was reported.

In every sense, then, the Shah's rule must be perceived as one of severe repression backed up by a willingness to use military and paramilitary power to contain the opposition of a hostile population. Heavy casualties were repeatedly inflicted on the Iranian citizenry by the use of modern weaponry against unarmed demonstrators.

Revolutionary Justice

In the aftermath of the revolution a series of summary executions occurred after brief trials before secret revolutionary tribunals. This process was authorized by the Revolutionary Council, originally without the evident knowledge or backing of Prime Minister Mehdi Bazargan, then head of the provisional government established immediately following the revolutionary victory. Bazargan denounced the process of "revolutionary justice" and threatened to resign, a threat he subsequently carried out after Ayatollah Khomeini endorsed the student seizure of the American embassy on November 4, 1979.

As matters then stood, there were approximately 1,000 executions that were directed mainly against the alleged principal agents of repression in the Shah era, leaders of the armed forces or SAVAK who were accused of being personally associated with massive crimes against the Iranian people. Several Iranians were also executed in this period according to the dictates of Quranic law for alleged criminal acts, including homosexual rape and violent crimes. This mode of assessing guilt and imposing punishment obviously violated the international human rights of the accused to be judged in open trials with due process protection. At the same time, given the revolutionary turmoil, the fear of private vengeance, and the long record of mass abuse associated with Pahlavi rule, extenuating circumstances existed.

The number of executions was relatively limited, and, as of early 1980, executions associated with criminal activity on behalf of the Shah's regime virtually ceased. Khomeini did not repudiate Bazargan despite the harshness of Bazargan's response ("irreligious, inhuman, and a disgrace") to this method of pursuing "revolutionary justice." On March 16, 1979, Khomeini called for an end to closed trials and summary executions, a call only partially heeded.[2]

Formation of an Islamic Republic

The Khomeini movement has been criticized because it assessed popular support for an Islamic republic by a simple yes–no question on a referendum. Critics allege that the choice should have been more subtle, asking whether the people preferred a monarchy, a constitutional monarchy, a nonreligious republic, or an Islamic republic. The constitutional referendum provided an insufficiently democratic sanction, it is argued, on which to base a mandate for an Islamic republic.

In response, however, it should be noted that the Khomeini movement made it clear throughout the revolution that an Islamic republic was its objective. This political outcome was promised to followers of Khomeini, and, in a sense, the extent of popular support for that promise is the only relevant question with regard to the reorganization of the Iranian state. The argument that a range of other options should be presented to the Iranian people is both an academic insistence, given the level of support for an Islamic republic, and probably an overstatement of the political sophistication of the Iranian people, so long victimized by a monochromatic tyranny.

The Role of the Left and Nonreligious Dissent

On numerous occasions before coming to power and shortly thereafter, Khomeini has affirmed the rights of Marxists and others to express their views and participate in the political life of an Islamic republic. Such an affirmation has been qualified to the extent that if the left were to establish links with foreign governments, its freedom to operate would be curtailed. The historical memory of the disruptive role played by the Tudeh Party in the early 1950s remains fresh, especially its apparent subordination to the will of Moscow and its contribution to the 1953 collapse of Mossadegh's government. As Khomeini put it, every country is entitled to protect itself "against those who would commit treason."

Underneath this expression of Khomeini's attitude lies another, given expression by the first elected president of the Islamic Republic, Abolhassan Bani Sadr: namely, the rather unrealistic view that when Marxists in Iran genuinely come to understand the goals of an Islamic republic, they would renounce Marxism and realize that Shi'ia Islam provided a better framework for the pursuit of social justice. And, indeed, the biography and ideas of Ali Shariati did have a great appeal for many progressive Iranians, convincing even some Marxists that Islam correctly understood provided a revolutionary ideology that was indigenous to Iran and enjoyed a mass following. One of the disappointments with the revolution as of early 1980 is the degree to which Shariati's person and ideas have been ignored, and more conservative conceptions of Islamic social and political policies insisted upon as integral to Islam. This Islamic shift to the right definitely alienated the secular left with its liberal values and outlook, and has even led some religious socialists within Iran into a position of opposition to the Khomeini leadership.

As matters have evolved, a substantial left has remained a critical presence within any Islamic republic; it will test the democratic character of the governing process both by its oppositional style and by the extent to which its rights of expression and activity are allowed. It may also seek to seize or reshape political power in the event the religious movement fails or is beset by deepening civil strife. These progressive inclinations have been able to express themselves largely within an Islamic framework, leading over time to increasing strength for a flexible view of Islam that is in large measure compatible with international human rights standards.

Several ambiguities exist. First of all, there existed the Fedayeen, that element on the extreme left that is now heavily armed and has engaged in armed struggle against the Shah. Will it renounce armed struggle at this new stage? Will it be suppressed? If so, by what means? Can this extreme left be integrated in any sense within the framework of an Islamic republic? Second, will the populist mainstream of the revolution tolerate an active left? There were many indications within university settings of interference by militant religious groups with meetings, with the distribution of literature, and with the carrying of Marxist placards at demonstrations and marches. It remained uncertain for years, despite some instances where official moves to repress the left occurred, whether the government will discourage such interference and protect the democratic rights of the left. Khomeini zigzagged with agility between tolerance and repression. Third, there is some degree of support for the view that the religious leadership moved to repress the left as soon as it consolidated its own power, and that the initial reassurances of tolerance were merely tactical. The death of Ayatollah Teleghani, the most liberal of religious leaders, was a serious blow to the hopes for a post-revolutionary government of unity and reconciliation. The interaction between the left and the emergent governing process in Iran did definitely reveal one dimension of the human rights situation. As suggested, however, this revelation was two-sided, depending on the political approach of the left (or segments of the left) toward opposition (renunciation of foreign links, of armed struggle), as well as on the attitudes of new political leaders, their religious guides, and the populist tides of the Islamic movement. In the short run, Ayatollah Khomeini's individual guidance turned out to be decisive in setting the tone of the governing process and imposing limits of opposition activity.

Ethnic Minorities

Iran is a multinational state. The Shah repressed these large minorities through military and paramilitary means. With the collapse of the armed forces and the weakening of the central state, these national groups have become insistent to varying degrees on improvements in their economic, political, and cultural situation in Iran. It seems indisputable that these national minorities have been victims of discrimination in the past, receiving a disproportionately low share of investment, social services, and so forth. Also, several of these minorities (e.g., Kurds, Baluchis) are predominantly adherents of Sunni Islam, and, therefore, additionally separate from the Shi'ia adherence of the great majority of Iranians, including virtually all of the leaders of the revolution. Some minority nationalities also contend that in exchange for their support of the Khomeini movement they had received assurances that a larger measure of autonomy and self-rule would be granted in an Islamic republic.

As with the left, it was difficult to assess the situation in the initial period of revolutionary rule. Signs of agitation have been evident throughout the minority territories, and serious fighting broke out in Kurdish areas. One issue is whether these minorities, or some of them, are secessionist in character, intend to rely on violence to achieve their goals, and maintain contact with outside forces (including transnational links with their own people—especially, with Kurds in Iraq and Turkey, Azerbaijanis and Turkomen in the Soviet Union, Baluchis in Pakistan). The separatist orientation also provided easy opportunities for covert operations by hostile foreign intelligence organizations seeking to destabilize an Islamic republic in Iran. So perceived, ethnic activism was viewed with suspicion, and regarded and treated as a security threat.

These national minorities together dominate the peripheral region of Iran, including the oil-producing region of Khuzistan. These minority populations live in distinct geographic areas, generally close to the borders of Iran, remote from the political and spatial center of the country. Clearly one test of human rights in an Islamic republic will be the capacity of the central government to deal fairly and nonviolently with these national minorities and to accommodate some of their claims to exercise a right of self-determination. At the same time, the role of foreign governments, the reliance by minorities or factional groups in their midst on armed struggle, and the extent to which self-determination becomes a euphemism for secession shaped the setting within which these issues were addressed by Tehran.

Religious Minorities

In Iran there are a number of religious minorities, including Sunnis,

Armenian Christians, Jews, Zoroastrians, Nestorians, and Bahais. For various reasons the most problematic relations concerned Sunnis, Jews, and Bahais. With the exception of the Bahais, the Khomeini leadership promised freedom of worship and an atmosphere of religious toleration.

The Sunni minority is troubled by the tension it perceives as likely to result from an Islamic republic drawn along strictly Shi'ia lines, especially given the strong hostility expressed by the Shi'ia leaders to Sunni Islam. Furthermore, the concentration of Sunnis among national minority groups hostile to the state may reinforce the perception of Sunnis by the leaders of the Republic as subversive elements.

With respect to the 80,000 or so Jews, the root of the problem involves the hostile relationship between an Islamic republic and Israel. One of the first diplomatic acts of the Khomeini movement was to invite PLO leader Yasir Arafat to Iran and pledge solidarity, symbolized by turning over the former Israeli embassy to the PLO. The situation is aggravated by the extent to which Israel is perceived as having been a bulwark of support of the Shah, including the role that the Israeli intelligence service, Mossad, is alleged to have played in setting up and working with the SAVAK.

Here again a key issue will be whether Iranian Jews are perceived as Zionists with operational emotional and material links to Israel. The government's capacity and will to discourage anti-Semitic attitudes within the population are also crucial. Khomeini has given the Jewish community repeated reassurances, including his assertion that it would be a tragedy for Iran if Jews leave. Fearing for their safety and well-being in an Islamic republic, five to eighteen thousand Jews left Iran in the early months after the fall of the Shah, and many more since then. Despite fears, the record of the Khomeini period toward the Jewish community as a whole was overall quite positive, if political trials of supporters of Israel who allegedly violated Iranian law are put aside. The issue disappeared as politically engaged Jews left Iran almost totally, and only a fraction of the original Jewish community remains in the country.

The circumstances of the 300,000 or so Bahais were of especial concern. Here, alone, Khomeini refused even to provide reassurance of tolerance. Indeed, he has said that Bahais have no place in an Islamic republic, that they constitute a political sect, and that they are not a genuine religion. Besides, many of their leading members were closely tied to Pahlavi rule. Reports of abuse of Bahais and their religious property in various parts of Iran by members of Revolutionary Committees were received and have elicited strong formal acts of protest by human rights groups.

In the background is the Shi'ia view of the Bahai religion (founded by Baha'u'llah, who is regarded by adherents as a subsequent and superior prophet to Mohammed) as heretical. Nevertheless, maintaining respect for the Bahai religion and people served as a test of adherence to human rights in an Islamic republic, a test that was largely failed.

Women

The status of women in Iran is another symbolic battleground. It is also a confusing one. Yardsticks for progress cannot be supplied on the basis of Western experience. Since the revolution is Islamic at its core, there are obvious tensions between religious convictions and achieving equality of treatment for women in Iran. The issue, like others in the human rights area, is susceptible to manipulation by those within and without the country seeking to destabilize the new governing process, or to rationalize its every act as dictated by Islam.

Khomeini and other religious leaders tried to be generally reassuring about the rights of women. After an initial insistence on traditional dress, Khomeini said that the chador was optional, but through time its use even by visitors to Iran has become mandatory. Demonstrations by women in Iran were not officially suppressed, and, in fact, those taking part early on were protected by a peculiar mixture of Fedayeen and some units of the Popular Militia working under the control of the Revolutionary Committees. At the same time, many incidents of harassment and intimidation of activist women were reported in the course of the first year of the revolution.

The main short-run issue is whether women will be able to advance their claims for equality, participation, and dignity within a democratic framework. It has been a difficult struggle, and by no means are women in Iran united as to their priorities or goals and in the evaluation of their experience. Also, no Islamic society has yet completely succeeded in producing a satisfactory readjustment of the traditional status and roles of women that fits smoothly into modern reality. Although there are a variety of shortcomings from the overall perspective of human rights and democracy, Malaysia, among Muslim countries, has probably done the best with regard to women.

Purges and Purity

In the media and government ministries, inflammatory allegations were being made that new revolutionary authorities in Iran instituted "purges."

Here again, the facts were difficult to sort out. The claims made on behalf of the revolution were that those who worked loyally for the old order needed to be replaced. The contention of the critics was that anyone who was not deferential and subordinate to the religious leadership was neither trusted nor wanted. A rather high degree of ideological conformity was initially imposed upon radio, television, and newspapers in a manner that certainly constrained the atmosphere of freedom in the new Iran. The first twelve months of revolutionary rule produced an inconsistent record, one in which the mood shifted back and forth.

Again it is important to note that the pre-revolutionary heritage of Iran has been one of censorship and control. Iranians were deeply moved in the early days of revolutionary victory when long lines formed at Tehran newsstands because finally newspapers and magazines contained real news with diverse interpretations. Later on, of course, liberal disenchantment occurred when newspapers and magazines critical of government policy or of divergent outlooks were periodically closed down, attacked, and censored.

The issue of "purity" is closely related to the general applicability of Islamic law. How strict and literal will be the lines drawn between Quranic text and behavioral compulsion in the new Iranian state? Already there are indications that liquor will be forbidden in public places and that entertainment featuring violence and sex will not be allowed in any form. Especially in provincial and rural Iran these new imperatives are likely to be supplemented by harsh punishment for violators. Law enforcement on these matters has been uneven and decentralized, with some very repressive regimes evidently operating in parts of the new Iran, but not uniformly in the country as a whole.

Assessment

This sketch of human rights prospects for Iran is incomplete and tentative, and somewhat dated. The unfolding of the Islamic republic will reveal the degree to which human rights will flourish. At present, outsiders should watch, learn, and wait, as well as judge and appraise. The process of post-revolutionary adjustment has been always difficult for every polity. There are enemies of the revolution that continue to be active. In Iran's case, outside states have an incentive to provoke the collapse of the Islamic government and the restoration of Western-oriented leadership, this time directly under military rather than dynastic auspices.

At least let us not confuse the tyranny of the past with the problems and disappointments of the present and future. Ayatollah Khomeini seems dedicated to evolving a form of governance for the people of Iran that includes a central commitment to social justice for the poor, a closing of gaps between social classes, and an elimination of the kinds of wasteful consumption and production patterns that grew up during the Shah's years. He continues to enjoy an intense popular mandate in pursuit of such goals. Success will enable Iran to demonstrate that a revolutionary victory need not be spoiled by the tensions raised in the post-revolutionary period of consolidation.

Claims Against the Shah & His Regime:
The Rights of Deposed Rulers & the Rights of the People

The international crisis built up around the seizure of American hostages in the United States embassy on November 4, 1979 suggests the importance of having some acceptable international mechanism to acknowledge and establish the responsibility of the ex-Shah for crimes against the Iranian people. In the background is a broader problem of dealing with deposed tyrants accused of crimes of state who are living more or less comfortably in exile. In addition to the Shah, there are such unsavory characters as Idi Amin, Emperor Bokassa I, Pol Pot, and General Anastasio Somoza Debayle at large in the world at the present time. The dramatic events in Iran, threatening lives of Americans, as well as creating a climate favorable to military intervention and even war, suggest the desperate need in international society for peaceful procedures of accountability, as well as limits on the right of states to provide asylum.

One of the great ideas born after World War II was the notion that even heads of state and top government leaders should be held criminally responsible for their gross violations of international law. As a result, war crimes trials were organized at Nuremberg and Tokyo, the surviving German and Japanese leaders prosecuted and, if convicted, punished, even, in some cases, by death. The trials have been criticized as "victors' justice" and for their failure to consider criminal allegations against the winning side in the war, especially the Allied reliance on strategic bombing techniques on a massive scale against German and Japanese cities and the use of atomic bombs. Nevertheless, the Nuremberg/Tokyo trials were a mechanism that answered the calls at the time for vindication and justice. More important, especially in the German case, the Nazi record of atrocity was publicly documented in a manner that facilitated German acknowledgment and democratic reconstruction. The Japanese experience, given the initial decision to exempt the Emperor and Emperor-system from legal and political scrutiny, was ambiguous from the outset.

The United States was centrally associated with this Nuremberg experiment. Our government at that time insisted, over Soviet and British objections, that an orderly, judicial method be relied upon to deal with the irresistible popular demands for some kind of retribution. After the trials the United States led the way in having the United Nations as a whole endorse the Nuremberg Principles as guiding rules of international law. And throughout this experience, prominent public figures, including the distinguished American prosecutor of the German defendants, former Supreme Court Justice Robert Jackson, insisted that the law laid down at Nuremberg included a promise to the future that similar behavior by other rulers and their cohorts would meet with a similar fate. We realize that many governments have violated the Nuremberg guidelines since 1946 and that their leaders could have been indicted if the Nuremberg promise had been kept. As the memory of World War II faded, so did the Nuremberg idea, although not completely. Within the United States, civil society militants kept the idea alive, particularly in the settings of the Vietnam War and in relation to reliance on nuclear weaponry. Until the altered experience of the 1990s, Nuremberg as an inter-governmental initiative seemed either unique to the special circumstances of that historical moment in 1945, or premature, or possibly a combination of both.

The events surrounding the embassy seizure in Tehran on November 4, 1979, have made many of us aware that we need a mechanism in international society to assess the criminal responsibility of deposed tyrants. I believe that such a mechanism could be brought into being in the present situation if the minimum political will existed. In other words, there are no legal or moral obstacles that block such action, provided only that the United States and Iran stand aside and allow such a process to come into being. What is possible, and I think desirable, is the establishment of a mechanism within the broad framework of authority provided by the United Nations for assessing the Shah's criminal responsibility.

The procedure I have in mind can be outlined to indicate its substance. As a first step a neutral delegation (say, Algeria or Venezuela) in the General Assembly or Security Council could introduce a resolution authorizing the secretary general of the United Nations to appoint a commission of inquiry composed of distinguished international jurists drawn from neither Iran nor the United States. This commission would have two broad functions. First of all, it would receive evidence of the Shah's alleged criminality and make a preliminary assessment as to whether there existed a reasonable basis for supposing the Shah guilty of gross violations of international law and crimes against the Iranian people. If the answer of the commission were affirmative, as is certainly likely, then it would proceed to its second task, that of proposing the establishment of a special tribunal and an operative legal framework for ad hoc trial of the Shah. The commission would complete its work by issuing a report containing findings and recommendations, calling upon the United Nations to act accordingly. At this point, assuming there was an affirmative recommendation by the commission, the United Nations would constitute a special tribunal. It could, perhaps, use the facilities, and conceivably even the personnel, of the International Court of Justice, the so-called World Court, that sits, often idly, in the quiet Dutch city of The Hague. The World Court, as such, is not a proper forum for a proceeding against the Shah. It is a tribunal limited to deciding legal disputes between sovereign states. Individuals can neither complain nor be the targets of complaint, and the scope of the World Court's activities is confined to noncriminal subject matter. Nevertheless, the independent creation of an emergency structure of adjudication located at The Hague is technically possible and politically attractive.

There are, at least, four problems of broad practical consequence that make this two-step proposal problematic: securing the participation of the Shah, obtaining the cooperation of the United States government, determining the applicable body of law, and enforcing the final decision. It is highly unlikely that the Shah would agree to participate in his own defense. Indeed, whoever heard of an accused criminal, especially an individual who acknowledges no guilt and accepts no accountability, voluntarily agreeing to appear before a court and accept the consequences? The two-step procedure outlined above could be flexible on this matter. It could invite the Shah to appear, and, failing this, it could urge the government in whose country the Shah was resident to cooperate with the United Nations procedure by turning over his person through some type of extradition process. In all probability, however, the government where the Shah is resident at the time of request will interpose its sovereign right to grant asylum to political leaders of foreign countries. Hence, it is highly likely that the United Nations procedure would have to go ahead in absentia. In this circumstance, appointing a counsel with strong professional credentials for the defense would certainly be appropriate. Such an appointment would add to the credibility and authority of the process.

Arranging for United States cooperation poses a formidable challenge. There is the matter of loyalty to an individual leader who was a close ally, and there is also the likelihood that any investigation of the Shah's rule and abuses would implicate the United States in serious respects.

The problem of applicable law is mainly a technical matter of prescribing for the commission and tribunal the legal criteria for use in their work. At Nuremberg, three categories of crimes were relied upon, specified in advance: crimes against peace, war crimes, and crimes against humanity. Here, the situation is different. The main burden of the charges against the Shah involve crimes against humanity in a context where no war existed. In the Nuremberg Principles, crimes against humanity are defined as follows:

> Murder, extermination, enslavement and other inhuman acts done against any civilian population, or persecution on political, racial or religious grounds, when such acts are done or such persecutions are carried on in execution of or in connection with any crime against peace or any war crime.[3]

The simplest approach would be for the commission to reformulate crimes against humanity by focusing on the relationship between ruler and population in a setting of international peace and drawing on the authority of the burgeoning international law of human rights, including the Universal Declaration of Human Rights. It would also be necessary, I think, to specify a special category of criminal conduct to cover plundering for private gain the public wealth of a country, possibly calling it "crimes against public well-being and wealth," or simply, "economic crimes of state." This last category is important in the case of the Shah, where a main line of allegation is the illegal removal of billions of dollars of Iranian public wealth and the existence of economic corruption as a pervasive feature of government. The challenge here is for the commission to find a legally satisfactory way to formulate authoritative standards without engaging in retroactive lawmaking.

The final practical issue is that of enforcement. How will the punishment be imposed? What is the point of such a procedure if there are no reliable means to exact the punishment? In essence, I believe, the value of this procedure is to give the Iranian people an opportunity to tell their story in a definitive way. It would, in effect, legitimate their rage over the American treatment of the former Shah as an individual deserving of sympathy and sanctuary. The tribunal could also, if so inclined, call upon domestic legal institutions, including relevant national courts, to give effect, especially in the property area, to findings establishing that many of the Shah's assets had been criminally acquired.

The most substantial of these problems are related to political issues. There is, as has been mentioned, above all the acute American sensitivity to the exposure of its role and that of its embassy and the CIA in putting and keeping the Shah in power between 1953 and 1979. Such sensitivity should have been balanced off against the lives and well-being of the American hostages, the threats of military intervention, and the growing isolation of the United States in the Moslem world. On a deeper level, it is time our citizenry were more fully informed about our actual foreign policy, and given the opportunity to endorse or reject it. In the dangerous situation associated with the hostage crisis, the prospect of official embarrassment should have seemed small indeed compared to the other risks involved. At the same time, governments are habitually reluctant to allow their dirty linen to be so washed in public, particularly as the cold war was in high gear, and the abandonment of the Shah in these circumstances would have been seen as extremely damaging to other United States liaisons with authoritarian leaders in Third World countries.

Another concern is whether such an internationalized procedure would have satisfied the leaders in Iran, the students holding the embassy, and the then all-powerful Ayatollah Khomeini. We will never know the answers because such an initiative was not attempted. There were indications early in the crisis of favorable response, including statements by two then leading members of Ayatollah Khomeini's inner circle—Abolhassan Bani Sadr, then acting foreign minister and later president; and also, Sadegh Ghotbzadegh, initially head of Iranian radio and television and later foreign minister after Bani Sadr's forced resignation. Both men suggested, perhaps incorrectly, that the other problems will go away, including the holding of the hostages and the embassy, if some impartial procedure under United Nations auspices can be agreed upon and taken seriously by all parties. It became increasingly doubtful whether such relatively secular voices of moderation carried any weight with Khomeini or the militants holding the hostages. Indeed, in retrospect, the opposite conclusion is persuasive. The militants occupying the embassy were primarily interested in the internal situation within Iran, including the ousting of Bani Sadr and other more liberal and secular individuals from positions of leadership, and only secondarily concerned about bringing the Shah to justice.

Finally, there was at the time an expressed anxiety that if the Shah were
to be prosecuted, then other former dictators could be pursued as well.
More serious than this, it is said, dictators will be disinclined to accept exile
if their prospect includes the possibility of criminal prosecution. Instead,
they will hang on to power, fighting against their opponents to the end no
matter how bloody the results. Such concerns raise questions about how
widespread the procedure proposed here is likely to become. Note that the
idea of Nuremberg has been confined to the special political circumstances
that existed at the end of World War II although many subsequent
international circumstances could logically have produced Nuremberg
prosecutions. In the end, the question is one of competing considerations
about the drift of world order. I am convinced that the lesser risks at that
time involve creating some procedure for the exposure and possible
punishment of deposed tyrants for their crimes of state.

In the end, the issue of political win is crucial. Whether the leaders of
Iran and the United States, now locked in a death embrace, have the
imagination and courage to disengage is the ultimate question. Iran would
have had to relinquish its literal claim for the physical body of the Shah
and the application of Islamic law in exchange for the satisfaction of its
most fundamental and principled demand that the responsibility of the
Shah for crimes against the Iranian people be established for all to see. The
United States would achieve its fundamental and principled demand that
all hostages be released, while relinquishing its tactical refusal to allow
inquiry into the criminality of the Shah's rule.

Despite difficulties, an international mechanism for investigating crimes
of state by deposed rulers seems to be an idea whose time has finally come.
And no better context than the then-existing anguish over the fate of the
hostages, of world peace, and of the Shah is likely to present itself.

The Iran Hostage Crisis: The Rights of Diplomats
and the Rights of Weak States

The United States government has insisted, since the Iran hostage crisis
commenced on November 4, 1979, that international law supports its
basic demand that Americans held captive be released. This insistence has
been confirmed by a unanimous finding of the International Court of
Justice, the highest organ for interpreting international law that exists in
the world. For the United States, then, the only inadequacy of
international law and the World Court in this setting has involved the
inability to enforce its legal mandate upon a defiant ruler. US attitudes

would shift abruptly when the World Court was invoked by Nicaragua during the period of Sandinista rule to uphold the sovereign rights of Nicaragua in the face of American interventionary activity, especially its support of the contra effort to stage a counter-revolution.

Ayatollah Khomeini's refusal to honor the rules of international law relating to diplomatic immunity were among the most serious international charges brought against his leadership. Even Hitler, it is alleged, never violated the diplomatic immunity of his enemies. In fact, one has to search the books of diplomatic history to find isolated precedents for the events that transpired at the American Embassy in Tehran during the period between November 4, 1979 and January 20, 1981. And, it was argued at the time that any of these earlier and lesser challenges to diplomatic decorum came from a source that could be credibly dismissed as "barbarian." Indeed, condemning Khomeini as a law-breaker and as a backer of terrorism gave rise quite naturally, on a popular redneck level in America, to the more virulent bumper sticker demands to "nuke Iran" or "hang Khomeini."

Yet one must wonder about this supposed clarity of international law. After all, is it not a serious matter that an embassy is used to subvert the constitutional order of a country, as was done by the United States in staging the coup that brought the Shah back to power in 1953? Is it not also serious that embassy personnel evidently helped establish and train the SAVAK, the secret police that committed over the years so many crimes against the people of Iran?[4] The response to these Iranian grievances is also clear: "Everybody knows that embassies are spy nests." True, vague prohibitions against intervening in the internal affairs of sovereign states exist, but no one takes them seriously. And besides, diplomacy is inevitably interventionary. It is argued that this is the game of politics as played by states on a global scale, for better or worse.

The law on the subject also supports the American refusal to extradite the Shah. First of all, it is claimed that the Shah was a recipient of the American prerogative to give asylum, especially on this occasion, where a supposed medical necessity existed.[5] Besides, on a more technical level, the absence of an extradition treaty between the United States and Iran would have made it virtually impossible to return the Shah to Iranian custody, even if United States President Jimmy Carter had wanted to do so.[6] Finally, even if an extradition treaty had existed, it is doubtful that an American court would have found the Shah extraditable. The evidence against him is connected with his repressive rule, but extradition is not normally available against someone accused of "political crimes." It is arguable, and has later been established by some national courts, that crimes against humanity are not political crimes, and extradition requests otherwise proper should be honored.

That is, international law as it exists generally supported the United States claim about the hostages, but it gives Iran almost no comfort. The very clarity of international law, given underlying inequities, raises questions about its one-sidedness. Why should the rules protecting diplomatic immunity be so much clearer and more authoritative than the rules protecting a weak country against intervention? Or why should "asylum" be available to a cruel tyrant associated with the massive commission of state crimes, including torture, arbitrary execution, and economic plunder? What kind of international law is it that protects foreign police and torture specialists by conferring upon them the status of "diplomat"?

In part, the drift of international law reflects the history of international relations since the birth of the modern state system in the middle of the seventeenth century. It is a law of, for, and by governments, and especially powerful governments. In that sense, all governments have a shared interest in upholding the absolute rights of their diplomatic representatives. Relations depend on communication, even in periods of stress, and hence the case for diplomatic immunity seems strong. The United Nations is, as an organization of governments, the world's strongest lobby for diplomatic immunity. On other aspects of the situation, interests are not so clearly shared. Intervention in an interdependent world is not altogether avoidable, and it represents one of the instruments by which the strong control the weak. Nonintervention generally helps the weak, as the prohibition is only meaningful as directed against the relatively stronger party to a conflict. The weaker side, regardless of its intentions, normally lacks an intervention option, although it could in a given instance theoretically ignore its handicaps of power. In fact, however, the history of interventionary diplomacy is overwhelmingly the story of how the strong have used their power in various ways against the weak. The struggle for norms and regimes based on nonintervention is the contrary story of how weaker states have tried to inhibit intrusions on their territorial integrity and political independence.[7] To renounce intervention seems for a superpower tantamount to renouncing the global extension of power politics. It can be done quite easily in words, but not consistently in deeds. Such interventionary patterns were particularly pronounced during the Cold War era.

In this regard, it is true that the protection of diplomatic immunity suggests an invariable constraint whereas the prohibition on intervention is fuzzy, vague, and necessarily conditional and contextual. The rationale for "humanitarian intervention," although itself controversial, suggests that even normative considerations can be ambiguous, as when, for instance, genocide or widespread abuse occurs in the target society. To make nonintervention into an absolute would be to endorse unlimited internal sovereignty, an endorsement quite inconsistent with the protection of fundamental international human rights. At the same time, there are some core instances of intervention that illustrate the abuse of sovereign rights, provided some limited assumptions are made. One of these, applicable to the Iranian case, is that in the absence of persistent and severe violations of human rights, the deliberate subversion of the constitutional process of a foreign state is an "illegal" intervention in its internal affairs, especially if a change of regime results in bringing to power an anti-democratic political leadership.

Regarding the treatment of deposed wandering tyrants, existing governments grow nervous, as well they might. Many rulers are potential defendants in trials alleging state crime. The idea of granting sanctuary to deposed leaders has some appeal as a matter of global policy, thereby creating the option of exile as an alternative to protracted civil strife and bloodshed. Even Idi Amin, Emperor Bokassa I, Pol Pot, and Anastasio Somoza Debayle have found foreign places of refuge; if returned home, they would all almost surely be executed.

What we find, then, is both a pro-imperial and a pro-governmental bias built into modern international law. This double bias is a natural consequence of states dominating the global scene and of some states dominating others in hegemonic fashion. Whether such a framework is adequate or not in the post-colonial world is one of the deeper, unexamined issues posed by the Iranian crisis. Khomeini clearly and vividly identified this historical bias embedded in international law:

> What kind of law is this? It permits the US government to exploit and colonize peoples all over the world for decades. But it does not allow the extradition of an individual who has staged great massacres. Can you call it law?[8]

Perhaps, however, Khomeini is here mixing up the law that should be with the law that could be. Given the way international diplomacy operates, is it reasonable to expect international law to be different than it is?

Let us not sit too quickly in judgment of Ayatollah Khomeini for his evident refusal to shape Iranian policy by reference to the law on the books. American leaders have had their own doubts about whether international law should interfere with the formation of foreign policy in crisis contexts. One recalls, of course, in this connection, Dean Acheson's famous remarks on the Cuban Missile Crisis made at the 1963 Annual Meeting of the American Society of International Law: "The power, position, and prestige of the United States had been challenged by another state; and law simply does not deal with such questions of ultimate power—power that comes close to the sources of sovereignty. I cannot believe that there are principles of law that say we must accept destruction of our way of life."[9] In fact, in the several narrations of the United States decision-making process over the course of the Cuban Missile Crisis, as written by non-lawyers, the legal factor is either not mentioned, or only so slightly as to be of no consequence.[10]

To similar effect, one recalls Leonard Meeker's "legal" defense of the United States' Dominican intervention in 1965 by counseling against "fundamentalist views on the nature of international legal obligations." Meeker was reacting to the fact that the non-defensive use of force in a foreign country was a clear violation of the United Nations Charter prohibitions of article 2(4).[11] Meeker, then legal adviser to the secretary of state, addressed this defense of American policy to the Foreign Law Association in June of 1965. My point here, as with my earlier reference to the Cuban Missile Crisis, is the willingness of American policymakers and their legal experts to bend or ignore international law under the pragmatic pressure of international circumstances. Why, then, be shocked when others do the same? Of course, the United States didn't violate this rule in the past, but why expect Iran to condition its exercise of sovereign rights by a literal imitation of our example? It is the more general example of subordinating legal inhibitions to claims of sovereign necessity that pertains here, and suggests the overall limits of law in relation to world politics.

And yet there is another set of possibilities. Why should governments alone establish the rules that govern behavior on the planet? Why should not citizens organize to insist on a framework of law that corresponds to a framework of minimum morality? Part of this pressure can come through the reform of international law, making it less one-sided. The non-Western governments of the Third World have exerted some pressure along these lines with respect to international economic relations, ocean rights and duties, and the status of irregular forces (guerrillas and liberation armies) in time of war.

Perhaps out of the Iranian encounter will eventually come increased possibilities for a more ambitious program of global reform. Perhaps we can look forward to a redrafting of the Vienna Convention on Diplomatic and Consular Immunity so as more nearly to balance the rights of the host country to political independence with the rights of the foreign country to diplomatic security. Already, a commission of inquiry has been established under United Nations auspices to investigate the Iranian grievances. Its role and impact are at this time problematic. From the outset it was evident that the United Nations commission, as established, could not expect to do more than investigate and report, and, as it turned out, even those expectations were never realized. What seems desirable is a permanent rather than an ad hoc mechanism, with a continuing competence to investigate charges of crimes of state filed against tyrants whether deposed or not, with the power to recommend, as appropriate, remedies, including even the formation of special tribunals competent to pass judgment. But to affirm the necessity of such a step should not be confused with a positive attitude toward feasibility. As with such other "necessities" as the Nuremberg enterprise and nuclear disarmament, the need is overcome by the intractable dynamics of statism, keeping power and authority fragmented when it comes to the use of force either internationally or intra-nationally.

It seems doubtful for a variety of reasons that global reform along the lines proposed above will be undertaken as a consequence of the Iranian hostage crisis. On the contrary. Efforts seem underway in the United States to revalidate the covert operations dimension of the CIA repertoire. The only open question in the public debate on the CIA is the degree of accountability to Congress and the stringency of the requirement that the president approve in advance proposed covert operations by the CIA. There is no serious prospect of conditioning CIA operations by the constraints of domestic and international law. Even more clearly, the United States is moving to establish military forces and doctrine for intervention in foreign countries. Indeed, the publicity surrounding the formation of the Rapid Deployment Force, designed especially for use in the Persian Gulf region, is very reminiscent of the 1960s enthusiasm for the Green Berets as the cutting edge of counterinsurgency doctrine, conceived of, especially in those early Kennedy years, as a way to defeat radical insurgencies in the Third World. This approach led to the Vietnam intervention, undertaken by Washington with only the most marginal attention to the constraining role of international law upon its sovereign discretion to use force as national policymakers saw fit. The one-sidedness of international law is but a reflection of the one-sidedness of international life in general.

Given this reality, have we not reached the stage where citizens, through voluntary associations, should organize to regulate the behavior of governments? At least, it would seem constructive to have a mechanism available for inquiring into the commission of state crime. Some past efforts in these directions exist. In Europe, the British philosopher Bertrand Russell established a "tribunal" to investigate charges of war crimes arising out of the American involvement in the Vietnam War.[12] More recently a group of international legal and cultural figures have joined in an effort to proclaim a legal framework for human rights, issuing the Algiers Declaration of the Rights of Peoples on July 4, 1976. Preliminary steps have been taken by an Italian entity, the Lelio Basso Foundation, to establish a tribunal that would investigate charges against governments and leaders flowing out of violations of the Algiers Declaration.

In other settings, individuals and groups have gathered together to put forward normative demands. In 1978 the Delhi Declaration condemned nuclear weapons and proposed a treaty for their renunciation as weapons of war. Earlier in 1975 a group of economists gathered in Mexico and issued the Cocoyoc Declaration, which called for a new global economic order that went well beyond the demands of governments for "a new international economic order."

How do these initiatives gain authoritativeness in international affairs? Suppose other groups issued less congenial declarations as to legal substance. How is it possible to choose among conflicting normative assertions? Would not chaos result if self-appointed law-makers were endowed with legitimacy? These are real concerns that require extended discussion. Suffice it to say here that government-generated law, to achieve effectiveness, also depends often on soliciting respect from the actors in international life. With populist initiatives, the path toward respect and observance is probably more difficult. Yet it is not essentially different from the growth of effective law on the basis of conventional sources. The law-making claim of non-governmental actors rests on the ultimate competence of individuals and groups to enact authoritative norms for behavior. Such norms do not enjoy an automatic validity and would not be valid at all in those arenas where validity is defined by reference to formal sources (for instance, the International Court of Justice). But in other arenas, including ones where international institutions and governments act, such populist norms can be invoked by participants, and if influential to some degree, then their role in shaping behavior is real and effective, and to that degree establishes part of the legal environment. Particularly with respect to crimes of state, there is an increasingly acknowledged institutional gap in the international legal order that is closed, if slightly, by private, non-governmental normative initiatives possessing a certain law-creating impact.

Because law is clear on the books does not prove that it deserves respect or that it is adequate. The events in Iran show us that some clear rules of international law have been broken, but they also suggest that the content and impact of this law is arbitrary and one-sided. Given the historical shifts in the world, including the upsurge of power in the Third World, it is not clear why the old law should be kept as is. But it is also not by any means certain that governments will create a more balanced law dealing with embassy use and abuse, as well as with whether someone accused of serious state crime should be entitled to asylum rather than, say, to a fair trial under impartial auspices. This may be the moment for individuals, churches, and voluntary associations of various kinds to assert a human concern—that the future of international law is not a matter for governments only.

In time this concern, born of frustration and anxiety, could become a powerful basis on which to impose on sovereign states an effective framework of morally conditioned restraint. At least, it is worth pursuing this way out of surrendering unconditionally our birthright as moral beings to the monopolizing tendencies of the sovereign state.

2001 Postscript

The above text was composed during the latter stages of the Iran hostage crisis in 1980, and has not been modified except for minor stylistic changes. The United States was definitely supportive behind the scenes of Iraq's initiation of war against Iran, a war that persisted with great human casualties, for most of the decade, without any serious effort by the UN Security Council to condemn Iraq's aggression or to encourage a cease-fire. This Iraq–Iran War led to unexpected results. Iran's capacity for self-defense was surprisingly robust given the turbulence associated with the revolution, including the dismantling of the Shah's military establishment. The Iraqi failure to prevail in a long and costly war also gave rise to Saddam Hussein's abortive aggression against Kuwait, which lead to a break with the United States, and eventually to the Gulf War in 1991 under United Nations auspices that succeeded in restoring Kuwaiti sovereignty. The effects linger as the UN has maintained a sanctions regime for more than a decade, inflicting great suffering on the people of Iraq without any evident weakening of Saddam Hussein's hold on power. During this period Iran has been treated by the United States as a so-called "rogue state," supposedly threatening the overall stability of the region and the world both by sponsoring anti-Israeli terrorism and by proceeding with a covert program to develop a nuclear weapons capability.

The resolution of the hostage crisis finally occurred at the end of the Carter presidency, with the release of the unharmed hostages coinciding with the inauguration of Ronald Reagan as President of the United States in January 1981. Various allegations have been made, although none with convincing evidence, that the hostage release was deferred until after the 1980 presidential elections by secret agreement negotiated between officials of the government of Iran and individuals representing the Republican Party, but such allegations remain in the realm of speculation.

The internal developments in Iran have led to significant changes, but also to impressive continuities. The Khomeini legacy remains strong, with no leader daring directly to challenge his approach to Islam and the Iranian State. His successor as spiritual guide, and ultimate authority, Ayatollah Khamenei, has maintained a lower profile, but has sided with the more conservative tendencies. At the same time, within theologically established boundaries, a democratic process has evolved. With the election and re-election of Mohamed Khatami by large margins, it has become evident that the people of Iran, while not rejecting the revolution, seek political moderation and cultural freedom, as well as the fullest possible protection of human rights and democratic practices. By and large, the conservative leadership has accommodated these popular wishes to an extent that has surprised outside observers, although the internal tensions in Iran persist, and reactionary backlashes of various sorts persist that include punishment of critics of Islamic features of the state and interference with intellectual and social activity. Islamic law is applied in an often draconian fashion, with the stoning to death of women convicted of adultery occurring this year.

Perhaps the most remarkable series of developments bearing on the analysis in the earlier text concerns the moves to establish procedures to hold political leaders criminally accountable. Two sets of developments have ensued in the 1990s that follow closely the recommendations proposed above in relation to the Shah. The first developments are associated with the bloody wars that accompanied the breakup of former Yugoslavia, and led to various accusations of official criminality, especially directed at the Serb leadership held responsible for initiating "ethnic cleansing" against the Bosnian Muslims in the 1990s. At the initiative of the UN Security Council an ad hoc tribunal was established at The Hague with the name International Criminal Tribunal for the former Yugoslavia. A second similar tribunal was established by the Security Council to deal with accusations against the perpetrators of genocide in Rwanda during 1994. This line of development has reached its climax during the present year with the arrest of Slobodan Milosevic? in Belgrade and his transfer to a prison in The Hague to await prosecution for alleged crimes in Kosovo. These initiatives inspired elements in global civil society, in collaboration with receptive governments, to push for the establishment of a permanent international criminal court. The result has been the Rome Treaty that will bring such an institution into being, despite reluctance by the United States, in the next year or so—that is, as soon as the requisite 60 ratifications are obtained.

An even more dramatic series of events relate to the indictment of Augusto Pinochet for crimes committed during his period of dictatorial rule in Chile by a Spanish court, and his detention in Britain for two years while British judicial bodies debated the proper response to a Spanish request for extradition. Although Pinochet was eventually returned to Chile for medical reasons, and has similarly been exempted from prosecution in Chilean courts on the same grounds, the idea of the accountability of leaders and the role of national courts in upholding such basic international norms as the prohibitions on genocide, crimes against humanity, and torture has moved forward. One step in this direction has been the formulation of "The Princeton Principles of Universal Jurisdiction" that set forth guidelines for judges to follow when confronted with issues of this sort. It remains too soon to assess this line of development, but it certainly constitutes an important advance over the situation that existed during the debate on the Shah's susceptibility to criminal prosecution in Iran or elsewhere.

Despite the long passage of years, the interest of many private sector actors in engaging with Iran, and the softening of political Islam as a force directed against the West, Iran's relationship to the world community has not been entirely normalized. Under the leadership of President Khatami, Iran has been responsible for inducing the United Nations to sponsor activities related to "a dialogue of civilizations." Europe and Japan seem inclined to normalize relations with Iran at this point, but as with so many potentially positive steps to improve the quality of world order, it is the United States that is most adamantly and effectively opposed.

The Iranian political drama continues to unfold. Its future remains uncertain except that it seems likely to retain its theocratic political and constitutional framework for the foreseeable future. Whether the democratizing mandate of the citizens can achieve results is a central issue. In this regard, allowing Iran to participate fully in the world economy is likely to have beneficial social and political effects within the country, and persisting with efforts at diplomatic isolation are likely to add to the influence of hardliners.

The relevance of religion to political life is central to the destiny of the region, and Iran's solution will be of great importance beyond its boundaries. Iran is situated between the ultra-rigid view of Islam associated with Taliban rule in Afghanistan and the anti-religious secularism of Turkey that seems to confuse religious devoutness with political subversion, disallowing Islamically oriented political parties to participate fully in the constitutional order. Iran has the opportunity to demonstrate that a religiously oriented Islamic state can bring to its society a form of humane governance that meets the challenges of modernity without rejecting the values and identities of tradition.

LIMERICK
COUNTY LIBRARY

Epilogue

ENDING THE DEATH DANCE

Few would deny that September 11 unleashed a fearsome sequence of reactions, and none so far worse than the anguishing fury of this latest cycle of Israeli–Palestinian violence. Surely the United States is not primarily responsible for this horrifying spectacle of bloodshed and suffering, but there is a gathering sense here and overseas that the US government has badly mishandled its crucial role for a long, long time, and especially since the World Trade Center attack. As the situation continues to deteriorate for both peoples, there is a rising chorus of criticism that paradoxically blames the United States for doing too much on behalf of Israel and also not enough to bring about a durable peace. Both lines of criticism seem justified.

There is little doubt that part of the recent escalation can be traced back to President Bush's overplaying of the antiterrorist card since day one of the response to al-Qaeda. By over-generalizing the terrorist threat posed by the September 11 attacks, Bush both greatly widened the scope of needed response and at the same time gave governments around the planet a green light to increase the level of violence directed at their longtime internal adversaries. Several important governments were glad to merge their struggle to stem movements of self-determination with the US war on global terror, and none more than Ariel Sharon's Israeli government. The Bush administration has made several costly mistakes. By not limiting the response to the al-Qaeda threat, it has taken on a mission impossible that has no end in sight; even worse, the administration embraces war in settings where it has no convincing relationship either to US or human security. Related to this broadening of the goal is the regressive narrowing of the concept of terrorism to apply only to violence by non-state movements and organizations, thereby exempting state violence against civilians from the prohibition on terrorism. Indeed, this statist approach has been extended so far that it calls non-state attacks on military targets such as soldiers or warships terrorism, while not regarding

This piece first appeared in The Nation, *29 April 2002.*

state violence as terrorism even when indiscriminately directed at civilian society, as seemed the case at times during the Russian response to Chechnya's drive for independence and with respect to Israel's approach to occupation. Such a usage is ethically unacceptable, politically manipulative, and decidedly unhistorical. It is important to recall that the usage of the word terrorism to describe political violence derives from the need to name the government excesses that spun out of control during the French Revolution.

The issue here is not one of political semantics but of analysis and prescription. By designating only Palestinian violence as terrorism, Israel's greater violence not only avoids stigma in the American context but has been officially validated by being treated as part of the struggle against terrorism. The point here is not in any way to excuse Palestinian suicide bombers and other violence against civilians, but to suggest that when a struggle over territory and statehood is being waged it can and should be resolved at the earliest possible point by negotiation and diplomacy, and that the violence on both sides tends toward the morally and legally impermissible. This contrasts with the challenge of al-Qaeda, a prime instance of visionary terrorism that can neither be neutralized by negotiation nor deterred, and must and can be disabled or destroyed in a manner that is respectful of moral and legal limits. To conflate these two distinct realities, as Bush has consistently done, is at the root of the US diplomatic failure to diminish to the extent possible the threats posed by the September 11 attacks and to offer the Palestinians and Israelis constructive guidance.

Another feature of the situation infects commentary from virtually every corner of the debate, also reflecting the mindlessness of a statist bias. Everyone from George Mitchell to George Bush seems entrapped in the mantra that it is of course to be expected that every sovereign state must react violently and punitively against any significant act of terror directed against it. Many of these commentaries also take note of the degree to which such counter terror gives rise to worse violence on the other side, revealing the bankruptcy of the approach. It is truly a vicious circle. At the same time, it never sees that the logic of such vengeful violence works reciprocally. If the dominant actor pursues such an approach, what of the weaker side? When the Palestinians strike, their actions are never understood here as reactive and understandable, always provocative. Never has this been truer than with respect to the horrifying Passover bombing at Netanya and the equally horrifying Israeli incursion with tanks and helicopters throughout occupied Palestine. If one is treated as essentially acceptable and the other condemned, it deforms our understanding.

The same dynamic applies to the endless discussion about Yasir Arafat's role. It is condemned, to varying degrees, while Sharon's bloody past is rarely mentioned. Sharon is usually treated with respect or, at most, Palestinian intransigence is given as the reason Israelis chose such an extreme leader in a democratic election.

But the problems of US leadership cannot all be laid at the feet of the Bush presidency. Just as crucial was the insufficiency of the Oslo peace process, and the blame game that has been played ever since the outbreak of the second intifada in late September 2000. It has been endlessly repeated, without any demonstration, that the Israelis under Prime Minister Ehud Barak made a generous offer at Camp David in the summer of 2000. It is then alleged that Arafat rejected an offer he should have accepted and resumed armed struggle. Further, it has been alleged that Arafat's rejection was tantamount to saying that the struggle was not about establishing a Palestinian state but about ending the existence of the Jewish state. It was this one-sided assessment, alongside others, that led to Sharon's election, which meant that Israel would henceforth be represented by a man with a long record of uncompromising brutality toward Palestinians and a disregard of their legitimate claims for self-determination.

But was Arafat to blame for the failure of the Oslo endgame? I think it was a most unfortunate failure of leadership by Arafat not to explain to the Palestinians, Israelis, and the world why Barak's Camp David proposals were unacceptable. It should be remembered that Arafat at one point seemed on the verge of accepting them but backed away only when confronted by the unhappiness of a large proportion of his own people with the sort of Palestinian state that would result. It should also be remembered that the entire negotiation concerned 22 percent of the original British mandated territory of Palestine, about which the Palestinians were expected to strike compromises while leaving the 78 percent that was Israel out of account. Further, the future of the settlements in the occupied territories was to be addressed by Israeli annexation of half of them, including 80 percent or more of the settlers, despite the settlements' illegality and the degree to which their existence was a daily irritant to Palestinian sensibilities. And on refugees, there were evidently some signs of a compromise in the making at the supplemental negotiations at Taba in January 2001, but nothing was written down, and it was far from clear that Barak could have delivered on what was offered even if re-elected, so strong were Israeli objections to any return by Palestinians to pre-1967 Israel. Beyond this, it was expected that the security of Israel was to be maintained in such a way as to put any emergent Palestine in a permanent position of subordination, thus denying the fundamental message of any genuine peace: insuring equivalence between the two states for the two peoples. The Palestinians would sooner or later challenge such a solution even if their leaders could be induced to sign on the dotted line. Many have forgotten that a widespread fear among Palestinians at the time of Camp David was that Arafat would sell his soul and that of his people (especially the more than 50 percent who were refugees) for the sake of a state, any state, as this was thought to be his sense of personal mission.

Similarly, the widespread contention in American circles that Arafat opted for terrorism is also seriously misleading. Such thinking deforms perceptions of what is reasonable. Arafat was up against more militant forces in the Palestinian movement throughout this period and was generally viewed as the most moderate voice among the Palestinian leadership; he had even shown an early willingness to incur the wrath of Hamas and Islamic Jihad militias by taking seriously his duty to prevent the territories under the administration of the Palestinian Authority from being used against Israel and Israelis. Beyond this, it was Sharon's own provocative visit to the al-Aqsa Mosque that started the second intifada. This visit proceeded despite fervent warnings about the explosion likely to happen, given privately to the Barak leadership by the most respected Palestinians, including the late Faisal Husseini, head of Orient House in Jerusalem.

The Palestinian demonstrations that followed were notably nonviolent at the outset. Israel countered from the beginning by using excessive force, killing and seriously wounding demonstrators in large numbers and by its practice of extra-judicial assassination of a range of Palestinians living in the West Bank and Gaza. At this point the escalatory spiral was initiated, with Israel acting with ever more force at each stage, ratcheting up the stakes to such a level that the Palestinians were being attacked with among the most sophisticated weapons of warfare, including very modern tanks and helicopter gunships. It was in the course of this process that Palestinian resistance gradually ran out of military options, and suicide bombers appeared as the only means still available by which to inflict sufficient harm on Israel so that the struggle could go on. I was a member of a human rights inquiry appointed by the UN Human Rights Commission a year ago; our report fully supported this line of interpretation in its study of the second intifada, as did the overwhelming majority of the Security Council membership. The basic conclusion of these efforts at impartial understanding was that Israel was mainly responsible for the escalations and that its tactics of response involved massive violations of international humanitarian law.

Closely related is the matter of continued Israeli occupation of the West Bank and Gaza, a reality that has been fully re-enacted in the past few weeks. It poses the question of what sort of right of resistance is enjoyed by an occupied people when the occupying power ignores international law and refuses to withdraw. Such a right of resistance does not permit unrestricted violence, but it certainly would seem to legitimize some armed activities. It puts in a different light the furor raised in January by the intercepted arms shipment that was evidently intended for Palestinian use. Should the opposition, in the context of the sort of struggle that has gone on for decades, have no right to gain the means of self-help while the occupying power can arm itself to the teeth, all the while denying international accountability and refusing UN authority?

Here is the essential point: The Palestinian mainstream learned via Oslo that its cease-fire would not produce a fair solution in the form of sovereign and equal states and that its real interests had been sacrificed on the altar of geopolitics. In effect, negotiations would be bargains reflecting the realities of power and control rather than either a pathway to some mutually acceptable form of parallel states or what many Palestinians had expected—namely, resolution by reference to international law. It is important to appreciate that on virtually every issue in contention, the Palestinians have international law on their side, including the Israeli duty to withdraw from land taken during a war, the illegality of the settlements under Article 49(6) of the Fourth Geneva Convention, the right of refugees to a safe return to the country that wrongfully expelled them, and the generalized support for a Jerusalem that belongs to everyone and no one. In other words, if fairness is understood by reference to international law, the outcome would look nothing like what was offered in the Barak/Clinton proposals. Such a result would come nowhere close to satisfying the right of self-determination as understood by almost all Palestinians and as achieved long ago by the Israelis. The failure of the US government to uphold Palestinian rights and the inability of the UN to implement its authority was extremely disillusioning for moderate Palestinians, and this tended to shift attention to the ouster of Israel from southern Lebanon through the use of force by Hezbollah.

What is worse, virtually all of the discussion about reviving the peace process, including that of the Palestinian leadership, is a matter of going back to a reconstituted Oslo—that is, negotiations between the parties after a cease-fire has been agreed upon. The Mitchell Commission report moves in this direction, as does the Tenet plan for putting a cease-fire into effective operation. Even these rather flawed initiatives have been stymied primarily by Sharon's hostility to the whole idea of peace negotiations under international auspices that would draw into question the settlements or address the grievances of the refugees and the sovereignty of Jerusalem in any way that would satisfy even the most moderate Palestinian expectations. The Palestinian Authority can also be faulted on the opposite basis for too readily subscribing to the "honest broker" claim of the United States in relation to the peace process, despite abundant evidence over the years of the degree to which the US government pursues an unabashedly pro-Israeli foreign policy that is underpinned by massive annual foreign assistance, mostly for weapons purchases. At the very least, Palestinian leaders should point to the problem and possibly seek more neutral auspices for these matters of life and death for their people. If real peace is the goal, we cannot get there from here!

It is this tragedy that continues to be played out in the most reprehensible ways. To say this is not to underestimate the difficulty of a good-faith peace process that meets the needs of both peoples. It would be a mistake to pretend that international law provides all the answers, although it does give guidance as to what is reasonable, given the overall controversy. On refugees, for instance, implementing international law would surely doom any agreement, since almost all Israelis would regard an unrestricted Palestinian right of return as tantamount to the destruction of the Jewish state. My conversations with many Palestinians suggest that there would be a great willingness to find a formula that both sides could accept, possibly relying on an Israeli acknowledgment of the wrongfulness of the expulsions, especially in 1948, provisions for compensation for lost property and limited opportunities for return phased in over time. If the Israeli leadership were prepared to work for the establishment of a Palestinian state equal to their own, I would anticipate an outpouring of Palestinian efforts to reassure Israel of its own sovereign identity.

Oddly, despite its record of partiality, only the United States seems to have the current capacity to put the two states on such a genuine peace track, but it is not likely to do so until pushed hard from within and without. An American civic movement of solidarity with the well-being of both peoples is essential, as is a more active independent European and Arab involvement. Both latter possibilities are becoming more plausible with each new atrocity. The belated yet still welcome Saudi initiative, offering normalization of Arab diplomatic relations in exchange for Israeli withdrawal to 1967 borders, is an important contribution. And Europe seems ready to propose a more independent alternative to what Washington has been offering if the White House cannot do better. Bush's call for Israel to withdraw its military forces from Palestinian areas "without delay" was somewhat encouraging, although it was immediately neutralized by Sharon's insistence on finishing the operation, and by the fact that Bush sent Secretary of State Colin Powell to exert pressure but allowed him to adopt the most non-urgent itinerary, including several intermediate stops in North Africa. Such a diplomatic pattern has been widely criticized as incoherent at best, but at least it is a modest improvement over backing Sharon's recent criminal assault on Palestinian cities and towns.

If the United States does do better, then these new forces of engagement could at last begin to draw the line between a process that merely puts the weaker side in the position of either accepting what is offered or getting blamed for not doing so, and a real process that gives both sides what they need: security and sovereignty. Of course, it will be difficult to move forward with the present cast of leaders and mainstream assumptions. But we should at least be clear that Sharon is a much bigger obstacle to real peace than Arafat is or ever was.

Acknowledgments

The first contact I had with the writings of Richard Falk was in 1993, while rummaging through a box of books that the librarian at the Inter-American Court of Human Rights had given me to sort. I was undertaking graduate research at the court in San José, Costa Rica, and was given the task of sorting out these English-language books to determine which should be placed on the library's shelves. I picked up a book of Richard Falk's and leafed through it; then, crouching between the stacks, I started to read segments, then chapters, and finally, I spent all of the working day and that evening going through the book cover to cover. Falk's words leapt out at me. It was as if he were speaking directly to me. His words on paper were like words in my ear; I could finish his sentences, and yet I could not wait to see what subject he would next tackle.

It was for me, as Edward Said has said about the writings of Jean-Paul Sartre or Bertrand Russell, "their specific, individual voices and presence that make an impression on me over and above their arguments because they are speaking out for their beliefs. They cannot be mistaken for an anonymous functionary or careful bureaucrat." It seems to me Richard Falk is the only prominent living scholar in the discipline of international law who does not seek the rewards of the state by trumpeting a party line. He does not mince words, he does not seek to make friends in high places—he simply speaks his mind about law and its place, not in solidifying the status quo, but in transforming ours into a just international society. Henceforth, whenever I undertook research, I took note of the relevant Falk writing. Although I sometimes disagreed with him, I always took his views into consideration.

When I heard Richard Falk speak for the first time, I must admit, I was disappointed. It was 1996, next door to the Graduate Institute for International Studies in Geneva where I was in the process of undertaking the coursework for a Ph.D. in international law. Falk spoke of the need for an entity other then the state to step forward with the benevolence that could create a social safety net. What I failed to see (as perhaps others failed to see that day) is that Falk is a work in progress. Each public speech or article is a way forward, a small piece of a much larger puzzle. He does not rehash old lectures or pull something out of the hat at the last minute. He is perpetually focusing on his next work, pushing forward with his Grotian quest to understand the world we live in and maybe leave it a better place than he found it.

The next contact I had with Falk was in late 1998 during a political science faculty meeting at the American University in Cairo (AUC), where I had just taken on a post as lecturer in public international law. Members of the faculty had been asked early in the semester to nominate eminent individuals to visit under our Distinguished Visiting Professor program. As a recent arrival, I thought it not my place to put a name forward, but I told myself that next year I would nominate Falk. Much to my delight, a senior colleague, Dan Tschirgi, beat me to it, and by a unanimous vote Falk was chosen. I brought Falk's curriculum vitae home for the weekend, and going through it I was astounded to count 50 pieces on the Middle East. I then remembered an exercise that James Patrick Sewell, who had supervised my Master's thesis in Canada, had once recommended. If I remember correctly, he had undertaken a study of the writings of Inis Claude, and proposed that I do the same with a scholar I respected. At the time I had balked, but with Falk as my subject, I warmed to the idea.

In May 2000, when Richard and his wife Hilal came to Cairo as our distinguished guests, Richard was agreeable, curious, and above all a good listener, interested and open to the many people who sought his time. I managed to spend an afternoon with him near the great pyramids of Giza, at the Mena House. This place, with its long history, including the wartime meeting between Winston Churchill and Chiang Kai-shek, made for an ideal place to interview Richard about the roots of his interest in the Middle East. That month, Richard gave a set of three lectures in the Oriental Hall of the American University in Cairo. His final lecture, asking the question "Can Political Democracy Survive the Religious Resurgence?" is the first piece in the section on Islam.

The appendix, which is the "2001 Report of the UN Commission on Human Rights on the Question of the Violation of Human Rights in the Occupied Arab Territories, Including Palestine," provides an interesting supplement to Falk's essays—for he is, in large part, the author of this impressive document. The rest of the book is comprised of the essays I culled from the 50 Middle East articles I found on his CV. I must thank Hoda el Ridi of the AUC Library, who managed to track down all those articles, leaving me only the pleasure of reading them.

I would also like to acknowledge with gratitude Ingy Kamel's assistance, which allowed me to coordinate getting the full manuscript to Phyllis

Bennis, despite the affair taking place on three continents. I would like to thank Phyllis, of Olive Branch Press and Washington's Institute for Policy Studies, and Pam Thompson, at Interlink, for guiding this project through the publishing process.

Finally, I would like to thank Richard Falk. This project has allowed me to interact with him, on paper and in person, for the last two years; I have been privileged to learn to look at the world through his eyes. I hope this anthology not only conveys the depth of Falk's understanding of the Middle East, but that it fosters, in some way, a new perspective on US policy in this part of the world.

Appendix

QUESTION OF THE VIOLATION OF HUMAN RIGHTS IN THE OCCUPIED ARAB TERRITORIES, INCLUDING PALESTINE

Report of the human rights inquiry commission established pursuant to UN Commission on Human Rights resolution S5/1 of 19 October 2000

From the 57th session of the Commission on Human Rights
Item 8 of the provisional agenda
E/CN.4/2001/121
16 March 2001
GE 0111872 (E)

Contents

I. Introduction

1. On 19 October 2000, the Commission on Human Rights adopted resolution S5/1 establishing a commission of inquiry to investigate violations of human rights and humanitarian law in the occupied Palestinian territories after 28 September 2000 and to provide the Commission on Human Rights with its conclusions and recommendations. In pursuance of this resolution, a human rights inquiry commission was established on 2 January 2001, comprising Professor John Dugard, (South Africa), Dr. Kamal Hossain (Bangladesh), and Professor Richard Falk (United States of America). Initially Professor Dugard and Dr. Hossain acted as Co-Chairpersons but, during the course of the visit to the occupied Palestinian territories (OPT), Professor Dugard was appointed as Chairman.

2. The Human Rights Inquiry Commission ("the Commission") held its first meeting in Geneva from 14 to 16 January 2001 to discuss its mandate, methodology, and programme of action. It then visited the occupied Palestinian territories (OPT) and Israel from 10 to 18 February 2001.

3. On the evening of its arrival in Gaza on 10 February 2001, the Commission met with the Palestinian Authority President, Yasir Arafat, who gave the Commission an account of the situation from the perspective of the Palestinian Authority. While in Gaza, the Commission held meetings and discussions with members of the Palestinian Authority, nongovernmental (NGOs), the Palestinian Red Crescent, the International Committee of the Red Cross (ICRC), international agencies (notably the Office of the United Nations High Commissioner for Human Rights (OHCHR), the United Nations Special Coordinator in the occupied territories (UNSCO) and the United Nations Relief and Works Agency for Palestine Refugees in the Near East (UNRWA)), journalists, lawyers and members of the Palestinian Legislative Council. It also interviewed several young men who had been seriously wounded during demonstrations by gunfire from the Israeli Defence Force (IDF) and visited a hospital in Khan Yunis where it saw persons hospitalized as a result of gas inhalation. En route to Khan Yunis, the Commission visited the Qarara area, near the Kusufim road leading to settlements, where it saw agricultural land that had been bulldozed and houses that had been demolished by the IDF and it spoke with the occupants of these houses, who are now living in tents. At Khan Yunis the Commission visited the Tufar checkpoint adjacent to the Neve Dekalim Jewish settlement. While the Commission members were speaking to journalists at this point, two shots were fired from a nearby building at the settlement. This evoked a heavy response from the IDF base attached to the settlement, resulting in three casualties, two of which were serious. Thereafter, the Commission interviewed persons who had suffered as a result of gunfire or the destruction of property.

4. The Commission spent Wednesday, 14 February interviewing Israeli NGOs and Israeli interlocutors who provided the Commission with a broader understanding of the context of the conflict and the legal position adopted by the government of Israel. On 15 and 16 February the Commission visited Ramallah, where it met with members of the Palestinian Authority, the Palestinian Legislative Council, the Palestinian Peace Negotiation Affairs Department, and Palestinian NGOs, lawyers and academicians. On the morning of 16 February, before leaving for Ramallah, the Commission met with the representatives of member states of the European Union, whose views confirmed many of the opinions expressed by other interlocutors interviewed by the Commission. Later in the morning of 16 February the Commission spoke with Christian and Muslim leaders (including those responsible for the management of the Al-Aqsa mosque) and met with Mr. Faisal El Husseini at Orient House. On Saturday, 17 February the Commission travelled to Hebron, where it met with the Temporary

International Presence in Hebron (TIPH) and the Mayor of Hebron. Owing to the tense security situation arising from the funeral of a person killed by IDF gunfire on the previous night, it was unable to visit "H2," the area of Hebron under Israeli military control. After leaving Hebron, it visited the Aida Refugee Camp near Bethlehem and inspected an UNRWA school and houses which had been heavily damaged by IDF shelling. Thereafter, it met with a wide range of interlocutors and journalists in Jerusalem.

5. While in Jerusalem, the Commission held evening meetings with widely respected Israeli academic and intellectual figures, who were able to inform the Commission about the legal context of the conflict and the Jewish settlements in the West Bank and Gaza and provide Israeli perspectives of the intifada. On the afternoon of 16 February, the Commission visited the East Jerusalem neighbourhood of Gilo, which had come under gunfire from the Palestinian town of Beit Jala. On the last day of its visit, the Commission met with an Israeli political scientist and a former Israeli IDF General.

6. At the request of the Commission, the staff of the United Nations Secretariat accompanying the Commission conducted a number of confidential interviews with victims in Gaza, Ramallah, Hebron and Jerusalem. The texts of these interviews were shared with members of the Commission.

7. The government of Israel made it clear from the outset that it would not cooperate with the Commission. Two letters were addressed to the government of Israel before the departure of the Commission for Israel requesting meetings with the government; a final letter containing a similar request was sent while the Commission was visiting the area. Despite these efforts, the government of Israel consistently maintained its policy of noncooperation with the Commission. The Commission is, however, pleased to report that the government did not in any way obstruct the work of the Commission and indeed facilitated its visit to Israel and the occupied territories by granting Dr. Hossain an entry visa. (The other two Commissioners did not require visas for their visit.)

8. Jewish settlements in the West Bank and Gaza feature prominently in this report. For this reason, the Commission approached the Council of Jewish Settlements of Judea, Samaria and Gaza (Yesha) in order to obtain their views at first hand. After consideration and consultation with the government of Israel, the Council decided not to cooperate with the Commission.

9. The Commission made a concerted effort to obtain information and opinions about human rights violations and violations of international humanitarian law from both the Palestinian and the Israeli perspectives. The Commission regrets the refusal of the government of Israel to cooperate with it. This meant that it could not obtain specific responses to allegations of human rights violations and violations of international humanitarian law or benefit from interaction on the concerns of the Commission. The Commission believes, however, that it was adequately informed as to the official Israeli position through its study of the Israeli submissions to the Mitchell Commission and the

government's response to the report of the High Commissioner for Human Rights and by speaking to informed Israeli interlocutors. It also had the benefit of a discussion with former General Shlomo Gazit, the Chief Military Coordinator of West Bank and Gaza Policy in the period 1967–1974 and a keen student of military affairs and security doctrine.

II. Methodology

10. The Commission has studied numerous reports on matters affecting human rights and humanitarian law in the occupied Palestinian territories since the start of the second intifada on 28 September 2000. During its visit to Israel and the occupied territories, it heard a considerable amount of evidence on such matters. In addition, it experienced violence at first hand, spoke to victims and inspected destroyed properties and the sites of some of the worst confrontations between demonstrators and the IDF. The impressions and interpolations of the Commission and the testimony received by the Commission confirm the views expressed by the most respected and reliable NGOs in the region. The Commission has, therefore, relied to varying degrees on the findings of respected NGOs where they were supported by reliable eyewitness accounts and where they coincide with other evidence received by the Commission. In other words, the Commission is guided in its report by the best available evidence. Most of this evidence is not disputed by either the Palestinian Authority (PA) or the government of Israel, although they tend to place an interpretation different from that of the Commission upon it.

11. In its report the Commission refers to facts and figures that show the magnitude of the violations of human rights and international humanitarian law in the OPT. These facts and figures have been taken from a wide variety of sources. Every attempt has been made to confirm their accuracy by reference to reports on the same incidents from other sources. Where there is any doubt about the accuracy of a particular factual situation, no statistics are given about it.

12. The present report will show that the IDF, assisted by settlers on occasion, has been responsible for most of the human rights violations and violations of international humanitarian law in the OPT. This is not to overlook the fact that human rights violations have been committed by Palestinians, either under the authority of the PA or by individual Palestinians acting seemingly without authority. Where necessary, the present report draws attention to these violations.

13. The mandate of the Commission is to report on violations of human rights and international humanitarian law in the OPT. Both the government of Israel and the PA allege that the other party has violated the Oslo Accords in fundamental respects during the present intifada. The Commission makes no attempt to pronounce on these allegations, except where they impinge upon matters falling within its mandate.

14. In the course of its investigation, the Commission met leaders of civil society in both Israel and the OPT. We were impressed with their understanding

and vision. Leaders of this kind offer the best prospect for the future of Palestine and the normalization of relations between Jews and Arabs.

15. The Commission hopes that its report will serve to advance the peace process. The attitude of the Commission is that, while there can be no human rights without peace, a durable peace is not likely to be attained if it is not founded on respect for human rights and the rule of law.

III. Clarifying the Context: Illusion & Reality

16. It was evident in all phases of our inquiry into the patterns of violations of human rights and international humanitarian law during the second intifada that an appreciation of the behaviour of the parties involved depended on having an understanding of the surrounding context. Each side has felt justified in taking the action that has accompanied recent moves, although each side gives its own self-serving interpretation of its legal, moral and political character. It is important to comprehend these differences in the process of seeking an objective assessment of the various allegations of violative conduct. It is just as important to avoid equating adversary positions as equally persuasive. In the setting of the Israeli-Palestinian relationship it is of pervasive significance that the Palestinian people are struggling to realize their right of self-determination, which by virtue of international law and morality provides the foundation for the exercise of other rights. Of comparable significance is the appreciation of the extent to which Israel's continued occupation of Palestinian territories has remained the most formidable obstacle to Palestinian self-determination.

17. The Commission came away from this inquiry with two overriding assessments that are at once discouraging and illuminating.

18. The first involves perceptions and focuses on the extent to which the two sides perceive the central reality of their respective positions from diametrically opposed constructions of the meaning of recent events. In essence, the government of Israel and most Israelis conceive of the breakdown of the Oslo process as creating for them a severe and novel security crisis. Most Israelis view the second intifada as an indication that Palestinians are unwilling to resolve their conflict by peaceful means, having rejected what is regarded as a generous offer by the government of Israel at the Camp David II and Taba stages of the Final Status negotiations. The nature of this crisis is such that, according to this dominant Israeli perspective, the encounter with the Palestinians has moved from a relationship between an occupying Power and an occupied people to one between conflicting parties in a state of belligerency or war, implying a virtual absence of legal and moral constraints, at least on the Israeli side, provided only that a self-serving argument of military necessity is set forth.

19. In the starkest possible contrast, the Palestinian Authority and most Palestinians perceive the current phase of their relationship with Israel as brought about by a combination of the distortions associated with the implementation of the Oslo principles, the failure to implement a series of authoritative United

Nations resolutions, most particularly Security Council resolutions 242 (1968) and 338 (1973), and grave breaches by Israel of the Fourth Geneva Convention. These aspects of the situation are further seen as responsible for the full harshness of Israeli occupation as it affects adversely the daily lives of the Palestinians. Such circumstances are regarded as profoundly aggravated by the continued expansion of Israeli settlements throughout the period of the Oslo process and by the IDF role in their protection. The combination of these elements is regarded by most Palestinians as the proximate cause of the escalating spiral of violence set off by the provocative events at Harem al-Sharif/Temple Mount on 28 September 2000. In this regard, the second intifada is viewed as a spontaneous series of moderate and proportional responses to an occupation that has been maintained and perpetuated in defiance of the authority of the United Nations since it was established in 1967. From this perspective, the Palestinians contend that they continue to seek a negotiated end to the conflict to attain a peaceful settlement that is fair to both sides and upholds the security of both peoples on the basis of mutuality.

20. Our second closely related conclusion is associated with the somewhat disguised link between the modality of Israeli occupation as a result of changes brought about by the Oslo process and the subsequent intifada, with its escalating spiral of violence. It is of critical importance to appreciate the interaction between the redeployment of the IDF since 1994 and the implementation of the Oslo Accords. In effect, the IDF withdrew by stages from most of the areas on the West Bank and Gaza inhabited by the bulk of the Palestinian population, and yet sustained, and even intensified, its control over the borders between the Palestinian territories and Israel and among the various districts internal to the OPT. Even more significantly, owing to the retention of the settlements situated throughout the Palestinian territories [...], the West Bank and Gaza were divided into "A," "B," and "C" areas, with the Palestinian Authority exercising full administrative control over A, while Israel exercises security control over B and retains exclusive control over C. In effect, a series of internal boundaries were established by agreements implementing the Oslo Accords, so as to enable Israel to provide protection to the settlements while withdrawing from areas densely populated by Palestinians. The effect of such a redistricting of the Palestinian territories was to produce a situation of extreme fragmentation, making travel very burdensome for Palestinians who went, for work or otherwise, from one part of the territories to another: checkpoints were maintained where detailed searches were carried out that resulted in long waits and frequent humiliation, greatly burdening Palestinian rights of movement even under normal circumstances. In the course of the second intifada, this already difficult situation has been severely aggravated by frequent closures and blockades that have prevented the movement of goods and persons across both internal and external borders. Most Palestinians described the situation of recent months as living under "a state of siege."

21. Such a pattern of control and security can only be understood in relation to the settlements and their need for safe access to and from Israel. The main IDF function in the occupied Palestinian territories is to guard the settlements and the access and bypass roads. The relationship is such that the settlers are given unconditional priority whenever their presence impinges upon that of the Palestinian indigenous population. For instance, all Palestinian traffic is stopped while a single settler vehicle passes on an access road, causing long delays and much resentment. While travelling, particularly in Gaza, the Commission had its own direct experience of this situation. When a violent incident occurs, Israeli closures further inhibit travel, often preventing or greatly detaining even emergency traffic, such as ambulances. The Commission verified several accounts of deaths due to an inability of Palestinians to receive timely medical attention. Israel has invested heavily in an elaborate system of bypass roads in the West Bank designed to provide most settlements and the IDF with the means to travel to and from Israel, and between settlements, without passing through Palestinian-controlled areas. Palestinians view these roads with alarm, both because of their substantial and symbolic encroachment upon the heart of a future Palestinian state and, more so, because the magnitude of the investment and effort involved in such a development seems to impart an Israeli view that most of the settlements on the West Bank will never be removed. This situation contrasts with Gaza, where access roads cut through Palestinian territory and have not been specially constructed. In this regard, the settlement structure in Gaza seems removable by negotiations on final status in a manner that at present does not appear likely in relation to the West Bank.

22. Part of the perceptual gap is associated with the effects and nature of the violence. Israelis appear to connect most of their casualties with the stonethrowing demonstrations, interspersed at times with Palestinian gunfire. The Palestinians associate casualties on their side mainly with what they view as Israeli/IDF overreaction to these demonstrations. It was the clear judgment of the Commission that Palestinian casualties were indeed mainly associated with these direct encounters, but that, to the best of our knowledge, the IDF, operating behind fortifications with superior weaponry, endured not a single serious casualty as a result of Palestinian demonstrations and, further, their soldiers seemed to be in no life-threatening danger during the course of these events. It was the definite view of the Commission that the majority of Israeli casualties resulted from incidents on settlement roads and at relatively isolated checkpoints at the interface between A, B, and C areas, that is, as a consequence of the settlements, and irritations resulting indirectly therefrom. In this regard, account must be taken of settler violence against Palestinian civilians in areas adjoining settlements, and of IDF complicity in such violence. A pervasive feature of the tensions associated with the second intifada is the clear affinity between the IDF and Jewish settlement communities, and the equally evident hostility between these communities and the surrounding Palestinian population.

23. The language associated with the second intifada is also relevant to an assessment of human rights violations and violations of international humanitarian law. Both sides tend to view the violence of the other side as comprising "terrorism." The Israelis view attacks by Palestinians, especially beyond "the Green Line" (pre-1967 Israel), as terrorism even if directed against official targets such as IDF soldiers or government officials. Palestinians regard the IDF tactics involving shooting unarmed civilian demonstrators (especially children) or relying on tanks and helicopters against demonstrators, in retaliation for shots fired from refugee camps, and assassinations of targeted individuals as state terrorism. The legal status of these patterns of violence is difficult to establish authoritatively. Part of the current complexity relates to the Israeli contention that a condition of armed conflict has replaced that of belligerent occupancy as a result of IDF withdrawals from A zones, and the transfer of governing authority in those areas to the PA. Another part of the complexity arises from the Palestinians' contention that they enjoy a right of resistance to an illegal occupation.

24. There is another fundamental discrepancy of perception. Israel believes that its security measures, including border and road closures, represent reasonable, even restrained, measures of response to Palestinian unrest and opposition. To the extent that Israel relies on the superiority of its weaponry or inflicts most of the casualties, such behaviour is rationalized as necessary to demoralize a numerically superior enemy, nipping its resistance in the bud. Such lines of explanation were set forth by Israeli witnesses to explain and justify even the use of live ammunition by the IDF against unarmed Palestinian demonstrators during the opening days of the second intifada. During these crucial days there was no evidence of Palestinian gunfire.

25. The Palestinians view this link between Palestinian acts of resistance and Israeli responses from an entirely different angle of interpretation. To Palestinians, the Israeli use of force from day one of the second intifada, and indeed before Ariel Sharon's visit on 28 September to the Al Aqsa mosque, was intended to crush any Palestinian impulse to oppose openly the continued Israeli domination and occupation of the West Bank and Gaza. For most Palestinians, the closures of roads and borders, destruction of homes and property, and accompanying measures of curfews and restrictions are regarded as clear expressions of an Israeli policy of inflicting collective punishment upon all Palestinian inhabitants. Palestinians also rejected the view that the Palestinian Authority, and its police, had the capacity to prevent hostile demonstrations or to ensure the absence of violent incidents involving targets within Israel. When Israel responded to such events by punishing the territories as a whole it was viewed by Palestinians as vindictive, unjust and illegal because such a response lacked any discernible connection to either the perpetrator or to prospects for deterrence of future violence.

26. Closely related to such perceptions are differences of viewpoint as to the nature of the second intifada. Israelis tended to contrast the first with second intifadas. The first intifada was seen in retrospect by Israelis as having been a

largely spontaneous, bottom-up and nonviolent expression of opposition to Israeli occupation. It was, in such circumstances, not reasonable to hold the Palestinian leadership responsible for the disorder. According to Israelis, the second intifada was instigated from above so as to mount a timely challenge to the Israeli leadership at a delicate moment in the peace negotiations. It was a calculated plan to improve upon an exceedingly weak Palestinian bargaining position and it also represented a serious failure by the Palestinian Authority to carry out its obligations under the Interim Agreements flowing from Oslo to maintain security for Israel in areas subject to its authority.

27. The Palestinians see the second intifada from an entirely different perspective, essentially from the outlook of an occupied people. They regard the demonstrations as spontaneous eruptions of pent-up hostile sentiment arising from years of frustration, disappointment and humiliation. Palestinians interpret the Israeli responses as consistent with the basic structure of the occupation of their territories, as onesided, lacking in empathy for the Palestinian civilian population, and designed to punish and crush any signs of resistance.

28. From this perspective, the Palestinians see the greater reliance by Israel on heavy weapons and deadly fire in the second intifada, as compared to the first, as seeking to discourage Palestinians from either raising the level of their resistance or resisting altogether. This reliance on the tactics of war is also perceived as providing Israel with a pretext for avoiding the restraints associated with the exercise of police responsibilities or relating to the application of standards of human rights.

29. In addition to these basic structural issues, it is of great importance to appreciate the added vulnerability of Palestinian refugees who comprise about 50 percent of the population in the Palestinian territories and whose number is increasing at a rate of more than 3 percent per annum. While the Israelis tend to perceive Palestinians resident in the territories as a single reality, without according any special attention to the refugees, the Palestinians are far more conscious of the acute suffering that Israeli security measures have brought to the refugee communities during this second intifada.

30. These refugees have been particularly victimized during the second intifada, often being trapped within their crowded confines by closure and curfew measures, which has made it impossible for many refugees to keep their jobs. Unemployment is high, savings almost nonexistent, with great suffering resulting. Also, for historical reasons, the Palestinian refugees, alone among refugee communities in the world, fall outside the protective regime of the Office of the United Nations High Commissioner for Refugees (UNHCR). UNRWA provides relief and humanitarian aid, but is not constitutionally or politically empowered to provide needed protection, a conclusion supported for us by discussions with leading United Nations officials and NGO experts.

31. A further fundamental question of human rights relates to the extreme differences between the parties on matters pertaining to the core dispute, the

wider refugee issue and its relationship to a successful peace process. The Israeli consensus regards the assertion of any serious demand to implement a Palestinian right of return in relation to Palestinians expelled from 530 villages in 1948 as a decisive complication in the search for "peace." The Palestinian approach is more varied and tentative. Some Palestinians do insist that the right of return be fully implemented in accordance with international law, which accords priority to repatriation to the extent desired. More frequently, Palestinians seem more flexible on this matter, seeking mainly a symbolic acknowledgement by Israel of the hardships associated with the expulsions, some provision for compensation and some possibilities for Palestinian family unification. This Palestinian view suggests that if there is Israeli good will on other outstanding issues, such as Jerusalem and the settlements, then controversy over the right of return can be addressed in a manner that takes account of practical realities that have developed in the course of the more than 50 years since the critical events.

32. Overall, the government of Israel and Israeli public opinion tend to regard all Israeli uses of force as reasonable measures of security, given the altered connection between the two societies as a result of the IDF redeployment associated with the Oslo process. Such security measures need to be stringent and intrusive so as to afford protection to the settlements, and to settler movement to and from Israel. Israeli security is a catch-all justification for all policies directed coercively at the people of Palestine. Such a major premise enables the Israeli outlook to view any Palestinian recourse to force as tantamount to "terrorism." The perceptual gap is greatest on this issue of violence and its interpretation, as Palestinians view their acts of opposition as reasonable responses to an illegal occupation of their homeland, treating their violence as produced by consistent Israeli overreaction to non-violent resistance. Additionally, Palestinians universally reject Israel's wider security rationale and view restrictions on movement, closures, property destruction, political assassinations, sniper shootings and the like as punitive and vindictive practices inconsistent with their fundamental human rights, as well as with the minimum restraints embodied in international humanitarian law.

33. There is one comprehensive observation bearing on the perception of United Nations authority by the two sides. Israelis tend to view the United Nations and most of the international community as completely unsympathetic to their quest for security, as well as biased in favour of Palestinian claims and grievances. On their side, the Palestinians feel disillusioned about the effectiveness of United Nations support and abandoned in their hour of need for elemental protection. Palestinians refer to the myriad United Nations resolutions supporting their cause, but never implemented. In this sense, both sides are currently suspicious about the role of the United Nations, its outlook, capacity and commitment.

34. Three conclusions follow from this consideration of Israeli-Palestinian perceptual gaps:

(a) The importance of encouraging better contact between persons of good will on both sides so that communication between the parties is more open and takes greater account of the views of the other side. This observation applies particularly to journalists, currently by and large confined within their respective societies, who tend to provide readers with partisan accounts of the interaction of Israelis and Palestinians that are uncritical of their respective official positions and to employ language that reinforces "enemy" stereotypes of "the other";

(b) The challenge to the organs of the United Nations to rehabilitate their reputation in relation to both Israel and the Palestinian Authority, and the two populations, by seeking to achieve objectivity in apportioning legal and political responsibility, in calling for certain conduct in the name of international law, and in fashioning proposals for peace and reconciliation. As important, or more so, is the need to take steps to ensure that United Nations directives, whether in the form of resolutions or otherwise, are implemented to the extent possible, and that non-compliance is addressed by follow-up action;

(c) An appreciation that a commitment to objectivity does not imply a posture of "neutrality" with respect to addressing the merits of controversies concerning alleged violations of human rights and international humanitarian law. Judgements can and must be made. It is useful to recall in this connection the statement of the Israeli Minister for Foreign Affairs, Shlomo Ben-Ami, on 28 November 2000 in the course of a Cabinet discussion, opposing the release of supposed Palestinian transgressors during the early stages of the second intifada: "Accusations made by a well-established society about how a people it is oppressing is breaking the rules to attain its rights do not have much credence" (article by Akiva Elder in *Ha'aretz*, 28 November 2000). Such a perspective underlies the entire undertaking of our report. We have attempted to the extent possible to reflect the facts and law fairly and accurately in relation to both sides, but we have evaluated the relative weight of facts and contending arguments about their legal significance. This process alone enables us to draw firm conclusions about the existence of violations of international legal standards of human rights and of international humanitarian law.

IV. The Legal Status of the Conflict

35. The legal status of the West Bank and Gaza and the legal regime governing relations between Israel and the people of Palestine have been in dispute ever since Israel first occupied the West Bank and Gaza in 1967. As the sovereignty of Jordan over the West Bank was questionable and Egypt never asserted sovereignty over Gaza, the government of Israel took the view that there was no sovereign Power at whose expense it occupied these territories. Consequently, although Israel is a party to the Fourth Geneva Convention of 1949, it maintained that it was not bound in law to treat the territories as occupied territories within the meaning of the Fourth Geneva Convention. Despite this, Israel agreed to apply certain of the humanitarian provisions contained in the Fourth Geneva Convention to the occupied territories on a de facto basis.

36. The peace agreements between Israel and the Palestinian Authority, hereafter referred to as the Oslo Accords, have superimposed an additional level of complexity on an already disputed legal situation. It is now argued by Israel that, despite the prohibitions contained in article 47 of the Fourth Geneva Convention on interfering with the rights of protected persons in an occupied territory by agreement between the authorities of the occupied territory and the occupying Power, the Oslo Accords have substantially altered the situation. In particular, it is argued by Israel that it can no longer be viewed as an occupying Power in respect of the "A" areas, accommodating the majority of the Palestinian population, because effective control in these areas has been handed over to the Palestinian Authority.

37. The status of the West Bank and Gaza raises serious questions, not only for the above reasons, but also because of the impact of human rights and self-determination on the territory. A prolonged occupation, lasting for more than 30 years, was not envisaged by the drafters of the Fourth Geneva Convention (see art. 6). Commentators have therefore suggested that in the case of the prolonged occupation, the occupying Power is subject to the restraints imposed by international human rights law, as well as the rules of international humanitarian law. The right to self-determination, which features prominently in both customary international law and international human rights instruments, is of particular importance in any assessment of the status of the West Bank and Gaza. The right of the Palestinian people to self-determination has repeatedly been recognized by the General Assembly of the United Nations and there can be little doubt that the ultimate goal of the Oslo peace process is to establish an independent Palestinian state. Indeed over 100 states already have relations with the Palestinian entity, not unlike relations with an independent state, while the Palestinian Authority has observer status in many international organizations. The Palestinian question is, therefore, seen by many as a colonial issue and the recognition of Palestinian statehood as the last step in the decolonization process initiated by the General Assembly in its resolution 1514(XV).

38. Uncertainty about the status of Palestine in international law has complicated the conflict between Israel and the Palestinian people since 29 September 2000. The government of Israel argues that it can no longer be seen as an occupying Power in respect of the A areas because it has ceded control over these territories to the Palestinian Authority. Moreover, it argues that, unlike the first intifada, in which the weapons of the Palestinian uprising were mainly stones, the weapons of the new intifada include guns and heavier weaponry, with the result that there is now an armed conflict between Israel and the Palestinian people led by the Palestinian Authority. This argument seeks to justify the use of force resorted to by the IDF in the present conflict. In essence, Israel argues that it cannot be seen as an occupying police power required to act in accordance with police law enforcement codes, but that it is engaged in an armed conflict in which it is entitled to use military means, including the use of lethal weapons, to suppress

political demonstrations, to kill Palestinian leaders and to destroy homes and property in the interest of military necessity.

39. Clearly, there is no international armed conflict in the region, as Palestine, despite widespread recognition, still falls short of the accepted criteria of statehood. The question then arises as to whether there is a non-international armed conflict, defined by the Appeals Chamber of the International Criminal Tribunal for the Former Yugoslavia in the Tadic case, as "protracted armed violence between governmental authorities and organized armed groups." The Israeli argument that the threshold for an armed conflict has been met is based on the fact that there have been some 3,000 incidents allegedly involving exchanges of gunfire and that Palestinian violence is organized and orchestrated by the Palestinian Authority. A contrary view advanced by the Palestinians is that the present intifada is to be categorized as an uprising of large elements of a civilian population against an occupying Power's unlawful abuses of its control over that population and its environment; that the uprising has been instigated by loosely organized elements of the population opposed to Israeli occupation of Palestine and the failure of the Palestinian Authority to improve the lot of the Palestinian people; and that there are no properly organized armed groups, let alone armed groups coordinated or organized by the Palestinian Authority.

40. It is difficult for the Commission to make a final judgment on this matter. However, it inclines to the view that sporadic demonstrations/confrontations often provoked by the killing of demonstrators and not resulting in loss of life on the part of Israeli soldiers, undisciplined lynchings (as in the tragic killing of Israeli reservists on 12 October 2000 in Ramallah), acts of terrorism in Israel itself, and the shooting of soldiers and settlers on roads leading to settlements by largely unorganized gunmen cannot amount to protracted armed violence on the part of an organized armed group. This assessment is confirmed by the peace that prevails in those areas of the West Bank and Gaza visited by the Commission. The Commission realizes that this assessment, based on a brief visit to the region and the views of witnesses and NGOs generally unsympathetic to the IDF, may not be fully accurate. However, there is enough doubt in the minds of the members of the Commission as to the prevailing situation to place in question the assessment of the situation as an armed conflict by the IDF justifying its resort to military rather than police measures.

41. In the opinion of the Commission, the conflict remains subject to the rules of the Fourth Geneva Convention. It does not accept the Israeli argument that the Fourth Geneva Convention is inapplicable by reason of the absence of a residual sovereign Power in the OPT. This argument, premised on a strained interpretation of article 2 of the Convention, fails to take account of the fact that the law of occupation is concerned with the interests of the population of an occupied territory rather than those of a displaced sovereign. The argument that Israel is no longer an occupying Power because it lacks effective control over A areas of the OPT carries more weight, but is likewise untenable. The test for the

application of the legal regime of occupation is not whether the occupying Power fails to exercise effective control over the territory, but whether it has the ability to exercise such power, a principle affirmed by the United States Military Tribunal at Nuremberg in *In re List and Others* (*The Hostages Case*) in 1948. The Oslo Accords leave Israel with the ultimate legal control over the OPT and the fact that for political reasons it has chosen not to exercise this control, when it undoubtedly has the military capacity to do so, cannot relieve Israel of its responsibilities as an occupying Power.

42. While an occupying Power or party to a conflict may be given a margin of interpretation in its assessment of the nature of the conflict, it cannot be allowed unilaterally to categorize a situation in such a way that the restraints of international humanitarian law and human rights law are abandoned. For this reason, the Commission suggests that the High Contracting Parties to the Geneva Convention should seriously address the nature of the conflict and Israel's obligations as a party to the Fourth Geneva Convention. The Commission is mindful of the Israeli objection to the "politicization" of the Geneva Conventions, but it sees no alternative to the exercise of the supervisory powers of the High Contracting Parties under article 1 of the Fourth Geneva Convention. Israel's objection that article 1 does not oblige a High Contracting Party to "ensure" respect for the Convention on the part of other states parties runs counter to the views of the ICRC and to the general obligation on the part of states to ensure respect for humanitarian law.

43. Even if the conflict is categorized as an armed conflict, entitling the IDF to greater latitude in the exercise of its powers, the IDF is certainly not freed from all restraints under international humanitarian law and human rights law. It is still obliged to observe the principle of distinction requiring that civilians may not be made the object of attack, "unless and for such time as they take a direct part in hostilities" (a principle reaffirmed in article 51 (3) of Additional Protocol I to the Geneva Conventions). Stone throwing by youths at heavily protected military posts hardly seems to involve participation in hostilities. Moreover, there is considerable evidence of indiscriminate firing at civilians in the proximity of demonstrations and elsewhere. In addition, the IDF is subject to the principle of proportionality which requires that injury to non-combatants or damage to civilian objects may not be disproportionate to the military advantages derived from an operation. The use of lethal weapons against demonstrators and the widespread destruction of homes and property along settlement roads cannot, in the opinion of the Commission, be seen as proportionate in the circumstances. Human rights norms also provide a yardstick for measuring conduct in the OPT, as there is general agreement that such norms are to be applied in the case of prolonged occupation. The 1979 Code of Conduct for Law Enforcement Officials and the 1990 Basic Principles on the Use of Force and Firearms by Law Enforcement Officials reflect the human rights norms applicable in the case of law enforcement and crowd control. It is against this background that allegations of

human rights violations and violations of international humanitarian law will be considered in the following section.

V. Excessive Use of Force

44. Casualties have been high in the present intifada. According to conservative estimates, as at 21 February 2001, 311 Palestinians (civilians and security forces) have been killed by Israeli security forces and civilians in the OPT; 47 Israelis (civilians and security forces) have been killed by Palestinian civilians and security forces; 11,575 Palestinians and 466 Israelis have been injured; 84 Palestinian children under the age of 17 years have been killed and some 5,000 injured; 1 Israeli child has been killed and 15 injured; 271 Palestinian civilians and 40 members of the security forces have been killed; while 27 Israeli civilians and 20 members of the security forces have been killed.

45. Most of the Palestinian deaths and injuries have been caused by live ammunition (deaths: 93 percent; injuries: 20 percent), rubber-coated bullets (deaths: 1 percent; injuries: 37 percent), and tear gas (deaths: 1 percent; injuries: 32 percent). Most of these deaths and injuries have occurred in confrontations/demonstrations held on the perimeters of A areas, roads to settlements or junctions on the road to settlements. There is no evidence that members of the IDF responsible for such killings or the infliction of such injuries were killed or seriously injured. On the contrary, the evidence suggests that members of the IDF, behind concrete bunkers, were in most cases not exposed to life-threatening attacks by stone- or Molotov-cocktail-throwers, or even by sporadic gunfire from gunmen in or around the demonstrations. This assessment is vigorously disputed by the IDF, which maintains that rubber-coated bullets and live ammunition have only been used in life-threatening situations.[1] However, statistics, reflected in the number of Palestinian deaths at demonstrations and the absence of IDF deaths or serious injuries at such confrontations, the evidence of eyewitnesses who testified before the Commission and the reports of NGOs and international bodies place the IDF assessment in serious question. It is difficult to resist the conclusion that most of these demonstrations could have been dealt with by methods normally used to suppress violent demonstrations, such as water cannons, tear gas and soft rubber bullets (of the kind used in Northern Ireland). Also, it is unclear why the IDF has not used riot shields to protect itself against stone-throwers. By and large the evidence suggests that the IDF is either not trained or equipped to deal adequately with violent demonstrations (despite its long experience in coping with such demonstrations) or that it has deliberately chosen not to employ such methods. For this reason the Commission shares the view expressed by many NGOs that the IDF is to be censured for failing to comply with the methods for law enforcement laid down in the law enforcement codes of 1979 and 1990 referred to above. The Commission likewise shares the concerns of NGOs about the failure of the IDF to comply with its own open-fire regulations relating to the use of live ammunition in situations of this kind.

46. Even if the above assessment is incorrect and the confrontations in question were manifestations of an armed conflict between the IDF and an organized Palestinian force, the Commission is of the view that the response of the IDF fails to meet the requirement of proportionality and shows a serious disregard for civilians in the proximity of the demonstrations.

47. The Commission received disturbing evidence about both the rubber-coated bullets and the live ammunition employed by the IDF. The former are, apparently, designed to target particular individuals and not to disperse crowds. Moreover, it is misleading to refer to them as "rubber bullets" as they are metal bullets with a thin rubber coating. The live ammunition employed includes high-velocity bullets which splinter on impact and cause the maximum harm. Equally disturbing is the evidence that many of the deaths and injuries inflicted were the result of head wounds and wounds to the upper body, which suggests an intention to cause serious bodily injury rather than to restrain demonstrations/confrontations.

48. International law obliges the military to be particularly careful in its treatment of children. Of the Palestinians killed, 27 percent have been children below the age of 18 years and approximately 50 percent of those injured have been below the age of 18 years. These children have been armed with stones or, in some cases, Molotov cocktails. The Israeli position is that the participation of children in demonstrations against the IDF has been organized, encouraged and orchestrated by the Palestinian Authority after thorough indoctrination against Israelis. While the Commission is prepared to accept that some children are likely to have been exposed to anti-Israeli propaganda in school or special training camps, it cannot disregard the fact that demonstrations are substantially the result of the humiliation and frustration felt by children and their families from years of occupation. The Commission heard evidence from parents and NGOs about the unsuccessful attempts of many parents to prevent their children participating in demonstrations and the grief caused them by the death and suffering of their children. In this respect, Palestinian parents are no different from Israeli parents. It is likely that the Palestinian Authority could have done more to restrain children from participation in stonethrowing demonstrations. The evidence suggests that, on occasion, the Palestinian police made attempts to prevent demonstrations, but these attempts were often unsuccessful. This can be ascribed to the incompetence of the Palestinian police, the fact that the Palestinian police were themselves targeted by stone-throwers when they attempted to curtail demonstrations, and an understandable identification of the Palestinian police with the goals and spirit of the demonstrators. History is replete with instances of cases in which young people, prompted by idealism, despair, humiliation and the desire for excitement, have participated in demonstrations that have confronted an oppressive regime. In recent times children have behaved in a similar way in Northern Ireland, South Africa, Indonesia and elsewhere. The insistence of the IDF that the Palestinian demonstrators, humiliated by years of military occupation which has become part

of their culture and upbringing, have been organized and orchestrated by the Palestinian Authority either shows an ignorance of history or cynical disregard for the overwhelming weight of the evidence.

49. The excessive use of force on the part of the IDF and the failure to comply with international humanitarian law is further demonstrated by the failure of the IDF to respect the vehicles of the Red Crescent and other medical vehicles. Statistics show that vehicles of the Red Crescent have been attacked on 101 occasions. The IDF has also prevented ambulances and private vehicles from travelling to hospitals. In this respect, it should be stressed that the Palestinians have likewise shown a lack of respect for medical vehicles and there have been 57 incidents in which Palestinians have attacked personnel and vehicles of the Magen David Adom.

50. In the present intifada, the IDF apparently on grounds of military necessity, has destroyed homes and laid to waste a significant amount of agricultural land, especially in Gaza, which is already land starved. Statistics show that 94 homes have been demolished and 7,024 dunums of agricultural land bulldozed in Gaza. Damage to private houses is put at US$ 9.5 million and damage to agricultural land at about US$ 27 million. Most of this action has occurred on roads leading to settlements, ostensibly in the interest of the protection of settlement vehicles. The Commission inspected some of the devastation caused by the IDF along settlement roads. On the Kusufim road, in the Qarara district, it inspected land that had been bulldozed for a distance of some 700 metres from the road. Houses situated on this land had been destroyed and families compelled to live in tents. Water wells in the vicinity had also been completely destroyed. The Commission found it difficult to believe that such destruction, generally carried out in the middle of the night and without advance warning, was justified on grounds of military necessity. To the Commission it seemed that such destruction of property had been carried out in an intimidatory manner unrelated to security, disrespectful of civilian well-being and going well beyond the needs of military necessity. The evidence suggests that destruction of property and demolition of houses have been replicated elsewhere in the West Bank and Gaza. Palestinians, like other people, are deeply attached to their homes and agricultural land. The demolition of homes and the destruction of olive and citrus trees, nurtured by farmers over many years, has caused untold human suffering to persons unconnected with the present violence. Even if a low-intensity armed conflict exists in the West Bank and Gaza, it seems evident to us that such measures are disproportionate, in the sense that the damage to civilian property outweighs military gain. Here it should be stressed that the Fourth Geneva Convention prohibits the destruction of private property by the occupying Power "except where such destruction is rendered absolutely necessary by military operations" (art. 53).

51. The Commission concludes that the IDF has engaged in the excessive use of force at the expense of life and property in Palestine. At the same time the Commission wishes to express its horror at the lynchings of Israeli military

reservists in Ramallah on 12 October 2000, the killing of Israelis at a bus stop in Tel Aviv by a Palestinian bus driver on 14 February 2001 and similar incidents that have done much to inflame Israeli public opinion against the Palestinian uprising.

52. There is no evidence that the IDF has taken serious steps to investigate the killing or wounding of Palestinians, except in a handful of cases, even where the circumstances strongly suggest that soldiers had behaved in an undisciplined or illegal manner. The excuse that no investigations are required on account of the characterization of the conflict as armed conflict is not convincing and shows a disregard for the provision of the Fourth Geneva Convention which requires the occupying Power to prosecute those guilty of committing grave breaches and other infractions of the Convention (art. 146). Equally unconvincing are the reasons given by the Palestinian Authority for its failure to investigate and prosecute the killings of Israelis, particularly those responsible for the Ramallah lynchings.

VI. Extrajudicial Executions/Political Assassinations

53. Extrajudicial executions or targeted political assassinations carried out by the IDF have resulted in only a small number of deaths and cannot compare in magnitude with the more widespread suffering caused to the Palestinian population. The Commission has, however, decided to pay special attention to these killings, because they have been officially acknowledged, promoted and condoned.

54. Israel has long been accused of being responsible for the assassination of targeted Palestinian individuals, but it is only during the second intifada that such a practice has been officially acknowledged and defended at the highest levels of the government of Israel. In early January 2001, the Israeli Deputy Minister of Defence, Ephraim Sneh, justified the policy in the following language: "I can tell you unequivocally what the policy is. If anyone has committed or is planning to carry out terrorist attacks, he has to be hit ... It is effective, precise and just." At a meeting of the Foreign Affairs and Defence Committee, Prime Minister Ehud Barak put the claim more broadly: "If people are shooting at us and killing us, our only choice is to strike back. A country under terrorist threat must fight back." And more directly, while visiting a military command on the West Bank, Mr. Barak was quoted as saying, "The IDF is free to take action against those who seek to harm us."

55. There is further official confirmation of the Israeli claim of right with respect to extrajudicial killings. When the IDF West Bank military commander, Brigadier-General Beni Gantz, was asked whether Israel was pursuing a "liquidation" policy with respect to the Palestinians, he responded as follows: "You said liquidation, not me. We will initiate action as necessary. We will not stop such action as long as there is a threat." Israel's Chief of Staff, Shaul Mofaz, invoked the legal opinion issued by the Military Advocate-General, Menachem Finkelstein, that it was permissible in exceptional cases to kill Palestinian terrorists, expressed in the following guarded language: "This is not routine, but an exceptional method whose goal is to save human lives in the absence of any other alternative

... It is used against people [who have] definitely [been] identified as having worked, and are working, to commit attacks against Israel." It should be noted that the Military Advocate-General uses more circumscribed language than do the political and military leaders, but his guidelines are self-applied, depending upon the accuracy of Israeli intelligence and upon good faith in limiting such tactics to circumstances of an exceptional character.

56. One prominent instance of a political assassination involved the sniper shooting of Dr. Thabat Ahmad Thabat in Tulkarem, West Bank, as he was driving his car from his house in the morning of 9 December 2000. Dr. Thabat, a dentist, 50 years of age, father of three, held official positions in the Palestinian Health Ministry and was a lecturer on public health at Al-Quds Open University. He was the Fatah secretary in Tulkarem and was in regular contact with Israeli NGOs working in the area of health and human rights. Several Israeli witnesses appearing before the Commission expressed dismay about the killing of Dr. Thabat, describing him as their "friend" and "partner" in the search for peace. Such expressions do not preclude the possibility that Dr. Thabat may have had a double identity, but Israel has produced no evidence of his complicity in violence against Israeli targets, beyond the vague allegation of his involvement in "terrorist activities." Press reports indicated that Israeli Special Forces undertook this action against Dr. Thabat as part of a military operation that consisted of "cleansing" Fatah security capacities in view of the demonstrations inside the Palestinian territories, and specifically at Tulkarem. Ms. Siham Thabat, the widow of Dr. Thabat, submitted a petition to the Supreme Court of Israel asking for an end to Israel's "cleansing policy," described as imposing "capital punishment without trial." The petition was dismissed. As far as is known, the prosecution submitted no further evidence specifically implicating Dr. Thabat.

57. While the Commission was present in the Palestinian territories, another prominent instance of extrajudicial killing occurred. It involved the use of a Cobra helicopter gunship to attack Massoud Iyyad with three rockets on 14 February 2001 while he was driving his car in Gaza near the Jabalya refugee camp. Mr. Iyyad was a lieutenant colonel and high-ranking member of Force 17, an elite security unit specifically assigned the task of protecting Yasir Arafat. Israeli security forces claimed credit for the assassination, contending that Mr. Iyyad was a leader of a Hezbollah cell in Gaza that was intending to transform the second intifada into a Lebanon-style war of attrition of the sort successfully waged by Hezbollah in the 1990s. Aside from the legality of such tactics, the allegations were never substantiated by the release of documentary or other evidence.

58. Such extrajudicial executions during the second intifada number at least 11, but the figure is probably much higher. Palestinian and independent sources put the figure at somewhere between 25 and 35. On at least one occasion, the killing of Hussein Ábayat on 9 November 2000 by anti-tank missiles fired at his car from helicopters, two women bystanders were also killed and three other Palestinians were seriously injured.

59. In a disturbing escalation of language associated with such violence, a designated spokesperson of the settler movement, Yehoshua Mor-Yosef, has been quoted as saying "Arafat is an enemy, he was never a partner. After seven years of war and him sending his own people to kill, we need to assassinate him."[2]

60. There have been several important political condemnations of extrajudicial killings. The government of the United States has expressed a critical attitude toward extrajudicial killing in a detailed exposition of the practice contained in the "occupied territories" section of the Country Reports on Human Rights Practices-2000 issued by the Department of State. On behalf of the European Union, its Presidency issued a declaration on extrajudicial killings, calling them "unacceptable and contrary to the rule of law," and urging Israel "to cease this practice and thus respect international law." (Brussels, 13 February 2001, 5928/01 (Presse 47)). This declaration was formally submitted by the Council of the European Union to the SecretaryGeneral of the United Nations with a request that it be circulated as a document of the General Assembly.

61. It is the view of the Commission that, whatever the truth of various allegations directed against specific individuals, the practice of political assassination is a fundamental violation of international human rights standards, as well as a grave breach of the Fourth Geneva Convention. Several human rights instruments, including the Universal Declaration of Human Rights and the International Covenant on Civil and Political Rights, affirm the right to life and specifically prohibit executions of civilians without trial and a fair judicial process.

62. Because the law of occupation also applies, provisions of this *lex specialis* take precedence over human rights. (For clarification of this conclusion, see the discussion on the legal status of the conflict in section IV above.) Thus, whether a particular loss of life is to be considered an arbitrary loss of life contrary to article 6 of the International Covenant on Civil and Political Rights can only be decided by reference to the law of occupation in the Fourth Geneva Convention. Article 4 of the Fourth Geneva Convention defines persons protected by the Convention as "those who, at a given moment and in any manner whatsoever, find themselves, in case of a conflict or occupation, in the hands of a Party to the conflict or Occupying Power of which they are not nationals." The phrase "in the hands of" simply means that the person is on territory that is under the control of the state in question and implies control that is more than mere physical control. Civilians lose the protection under the Fourth Geneva Convention when they become combatants by taking a direct part in hostilities (art. 51 (3) of Additional Protocol I). Israel contends that the victims of targeted political assassinations were combatants. This is unconvincing for two related reasons: they were not participating in the hostilities at the time they were killed; and no evidence was provided by Israel to back up its contention of a combat role despite their civilian appearance.

63. There is no legal foundation for killing protected persons on the basis of suspicion or even on the basis of evidence of their supposedly menacing activities

or possible future undertakings. On the contrary, article 27 of the Fourth Geneva Convention provides for the respect of protected persons, article 32 explicitly prohibits their killing under such conditions, and article 68 places restrictions on the application of the death penalty and, in any event, requires a prior judicial trial.

64. As the evidence indicates, Dr. Thabat and several others who were targets of political assassinations could have been arrested when, as was the case in this instance, he made almost daily trips to points under Israeli security control. The Commission concludes that the practice of targeted political assassination, which is fully acknowledged by the government of Israel at its highest levels, violates a number of provisions of the Fourth Geneva Convention. It also represents a grave breach of the Convention, which in article 147 refers to "willful killing" in this connection. Further, article 146 calls upon High Contracting Parties to enforce this prohibition in relation to those responsible for its violation.

VII. Settlements

65. Jewish settlements in the West Bank (including East Jerusalem) and Gaza feature prominently in the present conflict between Israel and the Palestinian people. This report focuses on the implications of the settlements for human rights and international humanitarian law during the second intifada.

66. Israel argues that the issue of Jewish settlements is a political one to be resolved in negotiations between Israel and the Palestinians over the political future of the OPT. Palestinians, on the other hand, see the settlement issue as a major impediment to the peace process and a question governed by international law. They argue that settlements are unlawful as they violate article 49 (6) of the Fourth Geneva Convention, which prohibits an occupying Power from transferring parts of its own civilian population into the territory it occupies. The international community has given its overwhelming support to the Palestinian position. Repeated resolutions of both the Security Council and the General Assembly condemn Jewish settlements in the West Bank and Gaza as a violation of the Fourth Geneva Convention. The same attitude is adopted by the International Committee of the Red Cross.

67. The Commission is itself of the opinion that Jewish settlements in the West Bank and Gaza violate article 49 (6) of the Fourth Geneva Convention and place a serious obstacle in the way of durable peace.

68. Since 1967, Israel has been responsible for establishing, financing and protecting Jewish settlements in the West Bank and Gaza. Initially this programme of creeping annexation pursued by means of the requisitioning and occupation of Palestinian land was justified by Israel on security grounds. This pretext has long been abandoned. Indeed, Yitzhak Rabin, while he was Prime Minister and Minister of Defence, acknowledged that most of the settlements added nothing to security and in fact were a burden on the army. Most settlements are today inhabited by civilian settlers motivated either by the ideology of Zionist expansion or by the comforts of a suburban way of life, subsidized by the government of

Israel. From the perspective of the government, settlements create factual situations on the ground that serve to establish political control over the occupied Palestinian territories.

69. Today there are some 190 settlements in the West Bank and Gaza, inhabited by approximately 380,000 settlers, of whom some 180,000 live in the East Jerusalem area. Settlements have expanded considerably since the start of the Oslo peace process and accelerated under the Prime Ministership of Mr. Barak. Settlements have continued to expand since the start of the second intifada. The map in annex III gives an indication of the extent to which settlements are scattered throughout the territories, and the population of the different settlements. Settlements differ considerably in size and location. Some number over 10,000 inhabitants, while others have fewer than 100 inhabitants. Some are situated at a considerable distance from Palestinian towns, whereas others are situated within a Palestinian city, as, most prominently, in the case of the Jewish settlement in Hebron, or on the doorstep of a Palestinian village or refugee camp. The settlement of Neve Dekalim, for instance, is situated adjacent to the crowded refugee camp of Khan Yunis. It was here that the Commission came under gunfire from the IDF.

70. In Gaza, settlement roads run through Palestinian territory and cross roads used by Palestinians, causing great traffic congestion for Palestinians whose vehicles are required to halt every time a settler or military vehicle approaches a crossroad. In the West Bank, on the other hand, Israel has built a vast road system, running for some 400 km, which bypasses Palestinian population centres and enables settlers and military forces protecting them to move speedily and safely through the West Bank. To achieve this, 160,000 dunums of land were requisitioned, much of it under cultivation by Palestinian farmers. Moreover, in some instances, Palestinian homes were demolished without compensation for the purpose of constructing this network of bypass roads. These roads prevent the expansion of Palestinian villages and undermine the economic development of Palestinians by restricting Palestinian movement and impeding the flow of commerce and workers from one Palestinian area to another. The scale of the investment in this road network raises troubling questions about Israel's long-term intentions for the West Bank.

71. The relationship between settlers and Palestinians is an unhappy one and each side views the other with hostility, anger and suspicion. Protected by the Israeli military, and exempt from the jurisdiction of the courts of the Palestinian Authority, settlers have committed numerous acts of violence against the Palestinians and destroyed Palestinian agricultural land and property. Israeli justice has often either turned a blind eye to such acts or treated them with leniency bordering on exoneration. Inevitably, this has fuelled the resentment of Palestinians, who regard Israeli justice as biased in favour of settlers. Since the beginning of the intifada on 29 September 2000, incidents of settler violence have dramatically increased. Palestinian hostility to settlers has grown alarmingly

since the start of this intifada and most of the Israelis killed in the present conflict have been settlers or soldiers charged with the task of protecting settlements and roads leading to settlements.

72. Settlements are a major obstacle in the way of peace between Israelis and Palestinians. First, they virtually foreclose the possibility of a viable Palestinian state as they, together with the road system connecting them, destroy the territorial integrity of Palestine. In this sense, they act as a major impediment to the exercise of the right to self-determination within the internationally recognized self-determination unit of Palestine, i.e., the territory occupied by Israel after the 1967 war. Secondly, settlements provide daily evidence of the violation of international law and the failure of the international community, acting through the United Nations and the High Contracting Parties to the Geneva Conventions, to remedy such a situation. The despair and cynicism in the Palestinian community about the willingness of the international community to enforce the rule of law is in large measure due to its failure to halt the growth of the settler population and to persuade the government of Israel to reverse this practice.

73. The link between settlements and violence in the present intifada is clear. Many of the acts of violence carried out by the IDF and settlers that have resulted in Palestinian deaths and injuries have occurred on the heavily defended roads leading to settlements or in the proximity of settlements. Settlements provide a visible and proximate target for the anger fuelled by years of Israeli occupation. The IDF convoys and bases in the proximity of settlements aimed at the protection of such settlements have been the focal point of Palestinian demonstrations, violence and sharpshooting. Likewise, much of the Palestinian property bulldozed by the IDF has been destroyed not in the interests of military security, but the security of settlers. Homes, fruit and olive trees, and crops have been destroyed by the IDF in order to make settlers feel more secure and to facilitate their access to their settlements by means of protected roads.

74. Settlers, too, have suffered from their proximity to the Palestinian people. As the most visible symbols of occupation, they are obvious targets for Palestinian gunmen.

75. Without settlements or settlers, there can be no doubt that the number of deaths and injuries in the present intifada would have been but a small fraction of their current number and, quite possibly, the present intifada might not have occurred. Both Israelis and Palestinians are therefore paying a high price in terms of life, bodily integrity and property for a programme that violates a cardinal principle of international humanitarian law.

76. Settlements act as a perpetual reminder to the Palestinian people of the humiliation of military occupation. This sense of humiliation is aggravated by the apparently comfortable way of life of the settlers, whose standard of living contrasts sharply with the poverty of their Palestinian neighbours. Refugees in crowded camps, with poor sanitation and limited water resources, inevitably view with envy and anger settlements with swimming pools and well-watered lawns.

77. Palestinian witnesses before the Commission, from all sections of the community, despite being of different political persuasions and from different income groups, spoke with equal anger and resentment about the presence of settlements and settlers in their territory. Many claimed settlements were a prime cause of the present intifada, a view shared by international organizations working in the West Bank and Gaza.

78. The Commission reaffirms that settlements in the West Bank and Gaza constitute a major violation of international humanitarian law and identify the presence of settlements and settlers as a primary cause of many violations of human rights in the OPT.

VIII. Deprivation of the Enjoyment of Economic & Social Rights: Effects of Closures, Curfews, Restrictions on Movement & Destruction of Property

Introductory note

79. It needs to be kept in mind that the Palestinian population in the occupied territories is, even under normal conditions, very poor, particularly the 50 percent of the Palestinians living in refugee camps. To impose additional burdens on such a population is inevitably to create patterns of severe material, social and psychological hardships. These hardships entail denials of basic human needs, as protected by international human rights standards, which raises important issues of international law. To claim a security justification for policies that inflict such pronounced harm imposes a heavy burden of persuasion on the claimant, in this case the government of Israel. The internal closures seem to have a mainly punitive character quite unrelated to security and are more likely to have the opposite effect of inflaming Palestinian resistance. Even external closures, especially for the import of building materials and the export of agricultural products, would seem to be unrelated to the maintenance of security. The condensed presentation of the effects of closure and related policies in this section of the report must be read with such considerations in mind.

Restrictions on movement

80. Since 29 September 2000, Israel has imposed severe restrictions on freedom of movement in the occupied territories. During the 123-day period from 1 October 2000 to 31 January 2001, the Israeli-Palestinian border was closed for labour and trade flows for 93 days, or 75.6 percent of the time. Internal movement restrictions and internal closures—partial or severe—were in place for 100 percent of the time in the West Bank and for 89 percent of the time in Gaza. The Dahania Airport in the Gaza Strip, the only Palestinian airport, was closed for over half of this period. During this 123-day period, the international border crossings to Jordan from the West Bank and to Egypt from Gaza were closed for more than 20 percent and 40 percent of the time, respectively. The safe

passage connecting the Gaza Strip and the West Bank was closed from 6 October, greatly obstructing travel for Palestinians and diminishing the governmental effectiveness of the PA.

81. The cumulative effect of these restrictions on the freedom of movement of people and goods is understandably perceived by the Palestinians affected as a siege. It has resulted in severe socio-economic hardships in the Palestinian territory. The internal closures have effectively sealed Palestinian population centres and restricted movement from one locality to another. The restriction on the entry of Palestinians into Israel has meant denial of access to their places of work in Israel to an estimated 100,000 Palestinians. The economic results have been devastating: the families of these workers are now suffering from a complete lack of income, threatening them with destitution. The World Bank's projection that the impact of closure will raise unemployment to 50 percent and the poverty rate to 43.7 percent in 2001 has almost been realized.

Internal closure

82. The internal closure has disrupted life within the territories. Workers are unable to reach their places of work. Produce from farms cannot reach markets. Shops and commercial offices are unable to open. From 8 October, numerous limitations were placed on passage between the north and the south of the Gaza Strip and movement between Gaza City and the cities of Khan Yunis and Rafah was prevented almost entirely. Movement within the West Bank has become nearly impossible. Hundreds of IDF checkpoints have been erected throughout the West Bank and entry to and exit from cities requires passing through them. The IDF has placed checkpoints at the entrances to all villages and entry and exit are possible only via dirt roads, entailing enormous hardships. Trips that once took 15 minutes now take several hours. In some of the villages, mostly in areas near settlements and bypass roads, the dirt roads have also been blocked with large concrete blocks and piles of dirt, and residents are imprisoned in their villages. The Commission itself observed such IDF checkpoints and concrete blocks and piles of dirt obstructing access.

External closure

83. The closure of the international border crossings with Jordan and Egypt, as well as the restrictions on movement of goods from Israel to the territories, has had a direct negative effect on all sectors of the economy. The near total interruption of the supply of basic construction materials has closed factories and plants dependent on these materials for their production activities. The construction and building sector in the Palestinian territories has been practically suspended owing to imports of basic construction materials such as cement, steel and timber being denied entry by the IDF through their control of border checkpoints. This, in turn, has resulted in the unemployment of tens of thousands of workers and employees in the construction and building sector. The overall

disruption of the economy and unemployment, together with mobility restrictions and border closures, have resulted in an average unemployment rate of 38 percent (more than 250,000 persons) as compared to 11 percent (71,000 persons) in the first nine months of 2000. According to one estimate, unemployment now directly affects the income of about 910,000 people or 30 percent of the population.

Curfews
84. Curfews have been imposed in certain areas of the occupied territories, which in effect imprisons an entire population in their homes. For example, Palestinians in the H2 area of Hebron have been under curfew almost continuously since October 2000. The curfews appear to be imposed for the convenience of settlers in the area as they do not apply to settlers. The character and timing of Israel's restrictions on the freedom of movement challenge the contention that these restrictions are dictated purely by security considerations: Israel has imposed a sweeping closure, curfew and siege on millions of people, rather than on individuals who pose a security threat. In addition, the policy of restrictions of movement discriminates between the two populations living in the occupied territories, namely Palestinians and non-Palestinians, since the restrictions are imposed exclusively on the Palestinian population. In many cases, the explicit aim of the restrictions is to ensure freedom of movement for the settler population at the expense of the local population.

Negative economic impacts
85. In the absence of border closures, per capita income was projected to be about US$2,000 in the Palestinian territories in the year 2000. As a result of border closures and internal movement restrictions, this is estimated to be reduced to US$ 1,680, a decline of 16 percent. The gravity of this negative impact is measured, however, by the disproportionately high impact on people living below the poverty line (estimated by the World Bank at US$ 2.10 per person per day in consumption expenditures). The number of poor is estimated to have increased from about 650,000 persons to 1 million persons, an increase of over 50 percent. Given the continuing closures and restrictions of movement of people and goods and the resultant unemployment and total deprivation of income to increasing numbers of the population, poverty and near destitution are mounting. Humanitarian assistance has dramatically increased.

Economic losses
86. The direct economic losses arising from movement restrictions are estimated at 50 percent of gross domestic product (GDP) for the four-month period of the second intifada and 75 percent of wage income earned by Palestinian workers in Israel. The GDP loss is estimated at US$ 907.3 million, while the loss of labour income from employment in Israel is estimated at US$

243.4 million. The total loss is estimated at US$ 1,150.7 million. The loss is about US$ 11 million per working day or US$ 3 per person per working day during the period 1 October 2000–31 January 2001. Significant decreases in earnings in the transportation sector have been reported as a result of the internal siege. The tourism sector has also reported significant decline.

Public sector revenue losses: revenue losses and increased social spending
87. There have been significant losses to the public sector in the form of lost revenues. Domestic income and value added tax (VAT) revenues have been reduced as a result of lower levels of domestic income caused by disruptions in production and reduced labour flows into Israel. External revenues, mainly customs and VAT revenues associated with imports from Israel and abroad, have been reduced by lower commodity flows caused by movement restrictions and reduced consumer demand. In 1999, 63 percent of all Palestinian Authority revenues were in the form of transfers of receipts collected by the authorities under the terms of the Paris Protocol on Economic Relations of 1994. VAT, customs, income tax, health fees and other taxes collected by Israel on behalf of the PA are estimated at US$ 53 million monthly. These revenues have been withheld from the PA since October 2000. As a result of the eroded revenue base, the PA has been unable to pay salaries to its employees.

Destruction of property
88. There has been continued destruction of property, in particular in the vicinity of settlements or bypass and access roads to settlements, allegedly on grounds of military necessity or security considerations. On 7 October 2000, Israeli tanks and bulldozers invaded the Netzarim Junction and destroyed two residential buildings comprising 32 apartments near the Israeli military outpost. On 8 October, the IDF destroyed an iron-processing factory in the Netzarim area, while in the same area bulldozers swept the agricultural land on the southeastern and southwestern sides of the junction. On 16 October, bulldozers swept land to the north of Neve Dekalim settlement. On 19 October, the IDF swept land leading to the Gush Katif settlement bloc. The Commission visited this area and observed the destruction of the farms, the sweeping of the land and the destruction of citrus and olive trees. This process of destruction of farms, cutting down of fruit trees and demolition of greenhouses planted with vegetables continues. The Commission received evidence from victims whose homes and greenhouses had been destroyed, citrus and olive trees uprooted and farmlands swept by bulldozers.
89. According to one estimate, the Israeli authorities demolished 223 Palestinian-owned buildings during 2000: 68 in the West Bank (including East Jerusalem) and 155 in the Gaza Strip.

Effect of closures and movement restrictions on health care

90. The Commission received evidence of the restrictions obstructing access by the sick and the wounded as well as pregnant women to hospitals. There have also been instances where the prolonged closure of outside borders, including the airport in Gaza, impeded the transfer of wounded Palestinians to other countries for treatment. An example of the effect of denial of access to hospitals is provided by statistical data from St. Luke's Hospital in Nablus, which reported a 38 percent decline in the admission rate, a 29 percent decline in the occupancy rate, a 53 percent decline in the number of surgical operations performed, a 20 percent decline in the number of babies delivered, a 48 percent decline in the number of patients in the intensive care unit, a 49 percent decline in the number of general practice patients, a 73 percent decline in the number of visits to specialty services and a 30 percent decline in the number of physiotherapy cases in the period October–November 2000 as compared to the same period in 1999.

Effect of closures and movement restrictions on education

91. Since the beginning of October 2000, more than 40 schools are reported to have been closed or unable to operate owing to curfews or closures. In the centre of Hebron, 34 schools have been closed, resulting in unemployment for more than 460 teachers, and 13,000 students were reported to be without educational facilities. Four Palestinian schools in Hebron have been closed by the IDF and turned into military bases: the M'aref School, Usama bin Munkez School, the Johar School and the Al Ukhwa School. Several thousand children are reported also to have had to be permanently moved from school premises as a result of damage to the school structure.

92. Schools near flashpoints—173 in the West Bank and 23 in the Gaza Strip— were the worst hit. They were subjected to several kinds of assault, including bombing by the Israeli army and shooting by settlers.

Violations of internationally recognized human rights norms & international humanitarian law

93. The measures of closure, curfew or destruction of property described above constitute violations of the Fourth Geneva Convention and human rights obligations binding upon Israel. Destruction of property is prohibited by article 53 of the Fourth Geneva Convention, unless such destruction is rendered absolutely necessary for military operations, which does not appear to be the case for much of the destruction carried out. Other obligations under the Fourth Geneva Convention affected by closures are those under articles 23, 55 and 56. These require the free passage of consignments of medical and hospital stores and the free passage of foodstuffs, clothing and medicines intended for certain vulnerable categories of persons and impose a duty to ensure food and medical supplies to the population and to ensure and maintain medical and hospital establishments and services, and public health and hygiene in an occupied territory.

94. Human rights norms are also apposite in the context of the closures because, in the Interim Agreement, Israel and the Palestinian Council accepted that they should exercise their powers and responsibilities pursuant to that Agreement with due regard to internationally accepted norms and principles of human rights and the rule of law.[3] Human rights violated by the closures include the right to work, internationally recognized in article 6 of the International Covenant on Economic, Social and Cultural Rights. The severe socio-economic hardships caused by the restrictions on movement constitute a violation of the right to an adequate standard of living recognized in article 11 of that Covenant. Destruction of houses that leaves the occupants homeless also violates this right, since it specifically includes the right to adequate housing. The closures and movement restrictions interfere with the right of everyone to education. Children and students are prevented from attending classes, despite the duty of states to make secondary and higher education accessible to all by every appropriate means. In addition, restrictions on movement are also placed on journalists. This affects their reporting of events and constitutes a violation of their freedom of expression and, indirectly, of the population's right to seek and receive information, recognized in article 19 of the Covenant. This right may be subjected to certain restrictions, but only in certain circumstances and not as a general rule. The Palestinian Authority has also restricted the freedom of movement of journalists.

95. Finally, attention is drawn to article 33 of the Fourth Geneva Convention, which prohibits collective punishment. Israel has invoked security considerations to justify closures and other measures described above. From the Commission's own observations, it would appear that while in some instances security considerations may justify temporary closures, the comprehensive and protracted closures, as well as the scale and nature of the destruction of property of Palestinian civilians, is best regarded as collective punishment.

IX. Palestinian Refugees & the Second Intifada

96. The Commission seeks to draw attention to the distinctive vulnerability of Palestinian refugees as a special case of hardship during the course of the second intifada, particularly as a result of the Israeli policies of closure and blockade. It needs to be appreciated that, according to UNRWA figures for 2000, there are 1,407,621 registered Palestinian refugees living in the West Bank and Gaza, comprising over 50 percent of the Palestinian population in these territories. That figure represents only 38 percent of the total Palestinian refugee population, the remainder being spread out mainly in Jordan, Lebanon and the Syrian Arab Republic. There are two sets of issues relevant to our inquiry: first, the vulnerability of Palestinian refugees living in refugee camps on the West Bank and Gaza, and second, the so-called "right of return" issue.

97. There is, first of all, the anomalous status of Palestinian refugees due to their exclusion from the protective mechanisms and responsibility of UNHCR. No other refugee community in the world is so excluded. UNRWA was established

in 1949 to address the specific concerns of Palestinian refugees and became operational in 1950. This special regime acknowledging the importance of the refugee dimension of the Israel–Palestine relationship was reinforced over the years by critical United Nations resolutions dealing with the conflict. UNRWA was given responsibility for humanitarian aspects of the international effort to alleviate the material suffering of Palestinian refugees, but it was not entrusted with any protective functions. These functions were assigned to a parallel entity called the United Nations Conciliation Commission for Palestine (UNCCP), which, ironically, was established in response to General Assembly resolution 194(111) calling for the protection of Palestinian refugees. Unlike UNRWA, UNCCP has been incapable of carrying out its functions, encountering political and financial obstacles from its inception. Although UNCCP continues to exist on paper, it lacks a budget and personnel, and is effectively defunct. Yet, this organizational structure continues to define the legal status of Palestinian refugees.

98. In accordance with the 1951 Convention relating to the Status of Refugees, protection is accorded to all refugees under the authority of UNHCR except for the Palestinians. They are excluded because of article 1D of the 1951 Refugee Convention, which provides: "This convention shall not apply to persons who are at present receiving from organs or agencies of the United Nations other than the United Nations High Commissioner for Refugees protection or assistance." Despite the failure of UNCCP to supply the anticipated protection, Palestinian refugees remain in limbo and have never in the more than half a century of their existence been incorporated within the UNHCR regime.

99. Such a result is particularly disturbing as article 1D explicitly recognizes the possibility that alternative forms of protection may fail for one reason or another. The language of the second paragraph of 1D is clear beyond reasonable dispute on this matter: "When such protection or assistance has ceased for any reason, without the persons being definitively settled in accordance with the relevant resolutions adopted by the General Assembly of the United Nations, these persons shall ipso facto be entitled to the benefits of this Convention." There is no discernible reason to refrain from implementing this inclusionary provision, which should have been implemented decades ago.

100. The issue is not trivial. For one thing, the Commission was repeatedly told by a variety of witnesses, supplemented by documentary materials, that the refugees in the camps in the occupied territories were enduring hardships that exceeded those being experienced by the general Palestinian population, and that UNWRA officials felt unable to raise questions of a protective nature, regarding them as outside their humanitarian mandate and of a "political" character.

101. These protective concerns are directly associated with the distinctive pressures exerted by Israeli responses to the second intifada. The refugee camps are often prominent flashpoints in relations with the IDF and the settlements, prompting retaliatory "security" measures, especially prolonged closures, including blockages of access roads. Refugees are trapped in these overcrowded camps,

prevented from going to places of employment and often denied access to educational and medical facilities. The incidence of destitution resulting from the impact of the second intifada is significantly higher for refugees than for non-refugees, and is felt more keenly, as refugees lack land for subsistence agriculture or within which to move about. Our visits to several Palestinian refugee camps revealed to us the special sense of material and psychological hardship associated with the confinement and curfews of this period of intifada. Under such conditions, it is hardly surprising that much of the support for Palestinian militancy and armed struggle is generated within the refugee camps.

102. The second, wider question, which is associated with the right of return, concerns the future of refugees outside the territories as well as those within, and is mostly beyond the scope of the Commission's central mandate. Its relevance arises from the degree to which Israelis insist that accepting such a right would be an act of suicide on the part of Israel and that no state can be expected to destroy itself. Such an apocalyptic approach to the refugee issue obstructs overall moves toward a just peace.

103. In conclusion, the Palestinian refugees within the territories seem worse off than the Palestinian refugee diaspora in neighbouring countries. Further, the deterioration of their circumstances throughout the West Bank and Gaza has been accentuated by the heightened tensions and violence of recent months. These refugees require a variety of emergency protections that can only be provided by a concerted effort on an urgent basis at the international level. UNRWA, with its resources already strained and its operating conditions subject to interference, is not capable of providing the necessary protection.

X. Conclusions & Recommendations

104. The commission of inquiry has been deeply mindful of its responsibility to exercise every care to be objective and impartial in gathering information and evaluating the evidence upon which it would base its conclusions and recommendations with the aim of calling attention to violations of human rights and international humanitarian law since 29 September 2000, and encouraging future compliance with international obligations to the extent possible.

105. In making its recommendations, the Commission from the outset emphasizes the need to understand the context and circumstances in which violations of human rights and breaches of international humanitarian law have occurred and the situation which has given rise to an ascending spiral of violence since the end of September 2000, resulting in a serious deterioration of the human rights situation.

106. The historical context is one of conflict and successive wars (over 50 years), prolonged occupation (over 30 years) and a protracted peace process (over 7 years). The peoples affected continue to suffer from a legacy of distrust, humiliation and frustration, only occasionally relieved by glimmerings of hope, which has all but disappeared of late.

107. The most worrying aspect of the recent escalation of violence leading to the loss of lives, disabling injuries caused to thousands, and the destruction of property and livelihoods is that the hopes and expectations created by the peace process are for the moment being smothered by mutual perceptions ascribing the worst of motives to each other, thus generating intense distrust and negative and destructive emotions.

108. It is important to emphasize that both the Palestinian people and the people of Israel have a yearning for peace and security, and that a precondition for achieving a just and durable peace is for every effort to be made on all sides to ease tensions, calm passions and promote a culture of peace. This could be helped if the process through which negotiations for peace are pursued is transparent, so that both Palestinian and Israeli public opinion can be built up in support of the process and of its eventual outcome. In this way, the mutual confidence upon which a durable peace must rest could be nurtured.

109. The Commission was encouraged by the extent to which its own assessments of the main issues addressed in the report substantially coincided with the most trustworthy third party views, including those of diplomatic representatives of the European Union and senior international civil servants with years of experience in the region. Thus, an informed and impartial consensus reinforces the conclusions and recommendations set forth here.

110. It is with an understanding of the tragic history of the peoples involved, and its psychological legacy, that our recommendations, aimed at discouraging the persistence of recent violations of human rights, are set out in four parts. The first part seeks to address the root causes that need to be resolutely addressed and resolved. The second part lists safeguards and procedures that need to be observed while negotiations aimed at a comprehensive, just and durable peace are pursued in good faith. The third part presents a series of measures which can be taken immediately to deter further violence and to end the destruction of lives, property and livelihoods. The fourth part is more ambitious, recommending steps for establishing a climate conducive to the emergence over time of a just and durable peace for the peoples of Israel and Palestine.

I. Conditions for a just and durable peace

111. A comprehensive, just and durable peace is to be sought through negotiations in good faith that would end the occupation and establish a dispensation that meets the legitimate expectations of the Palestinian people concerning the realization of their right to self-determination and the genuine security concerns of the people of Israel.

112. While noting that it is the Israeli position that occupation has in effect ended in much of the occupied territories following the agreements reached leading to the establishment of the Palestinian Authority, as well as the fact that the ultimate disposition of the settlements in those territories is a matter for negotiation between the parties, it needs to be recognized that, from the

Palestinian perspective, so long as the settlements remain as a substantial presence in the occupied territories, and Israeli military forces are deployed to protect those settlements, no meaningful end to occupation can be said to have taken place.

II. Human rights and humanitarian law imperatives

113. The framework for a final peaceful settlement and the process through which it is pursued should be guided at all stages by respect for human rights and humanitarian law and the full application of international human rights standards set out in the Universal Declaration of Human Rights and in applicable human rights instruments, in particular those relating to women, children and refugees.

114. An adequate and effective international presence needs to be established to monitor and regularly report on compliance by all parties with human rights and humanitarian law standards in order to ensure full protection of the human rights of the people of the occupied territories. Such an international mechanism should be established immediately and constituted in such a manner as to reflect a sense of urgency about protecting the human rights of the Palestinian people.

115. Protection needs to be accorded to the people of the occupied territories in strict compliance with the 1949 Geneva Convention Relative to the Protection of Civilians in Time of War (Fourth Geneva Convention). The High Contracting Parties, individually and collectively, need urgently to take appropriate and effective action to respond to an emergency situation calling for measures to alleviate the daily suffering of the Palestinian people flowing from the severe breaches of the Fourth Geneva Convention. Article One of the Convention places a duty on the High Contracting Parties "to respect and ensure respect" of the provisions of the Convention "in all circumstances." The Commission recalls that the Conference of the High Contracting Parties to the Fourth Geneva Convention, convened in Geneva on 15 July 1999, in its concluding statement reaffirmed the applicability of the Fourth Geneva Convention to the occupied Palestinian territory, including East Jerusalem, and reiterated the need for full respect for the provisions of the Convention in that Territory, and further recorded the following decision: "Taking into consideration the improved atmosphere in the Middle East as a whole, the Conference was adjourned on the understanding that it will convene again in the light of consultations on the development of the humanitarian situation in the field." In view of the serious deterioration of the humanitarian situation in the Territory, the Commission recommends that the High Contracting Parties should act with urgency to reconvene the Conference. Such a Conference should establish an effective international mechanism for taking the urgent measures needed.

III. Urgent measures for the protection of human rights

116. It seems incontestable that the Israeli Security Forces (i.e. the IDF and the Israeli Police Force) have used excessive and disproportionate force from the

outset of the second intifada, whether their conduct is measured by the standards of international humanitarian law applicable to armed conflict, the codes of conduct applicable to policing in situations not amounting to armed conflict or by the open-fire regulations binding upon members of the Israeli Security Forces. In these circumstances there is an urgent need for the Israeli Security Forces to ensure that, even in life-threatening situations, great care is taken not to inflict injury on civilians not directly involved in hostile activities and not to cause disproportionate harm and injury. In non-life threatening situations, particularly demonstrations, the security forces should comply fully with the policing codes of 1979 and 1990, as well as their own open-fire regulations. Every effort should be made by the government of Israel to ensure that its security forces observe these rules, that such rules are made effectively known to members of the security forces, that the rules are not arbitrarily and summarily altered and that it is made clear to the security forces that violations will result in meaningful disciplinary action being taken against them.

117. The Israeli Security Forces should not resort to the use of rubber-coated bullets and live ammunition, except as a last resort. Even in life-threatening situations minimum force should be used against civilians. The Israeli Security Forces should be amply equipped and trained in non-lethal means of response, particularly for dealing with violent demonstrations. Every effort should be made to use well-established methods of crowd control.

118. The use of force by the IDF in the exercise of its role of providing security to settlers is also subject to international humanitarian law standards, including the Fourth Geneva Convention, and cannot be used for preemptive shooting of unarmed civilians in areas near settlements or on access and bypass roads leading to settlements or for the destruction of Palestinian property, including the demolition of homes, the cutting down of trees and the destruction of farms, and appropriate instructions to that effect should be issued to all concerned.

119. Targeted shooting of individuals by the IDF or by settlers or by sharpshooters of either side amounts to extrajudicial execution, which is a gross violation of the right to life, constitutes a breach of international humanitarian law and would attract international criminal responsibility. Instructions should be urgently issued and disseminated by all the concerned authorities immediately to end such targeted killing.

120. Complaints regarding the use of lethal force or the excessive use of force which has caused death or serious injury should be investigated and persons found responsible should be held accountable and should not enjoy impunity.

121. Immediate and effective measures need to be taken to end closures, curfews and other restrictions on the movement of people and goods in the occupied territories so that the right to livelihood and normal economic activities are restored, as also the right of access to education and health.

122. Immediate and effective measures need to be taken to prevent the destruction of property in the occupied territories, including the demolition of

houses, the cutting down of fruit and other trees, and the destruction of farms and standing crops by the use of bulldozers and other means.

123. Prohibitions and restrictions derogating from the rights of the Palestinian people, including economic and social rights, imposed by invoking security considerations must be specifically justified and are in all cases subject to compliance with international humanitarian law standards.

124. All concerned authorities must refrain from measures that amount to collective punishment. This would include withholding transfer to the Palestinian Authority of taxes and duties collected by the government of Israel, the imposition of restrictions on movement, or violent acts of reprisal by either side.

125. Instructions need to be issued immediately by all concerned authorities to security forces strictly to refrain from using force against or impeding the provision of medical relief and treatment by those working for the Red Cross, the Red Crescent and Magen David Adom, and in hospitals, and to ensure protection to ambulances and hospitals. These instructions should require all concerned to ensure unimpeded access for the sick, the injured and pregnant women to hospitals.

126. Compensation should be provided to victims of unlawful use of force where this has caused death, disablement, destruction of property or economic loss.

127. All impediments to the flow of humanitarian assistance, now even more urgently needed, should be removed as a matter of urgency and every effort should be made to facilitate the work of the United Nations and other bodies involved in providing humanitarian assistance and medical relief.

128. The life and safety of children and their access to education and health care should be especially protected. Special instructions should be urgently issued prohibiting shooting at unarmed children and pointing out that such acts would engage international and national criminal responsibility. Every care should be taken to ensure that children are not involved in situations where they expose themselves to risk of becoming victims of acts of violence.

129. Steps should be taken to apply article 1D of the 1951 Convention relating to the Status of Refugees to ensure that a regime of protection under the authority of the United Nations High Commissioner for Refugees is extended to Palestinian refugees, especially those currently residing in West Bank and Gaza camps. These refugees have been particularly victimized during the second intifada, are not now protected by the application of the UNRWA framework and urgently require international protection on a priority basis.

130. A mutually acceptable comprehensive settlement must deal equitably with the issue of Palestinian refugees and their rightful claims, including those refugees living outside of the Palestinian Territories. Such arrangements should be negotiated in a manner that is sensitive to legitimate Israeli concerns.

131. All restrictions on access to places of worship and all holy sites should be removed and access to them by all faiths should be respected.

IV. Transforming the climate of hostility

132. The Euro-Mediterranean Agreement between the European Communities and their Member States and the state of Israel declares in article 2 that their relationship is to be based on respect for human rights and democratic principles which guide their internal and international policy; this could provide the basis for an initiative by the former to play a more pro-active role in promoting acceptance and implementation of these recommendations and in supporting the holding of consultations and dialogue at all levels between the Palestinian people and the Israeli people.

133. To improve prospects for durable peace, especially given the fundamental gaps in perception that currently separate the two sides, it is strongly recommended that the Commission on Human Rights take concrete steps to facilitate dialogue between representative Israelis and Palestinians at all levels of social interaction, formally and informally. In this regard, the Commission on Human Rights is urged to convene a consultation between leaders of Israeli and Palestinian civil society on a people-to-people basis in Geneva at the earliest possible time. In a similar spirit, to engage Europe more directly in the realities of the crisis the Commission on Human Rights is urged to convene a round table of representatives of European civil society and government to discuss steps that can be taken to alleviate the suffering of the Palestinian people and to ensure greater respect on both sides for human rights standards and for international humanitarian law.

134. In view of the comprehensive denial of human rights and the continuing pattern of behaviour violative of international humanitarian law, this Commission recommends to the Commission on Human Rights that it establish a high-profile periodic monitoring and reporting undertaking to consider the degree to which the recommendations of this report to the parties are being implemented.

Notes

The following abbreviations are used in these notes:
AJIL: American Journal of International Law
ICAO: International Civil Aviation Organization
UNGA: United Nations General Assembly

INTRODUCTION

1 "The Middle East: What is Our Long-Term Vision?" *Middle East Policy* 3 (1994): 9.

2 "The Grotian Quest," in a special edition entitled "The Grotian Moment: Unfulfilled Promise, Harmless Fantasy, Missed Opportunity?" of *International Insights* 13 (1997): 39.

3 "Grotian" 37.

4 "Grotian" 36.

5 "Comments on International Law and the United States' Response to the Iranian Revolution," *Rutgers Law Review* 33 (1981) 399–409.

6 "Trusting Khomeini," editorial, *New York Times*, 16 February 1979: 27.

7 Edward Said, *Representations of the Intellectual* (New York: Vintage Books, 1994) 11.

8 This type of analysis, developed from what has come to be known as the New Haven School, of which Falk is a leading exponent, seeks to emphasize international law as a process rather than simply as rules.

9 The second item that Blum mentions—not of relevance to this study—relates to Falk's use of the process-orientated approach in considering the raid. See Yehuda Blum, "The Beirut Raid and the International Double Standard: a Reply to Professor Richard A. Falk," in John Norton Moore, ed., *The Arab-Israeli Conflict*, vol. 2 (Princeton: Princeton University Press, 1992) 255.

10 *Israel in Lebanon*: The Report of the International Commission to Enquire into Reported Violations of International Law by Israel During its Invasion of Lebanon, 1983.

11 Richard Falk and Burns H. Weston, "The Relevance of International Law to Palestinian Rights in the West Bank and Gaza: In Legal Defense of the Intifada," *Harvard International Law Journal* 32 (1991): 129–157.

12 Michael Curtis, "International Law and the Territories," *Harvard International Law Journal* 32 (1991): 457–495.

13 Richard Falk and Burns H. Weston, "The Israeli-Occupied Territories, International Law, and the Boundaries of Scholarly Discourse: A Reply to Michael Curtis," *Harvard International Law Journal* 33 (1992): 190–204.

14 "The Middle East: What is Our Long-Term Vision?" *Middle East Policy* 3 (1994): 10–11.

CHAPTER 2: THE CRUELTY OF GEOPOLITICS

1 Geopolitics is used in this article to designate prevailing patterns of hegemonic structures and processes, and not in the more restricted sense of referring to the geopolitical school of thought that is particularly associated with Halford Mackinder, who emphasizes the strategic implications of "heartland" and "islands" as unlocking the mysteries of world politics. For a spirited exposition and application of geopolitics in this latter sense, see Colin S. Gray, *The Geopolitics of Super Power* (Lexington, KY: University of Kentucky Press, 1988) 4–12.

2 Political regions, especially the Middle East, would benefit by subordinating intra-regional conflict among states to a common interest in achieving insulation from global intrusions. For reasons argued, however, in the Middle East the presence of oil reserves and Israel make this task almost impossible.

3 The hostage crisis of 1979–1980 was provoked by the United States' willingness to grant asylum to the Shah of Iran after his departure from Iran.

4 The vision was otherwise flawed, drawing its strength from an Islamic tradition of confessional severity that was applied in a manner antagonistic to the most elementary protection of human rights.

5 That is, the Islamic confessional impulse has spread among the distinct peoples of the region, but the leadership of such Islamic political movements is decidedly nationalistic and does not look to Tehran for inspiration and guidance.

6 Other concerns were alleged by the United States government and others to be relevant. These included resisting further expansion by Saddam, upholding the sovereign character of Kuwait, resisting and deterring aggression, validating the United Nations' claim to protect the security and existence of its members, and asserting United States' leadership in the post-Cold War world.

7 Yasir Arafat aggravated the Palestinian plight by his emotive and intense pro-Saddam rhetoric, particularly after the Gulf War began. The role and position of the Palestine Liberation Organization (PLO) was nuanced more than the media allowed. The PLO favored Iraqi withdrawal from Kuwait and used its energies to promote a negotiated settlement right up to the January 15th deadline.

8 The Armenian story is probably worse. Caught in the maelstrom of Turkish nationalism, the Armenian peoples endured genocide in 1915, the survivors being dispersed and left essentially with only their memories.

9 Arguably, the Kurds have allowed themselves to be too easily divided into distinct national groupings (i.e., the Iraqi Kurds, the Turkish Kurds), making them especially vulnerable to geopolitical manipulation and suppression by state power in the region and by global forces.

10 See Ernest Gellner, *Nations and Nationalism* (Oxford: Basil Blackwell, 1983) for a dogmatically propounded, yet insightful, argument.

11 See Mary Kaldor, *The Imaginary War: Understanding the East–West Conflict* (Oxford: Basil Blackwell, 1990) for a brilliant reinterpretation of the Cold War as political experience.

12 The shape of the new Europe remains sharply contested: whether it will

move toward federation or confederation; whether unity will be mainly the outcome of intergovernmental negotiations or, more centrally, the product of civil initiatives organized at the societal level; whether limited to affluent industrial Europe or moving to incorporate the less affluent European periphery, including even breakaway republics from the Soviet Union.

13 For limited horizons of political hopes, even by those most militantly engaged in democratization initiatives and perspectives, see George Konrad, *Anti-Politics* (London: Quartet, 1983); and Mary Kaldor and Richard Falk, eds., *Dealignment: A New Foreign Policy Perspective* (Oxford: Basil Blackwell, 1987).

CHAPTER 3: CAN POLITICAL DEMOCRACY SURVIVE THE RELIGIOUS RESURGENCE?
1 See Falk's *Predatory Globalization* (Cambridge, UK: Polity, 1999).
2 Dr. Saad Eddin Ibrahim is a professor of sociology at the American University in Cairo and head of the Ibn Khaldoun Centre for Development Studies. Ibrahim was sentenced on May 21, 2001 to seven years' imprisonment on charges stemming from the monitoring of the national parliamentary elections of 2000, and branded a "traitor" by the Egyptian President Mubarak. Amnesty International and Human Rights Watch consider his trial by the Supreme State Security Court to have been "contrary to international standards for fair trials." See *Amnesty International New Release*, "EGYPT: Human Rights Defender Sentenced to Seven Years Imprisonment in Unfair Trial," 21 May 2001.

CHAPTER 4: FALSE UNIVERSALISM & THE POLITICS OF EXCLUSION
1 Of course, this orientation was hardly original to Huntington, but rests upon a civilizational exploration by many others, most notably the extraordinarily important depiction of civilizational reality by Fernand Braudel, *The Mediterranean and the Mediterranean World in the Age of Philip II* (New York: Harper Collins, 1972) 545–596. See also the monumental achievement of Arnold Toynbee, *A Study of History*. For a negative perception of the impact of resurgent Islam see Adda B. Bozeman, *Politics and Culture in International History* (New Brunswick, NJ: Transaction, 1994), especially pp. xix–xxi. For a favorable Islamic orientation and perspective see Ahmet Davutoglu, *Civilizational Transformation and the Muslim World* (Kuala Lumpur, Malaysia: Mahir Publications, 1994).
2 Stephen C. Toulmin, *Cosmopolis: The Hidden Agenda of Modernity* (New York: Free Press, 1990). For other presentations of contemporary world order see James N. Rosenau, *Turbulence in World Politics: A Theory of Change and Continuity* (Princeton, NJ: Princeton University Press, 1990); R.B.J. Walker, *One World/Many Worlds: Struggles for a Just World Peace* (London: Zed Press, 1988); and Richard Falk, *On Humane Governance: Toward a New Global Politics* (College Park, PA: Penn State University Press, 1995).
3 The character of "significant difference" is substantively complex, but procedurally relatively simple, referring to relatively equal access, representation, and status in principal arenas of formal authority, as well as relatively equal

treatment in the application of norms of behavior and regimes of prohibition, for instance, the regime prohibiting the proliferation of nuclear weaponry. The qualification of a civilization as "major" is also potentially troublesome, raising the question "What counts as a civilization?"

4 David Held, *Democracy and the Global Order: From the Modern State to Cosmopolitan Governance* (Cambridge, UK: Polity, 1995), especially pp. 219–286; and Daniele Archibugi and David Held, eds., *Cosmopolitan Democracy: An Agenda for a New World Order* (Cambridge, UK: Polity, 1995.)

5 The argumentative assertion here is the insistence on the word "essential," reflecting a psycho-political, as well as a legal and moral, assessment. There is, of course, no implication that Islam (or any other civilization) is monolithic, but only that the collective identity expressed by the label "Islam" is a meaningful category in a manner analogous to the label "Britain" or "France."

6 An eloquent and persuasive Muslim expression, both critical toward the West and visionary in relation to an Islamic contribution to an enhanced world order, is Chandra Muzaffar, *Human Rights and the New World Order* (Penang, Malaysia: Just World Trust, 1993). In his role as founder and director of Just World Trust, Muzaffar has convened a series of meetings and issued many commentaries on world policy issues that react against what I am describing as "the geopolitics of exclusion." A particularly notable effort was an international workshop, "Images of Islam: Terrorising the Truth," 7–9 October 1995, Penang, Malaysia. See also his collection of essays that are more geopolitical than inter-civilizational in tone, *Dominance of the West over the Rest* (Penang, Malaysia: Just World Trust, 1995).

7 For rather enlightened examples of recent literature, invoking as well the deep historical roots of the encounter, see Graham E. Fuller and Ian O. Lesser, *A Sense of Siege* (Boulder, CO: Westview/RAND, 1995); John L. Esposito, *The Islamic Threat: Myth or Reality* (New York: Oxford University Press, 1992); and Fred Halliday, *Islam and the Myth of Confrontation* (London: I. B. Tauris, 1996). In the context of human rights, the uncritical call for universal human rights, without reference to inter-civilizational agency, is problematic. See, for example, Ralf Dahrendorf, *The Modern Social Conflict* (London: Weidenfeld and Nicolson, 1988) 181.

8 But see an important caveat relating to their contention that overlooking the inter-ideological cleavages of the Cold War was a dangerous instance of false universalism. Harold D. Lasswell and Myres S. McDougal, "Diverse and Contending Public Order Systems," in McDougal and Associates, *Studies in World Public Order* (New Haven, CT: Yale University Press, 1960): 3–42.

9 These efforts involved trying to insist upon sovereignty rights as a balance against interventionary claims associated with the jurist or diplomat responsible for the assertion—as, for instance, "the Calvo Clause," "the Drago doctrine"—as well as efforts to put foreign and domestic investors on a level of parity in relation to expropriation controversies.

10 The most prominent of these were the Declaration on the Establishment of a New Economic Order, Programme of Action on the Establishment of a New

International Economic Order, and the Charter on the Economic Rights and Duties of States. For a convenient text see Burns H. Weston et al., eds., *Basic Documents in International Law and World Order* (St. Paul, MN: West Publishing, 1990) 550–575.

11 For the most authoritative formulation, see "Declaration on the Right to Development," adopted as UNGA Res. 41/128, 4 December 1986, in Weston, *Basic Documents* 485–488.

12 For a powerful argument along these lines, emphasizing the importance of the acceptance of the right to development as an integral element of human rights, at the UN Conference on Human Rights held in Vienna, June 1993, see Upendra Baxi, *Mambrino's Helmet?: Human Rights for a Changing World* (New Delhi: Har-Anand Publications, 1994) 1–17, 22–54.

13 See Rosanne Ortiz, *Indians of the Americas: Human Rights and Self-Determination* (London: Zed Books, 1984).

14 See ILO Convention No. 107, "Concerning the Protection and Integration of Indigenous and Other Tribal and Semi-Tribal Populations in Independent Countries," text in Weston, *Basic Documents* 335–340, for a prime instance of paternalism; compare ILO Convention No. 169 for a vastly improved formulation that reflects pressure from and participation by representatives of indigenous peoples, completed in 1989 (see pp. 489–497 of the same book). For a sensitive account of the consequences over a period of centuries see James Anaya's contribution to the Report of the Canadian Royal Commission on Aboriginal Peoples, 1995.

15 For a helpful account of the obstacles in the path of acceptance within the UN system see the newsletter *Nouvelles Internationales* 4.1–2 (1996): 2–5.

16 The comparison is meaningful along a number of axes, including the tendencies toward "Orientalism" and "Occidentalism," that is, the mutually demeaning, if not demonizing, stereotypic images of the other that are characteristic of inter-civilizational encounters, especially if combined with relations of domination and subordination. Basic here, of course, is Edward Said's *Orientalism* (New York: Pantheon, 1978). Also suggestive is Jean-François Lyotard, "The Other's Rights," in Stephen Shute and Susan Hurley, eds., *On Human Rights* (New York: Basic Books, 1993) 135–146. Also of relevance may be the shared element of anti-modernism in both the indigenous/traditional and Islamic challenges, which may be one aspect of an explanation for their co-emergence. For valuable varying perspectives on Islamic attitudes, see Akbar S. Ahmed, *Postmodernism and Islam: Predicament and Promise* (London: Routledge, 1992) and Fatima Mernissi, *Beyond the Veil: Male–Female Dynamics in Modern Muslim Society* (Bloomington, IN: Indiana University Press, 1987).

17 Davutoglu, Ahmet. *Civilizational Transformation and the Muslim World* 101; see also the discussion in immediately subsequent paragraphs.

18 Davutoglu 103–104.

19 Davutoglu 27.

20 Davutoglu 114–117.

21 It should be noted that leading thinkers of indigenous peoples make similar claims.

22 Esposito, *The Islamic Threat*; and Fuller and Lesser, *A Sense of Siege*.

23 It is true that the Bosnian government understated Bosnia's Islamic identity throughout the war, emphasizing its pluralistic character and its refusal to emulate the ethnic cleansing of its Serbian and Croatian adversaries.

24 On media bias see Edward Said, *Covering Islam* (New York: Pantheon, 1981).

25 For an excellent overall presentation of the non-proliferation regime that accords with my own analysis, see Michael Klare, *Rogue States and Nuclear Outlaws* (New York: Hill and Wang, 1995) 156–157. Klare points out that Pakistan's strategic relationship with the West definitely moderated to some extent efforts to obstruct Pakistan's efforts to acquire a nuclear weapons capability. On the Israeli weapons program as facilitated by anti-proliferation states see Seymour Hersh, *The Sampson Option* (New York: Random House, 1991).

26 For a balanced analysis that supports this assessment, although not phrased in civilizational categories, see Janna Nolan's "Sovereignty and Collective Intervention: Controlling Weapons of Mass Destruction," in Gene M. Lyons and Michael Mastanduno, eds., *Beyond Westphalia: State Sovereignty and International Intervention* (Baltimore, MD: Johns Hopkins University Press, 1995) 170–187. Nolan's conclusion is pertinent: "The Achilles heel of nonproliferation initiatives, as such, is emerging regional powers' perception of discrimination in a system that continues to place a high value on weapons of mass destruction as an indicator of state power and prestige, even while trying to promote the global prohibition of such weapons"(187).

27 See especially the Harvard report based on field assessments by health specialists, International Study Team, *Health and Welfare in Iraq after the Gulf War: An In-Depth Assessment* (Cambridge, MA: Harvard University, October 1991). See also the report prepared by Eric Hoskins, Calvin Bauman, and Scott Harding of Gulf Peace Team Special Mission to Iraq: Health Assessment Team, Amman, Jordan, 30 April 1991; and Francis A. Boyle, "Indictment, Complaint, and Petition by the 4.5 Million Children of Iraq for Relief from Genocide by President George Bush," document, 18 September 1991. A useful discussion is to be found in Sarah Graham-Brown's "Intervention, Sovereignty, and Responsibility," *Middle East Report* 25.139 (1995): 2–12, 32. For a more general condemnation by way of international law see Hans Kochler, *The United Nations Sanctions Policy and International Law* (Kuala Lumpur, Malaysia: Just World Trust, 1995). An excellent overview, with useful chapters on the impact of sanctions on Iraq is contained in David Cortright and George A. Lopez, eds., *Economic Sanction: Panacea or Peacebuilding in a Post-Cold War World?* (Boulder, CO: Westview, 1995); and Fred Tanner, ed., *Effects of International Sanctions* (Malta: Mediterranean Academy of Diplomatic Studies, January 1996).

28 Nolan, "Sovereignty and Collective Intervention" 175.

29 This impression is supported by the unquestionably hostile treatment of the scandal by two sophisticated books written by leading writers for the *Wall Street Journal* and the *Financial Times*, which nonetheless make the striking point that many of BCCI's most dubious practices were in most respects identical with those of mainstream international banking. See Peter Truell and Larry Gurwin, *False Profits: The Inside Story of BCCI, the World's Most Corrupt Financial Empire* (Boston: Houghton Mifflin, 1992); and Jonathon Beaty and S. C. Gwynne, *The Outlaw Bank: A Wild Ride into the Secret Heart of BCCI* (New York: Random House, 1993). Also relevant is the much less traumatizing approach taken to dealing with the savings and loan scandal of the 1980s in the US. See Kathleen Day, *S & L Hell: The People and the Politics Behind the $1 Trillion Savings and Loan Scandal* (New York: Norton, 1993).

30 For a fuller discussion see Falk, "Contradictory Images and Conceptions of International Terrorism," unpublished paper, 1994.

31 For a critique of Libyan policy by a non-Muslim, see Fan Yew Teng, *The Continuing Terrorism Against Libya* (Kuala Lumpur: Egret Publications, 1993).

32 See Fuller and Lesser, *A Sense of Siege* 49–50.

33 This gambling metaphor is borrowed from Mary Catherine Bateson's illuminating use of it in connection with bias against and demoralization of women. See Bateson, *Composing a Life* (New York: Atlantic Monthly Press, 1989) 205.

34 For the complexity of this latter extension of Westphalian thinking, see James Crawford, ed., *The Rights of Peoples* (Oxford: Clarendon Press, 1988); and William Felice, *Taking Human Rights Seriously: The Importance of Collective Human Rights* (Albany, NY: State University of New York Press, 1996).

35 A recent discussion of these conceptual issues in relation to the alleged erosion of sovereignty, with particular reference to intervention under the auspices of the international community, is to be found in Lyons and Mastanduno, *Beyond Westphalia?*

36 For important extensions of the scope and orientation of human rights see Abdullahi Ahmed An-Na'im, ed., *Human Rights in Cross-Cultural Perspectives: A Quest for Consensus* (Philadelphia, PA: University of Pennsylvania Press, 1992), especially the chapter by An-Na'im: 19–43; Smitu Kothari and Harsh Sethi, eds., *Rethinking Human Rights: Challenges for Theory and Action* (New York: Horizons, 1989); Myres S. McDougal, Harold D. Lasswell, and Lung-chu Chen, *Human Rights and World Public Order* (New Haven, CT: Yale University Press, 1980); and Felice, *Taking Human Rights Seriously.*

CHAPTER 5: IMPLICATIONS OF THE OSLO/CAIRO FRAMEWORK FOR THE PEACE PROCESS

1 See the full text of the Oslo agreement in *Palestine Yearbook of International Law* 7 (1992/94): 232.

2 Illustrative of this role for external political actors was the high-profile US government initiative to induce Israel and the PLO to do more on behalf of both

the negotiating progress and the implementation of what had been previously negotiated (including arrangements for elections and Israeli troop withdrawals). Greenhouse, "Clinton Intervenes to Help Revive Stalled Mideast Peace Talks," *New York Times* 13 February 1995; Graham, "Clinton Pledge in Mideast," *Financial Times* 13 February 1995.

3 Such initiatives seem peculiarly relevant at this stage with respect to human rights as neither negotiating party appears motivated to support compliance in self-rule areas. See "The Gaza Strip and Jericho: Human Rights under Palestinian Partial Self-Rule," *Human Rights Watch: Middle East*, February 1995.

4 The contention is not that there was a settler conspiracy, but that settler attitudes generate and ratify terrorist acts against Palestinians. See Said, "Hebron Was Inevitable," *The Progressive* (May 1994): 25–27.

5 Original Editor's Note: Jordan and Israel signed a Peace Treaty on October 26, 1994, and both countries have been moving steadily toward normalizing their bilateral relationship.

6 See Ibrahim, "Gulf Nations Balk at Proposal for Mideast Development Bank," *New York Times* 17 February 1995.

7 Fletcher, "Israel's Great Wall? Critics Belittle a Barrier Against Palestinians," *Christian Science Monitor*, 27 January 1995; Friedman, "It's Time to Separate," *New York Times* 29 January 1995.

8 Indeed, the Rabin government has been reluctant to directly challenge efforts to memorialize the memory of Baruch Goldstein at the Kiryat Arba settlement. See Gellman, "Palestinian Killed in Clash on Massacre Anniversary," *Washington Post* 15 February 1995.

9 Article V(2) commits the parties to begin negotiations "as soon as possible… but no later than the *beginning* of the third year of the interim period"—that is, after two years. Emphasis added.

10 For example, see Kohen, "Invitation to a Massacre in East Timor," *The Nation* 7 February 1981.

11 For background, see the notes to the Introduction on the Falk and Weston and Curtis articles in the *Harvard International Law Journal*.

12 B'tselem's report *Neither Law Nor Justice* (August 1995) traces events and cases of unlawful arrest and torture by the Palestinian Preventive Security Service.

13 In addition to the absence of deadlines (contrasting with the specified date for holding elections), there is no assurance in the Arafat letter that, in fact, the PNC will accept the proposed changes, and no indication that its failure to do so is a violation of Palestinian obligations or gives Israel a legal pretext for not fulfilling its commitments.

14 Gaza-Jericho Agreement, Article VI (2) (B).

15 See the UNGA Resolution A/RES/43/177 of 20 December 1988 whereby the Assembly "*Decides* that, effective as of 15 December 1988, the designation "Palestine" should be used in place of the designation 'Palestine Liberation Organization' in the United Nations system…" Text reproduced in the

Palestine Yearbook of International Law 4 (1987/88): 312. For a list of diplomatic recognition accorded the PLO, see *Palestine Yearbook of International Law* 2 (1985): 189–190. More states than the list referred to above have extended their respective recognition to the newly declared state of Palestine.

16 See Dajani, "The September 1993 Israel-PLO Documents: A Textual Analysis, *Journal of Palestine Studies* 23 (1994): 5–23; Shehadeh, "Questions of Jurisdiction: A Legal Analysis of the Gaza-Jericho Agreement," *Journal of Palestine Studies* 23 (1994): 18–25.

17 I have elsewhere drawn a distinction between "a bargain" struck on the basis of inequality, and "a solution" that meets the reciprocal needs of both sides, and is likely to be politically viable over time; a peace treaty that embodies the results of victory and defeat is likely to be an unstable bargain if the stronger side exacts maximum advantage and the weaker side is denied basic rights. The Versailles Agreements after World War I are an exemplary instance of the vulnerability of one-sided arrangements to subsequent repudiation, as well as to links between one-sidedness and political extremism as a reaction to such perceived weakness and humiliation. See Falk, "Can US Policy Toward the Middle East Change Course?" *Middle East Journal* 47 (1993): 11–20.

CHAPTER 6: THE KURDISH STRUGGLE FOR SELF-DETERMINATION

1 See, for example, Chris Hedges, "An Odd Alliance Subdues Turkey's Kurdish Rebels," *New York Times*, 24 November 1992: A1 (reporting that Iraqi Kurds are helping Turkish forces fight Turkish Kurds).

2 See, for example, Lee C. Buchheit, *Secession: The Legitimacy of Self-Determination* (New Haven: Yale University Press, 1978) 153. The transition from tribal to national consciousness may have been both deferred and prolonged by a variety of Kurdish circumstances, including the geographic setting, the presence of strong contending non-Kurdish regional forces, and the relatively noninterventionary quality of Ottoman administration.

3 Iraqi Kurdistan has become dependent on official Turkish benevolence since 1991 as a consequence of Baghdad's continuing hostility and internal blockade of the Kurdish region. See Chris Hedges, "Kurds in Iraq Warned by Turkey, Iran, and Syria," *New York Times*, 15 November 1992: A9. International protection of Iraqi Kurdistan has depended on Turkish permission to use bases integral to Operation Provide Comfort. [Original Editor's Note: Operation Provide Comfort was a humanitarian operation begun by the US military in April 1991 to provide relief to Kurds fleeing Iraqi forces in the aftermath of the Gulf War. See Michael E. Harrington, "Operation Provide Comfort: A Perspective in International Law," *Connecticut Journal of International Law* 8 (1993): 635.

4 See the Institut Kurde de Paris *Information and Liaison Bulletin* 91–92 (October–November 1992): 2.

5 "Treaty of Peace Between the British Empire and Allied Powers (France, Italy, Japan, Armenia, Belgium, Czecho-Slovakia, Greece, the Hedjaz, Poland, Portugal, Roumania and the Serb-Croat-Slovene State) and Turkey," 10 August 1920, *British*

& *Foreign St. Papers* vol. 113, part. 652 [hereinafter Treaty of Sèvres].

6 The Republic of Mahabad constituted the only successful attempt at an independent Kurdish State in the period since World War I. It was created in what is now western Iran in December 1945. It ceased to exist in December 1946 when it was occupied by Iran. Gerard Chaliand, ed., *People Without a Country: The Kurds and Kurdistan* (Northampton, MA: Interlink, 1980) 135–52.

7 Chaliand.

8 A dramatic expression of this regional consensus was the extraordinary meeting in Ankara on November 14, 1992 of the foreign ministers of Turkey, Iran, and Syria that openly condemned the establishment of a de facto state in northern Iraq, declaring such a development a threat to the territorial integrity of Iraq, a likely zone of chaos, and a threat to the national security of the three countries. See Hedges, "Kurds in Iraq" A9. The meeting was extraordinary because it brought together governments united by little else than their common anti-Kurdish consensus, and because the inclusion of Iran—which contravened US foreign policy aimed at isolating Iran from regional frameworks—was not cleared with Washington.

9 Treaty of Peace, July 24, 1923, between the British Empire-France-Italy-Japan-Greece-the Serb-Croat-Slovene State, and Turkey, *Treaty Series of the League of Nations*, vol. 28, pt. 11.

10 Treaty of Sèvres.

11 There was evidently significant Kurdish resistance activity, but it was effectively suppressed, and either ignored or misconstrued by later historical accounts. For an effort at revisionist historical assessment, see Kamal Madhar, "The Kurdish Revolt of 1925," *Kurdish Culture Bulletin* 1.68 (1988).

12 See typical analysis along these lines in Stephen C. Pelletiere, *The Kurds: An Unstable Element in the Gulf* (Boulder, CO: Westview, 1984) 57–61.

13 For an account of the early stages of the breakup of the Yugoslav federation, see Morton H. Halperin and David J. Scheffer, *Self-Determination in the New World Order* (Washington, DC: Carnegie Endowment for International Peace, 1992) 32–38.

14 Internal self-determination is also used as a way to reinforce the norm of nonintervention in the internal affairs of a state and to ground legitimate sovereignty on respect for fundamental human rights. In effect, as self-determination inheres in the people rather than the state, it presupposes a measure of internal freedom. For helpful discussion see Antonio Cassese, "Political Self-Determination: Old Concepts and New Developments," *UN Law/Fundamental Rights*, ed. Antonio Cassese (Alphen aan den Rijn : Sijthoff & Noordhoff, 1979) 137–165.

15 Both the relative achievements and the anguishing vulnerabilities of Iraqi Kurds are expressive of the broader issues at stake. The autonomy agreement of March 1970 between the Iraqi Kurdish representatives and the Baghdad government was most forthcoming compared to Kurdish circumstances

elsewhere, but the subsequent disregard of the commitments and genocidal suppression of Kurdish resistance in both the late 1970s and again in the late 1980s visited a worse fate on Iraqi Kurds than was being endured elsewhere. For a brief account of both aspects, see Hurst Hannum, *Autonomy, Sovereignty, and Self-Determination: The Accommodation of Conflicting Rights* (Philadelphia, PA: University of Pennsylvania Press, 1992) 190–194.

16 A major theme of the concluding part of this essay is the extent to which self-determination prospects are arbitrarily conditioned by the vagaries of geopolitics. These vagaries work grave historic injustices on certain peoples; the Kurdish people have been and continue to be victimized. The state of Israel was effectively established in the aftermath of World War II, facilitated by the grim revelations of massive genocide against the Jewish peoples. See Chapter 2.

17 Hannum 28. As will be considered in the next part of this essay, the abandonment of the Sèvres pledge to establish Kurdistan was almost completely a matter of changing British colonial calculation between 1920 and 1923 and had virtually nothing to do with any sense of a reduced justification for establishing a Kurdish state.

18 Hannum 29, 370–71.

19 UNGA, 15th Session, Official Records, Supplement 16, *Declaration on Colonial Countries*, in pursuance of UNGA Resolution 1514, A/4684, 1961.

20 *Declaration on Colonial Countries*, 67. The vote was 89 in favor, 0 in opposition, with 9 abstaining including the United States, United Kingdom, and France. Subsequent developments have authoritatively embodied the right of self-determination as specified in the Declaration as an operative norm of international law. See Hannum, 27–49.

21 *Declaration on Colonial Countries*, para. 6.

22 Opened for signature 19 December 1966, S. Ecex. Doc. E, 95th Cong., 2d Sess. (1979), 999 UNTS 171 [hereinafter CPRC].

23 Opened for signature 19 December 1966, S. Exec. Doc. D, 95th Cong., 2d Sess. (1979), 993 UNTS 3 [hereinafter ESCRC].

24 CPRC, art. 1(1); ESCRC, art. 1(1).

25 UNGA, 25th Session, Official Records, Supplement 28, Resolution 2625, A/8028, 1970.

26 UNGA Res. 2625.

27 UNGA Res. 2625.

28 For helpful surveys of practice see Halperin and Scheffer, and also Hannum.

29 But see Halperin and Scheffer, 27–38 (noting US reluctance to validate self-determination claims resulting in secession, even in relation to the former Soviet and Yugoslav federations).

30 See, for example, Amitai Etzioni, "The Evils of Self-Determination," *Foreign Policy* 89 (1992): 21–35.

31 For an attempt at a more systemic explanation, see Chapter 2.

32 President Woodrow Wilson, address by the President of the United States on

18 January 1918, in *Congressional Record* 56 (1918): 680–681.
   33 Treaty of Sèvres.
   34 Treaty of Sèvres, art. 62.
   35 Treaty of Sèvres, art. 64.
   36 For background on oppression generally, see Peter W. Galbraith and Christopher Van Hollen, Jr., *Chemical Weapons Use in Kurdistan: Iraq's Final Offensive*, 100th Cong., 1st sess., S. Doc. 148. For subsequent reports, see Peter W. Galbraith, *Saddam's Documents*, 102nd Cong., 2nd sess., 1992, S. Doc. 111; Peter W. Galbraith, *Kurdistan in the Time of Saddam Hussein*, 102nd Cong., 1st sess., 1991 S. Doc. 56; Peter W. Galbraith, *Civil War in Iraq*, 102nd Cong., 1st sess., 1991, S. Doc. 27.

CHAPTER 7: PROTECTING PALESTINIANS
   1 One of the members of the Commission was former Foreign Minister of Bangladesh and the third member of the Commission was a South African human rights expert currently on the faculty at Leiden, who is a member of the International Law Commission, the expert body on international law of the UN.

CHAPTER 8: LEGAL REFLECTIONS ON THE ISRAELI OCCUPATION
   1 For useful analysis see John Dugard's lecture, "The Enforcement of Human Rights in the West Bank and Gaza Strip," Rights of Man Conference, Jerusalem, January 1988, published in Emma Playfair, ed., *International Law and the Administration of Occupied Territories: Two Decades of Israeli Occupation of the West Bank and Gaza Strip* (Oxford: Oxford University Press, 1995); along with Falk and Weston, "The Relevance of International Law" (see Introduction, note 11).
   2 Such analysis is not, of course, intended to cast doubt on these underlying Palestinian claims; indeed, these claims enjoy widespread moral, political, and legal backing in international society at the level of both governmental policy and public opinion. The argument in the text is rather that the abuse of the Palestinians caught in the reality of the occupation since 1967 establishes, on the basis of authoritative treaty rules, a distinct basis of criminality.
   3 These issues were discussed in several cases before US military tribunals at Nuremberg, especially the *Hostages* case (USA v. Wilhelm List et al.) and the *Einsatzgruppen* case (USA v. Otto Ohlendor et al.), Trial of War Criminals Before the Nuremberg Military Tribunals, vol. 2 (1950): 1243ff; US Military Tribunal II (1950): 493ff.
   4 For materials on this development of international law see R. Falk, G. Kolko, R. J. Lifton, eds., *Crimes of War* (New York: Random House, 1971).
   5 For a helpful collection of material from a professedly Palestinian perspective see League of Arab States, *The Israeli Settlements in the Occupied Arab Territories* (1988). For a more objective, yet equally condemnatory, assessment see report of the International Commission of Jurists, "Israeli Settlements in Occupied Territories," 1977: 27–36.
   6 The factual developments associated with Israeli encroachment upon

Palestinian sovereign rights in the occupied territories are comprehensively depicted in Meron Benvenvisti, "1987 Report of the West Bank Data Base Project," *Jerusalem Post* 1987.

7 Arguments to the contrary by partisan Israeli commentators are so contrived legally and so contrary to the weight of international official opinion and expert commentary as to lack credibility. For a sampling of such argumentation see Y. Blum, "The Missing Reversioners: Reflections on the Status of Judea and Samaria," *Israel Law Review* 279 (1968); E. V. Rostow, "Palestinian Self-Determination: Possible Futures for the Unallocated Territories of the Palestinian Mandate," *Yale Studies in World Public Order* 5 (1979): 147–72; A. Gerson, "Trustee-Occupant: The Legal Status of Israel's Presence in the West Bank," *Harvard International Law Journal* 14 (1973): 1–49.

8 See Adam Roberts, "The Applicability of Human Rights Law during Military Occupation" *Review of International Studies* 13 (1987): 39–48.

9 Such has been UN practice in relation to South Africa's prolonged "illegal" occupation of Namibia, reinforcing both the illegitimacy of the South African role and safeguarding the sovereign rights of the inhabitants of the occupied territory.

10 For a useful compilation on Camp David diplomacy, including the texts of the agreements and the formal position of the main relevant non-participants, including the PLO, see *The Egyptian-Israeli Treaty: Text and Selected Documents* (Beirut: Institute for Palestine Studies, 1979).

CHAPTER 9: THE STATUS OF ISRAELI SETTLEMENTS UNDER INTERNATIONAL LAW

1 For a convenient crystallization of their basic legal analysis, see Sally V. Mallison and W. Thomas Mallison, "Settlements and the Law: A Juridical Analysis of the Israeli Settlements in the Occupied Territories," a pamphlet published by the American Educational Trust, 1982: 1–27.

2 See Blum, "The Missing Reversioners" (see Chapter 8, note 7).

3 Rostow, "Palestinian Self-Determination: Possible Futures for the Unallocated Territories of the Palestine Mandate," *Yale Studies in World Public Order* 5 (1979): 147–172.

4 The formal US position on the international law status of the settlements was clearly outlined in a letter written in 1978 by Herbert J. Hansell, then legal advisor to the secretary of state. The letter was addressed to two important congressmen, chairmen of subcommittees of the International Relations Committee of the House of Representatives. Hansell's letter, after referring to expert opinion, concluded with this key paragraph: "On the basis of the available information, the civilian settlements in the territories occupied by Israel do not appear to be consistent with these limits on Israel's authority as belligerent occupant in that they do not seem intended to be of limited duration or established to provide orderly government of the territories and, though some may serve incidental security purposes, they do not appear to be required to meet military needs during the occupation." *International Legal Materials* 17.1–3 (1978): 777–779.

The letter proceeds to regard the settlements as inconsistent with Article 49 (6) of the Fourth Geneva Convention, and supports the view that however long the occupation lasts, these obligations remain; it also accepts the standard view that since the intention of these limits on occupying authority is for the benefit of the civilian population they apply whether or not Jordan is regarded as "the legitimate sovereign" with respect to the territory in question. The conclusion reached at the end of the letter is that "for the reasons indicated above, the establishment of the civilian settlements in these territories is inconsistent with international law" (779). See also statements by US representatives before various UN bodies to the effect that Israel's actions in the occupied territories, including Jerusalem, are to be considered only as interim measures that should not in any way prejudge the outcome of future negotiations between the parties. See, for example, US Representative William Scranton's statements before the UN Security Council on March 22, 23, 25, 1976 in *US State Dept. Bulletin* 19 April 1976: 526–530; earlier statements by US Representative Daniel P. Moynihan can be found in the *Bulletin* 5 January 1976: 21, and 16 February 1976: 189.

5 Gerson, "Trustee-Occupant: The Legal Status of Israel's Presence in the West Bank," *Harvard International Law Journal* 14 (1973): 1–49.

6 See, for example, "Israeli Settlements in Occupied Areas," *International Commission of Jurists* (1977): 27–36.

7 See Hansell's letter, above, for succinct analysis of the applicability of Article 49 (6).

8 See, for example, the statement by Allan Gerson, US representative in Special Political Committee, 30 November 1981 on "Israeli Practices in the Occupied Territories": "The issue of whether the settlements are legal or illegal has received so much attention that it has effectively diverted debate from what should be the fundamental issue—Does the continued establishment of Israeli settlements advance or hinder progress toward 'just and lasting peace'?" And "… my government has decided, as reflected in our vote, to eschew participation in the legal debate and to focus instead on the policy aspects of the problem. We hope other members of this body will decide to do so as well."

9 For Benvenisti's interpretation of the effects of the settlements process see *The West Bank Data Project: A Survey of Israel's Policies* (Washington: American Enterprise Institute, 1984), especially pp. 64–69; see also subsequent report of Israeli land alienation practices on the West Bank that reinforces the conclusions of the earlier report as discussed in the *New York Times* 1 April 1985: A1, 6.

CHAPTER 10: THE BEIRUT RAID & THE INTERNATIONAL LAW OF RETALIATION

1 According to the *New York Times*, 5 January 1969, the owners of the airlines whose planes were destroyed were not only the Arab governments. Middle East Airlines, which lost eight aircraft, is owned 30 percent by Air France, 5 percent by Lebanese individuals, and 65 percent by Intra Company, an inter-governmental corporation constituted by the Kuwaiti, Qatari, Lebanese, and US governments.

The United States is evidently represented by the Commodity Credit Corporation, which is owed money for wheat sales by Intrabank, a predecessor of Intra Company. Lebanese International Airways, which lost three planes, is 58 percent American-owned. Trans-Mediterranean Airways, which lost two planes, is owned by private Lebanese interests. Early reports indicated that British insurance underwriters had agreed to accept $18 million in claims, rejecting claims from policies that did not cover war risks. Note that, aside from Lebanon, none of the interests affected by the Beirut raid involved principal Arab countries. For a detailed inventory of the damage done in the raid, including damage to terminal facilities, see letter of 14 January 1969, from Assad Kotaite, the Lebanese representative on the Council of the ICAO, to the secretary general of that organization (1 January, 1969: WP/4945).

2 There are several "liberation" groups constituted by Palestinian refugees. The most important group is the Palestine Liberation Organization, now presided over by Yasir Arafat. Arafat earned his reputation, and remains, as the leader of Al Fatah, the military commando section of Al Asifa. Then there is a group called the Popular Liberation Corps, with anonymous leadership, and associated with the Palestinian branch of the Ba'ath party. Finally, there is the Popular Front for the Liberation of Palestine headed by George Habbash. It is the Popular Front, a relatively secondary liberation group, that has claimed credit for the attacks on El Al planes. This Popular Front has been weakened by an internal split which led 600 of its estimated 2,000 members to join the Marxist-Leninist Popular Democratic Front for the Liberation of Palestine in late 1968 and early 1969. See articles by Dana Adams Schmidt, mentioned below.

3 See Ambassador Shabtai Rosenne of Israel, ICAO, Minutes of Third Meeting of the Extraordinary Session of the Council, 23 January 1969: 5.

4 This account of the arraignment proceedings is based on an article in the *New York Times*, 31 December 1968: 3. This contention must be set off against some of the elements of the attack itself. The assailants evidently could have proceeded more easily to destroy the plane when it was empty and yet chose to wait until it was loaded for take-off. In fact, the semi-official Egyptian newspaper, *Al Ahram*, praised the members of the liberation group for their willingness to wait at the airport at risk to themselves until their attack would have maximum effect, and exaggerated the damage done by falsely reporting that the El Al plane was destroyed by fire. *Al Ahram*, 27 December 1968: 1.

5 For the text of the two letters, both dated 29 December 1968, requesting an urgent meeting of the Security Council, see S.8945, S.8946.

6 UN Doc. S/Res/262 (1968). For the reactions of various delegations to this resolution, see S/PV. 1462, 31 December 1968: 7–88. The factual circumstances surrounding the Beirut raid, as well as their divergent interpretations, are well stated by the representatives of Lebanon and Israel in their presentations to the Security Council. See UN Doc. S/PV. 1460, 29 December 1968: 6–27, S/PV. 1461, 30 December 1968: 11–20, 43–62.

7 For full text see UN Doc. S/PV. 1462: 6; 6 *UN Monthly Chronicle* 19 (January 1969); also reprinted below: 681.

8 Ambassador Rosenne's initial statement in the UN Security Council specifically invoked this earlier interference with an international flight of El Al Airlines as a part of the context that conditioned the decision to make the Beirut reprisal raid. See debate of December 29, 1968, in the Security Council, S/PV. 1460: 23. Note that Lebanon was not the sole target; all Arab-owned aircraft at the airport were destroyed. See second note in this chapter for details. As was made clear at various points by Mr. Rosenne and later by Mr. Tekoah, the Beirut raid was intended as a warning directed at all Arab governments.

9 For statistics on comparative arms expenditures in the Middle East, see Nadav Safran, *From War to War: The Arab-Israeli Confrontation, 1948–1967* (New York: Pegasus, 1969) 433–434.

10 For an account of the Iraqi hangings see *The Economist*, 1 February 1969: 20. Eight more persons, all Moslems, were reportedly executed for similar crimes on 20 February 1969. A further report indicates that in a third Iraqi spy trial seven more persons have been condemned to death, including two or three Jews and a former premier of Iraq, Abdel Rahman al-Bazzaz. *New York Times*, 1 March 1969: 9.

11 "There is still little talk here of an Israeli military reaction to the hangings, in part because this would contradict the Israeli policy of using raids as warnings rather than reprisals, and also because this might do more harm than good." James Feron, "Israeli Consulting on Ways to Assist the Jews of Iraq," *New York Times*, 30 January 1969: 2.

12 See article by James Feron, "Israel Ponders Issue of Reprisal," *New York Times*, 2 February 1969.

13 For various accounts of the Zurich attack and reactions to it, see *New York Times*, 19 February 1969: 1, 2, 3; 20 February 1969: 1, 3.

14 *New York Times*, 1 March 1969: 1, 14.

15 See James Feron, "New Israeli Strategy Seen in Raid Near Damascus," *New York Times*, 25 February 1969: 3.

16 For some discussion of the differences between the activities of these Arab guerrilla groups, see Dana Adams Schmidt, "An Arab Guerrilla Chief Emerges," *New York Times*, 4 March 1969: 6. On the different ideas of tactics between the two main Arab organizations, Al Fatah and the Popular Front, see another report by Schmidt, *New York Times*, 20 February 1969: 2.

17 Mr. Boutros, the Lebanese representative who appeared before the Security Council, offered a categorical denial of any governmental responsibility for the Athens incident in the following principal language: "...Lebanon cannot be held responsible for acts which were committed by Palestinian refugees outside its territory and of course without its knowledge, and which were committed by Palestinian refugees whose intentions were not known to Lebanon..." Furthermore, "... If Israel really felt that Lebanon was responsible for the incident at Athens, [why] did it not immediately file a complaint against Lebanon in the

Council?" UN Doc. S/PV. 1461, 30 December 1968: 12.

18 See *New York Times*, 5 January 1969: IV.1; for further documentation of Lebanese praise for the work of the Popular Front (and other liberation efforts), see release of Israel's Information Office, "The Israeli Action at the Beirut Airport," 28 December 1968. This document included the following quotation attributed to Mr. Yam, the Lebanese prime minister, on 2 November 1968: "Fedayeen action is legitimate, and no one can condemn the fedayeen for what they are doing. Their aim is to retrieve their homeland and their plundered rights.... Thus, I say, fedayeen action is legal." Israeli sources have also quoted specific Lebanese praise for the perpetrators of the Athens incident. See Mr. Tekoah's statement before the Security Council (UN Doc. S/PV. 1461: 52–55), especially the following excerpt: "The attention of the Lebanese government has been drawn on numerous occasions to the activities of the terror organizations within its borders. The Lebanese government, however, has not only continued to condone these activities, but has publicly identified itself with them. Prime Minister Al-Yaft has announced several times that his government supports terror operations against Israel." UN Doc. S/PV. 1461: 52.

19 Mr. Boutros indicated that he had "reservations" about the action of the Security Council because "it did not draw the conclusions to which the findings should have led and it hesitated to order the application of Chapter VII of the Charter to Israel." UN Doc. S/PV. 1462: 81.

20 Mr. Tekoah, in reacting to the adverse judgment of the Security Council, said: "Let no one make the mistake of thinking that the people of Israel might be swayed by inequitable pronouncements." Further, "... not Security Council resolutions, but the attitude and actions of the governments in the area will determine the destiny of the Middle East." (UN Doc. S/PV. 1462: 52.)

21 A somewhat more balanced debate took place at ICAO. See the minutes of the First, Second, Third, and Fourth Meetings of the Extraordinary Session of the Council, 20, 21, 23, 31 January 1969.

22 For overall legal perspective, with representative statements by adversary analysts, see the symposium published under the title "The Middle East Crisis: Test of International Law," *Law and Contemporary Problems* 32 (Winter 1968): 1–193; W. V. O'Brien, "International Law and the Outbreak of War in the Middle East," *Orbis* 11 (1967): 692, 723. For general background see Nadav Safran, *From War to War: The Arab-Israeli Confrontation, 1948–1967* (New York: Pegasus, 1969); Fred J. Khouri, *The Arab-Israeli Dilemma* (Syracuse, NY: Syracuse University Press, 1968). On problems of biased and incompatible perception of identical circumstances in relation to international conflict, see Ralph K. White, *Nobody Wanted War: Misperception in Vietnam and Other Wars* (Garden City, NY: Doubleday, 1968).

23 There are problems of characterization arising from contradictory interpretation of the facts (e.g., extent of knowledge by Lebanese officials of the activities of the Popular Front), of the legal duties (e.g., extent of obligation to regulate activity of liberation activities within territory), and of policy issues (e.g.,

conflict between security of territory and recourse to retaliatory force).

24 Although variations of terrain, tradition, and political milieu make certain societies very susceptible to internal opposition of an insurgent character; also, of course, in many parts of Asia, Africa, and Latin America the central government is not able to exert its control over the entire expanse of national territory. Of course the logic of governmental control involves the capacity to control liberation activity as well as the incentive to engage in it.

25 There is also absent any consensus as to the character of political legitimacy in international society. The presence of such a consensus induces moderation in the choice of means and ends of political conflict; its absence induces extremist tactics and strategy, making compromises difficult to specify, and giving a prominent role to violence and warfare. See Henry A. Kissinger, "Central Issues of American Foreign Policy," in Kermit Gordon, ed., Agenda for the Nation (Washington: Brookings Institution, 1968) 585–614, esp. 585–589. The sharpest global cleavage related to political legitimacy is concerned with the status of radical socialism as the basis for organizing a sovereign state. The Arab-Israeli conflict that can be expressed in several distinct fashions, perhaps most fundamentally in terms of the status of Zionist claims, is one in which there is almost no consensus as to legitimacy. There is not even a willingness to accept as settled the right of Israel to exist as a distinct sovereign state.

26 One might also mention the psychological support given exile groups from East Europe by the official congressional celebration of "Captive Nations' Week" each year. For legal critique see Q. Wright, "Subversive Intervention," AJIL 54 (1960): 521. In Sec. 101 of the Mutual Security Act of 1951 (and in similar legislative enactments of several subsequent years) the US Congress appropriated and earmarked 100 million dollars for escapees from Eastern Europe for a Liberation Legion for Eastern Europe, specifically "to form such persons into elements of the military forces supporting the North Atlantic Organization or for other purposes." AJIL 46, Supp. 14 (1952). For citations see American Foreign Policy, 1950–1955, Basic Documents 3060, 3119.

27 There is some polemical treatment of these issues in relation to the controversy over the legal status of support for various kinds of "wars of national liberation." But there has been no effort to deal with the generality of claims in light of some consistent body of doctrine.

28 In this regard, see the Declaration on Inadmissibility of Intervention, adopted as Resolution 2131 (XX) of the UNGA on 21 December 1965; AJIL 60 (1966): 662. In recounting the grave concern of the membership with "the increasing threat to universal peace due to armed intervention and other direct or indirect forms of interference," the Declaration "solemnly declares" in its second numbered paragraph: "...Also, no State shall organize, assist, foment, finance, incite or tolerate subversive, terrorist or armed activities directed towards the violent overthrow of the regime of another State, or interfere in civil strife in another State." Such a contradiction between Assembly assertion and liberation practice helps discredit

the guidance role of international norms and to give comfort for those who would dismiss restraints upon violence as "legalisms."

29 Compare Security Council statements of Mr. Boutros and Mr. Tekoah on the issue of responsibility. UN Doc. S/PV. 1461: 12–20, 46–56.

30 A consensus within the UNGA is strongly supportive of anti-colonial and anti-racist liberation movements. This attitude of support has assumed a quasi-legislative status because of the law-creating role of the organization. See, generally, Chapter 6 in Falk, *The Status of Law in International Society* (Princeton, NJ: Princeton University Press, 1969).

31 The statement in the text is a very crude generalization. The effect of exerting governmental control of varying degrees over different categories of liberation group activity varies from country to country in the Arab world and through time in each country. In general, Jordan has been most vulnerable to a takeover from the liberation movement as a result of the strong Palestinian influence within the Jordanian armed forces. The governments of Syria and the United Arab Republic enjoy greater freedom of action, although within each government elite there is a faction strongly committed to the liberation cause that would be deeply alienated by any interference with the freedom of action of the guerrilla group. The same comment also seems true for Lebanon. In all Arab countries the liberation movement seems popular with the masses, and governmental regulation or suppression would be regarded as a very unpopular policy.

32 For a profound inquiry into these problems, see Myres S. McDougal and Florentino P. Feliciano, *Law and Minimum World Public Order* (New Haven: Yale University Press, 1961) 97–260. See also the French explanation of their refusal to supply arms to Israel, at first as a consequence of Israel's initiation of force in June 1967, and recently in reaction to Israel's action at the Beirut Airport. *New York Times*, 8 January 1969: 1, 19.

33 This assertion rests on two considerations: (1) the inability of the UN to implement its decisions; and (2) the political factors that act to shape such a decision. The problems of control are particularly severe in the Middle East because of the rivalry between the United States and the Soviet Union for influence within the region.

34 See speculation to this effect as part of the Israeli reaction to censure by the Security Council and imposition of an arms embargo by France, *New York Times* 12 January 1969: 1, 9. A state such as Israel might also seek to avoid inter-regional trade-offs at its own expense if the settlement bargain is achieved by superpower consensus (that is, in simplistic terms, the Soviet position on Middle Eastern problems is accepted in exchange for Soviet acceptance of the US position on South Asian problems).

35 Ian Brownlie, *International Law and the Use of Force by States* (Oxford: Oxford University Press, 1963) 281. Brownlie's statement is supported with additional citations and discussions in R. Higgins, *The Development of International Law*

Through the Political Organs of the United Nations (Oxford University Press, 1963) 217–218. For general background, see Evelyn Speyer Colbert, *Retaliation in International Law* (New York: King's Crown Press, 1948).

36 But for more flexible views of what is permitted under the Charter in the name of self-defense, see McDougal and Feliciano, 1–260 and 679–689; Julius Stone, *Aggression and World Order* (Berkeley: University of California Press, 1958); D. W. Bowett, *Self-Defense in International Law* (New York: Praeger, 1958).

37 UN Doc. S/RES/188 (1964). The next clause of the resolution "deplores the British military action at Harib on 28 March 1964." And the Charter basis of the condemnation is suggested by language in the preambular section "Recalling Article 2, paragraphs 3 and 4 of the Charter of the United Nations." The Security Council resolution here, unlike the one condemning Israel for the Beirut raid, does widen the context and establish some kind of reciprocal obligation on the part of Yemen. For instance, the fourth operative paragraph "Calls upon the Yemen Arab Republic and the United Kingdom to exercise the maximum restraint in order to avoid further incidents and to restore peace to the area." And in the last paragraph, the secretary general is called upon to use his "good offices to settle outstanding issues, in agreement with the two parties." Thus, although the United Kingdom is censured, the sense of mutual responsibility is stressed in a way that it is not in the December 31 resolution. See also I. F. Stone, "International Law and the Tonkin Bay Incidents," in Marcus G. Raskin and Bernard B. Fall, eds., *The Viet-Nam Reader* (New York: Vintage, 1965).

38 See *New York Times*, 5 January 1969: IV.1; General Bar Lev said that "the large-scale operation" against the fedayeen bases of Karameh and Es-Salt in Jordan during 1968 "were not reprisals." He went on to say that "these were actions intended to strike directly at the heart of the terrorists." As an earlier example of a reprisal, General Bar Lev cited the Israeli commando attack upon Egyptian bridges and upon a transformer station serving the Aswan Valley, the destruction taking place in the Nag Hamadi area. This reprisal was in retaliation for alleged Egyptian violations of the cease-fire along the Suez Canal. For a summary of the meetings of the Security Council devoted to this question on 1 & 4 November 1968, see *UN Monthly Chronicle* 5 (November 1968): 3–16. Another prominent Israeli reprisal action occurred in October 1967, after Egyptian rockets sank an Israeli destroyer, Elath, leading to the death of most of the crew. Israel alleged that the Elath, the largest ship in the Israeli Navy, was on "a routine patrol" and sailing in international waters, more than twelve miles from the Egyptian shore. Egypt contended that the Elath was only ten miles from shore and heading for Port Said in a "provocative" manner. The Elath was sunk on 21 October 1967 and the Israelis retaliated three days later with a heavy artillery barrage directed at the city of Suez, near the cease-fire line. One result of the barrage was to destroy or badly damage the two most important oil refineries in Egypt, which supplied 80 percent of the country's gasoline and cooking fuel. The Elath reprisal contrasts with the Beirut raid because the

provocative action—sinking the ship—was clearly governmental in character. Hence, there was no issue as to whether Egypt was responsible, if in fact it was "illegal" to sink the Elath, itself a complicated issue of both fact and law. A resolution in the Security Council condemned both acts as violations of the cease-fire and called for strict adherence by all governments in the future. Account of the Elath incident is based on Khouri, 279.

The principal purpose of retaliatory uses of force by Israel is to influence decision-making by Arab governments, especially with respect to their encouragement of terroristic tactics on the part of liberation groups located on their territory. Mr. Tekoah's conclusion of his final statement in the Security Council makes the centrality of this objective very clear. He says: "Israel's action in Beirut, taken in defense of its rights, should bring the Arab governments to understand the full depth of Israel's determination to ensure its right to peace and security. When the Arab states realize that determination, become persuaded by its tenacity, and draw the appropriate conclusions, there will be peace in the Middle East." UN Doc. S/PV. 1462: 52. Arab spokesmen, in contrast, refused to treat the Beirut raid as raising any issue that was broader than the permissibility of such an attack by the Israeli government, given the absence of any prior governmental act of provocation on the part of Lebanon. Both the Beirut and the Elath reprisal raids seemed to include an element of punitive action, a policy of inflicting losses on Arab governments that exceed those inflicted upon Israel by prior action.

39 As a technical matter, charter law is properly accorded priority over inconsistent rules of customary international law. Therefore, the clear rejection of the right of reprisal in UN practice seems to establish the general authority of this conclusion in positive international law. However, the inability of the United Nations to impose its views of legal limitation upon states leads to a kind of second-order level of legal inquiry that is guided by the more permissive attitudes toward the use of force to uphold national interests that is contained in customary international law. This point has considerable jurisprudential importance, as it suggests the usefulness of a method of successive legal approximations. If the Charter status of reprisals exhausted legal inquiry, then there would be no prospect of moderating force in retaliatory settings wherein the Charter approach was ineffectual. Specifically, in the Arab-Israeli setting it appears useful to maintain second-order levels of legal inquiry so as to retain criteria of reasonableness in a situation that threatens at many points to deteriorate into intense and limitless forms of violent conflict. The customary international law of reprisal is a very important illustration of such second-order legality. Note, especially, that this kind of inquiry is associated with the contention of Israel that the purpose of a reprisal is not to inflict a punishment, but to communicate a claim with respect to future behavior. Even second-order legal inquiry may be ill-adapted to the kind of retaliatory claim being made by Israel, see above, Sec. II, and a third-order legal inquiry involving the specification of considerations bearing on the relative legal status of a particular retaliatory claim, see below, Sec. IV.

40 A useful short discussion of the background and character of the right of reprisal is given by Gerhard von Glahn, ed., *Law Among Nations* (New York: Macmillan, 1965) 498–501.

41 Many international documents that formulate governmental duties of conduct include the responsibility to prevent the use of territory as a base for liberation activities against a foreign state. For example, the *Declaration on Inadmissibility of Intervention* declares that "no state shall... tolerate subversive, terrorist, or armed activities." See also citations in note 69 below, especially Garcia-Mora and Lauterpacht.

42 Note that Israeli representatives in the Security Council indicated that Arab countries other than Lebanon were also intended as targets of the Beirut raid. All Arab aircraft were destroyed, and not only those associated with Lebanese interests. Also the context was defined by Israel to include (1) the Athens incident, (2) the diversion of an El Al plane to Algiers in July 1968, and (3) the overall Arab policy of supporting the activities on their territory of the liberation groups. As Mr. Rosenne suggested to the Security Council: "Without in any way belittling the gravity of this terrorist warfare being conducted against Israel's civil aircraft, wherever they might be, the complaint that we are discussing must also be seen in the broader context of the continuation by the Arab states, including Lebanon, of active belligerency and warfare against Israel through the instrumentality of irregular forces and organizations armed, trained and financed by the Arab governments, including the government of Lebanon." UN Doc. S/PV. 1460: 24–25.

43 On the comparatively low level of Lebanese hostility toward Israel, see Khouri, 191, 230–231; Safran, 182–185, 245–247. On its more recent increase, however, see "The Israeli Action at the Beirut Airport," Israeli Information Office, undated release, and the statement by Prime Minister Eshkol in Jerusalem on 29 December 1968, bearing the title, "Lebanon Cannot Disclaim Responsibility for Terrorism."

44 The Arab governments, and even more pointedly the Soviet Union, took the position that the Athens incident was a matter for Greek internal criminal law, and of no relevance at all to the debate on the Beirut raid. As Mr. Ghorra of Lebanon said, "In our view, that incident which took place at the Athens airport is a matter of common law, and the Greek courts have sole jurisdiction in the matter." UN Doc. S/PV. 1460: 61. Mr. Malik of the Soviet Union put his view as to the territorial, non-governmental character of the Athens incident very forcefully: "This incident, which took place in Athens, relates to the sovereignty and competence of Greek authorities; it occurred on Greek territory. According to the press reports, the competent authorities of that country are dealing with this matter; they are studying it, and apparently they have taken some measures. They have executive as well as judiciary authorities there. How is this matter at all related to the Security Council? As I have already pointed out in my observations following the adoption of the agenda, if the Security Council were to begin to

consider all the terrorist acts which are being perpetrated, no matter where, including even this country [the United States], then the Security Council would simply cease to be a Security Council... The representative of Israel is dragging the Security Council into the consideration of events which took place on the territory of a sovereign power which is certainly entitled to deal with this matter... and that country has not appealed to the Security Council." UN Doc. S/PV. 1460: 13.

And later, on the last day of the debate, Mr. Malik reiterated his position in more succinct form: "It must be stressed that the attack against the Israeli airplane was indeed carried out by citizens of a third state on the territory of yet another state; and, in accordance with international law, a state can be held responsible only for acts of its own organs, such as its armed forces or its citizens, on the territory of that given state." UN Doc. S/PV. 1462: 22.

Mr. Wiggins, the representative of the United States, did take the position that "Israel was rightly aroused and legitimately concerned about the attack upon an Israeli aircraft in Athens on 26 December" but, nevertheless, he concluded that "[N]othing that we have heard has convinced us that the government of Lebanon is responsible for the occurrence in Athens." UN Doc. S/PV. 1460: 28–30.

45 Mr. Rosenne did tell the Security Council that "[A]ll through 1968 Lebanon, turning a deaf ear to Israel's appeals has been playing an ever increasing role in the overall Arab belligerency against Israel." UN Doc. S/PV. 1460: 21. There is no indication of any specific Israeli effort to persuade the Lebanese government to exercise stronger control over the Popular Front in view of the Athens incident. Israel's justifications for focusing the attack upon Lebanon rested on allegations involving (1) the departure of the Arab perpetrators from Beirut; (2) the Lebanese toleration of increasing activity by the Popular Front on its territory; and (3) official and semi-official Lebanese endorsement of the use of terroristic methods by the perpetrators of the Athens incident.

46 Mr. Wiggins, the US representative to the Security Council, made this point forcefully when he said that the Beirut raid was "an unacceptable form of international behavior. In magnitude it is entirely disproportionate to the act that preceded it. It is disproportionate in two ways: first, on the degree of destruction involved; and secondly, in a more fundamental way, in the difference between the acts of two individual terrorists and those of a sizable military force operating openly and directly under governmental orders." UN Doc. S/PV. 1460: 28–30.

47 The visibility of the two occurrences can be gauged by comparing their treatment in newspapers around the world. The Athens incident was reported as a relatively minor terroristic act, whereas the Beirut raid received headlines and the damage done was shown in large photographs.

48 There are underlying the specific allegations of terror and counter-terror the more general allegations about bringing the conflict to an end either by "disintegrating" Israel and replacing it with the secular state of Palestine, by carrying out the provisions of Security Council Resolution 242 of 22 November

1967, by working out an agreed solution through the good offices of Gunnar V. Jarring, the special representative of the secretary general, or by accepting a solution for the area that is worked out by guarantor Powers such as the United States, the Soviet Union, France, and the United Kingdom.

49 As pointed out already, Israel, in particular, objected throughout to the effort to restrict the scope of inquiry to the Beirut raid. See note 8.

50 The problem is fully depicted from an Israeli viewpoint in an article by Amnon Rubinstein, "'Damn Everybody' Sums up the Angry Mood of Israel," *New York Times Magazine*, 9 February 1969: 24–27, 93, 96–99. See especially page 98, on which there is a discussion of why Israel does not engage in counter-terror against Arab interests by organizing irregular military forces of its own, thereby cutting the overt link between retaliation and the Israeli government. A senior officer is quoted as saying "[t]error for terror is the only solution," but Rubinstein writes, "This solution is unacceptable in the Israeli government." He advances three arguments: (1) "The whole philosophy" of Israeli resistance "runs contrary to any suggestion of counter-terror." (2) Recourse to irregular forces would weaken Israel's contention that Arab incitement of irregular forces is a violation of the cease-fire agreement reached at the end of the June war; this reasoning is attributed to Moshe Dayan. (3) Regular troops can be militarily protected in the course of their mission in a way that irregular forces cannot; this view is attributed to General Bar Lev.

51 For somewhat similar suggestions in different circumstances of conflict, see Philip C. Jessup, "Should International Law Recognize an Intermediate Status between Peace and War?" *AJIL* 48 (1954): 98; McDougal and Feliciano, 97–120.

52 The duty of respect arises from the obligation of a member of the United Nations to accord respect to acts of the Security Council when that organ is acting, as it was here, within its sphere of competence. As the Council was acting under Chapter VI, not VII, its resolution was formally a "recommendation" rather than a "decision." On this point see further discussion in note 59 below.

53 There were extended discussions of the legal consequences of the Beirut raid in the ICAO. These discussions resulted from a Lebanese complaint that the Israeli action was a violation of the Chicago Convention on Air Transport and that Israel should be condemned and made to pay for the damage done. Although questions about the competence of ICAO to deal with a complaint of this character dominated the debate, the issues were discussed generally in a manner more favorable to the Israeli position than was the case in the Security Council. The outcome of these discussions was a decision *sine die*, which is quite a contrast with the result within the UN forum.

54 An interview published in *Time*, 10 January 1969: 28.

55 In violation of the 22 November 1967 resolution of the Security Council and of the stated objectives of all states other than Israel, there does not seem to be any serious disposition by the Israeli government to re-establish the *status quo ante* 5 June 1967. In particular, the retention of administrative control over

Jerusalem, of the Golan Heights, a strip of Sinai needed to assure control over the Straits of Tiran, and of a portion of the West Bank of the Jordan and of the Gaza Strip seems to be insisted upon by Israel. There is, then, on the Arab side an unwillingness to accept the existence of the state of Israel and on the Israeli side an insistence upon expansion through conquest. For an assessment of Israel's intention to retain conquered Arab lands, see interview with Levi Eshkol published in *Newsweek*, 17 February 1969: 49–56; see also analysis of these claims by James Feron, "Eshkol Mentions the Unmentionable," *New York Times*, 16 February 1969: IV: 2. Israel's claims are a mixture of security demands of a defensive nature and of territorial demands of an expansionist nature.

56 The position of Israel before the political organs of the UN is coming to resemble that of South Africa in certain critical respects, especially with regard to the degree of its diplomatic isolation. Israel does continue to enjoy some diplomatic support from the United States and from some countries in Western Europe, but, since the end of the 1967 war, even these governments have grown increasingly critical of Israel's expanding demands and exercise of prerogatives.

57 See Julius Stone, *No Peace—No War in the Middle East* (Sydney, Maitland, 1969), especially pages 4–5: "Everyone knows that too many present Security Council Members are committed to voting on the Arab side, for pro-Israel resolutions to be adopted, no less than five of these Members refusing even to maintain diplomatic relations with her."

58 Abba S. Eban, Foreign Minister of Israel, suggested that anti-Jewish discrimination is embodied in the recent diplomatic attacks upon Israel: "I have no other explanation for the fact that the Soviet Union, which invaded Czechoslovakia, can condemn alleged Israeli 'aggression' at the UN without the public gallery bursting into laughter." Interview, *Time* 10 January 1969: 28.

59 There is a certain legal ambiguity created by the status of various actions taken by the Security Council. In a formal sense, the judgments of the Security Council have the status of "recommendations" unless they are made under Chapter VII of the Charter. Except for "decisions" relating to the observation of the cease-fire, the Security Council has relied upon its "recommendatory" powers under Chapter VI. The resolution censuring Israel after the Beirut raid was a "recommendation." As such, it can be argued that Israel has no formal obligation to obey it. On the other hand, a resolution of censure involves an authoritative act of community review that constitutes strong evidence as to the respective rights and duties of parties to an international controversy.

60 Countries that have been the targets of UN directives have almost invariably refused to comply. In fact, when an international conflict gets to the point where the UN takes sides, it is almost assured that "the losing side" will not voluntarily obey the will of the Organization.

61 That is, in strategic parlance, the objective is one of deterrence rather than defense. The primary effort is to influence decision-making in the target state's government rather than to diminish its capabilities for action. The Beirut raid aimed

at shaping the policies of Arab governments with respect, in particular, to terroristic activities directed at the operations of El Al Airlines by liberation movements based within their territory. There was no intention to deprive Arab countries of commercial aircraft, which were obviously replaceable at relatively little cost.

62 Ambassador Tekoah's statements to the Security Council confirm the conclusion that the Israeli government sought, above all else, to induce Arab governments to prohibit liberation movements operating within their territory from interfering with El Al flights.

63 See the *New York Times* 12 January 1969: 1, 9; see, especially, article by Rubinstein cited above. However, the Israeli response to the Zurich incident casts some doubt on the generality of the statement in the text.

64 The objective factors are those that can be formulated in general terms, whereas the subjective factors are those that involve the perceptual framework of the participants in the situation and are subject to wide variation depending on personality, cultural, and ideological considerations.

65 This tendency would be strengthened if the claimant state executed its operation in such a way as to minimize the injury to innocent civilians and third-party interests. The United States claiming pattern in the Cuban missile crisis is a model for this contention. A novel claim by the United States to use force on the high seas was made to appear so reasonable in assertion and execution that critical reaction, even though the Soviet Union was the target of the claim, was kept to a minimum. For two legal arguments by government officials in support of the United States claim, see Leonard C. Meeker, "Defensive Quarantine and the Law," *AJIL* 57:515 (1963); Abram Chayes, "The Legal Case for U.S. Action on Cuba," 47 Dept. of State Bulletin 763 (1962).

66 I have elsewhere analyzed the reactions of African countries to the so-called Stanleyville operation of December 1964, in these terms. See Falk, *Legal Order in a Violent World* (Princeton University Press, 1968) 324–335.

67 There are certain other factors that explain censure from third-party sources: (1) prior uses by Israel of excessive force in response to terroristic provocation; (2) the selection of Lebanon as the target of retaliation, given the long period of non-involvement by the Lebanese government in the Arab-Israeli conflict; (3) the growing realization that Israel was insisting upon retaining some of the territorial fruits of the 1967 war; (4) the timing of the Beirut raid seemed to be damaging prospects for either a Great Power or UN initiative to bring some measure of stability, if not real peace, to the Middle East.

68 A subsequent article will attempt to evolve a suitable framework for the assessment of acts of violence relied upon by liberation groups to achieve their political ends. Such a framework would involve, necessarily, some assessment of the compatibility between the aims of these groups and appraisal of these aims by regional and global institutions and their conformity with norms of international law. In addition, the choice of means used to pursue such aims requires an innovative legal analysis that reconsiders paramilitary violence as an instrument of

political change. Eventually the two frameworks of legal appraisal will need to be integrated into a single coherent approach to the relevance of international law to this species of international conflict that has assumed such great importance in world affairs.

69 For some relevant legal background see Fritz Grob, *The Relativity of War and Peace* (New Haven: Yale University Press, 1949); Albert E. Hindmarsh, *Force in Peace: Force Short of War in International Relations* (Cambridge: Harvard University Press, 1933); M. R. Garcia-Mora, *International Responsibility for Hostile Acts of Private Persons against Foreign States* (The Hague: Nijhoff, 1962); Hersch Lauterpacht, "Revolutionary Activities by Private Persons against Foreign States," *AJIL* 22:105, 130 (1928). For some specification of support given terroristic groups in Egypt and Jordan since the June war, see Stone 4–6. According to Israeli sources there have been 1,288 acts of sabotage and border incidents between June 6, 1967, and December 31, 1968; 920 of these acts occurred in the Jordanian-Israeli sector, 166 in the Egyptian sector; 37 in the Syrian; 35 in the Lebanese; and 130 in the Gaza Strip sectors. Israeli losses have been put at 234 soldiers and 47 civilians killed and 765 soldiers and 330 civilians wounded. Arab losses are reported by Israel as considerably greater than these figures. See *New York Times*, 13 February 1969: 1, 4. There are indications of a rising Israeli concern about the growing capacity of the guerrilla groups to impair Israel's security, including especially the character of its administration of occupied territories inhabited largely by Arabs. See James Feron, "Israel Concerned over Guerrillas," *New York Times* 9 March 1969: 12.

70 Israeli statements before the Security Council emphasized the effort to carry out the Beirut raid without inflicting casualties upon Lebanese citizens. See, for example, UN Doc. S/PV. 1460: 23. And in the official release of the Israeli Information Office in New York, the following language appears: "At great risk to themselves, Israeli troops at the Airport exercised the strictest precautions to prevent civilian casualties. The planes were emptied of passengers and ground crews, and people in the vicinity were led away to safety. Loudspeakers were employed to issue instructions in Arabic and English. The only shots fired were warning shots in the air." Release dated 28 December 1968.

71 Israeli attacks against Arab paramilitary bases associated with guerrilla activities have occasioned little adverse reaction, especially if "provoked" by an upsurge in miscellaneous incidents of terrorism within Israel. See paragraphs on the air strike against Syrian bases of Al Fatah on 24 February 1969, above. To some extent the governmental character of a retaliation against non-governmental provocation is neutralized if the targets are military. This is especially true if the victims of the terrorism were civilians and damage done to non-military targets. The choice of a non-military target for Israeli retaliation after the Athens incident seems to be a very significant element in explaining the strong adverse international reaction to the Beirut raid.

72 Consider the analysis of Safran xii–xv, 21–142, in terms of the levels: (1) Arab–Israeli; (2) inter-Arab; (3) US–USSR.

73 The significance of this role, it should be noted, depends on a conception of international law that is wider than one concerned with rules of behavior. Neither the Charter norms nor the norms of customary international law delimiting the right of reprisal, come to grips with the kind of choice that confronts a government that needs to design responses to persistent terrorism directed at the security of its national territory. In such circumstances, the exigencies of response cannot be cast aside by the invocation of legal rules. At the same time, retaliatory claims can be asserted in accordance with a framework of restraint that is designed to minimize disruption, to maximize the clarity of the message conveyed, and to solicit the sympathy of the organized world community.

74 Consider problems associated with the effort by the United States to extend its antitrust regulation to govern the foreign operations of business firms that have an anti-competitive impact on the U.S. economy.

CHAPTER 11: RETHINKING US–ISRAEL RELATIONS AFTER THE LEBANON WAR
1 *New York Times*, 6 October 1982.
2 "Lebanon: The Case for the War," *Commentary* October 1982: 21.
3 Loren Jenkins, "Phalangists Implicated in Massacre," *Washington Post*, 30 September 1982.
4 "Lebanon: The Case for War."
5 *Wall Street Journal*, 11 November 1982.
6 "Lebanon: The Case for the War."
7 *New York Review of Books*, 18 November 1982: 74.
8 *New York Review of Books*, 75.
9 "J'Accuse," *Commentary* September 1982: 31.
10 "J'Accuse," 31.
11 "The Massacre: Who Was Responsible?" *Washington Post*, 24 September 1982.
12 Claudia Wright, "Pre-Invasion Surge of Arms to Israel," *Pacific News Service*, September 1982.
13 Excerpts from Begin's testimony before panel on West Beirut massacre, *New York Times*, 9 November 1982.
14 *Time*, 15 November 1982: 47.
15 "Reply," *New York Review of Books*, 18 November 1982: 77.

CHAPTER 13: INTERNATIONAL LAW & THE US RESPONSE TO THE IRANIAN REVOLUTION
1 Acheson, Remarks, *Proceedings of the American Society of International Law* 57 (1963): 14.
2 Meeker, "The Dominican Situation in the Perspective of International Law," *Department of State Bulletin* 53 (1965): 60.

CHAPTER 14: HUMAN RIGHTS AFTER THE IRANIAN REVOLUTION

1 On executions, see the *New York Times*, 17 March 1979: 1.

2 *New York Times*, 17 March 1979.

3 Text in *Crimes of War* (see Chapter 8, note 4).

4 Perhaps the most reliable interpreter of Iranian political developments refers to the Shah as having come to power in 1953 "as a result of a CIA-backed and in large part CIA-directed coup...." Richard Cottam, *Nationalism in Iran* (Pittsburgh: Pittsburgh University Press, 1979): 332; for an insider account see Kermit Roosevelt, *Counter-Coup: The Struggle for the Control of Iran* (New York: McGraw Hill, 1979).

5 For a convincing dissent on the claim of medical necessity see Bloom, "The Pahlavi Problem: A Superficial Diagnosis Brought the Shah into the United States," *Science* 270 (1980): 282–286; see also front page journalistic account by Richard A. Knox to same effect, *Boston Globe,* 24 November 1979: 1, 4.

6 According to US law, extradition cannot be granted by the president apart from treaty, unless authorized by legislation. Even if a special statute authorizing extradition of the Shah had been validly enacted, it would almost certainly have been struck down by the courts as an *ex post facto* law. For brief summary of legal situation pertaining to extradition in absence of treaty see Marjorie Whiteman, *Digest of International Law* 6 (1968): 732–737; see also *Valentine v. United States ex rel. Neidecker,* 299 US 5 (1936) esp. 8–9.

7 An excellent analysis of the dependence of international order upon upholding the norm of nonintervention as much as possible is to be found in R. J. Vincent, *Nonintervention and International Order* (Princeton, NJ: Princeton University Press, 1974).

8 Interview, *Time* 7 January 1980: 27.

9 Remarks, *Proceedings of the American Society of International Law* (1963): 13–15, at 14.

10 For skeptical assessment of the relevance of international law to the Cuban missile crisis see W. P. Gerberding, "International Law and the Cuban Missile Crisis," in L. Scheinman and David Wilkinson, eds., *International Law and Political Crisis* (Boston: Little, Brown & Co., 1968) 175–210. For a much more positive view, see Abram Chayes, *The Cuban Missile Crisis* (New York: Oxford University Press, 1974).

11 Leonard Meeker, "The Dominican Situation in the Perspective of International Law," *Department of State Bulletin* 53 (1965): 60–66, at 60.

12 The results of this investigation remain impressive as a moral and legal indictment of US tactics in the Vietnam War. See John Duffett, ed., *Against the Crime of Silence: Proceedings of the International War Crimes Tribunal* (New York: Simon & Schuster, 1970).

APPENDIX: THE 2001 REPORT OF THE UN HUMAN RIGHTS COMMISSION

1 The resort to shooting by the Israeli police at Harem-al-Sharif/Temple Mount on 29 September 2000 that started the second intifada was, by reliable accounts, not a response to Palestinian gunfire. This raises a serious question about the insistence on the part of the government of Israel that lethal weapons have only been used in response to Palestinian gunfire.

2 *International Herald Tribune*, 27 February 2001: 8.

3 Interim Agreement of 28 December 1995, Article XIX. Without this agreement, Israel would still be bound to ensure civil and political rights that are nonderogable to the population of the occupied territories. Article 1 of the International Covenant on Civil and Political Rights requires that it protect the rights of all individuals subject to its jurisdiction, that is individuals under its effective control. The International Covenant on Economic, Social and Cultural Rights does not refer to individuals under the state's jurisdiction, which makes its application to the population of the occupied territories more doubtful. Israel became a party to the two International Covenants in 1991.

Index